LIBRARY OF HEBREW BIBLE/ OLD TESTAMENT STUDIES

698

Formerly Journal for the Study of the Old Testament Supplement Series

Editors
Claudia V. Camp, Texas Christian University, USA
Andrew Mein, Durham University, UK

Founding Editors
David J. A. Clines, Philip R. Davies and David M. Gunn

Editorial Board
Alan Cooper, Susan Gillingham, John Goldingay,
Norman K. Gottwald, James E. Harding, John Jarick, Carol Meyers,
Daniel L. Smith-Christopher, Francesca Stavrakopoulou,
James W. Watts

ETHICAL GOD-TALK IN THE BOOK OF JOB

Speaking to the Almighty

William C. Pohl IV

LONDON • NEW YORK • OXFORD • NEW DELHI • SYDNEY

T&T CLARK
Bloomsbury Publishing Plc
50 Bedford Square, London, WC1B 3DP, UK
1385 Broadway, New York, NY 10018, USA
29 Earlsfort Terrace, Dublin 2, Ireland

BLOOMSBURY, T&T CLARK and the T&T Clark logo
are trademarks of Bloomsbury Publishing Plc

First published in Great Britain 2020
This paperback edition published in 2021

Copyright © William C. Pohl IV, 2020

William C. Pohl IV has asserted his right under the Copyright, Designs and Patents Act, 1988, to be identified as Author of this work.

For legal purposes the Acknowledgements on p. ix constitute an extension of this copyright page.

All rights reserved. No part of this publication may be reproduced or transmitted in any form or by any means, electronic or mechanical, including photocopying, recording, or any information storage or retrieval system, without prior permission in writing from the publishers.

Bloomsbury Publishing Plc does not have any control over, or responsibility for, any third-party websites referred to or in this book. All internet addresses given in this book were correct at the time of going to press. The author and publisher regret any inconvenience caused if addresses have changed or sites have ceased to exist, but can accept no responsibility for any such changes.

A catalogue record for this book is available from the British Library.
Library of Congress Control Number: 2019956638.

ISBN: HB: 978-0-5676-9302-0
       PB: 978-0-5677-0331-6
       ePDF: 978-0-5676-9303-7

Series: Library of Hebrew Bible/Old Testament Studies, volume 698

ISSN 2513-8758

Typeset by: Forthcoming Publications Ltd

To find out more about our authors and books visit www.bloomsbury.com
and sign up for our newsletters.

For Shaunté, Samuel, Abigail, and Hannah

Contents

Acknowledgments	ix
Abbreviations	xi

Chapter 1
ETHICAL SPEECH IN JOB:
AN INTRODUCTION ... 1
   Foundations for the Study ... 2
   Contextualizing the Study ... 5
   The Methodology of the Study ... 11
   The Argument of the Study ... 19

Chapter 2
"JOB DID NOT SIN WITH HIS LIPS":
THE EXTERNAL RHETORIC OF THE BOOK OF JOB—
A PRELIMINARY INVESTIGATION ... 21
   Methodological Considerations ... 21
   External Rhetorical Analysis of the Book of Job ... 25
   Summary ... 42

Chapter 3
"I WILL COMPLAIN IN THE BITTERNESS OF MY SOUL":
JOB'S INTERNAL RHETORIC IN THE FIRST SPEECH CYCLE (JOB 3–14) ... 44
   "Why Is Light Given to a Man Whose Way Is Hidden?":
      The Rhetoric of Job's Opening Speech (Job 3) ... 45
   "Is There Any Injustice on My Tongue?":
      The Rhetoric of Job's Second Speech (Job 6–7) ... 59
   "I Will Speak in the Bitterness of My Soul":
      The Rhetoric of Job's Third Speech (Job 9–10) ... 79
   "All the Days of My Hardship I Will Wait Until My Renewal Comes":
      The Rhetoric of Job's Fourth Speech (Job 12–14) ... 100
   Summary of the First Speech Cycle ... 127

Chapter 4
"Why Do You Pursue Me Like God?":
Job's Internal Rhetoric in the Second Speech Cycle (Job 15–21)   132
   "To God My Eye Leaks":
      The Rhetoric of Job's Fifth Speech (Job 16–17)   132
   "Be Afraid of the Sword":
      The Rhetoric of Job's Sixth Speech (Job 19)   149
   "Treachery Remains of Your Answers":
      The Rhetoric of Job's Seventh Speech (Job 21)   165
   Summary of the Second Speech Cycle   179

Chapter 5
"Even Today My Complaint Is Bitter":
Job's Internal Rhetoric in the Third Speech Cycle (Job 22–27)
and His Final Speech (Job 29–31)   183
   "I Am Not Destroyed before Darkness":
      The Rhetoric of Job's Eighth Speech (Job 23–24)   184
   "How You Have Helped Him Without Power!":
      The Rhetoric of Job's Ninth Speech (Job 26:2-4)   198
   "Until I Die I Will Not Turn My Integrity Away from Me":
      The Rhetoric of Job's Tenth Speech (Job 27)   203
   "Does Not One on a Heap of Ruins Stretch Out His Hand?":
      The Rhetoric of Job's Eleventh Speech (Job 29–31)   210
   Summary of the Third Speech Cycle and Job's Final Speech   225

Chapter 6
"Words Without Knowledge"?
The External Effect of the Elihu and Yahweh Speeches   228
   The Elihu Speeches (Job 32–37)   228
   The Yahweh Speeches and Job's Responses (Job 38–42:6)   236
   Summary   246

Chapter 7
Ethical God-Talk:
Conclusions and Implications   247
   The Book's Contribution to Ethical God-Talk   249
   The (Reconstructed) Rhetorical Situation of the Book of Job   251

Bibliography   257
Index of References   269
Index of Authors   288

Acknowledgments

My fascination with the book of Job took deep root during my doctoral coursework in an advanced Hebrew reading course with Dr. Dennis Magary at Trinity Evangelical Divinity School. One evening, while preparing for the next day's class, I was reading Job's visceral prayer of protest in Job 3 and was hooked. I had to figure this book out (to some degree). This monograph is the fruit of that journey.

This project is a revision of my dissertation completed at TEDS, under the supervision of Dr. Magary, with Dr. Eric Tully and Dr. Richard Averbeck serving as astute readers. I am grateful to each of them for their direction, feedback, and encouragement throughout the process. I am also thankful to numerous colleagues during my time at TEDS, with whom I shared my thinking and writing. Their encouragement was instrumental in helping me reach the completion of the dissertation. Thanks especially are due to David Bryan, John Simons, Oliver Hersey, Patrick Jones, Michael Cox, Michelle Knight, and Cooper Smith. At the publication stage, I was blessed to continue to receive encouragement from my colleagues at Cincinnati Hills Christian Academy, in particular Dr. Dean Nicholas, Dr. Pete Dongell, Aaron Turvey, Drew Baker, and Jordan Kramer. For their support and friendship, I am grateful.

I owe a debt of gratitude also to Claudia Camp and Andrew Mein for their expert help in the publication process. Their patience and advice have proven invaluable. Furthermore, I want to express my deep gratitude to the reviewers for their thorough feedback, which has assuredly made this project better. Of course, whatever deficiencies that remain are my own.

Thanks also to my family for their love and support throughout this process. The visits to Chicagoland from my parents, Bill and Colleen, and my wife's parents, Stan and Deb, while at TEDS were life-giving for my wife and me during the doctoral program. We feel blessed now to live so close, where weekend visits are no longer needed. Thanks also to my kids—Samuel, Abigail, and Hannah—for their patience and enthusiasm for life. They've kept me grounded throughout this entire process. And last, but certainly not least, thanks to my wife, Shaunté. More than anyone else, she has supported, loved, and encouraged me. I've been profoundly blessed. Praise be to God!

ABBREVIATIONS

AIL	Ancient Israel and Its Literature
ASV	Authorized Standard Version
BASOR	*Bulletin of the American Schools of Oriental Research*
BBR	*Bulletin for Biblical Research*
Bib	*Biblica*
BibInt	*Biblical Interpretation*
BCOT	Baker Commentary on the Old Testament
BZAW	Beihefte zur Zeitschrift für die alttestamentliche Wissenschaft
CBQ	*Catholic Biblical Quarterly*
COS	*The Context of Scripture*. Edited by William W. Hallo. 3 vols. Leiden: Brill, 1997–2002
DBSJ	*Detroit Baptist Seminary Journal*
ESV	English Standard Version
FOTL	Forms of the Old Testament Literature
GKC	*Gesenius' Hebrew Grammar*. Edited by Emil Kautzsch. Translated by Arther E. Cowley. 2nd ed. Oxford: Clarendon, 1910
GW	God's Word Translation
HALOT	*The Hebrew and Aramaic Lexicon of the Old Testament*. Ludwig Koehler, Walter Baumgartner, and Johann J. Stramm. Translated and edited under the supervision of Mervyn E. J. Richardson. 4 vols. Leiden: Brill, 1994–1999
HAR	*Hebrew Annual Review*
HBT	*Horizons in Biblical Theology*
HCSB	Holman Christian Standard Bible
HUCA	*Hebrew Union College Annual*
ICC	International Critical Commentary
Int	*Interpretation*
ITQ	*Irish Theological Quarterly*
JAJSup	Journal of Ancient Judaism Supplements
JBL	*Journal of Biblical Literature*
JETS	*Journal of the Evangelical Theological Society*
JHS	*Journal of Hebrew Scriptures*
Joüon	Paul Joüon. *A Grammar of Biblical Hebrew*. Translated and revised by T. Muraoka. 2nd ed. Rome: Gregorian and Biblical, 2009
JPS	Jerusalem Publication Society: *Tanakh*
JSNTSup	Journal for the Study of the New Testament: Supplement Series

JSOT	*Journal for the Study of the Old Testament*
JSOTSup	Journal for the Study of the Old Testament: Supplement Series
JTS	*Journal of Theological Studies*
KAT	Kommentar zum Alten Testament
KJV	King James Version
LHBOTS	Library of Hebrew Bible/Old Testament Studies
LXX	Septuagint
MT	Masoretic Text
NASB	New American Standard Bible
NCV	New Century Version
NET	New English Translation
NICOT	New International Commentary on the Old Testament
NIDOTTE	*New International Dictionary of Old Testament Theology and Exegesis*. Edited by Willem A. VanGemeren. 5 vols. Grand Rapids: Zondervan, 1997
NIV11	New International Version, 2011 Update
NIV85	New International Version, 1985 Edition
NIVAC	New International Version Application Commentary
NRSV	New Revised Standard Version
NVI	Nueva Versión Internacional
OBT	Overtures in Biblical Theology
OTE	*Old Testament Essays*
OT	Old Testament
OTL	Old Testament Library
PRSt	*Perspectives in Religious Studies*
PSB	*Princeton Seminary Bulletin*
RBL	*Review of Biblical Literature*
RSV	Revised Standard Version
RTR	*Reformed Theological Review*
RVR1995	Reina-Valera, 1995 Update
SCH2000	Schlachter, 2000 Update
SG21	Segond 21
SJT	*Scottish Journal of Theology*
TrinJ	*Trinity Journal*
TTJ	*Trinity Theological Journal*
VT	*Vetus Testamentum*
WBC	Word Bible Commentary
WO	Waltke, Bruce K. and M. O'Connor. *An Introduction to Biblical Hebrew Syntax*. Winona Lake, IN: Eisenbrauns, 1990
WTJ	*Westminster Theological Journal*
WUNT	Wissenschaftliche Untersuchungen zum Neuen Testament
WW	*Word and World*
ZAW	*Zeitschrift für die alttestamentliche Wissenschaft*

Chapter 1

ETHICAL SPEECH IN JOB: AN INTRODUCTION

The bold, brash way that Job talks about and to God leaves most readers bewildered. Job says to Eliphaz, "For the arrows of the Almighty are in me, from which my spirit drinks poison; the terrors of God are arrayed against me" (6:4).[1] Job also says to God, "Your hands shaped me and made me; but now you have destroyed me completely" (10:8). The tenor of these statements is not unique; Job consistently describes God's actions against him as violent and destructive (3:23; 7:12-15, 17-20; 9:17-18; 10:10-13; 13:20-28; 16:7-17; 17:6; 19:6-22; 23:15-16; 27:2; 30:18-23). Job even suggests God is unjust (9:22-24; 21:7-33; 24:1-17, 21-23). These shocking statements offend his friends and make the reader uncomfortable. These statements, though, also contrast with Job's initial statements in the prologue as well as some of Job's other statements in his dialogue with his interlocutors (1:21; 2:10; 13:15; 16:19; 19:25). Even more amazing is that Yahweh assesses Job's speech throughout the book as נְכוֹנָה—truth (42:7-8). Job's talk to God and about God throughout the book raises questions. Is this speech ethical? Should one talk this way? Is Job a model? Is Job paradigmatic in some ways but not in others? Has Job sinned in his speech? How are Job's words related to the (implied) author's communicative goals? The present study seeks to investigate this issue of ethical God-talk in the book of Job, that is, the rightness or wrongness of discourse to God and about God.

---

1. All translations are my own unless otherwise noted.

Foundations for the Study

For the past three decades, speech ethics has been an area of scholarly interest in biblical studies. In pursuing the study of speech ethics, the book of Job has received some attention, though there is no full-length study that explores the question of the book's contribution to the ethics of God-talk. William Baker defines speech ethics as "the idea of ethics or morality as applied to interpersonal communication. Simply put, it is the rights and wrongs of utterance. It involves when to speak, how to speak, and to whom to speak, as well as when, how, and to whom not to speak" (Baker 1995: 2).[2] In other words, propositional content and context are crucial factors in assessing ethical speech. Context includes addressee, timing, and rhetorical situation. Context matters because certain speech may be acceptable in certain contexts, but not in others. For example, certain utterances are acceptable in an informal gathering of friends at a local restaurant that are not acceptable in the formal setting of a workplace. In this study, a rhetorical situation defines this context.[3] Identifying the situation provides a way to assess the content, form (genre), and illocution of an utterance.

In the context of the Old Testament, something that is ethical is consistent with or conforms to God's standard; it is approved by God. God is the norm of what is ethical (Kaiser 1983: 5–6; Wright 2004: 23–47). God as the arbiter of ethical speech especially makes sense for a study of the book of Job, where we have two divine speech acts at the end of the book, both of which assess the ethics of speech. These divine verdicts are instrumental in assessing the book's contribution to ethical God-talk.

Ethical speech, like an ethical act, may be obligatory or permissible. It is praiseworthy—commendable, laudable, admirable, and exemplary. Ethical God-talk is speech to God or about God that is right, appropriate, true, and in alignment with God's standards.[4] The content of ethical

---

2. See also Härle (2011: 435–40) where he suggests (1) that a right word is a true word, that is, not an ignorant (unknowing) word, an erring word, or a lie; (2) that a right word corresponds to reality; and (3) that the right word should be said, noting that not all true words need to be said at all times.

3. See methodology below.

4. With this in mind, speech *to* God is understood as an utterance addressed to God; this is, in a word, prayer. Speech *about* God is an utterance that uses a third person form to predicate something about God, for example, his character or his actions. This requires a third person statement: "God is X" or "God does Y." This can be found in prayer (e.g., in the context of prayer one might say, "God is majestic; praise be to him") but can also be found in the context of address to another person. Both types of utterances—to God and about God—constitute God-talk.

God-talk is propositionally true and consistent with the reality of who God is and how he acts. It must also fit within one's situation, the context. For example, a situation in which one is suffering allows for the genre of lament, which permits a different range of acceptable aspects of utterances that may not be appropriate in other forms of discourse or in other contexts. The illocution—that is, communicative goal or intention—and addressee of lament are reasons that the standard of acceptable speech changes: it is an utterance addressed to God in faith seeking relief from suffering. Unethical speech, on the other hand, is an utterance that deviates from this norm, is inappropriate, or is sin. It is blameworthy—culpable, erring, and deserving of censure. Just as there are different degrees of ethical speech (e.g., permissible, obligatory, or supererogatory), so also are there different degrees of unethical speech (e.g., mistaken, culpably ignorant, or morally repugnant).[5]

Ethics are meaningful on both the individual level and at the level of the community. The book of Job focuses on the individual, specifically the individual innocent sufferer, but as canonical Scripture for a believing community, it has implications that reach to the level of that community. In other words, the book of Job teaches individual innocent sufferers amidst the believing community what ethical God-talk is.

The genre of wisdom, to which the book of Job traditionally belongs, has two implications for this study. First, speech ethics is a prominently featured theme in wisdom works (see Baker 1995). In fact, a cursory reading of the book of Proverbs indicates a major concern for appropriate speech and its various manifestations. Baker's background sections in his monograph highlight this well, while also showing how this was a major concern in other ancient cultures (3; see his background chapters). Second, wisdom literature is concerned with living well in God's world—living in light of the fear of Yahweh—and so the sense of ethics used in this study coheres with the concerns of the genre as a whole.

Recently, however, the notion of a collection of wisdom writings has been challenged.[6] On the one hand, the conclusions of the present study correspond to the encouragement of these scholars not to limit our understanding of the book of Job to a wisdom corpus. On the other hand, the theme of speech ethics also links the book of Job with other so-called wisdom texts. In other words, the book of Job fits naturally within at least

---

5. For this study, ethics and morality are synonymous; see Baker's usage of these terms (1995: 2).

6. See Kynes 2015: 11–38; 2018: 1–24; 2019; cf. Weeks 2015: 160–77, among others (see the entire collection of essays on this topic in Sneed 2015).

a couple of different families of texts. There is value in seeing how Job relates to other types of texts in the Hebrew Bible. Nevertheless, there is much to be gained by following the traditional designation as well, given that the topic that is the focus of this study, speech ethics, fits within the traditional designation of Job as wisdom: the book, like other wisdom books, deals with ethical speech and how to live well in God's world.

In light of these foundational concerns, this study examines the ethics of God-talk in the book of Job by asking this question: What does the book of Job contribute regarding the ethics of God-talk for the innocent sufferer?[7]

This study argues that the book's contribution to ethical God-talk is that it is right and good to engage God in protest prayer.[8] This study establishes that it is Job's discourse that is the primary vehicle by which the book makes its contribution regarding this theme. Building on this finding, I demonstrate that the shape and content of the book affirm both Job's protest prayer itself and his defense of protest prayer as ethical, though aspects of each are deemed unethical. More specifically, the narrative frame, especially Job 42:7-8, establishes the ethical nature of Job's protest prayer and his defense of it. Another divine assessment, however, is found in the whirlwind speeches, which nuances the frame's assessment by highlighting aspects of Job's protest prayer and his defense of his protest prayer as unethical. Job's unethical speech includes his propositional content of cosmic divine injustice and Job's intention in using his oath to constrain God to act. The argument thus first establishes the saliency of the theme of ethical God-talk and that Job's discourse is the primary rhetorical means for the (implied) author regarding this theme (Chapter 2). Next, I analyze Job's discourse and its rhetoric (Chapters 3 through 5). This analysis is then considered in light of the Elihu and Yahweh sections and their effect on the reader (Chapter 6). In light of the arrangement of the book of Job, the divine assessments balance each other to affirm protest prayer as ethical speech for the innocent sufferer.

---

7. The qualification "for the innocent sufferer" is important in that it takes seriously the prologue of the book.

8. The phrase "protest prayer" refers to a broad category, often described as lament in the scholarly literature, broadly understood. To avoid confusion, I use "lament" to refer to a specific kind of protest prayer, related to, yet distinct from, "complaint." In other words, protest prayer is a broad term that encompasses two related but distinct kinds of prayer, the lament and the complaint. By choosing this terminology, I am able to reserve the terms "lament" and "complaint" to designate specific form-critical categories. These are defined below on pp. 15–17. I also use the term prayer to refer to any verbal communication directed to God.

Contextualizing the Study

There are five pillars of literature that provide the foundation upon which this study builds. The following review surveys the works most germane, beginning with the significant work of Gustavo Gutiérrez, and then turns to rhetorical studies on the book of Job, recent commentaries that stress the ethics of God-talk as a theological contribution of the book of Job, form-critical work on the book of Job, and, finally, literature on protest prayer.

More than thirty years ago, Gustavo Gutiérrez published *On Job: God-Talk and the Suffering of the Innocent* (1987). It remains the seminal work to date for the study of ethical God-talk in the book of Job. He suggests that the book is about how to talk about God, arguing that this is the preeminent theme in the book of Job (xviii, 11–13).[9] Job, he suggests, both in his piety and his protest, is a paradigm for those who suffer (4). He broadly analyzes the dialogues to show Job's movement as he connects with the poor. Job's identification with the poor provides the foundation for Job's correct God-talk (19–49). Job's confrontational complaint, Gutiérrez contends, exhibits his faith and leads to his encounter with Yahweh that pushes him to understand Yahweh's freedom (51–92). He concludes that the book of Job encourages its readers to speak out prophetically against the lot of the poor while also engaging God in honest, confrontational, yet hope-filled ways (93–4, 101). Although Gutiérrez's work has been a catalyst in the study of ethical God-talk, its limited size, scope, and methodology leave room for more comprehensive analysis.[10] In particular, Gutiérrez leaves unexplored the rhetoric of the book as it relates to ethical God-talk.[11]

---

9. Cheney (1994: 24–83, esp. 67–9) has argued similarly in his literary study, though his study focuses more on characterization than developing the insight regarding the issue of proper speech.

10. One issue is how Gutiérrez understands Job's commitment to the lot of the poor as the foundation for his contemplation of God's freedom (see 1987: 31–4, 51, 56). This interpretation struggles to make sense of the order of the book: how are Job 21 and Job 24 a foundation for Job's reflection in Job 9, 16, and 19? It is unclear to me how what Job says in Job 21 and 24 can help him come to terms with God's freedom when these chapters come *after* what Job has already said about his hope in God.

11. A number of other studies pertain to ethical God-talk as well, though less directly. One such study is Greenstein (2006: 238–58), where he argues, building on Gutiérrez, the book of Job's primary topic is discourse—"discourse is not only [the book's] medium but its topic" (240). Another study is Harding (2010: 523–47), where he argues that the book of Job, based on its focus on speech, is a "metaprophecy,"

The second pillar of literature includes the works that apply rhetorical criticism to the book of Job. The rhetoric of the book as it relates to proper speech has been treated recently by Charles Yu (2011). Employing the rhetorical theory of Lloyd Bitzer (1992: 1–14), Yu contends that ancient Israelite mourning practices provide the background for understanding the rhetoric in the book (i.e., the book's rhetorical situation) (15–17; see also 29–74, 151–96).[12] With this sociological framework in mind, Yu outlines the motives, goals, and rhetorical strategies for each speech. He suggests Job is seeking to provoke God into action; the friends, meanwhile, are seeking to renegotiate Job's social status in light of his suffering (176–95). Yu's rhetorical analysis of the speech acts of the book provide an important dialogue partner for this study on a number of levels. First, his analysis of the friends' speeches helps establish the literary rhetorical situation for Job's speeches. Second, his analysis of Job's speeches provides an important starting point for considering Job's rhetoric within the book, though his analysis is lacking at certain points due to the scope of his study. Third, though the majority of the rhetorical analysis in Yu's study is what I am referring to as "internal" rhetoric, his conclusion has some brief musings regarding the "external" rhetoric of the book, which relate to speech ethics.[13] He concludes that the book provides a warning to sages

wrestling with (and critiquing) themes found in the prophetic books. Harding suggests, based on 9:33, 13:7-9, and 23:12, that "trustworthy speech about the deity is impossible because the deity is free to act in unpredictable ways of which humans may never be granted knowledge" (537). My study focuses not on the impossibility of speech about God, but the ethics of speech to and about God. Additionally, there is Nam's work (2003). His contention that Job is commended for speaking to God (i.e., constructively) has been echoed with slight variation by other scholars. See Oeming 2000: 103–16; van Hecke 2003: 115–24; Seow 2011b: 70–92. A number of scholars have assessed the rightness (or wrongness) of Job's speech. For example, see Newell 1984: 298–316; Baker 1995: 30–1, 194–5; Balentine 1998: 259–78; Fox 2011: 145–62; Walton 2012: 173–4, 188–9, 229–30, 270–2, 291, 331–5, 433; Longman 2012: 98, 104–7, 173, 181–3, 203, 215–16, 243–5, 280–2, 304–5, 365–6, 459; Kynes 2013d: 174–91; Fox 2013: 1–23. Newell emphasizes Job's need for repentance, while Walton and Longman highlight deficiencies in Job's God-talk. Baker understands Job to be a blasphemer, a negative paradigm for speech ethics. Fox thinks Job's words "are less than laudable" at points. Kynes and Balentine, on the other hand, emphasize the rightness of Job's lament. These assessments notwithstanding, Clines suggests that the patient Job of the prologue and the impatient Job of the dialogue can both be paradigms for the reader, depending on one's needs (Clines 1989: xxxviii–xxxix).

12. See Lambert (2015: 557–75), which is discussed below.

13. On the distinction between "internal" and "external" rhetoric, see Howard 2008: 132–46. Howard defines "external" rhetoric as the text's rhetoric toward the

and to comforters, namely, that they should recognize and respect their epistemic limits and not be cruel by imposing rigid dogma upon those who are despairing (415–16, 418). His focus is on what might be termed comforter speech ethics, what he calls "comforter malpractice" (285–6, 307, 311, 329, 338, 361–4). Yu's study demonstrates that speech ethics is a persuasive concern of the book, that the book is concerned with shaping the reader in regards to how to think about proper speech and act accordingly. The warning to sages and comforters is the obverse side of the same coin to the topic treated in this study, ethical God-talk. Yu's contribution regarding the internal rhetoric provides an important foundation for this study.

Another rhetorical-critical study that pertains to the ethics of God-talk is Dale Patrick and Allen Scult's brief treatment in *Rhetoric and Biblical Interpretation* (1990: 81–102). Patrick and Scult argue that the book of Job is primarily about proper expression of faith in the midst of suffering (95–6). They come closest to dealing with the rhetorical nature of the theme of ethical God-talk, though their study of the book of Job is dominated more by exploring methodological concerns than a rhetorical reading of the book as a whole.[14]

Pieter van der Lugt's (1995) book-length rhetorical-critical study of the book of Job is also worth mentioning. Van der Lugt's study is more along the lines of Muilenburg's proposal for rhetorical criticism, with his focus on stylistics and structuring speeches in the book of Job, offering only brief comments on what this analysis indicates about the main ideas of

---

reader, and "internal" rhetoric as the rhetoric of the psalmist in his prayer to God. Both aspects of rhetoric will be addressed in this project. The internal rhetoric (Job's persuasion of God and the friends) provides the foundation for the external rhetoric (the book's contribution regarding the ethics of God-talk). Though he does not use these terms, Yu's argument proceeds along the same lines (2011: 411–18). In other words, one of the persuasive strategies of the author is his manipulation of the characters in the book. This will be further established in Chapter 2 below, particularly as it relates to Job and his discourse and the role this discourse plays in the author's rhetorical strategies regarding ethical God-talk.

14. Scholars have discerned and interpreted a number of Job's rhetorical strategies, though few studies bring them together. For Job's rhetorical use of the Psalms, see Kynes 2012; 2013a: 201–13; 2013c: 34–48. For Job's rhetorical use of Isaiah, see Kynes 2013b: 94–105. For Job's use of a pseudosorites, see O'Connor 1987a: 239–53; 1987b: 161–72; Patterson 2010: 19–36. For the use of interrogatives in the speech cycles, see Magary 2005: 283–98. On the rhetoric of conceptual metaphor, see Hawley 2018. The commentaries treat rhetoric on occasion as well; see Habel 1985; Clines 1989; Newsom 1996; Clines 2006, 2011.

any particular speech. The current study, by contrast, focuses on rhetorical criticism by looking at persuasion (see the methodology below).

The third pillar of literature upon which this study builds is the commentaries on the book of Job. In particular, two recent commentaries have been attentive to the question of ethical God-talk, focusing on protest prayer. The first is C. L. Seow's magisterial commentary in the Illuminations series (2013). Seow is attentive to the theological contribution of different voices within the book. Summarizing the theology of the character Job, Seow argues, "Job's theology has ethical implications. This is true not only for those who suffer but also for those in their community… The lament tradition is…reaffirmed, even for laments *in extremis*, even for words that border on blasphemy" (91–2). His analysis of Job 6 is especially insightful in this regard, as he highlights how ethical speech is at the center of the debate between Job and his friends (452–68), though exactly how the book focuses on this theme and a more robust understanding of what this contribution regarding the ethics of God-talk is remain topics for further investigation. The second is Lindsay Wilson's commentary in the Two Horizons Old Testament Commentary series (2015).[15] Wilson argues one of the purposes of the book is to show that "complaints and questioning" can be "legitimate expression[s] of the faith of a righteous person," and thus "can in some circumstances be appropriate" (10). Accordingly, Wilson outlines the book's theological contribution regarding protest prayer (242–57, 368–82). This attention to the book's contribution to protest prayer indicates the traction of Gutiérrez's contention among recent interpreters.

Fourth, in light of this study's methodology, form-critical studies on the book of Job deserve mention. The work of Westermann (1974) is significant in this regard. He suggests the dominant form of Job's speeches is lament. But Job uses other forms as well: wish, hymn, asseveration of innocence, and avowal of trust (1981b: 42–59). Westermann's contribution remains the seminal form-critical work on the book of Job, though Murphy (1981), Hartley (1988), and Clines (1989, 2006, 2011) are also sensitive to form-critical concerns. While the analysis in this study is not merely form-critical, the insights of these scholars provide a foundation from which to evaluate Job's use of forms (i.e., genres) to discern Job's rhetorical goals, as noted in the discussion of methodology below.

The fifth and final pillar upon which this study builds is the voluminous literature on protest prayer. Westermann's contributions are seminal for the scholarly work on a theology of lament that has emerged in recent

---

15. See also Wilson's shorter articles (2003: 121–38; 2005: 384–9).

years.[16] He draws attention to the centrality of the lament tradition for OT theology given its significance in the exodus event: the people cry out in distress (i.e., lament) and are delivered. Thus, lament plays a major role from the inception the nation of Israel; the pattern of cry and deliverance is set in the Pentateuch (Westermann 1974: 20–30; cf. Brueggemann 1995a: 77–82). Westermann (1974: 23) argues that the book of Job continues this trajectory as "a mighty fugue based on the cry of lamentation; it alone indicates the underlying significance that the lament had in Israel for talk of God, that is, for theology." He is also attentive to the rhetorical nature of the lament as it seeks to move God to act on the sufferer's behalf (24–6; cf. Westermann 1998: 239; Wilson 2015: 251).

Brueggemann subsequently develops Westermann's contributions in a number of publications. He stresses how lament testifies to Israel's (and the OT's) insistence that life is lived authentically in a dialogic relationship with Yahweh, and suggests that the covenant relationship between God and his people is negatively affected without lament (Brueggemann 1995a: 67–8; 1995c: 102–3; cf. Balentine 1993: 9). Biblical lament testifies and gives expression to life in this fallen world, providing language for seasons of turmoil. The lament tradition gives innocent sufferers an avenue by which they can articulate that things are not as they ought to be, arguing with God to change the situation in accordance with his covenant promises. Yet, biblical lament is not merely the expression of negative feelings; it includes the petition to God to deliver (Wilson 2015: 244).

Because OT lament wrestles with God, Brueggemann (1985: 400–401) also notes that it challenges what is considered acceptable speech. But as speech directed to God it is acceptable, even if daring, because it appeals to the only one who can change the circumstances (Ross 2013: 150). Although lament is a minority voice in the OT it is not insignificant (Brueggemann 1985: 395–415). The extensive use of lament in the OT commends this kind of prayer as fundamental to the life of faith in this fallen world, not something to be suppressed or overcome by spiritual growth (Moberly 1997: 879). Significantly, God honors this kind of language (Brueggemann 1995a: 69; Balentine 1993: 147).

A number of other scholars have contributed to our understanding of the workings of protest prayer. In particular, the works of Miller (1993: 356–62; 1994: 55–225; 1998: 211–32), Broyles (1989), Balentine (1993: 146–98), and Janowski (2009) provide rich biblical, theological,

16. See, e.g., Westermann 1974: 20–38; 1998: 233–41; Broyles 1989; Balentine 1993: 118–98; Miller 1994: 55–143; Brueggemann 1995a: 67–83; 1995b: 3–32; 1995c: 98–111; 1995d: 84–97; Billman and Migliore 1999; Wolterstorff 2001: 42–52; Brown and Miller 2005b; Morrow 2006a; Billings 2015.

and anthropological understanding of protest prayer. From a Jewish perspective, Laytner's study, *Arguing with God* (1990), shows how frequently the arguing-with-God motif materialized in Jewish history and religious practices, establishing how, from the biblical period through the rabbinic period to post-Holocaust writers, the protest prayer motif is a significant way to engage God—arguing with God against God.[17]

More recently, Lambert (2015: 557–75) helps connect the practice of lament with ritual mourning. He argues that the book of Job should be understood as a work featuring ritual mourning, "a sort of fable of failed consolation and its development" (562). He suggests the dialogue is about encouraging Job to emerge from his ritual mourning when he fails to do so after seven days and night of silence. Lament—or protest prayer—is mourning verbalized, according to Lambert (563).

A number of key insights and themes run through this literature. In particular, protest prayer is an inherently faith-filled act. The one who protests in prayer is bringing their concerns to the only one who can change their circumstances—God—testifying to a radical faith.[18] Brueggemann describes protest prayer as an act "of relentless hope" (1985: 402).[19] Thus, Wilson argues that OT laments encourage a "genuine faith in the midst of trouble, a faith that knows that, even when God seems silent, help can come from no one else except God. This is not a failure of faith, but a part of genuine faith that has the courage to doubt, to complain, to protest—knowing that God and God alone can meet him in his utter darkness"; the act of lament is a "desperate struggle of faith, for faith" (2015: 250–1). He concludes, "The laments are a legitimate part of a robust adult faith that knows that God will not be shattered or provoked by strong words of protest... Yet the book of Job presents [protest prayer] as a legitimate part of faith when a righteous person, not being punished for his sin, undergoes unspeakable loss and suffering and experiences God as silent or absent" (255). Relatedly, at the heart of protest prayer is the petition. All of the elements of these prayers build upon and reinforce the petition for God to change the complainant's situation. These will be important ideas as we study protest prayer in the book of Job.

One final aspect of protest prayer is worth mentioning, namely, the historical development of the practice. Westermann seems to be the first to develop an understanding of the historical development of protest

---

17. See also Blumenthal (1993), who develops these insights in an interdisciplinary way, combining theology with psychology.

18. Wolterstorff (2001: 45) argues that without faith lament is impossible.

19. See also Brown and Miller 2005a: xv; Wolterstorff 2001: 43–4.

prayer (1981a: 165–213). He suggests that the exilic experience, where God judged Israel according to her sin, established a milieu in which "complaint against God was absolutely disallowed" (171). This understanding has been developed and qualified by others,[20] with William Morrow in particular developing these insights as they pertain to the book of Job (2006a: 129–46). Building on the work of Karl Jaspers, Morrow suggests broader intellectual and philosophical movements are at play (what he calls the "Axial Age") where "[t]he book of Job is responding to a crisis in the liturgical economy of early Judaism: the complaint against God became theologically problematic in the post-exilic era" (129). He concludes, "[t]he intransigent refusal of Job's comforters to entertain the force of his complaint against God and his declarations of innocence points to their engagement with Axial Age influences. In the pre-exilic period, wisdom discourse as well as complaint rhetoric existed in Israel. It is the assertion of wisdom theology to the exclusion of complaint rhetoric by Job's comforters that marks a theological turning point in the history of biblical thought" (138). Morrow does not think, however, that the writer of the book intends to resolve the question of the ethics of protest prayer (146). In any event, according to Morrow, the book of Job testifies to a shift away from protest prayer to penitential prayer, which is suggestive of when the book was written.[21] I will return to these historical insights in Chapter 7 as we consider the rhetorical situation of the book of Job.

The Methodology of the Study

This study moves through three phases of investigation. The first phase of investigation is a literary-rhetorical analysis of the book of Job. A rhetorical analysis of the book of Job demands a literary approach, meaning it approaches the book as a unified composition, a narrative with narration and dialogue.[22] This view of the book has become more common

---

20. See Werline 1998; Boda 1999; 2001: 186–97; 2003: 51–75; cf. the collection of essays in Boda et al. 2006. In particular, see Balentine 2006b: 1–20; Boda 2006a: 21–50; Rom-Shiloni 2006: 51–68; Bautch 2006: 83–99; Morrow 2006b: 101–17; Boda 2006b: 181–92; and Balentine 2006a: 193–204.
21. Though I disagree with Morrow's exegesis of many of the sections of the book of Job (as the study below will elucidate), his historical insights are keen.
22. See Watson and Hauser 1994: 4–7. Hauser notes that the relationship between rhetorical criticism and literary criticism is sometimes hard to distinguish, especially in that rhetorical critics must pay attention to the literary artistry of the text being analyzed. The literary features of the text are the means by which the (implied)

in recent years (Habel 1985: 35–7; Seow 2013: 26–39). The question this project addresses needs to be answered by understanding the implied author's intent. The implied author, as Booth articulates, is the projection of the author the reader establishes in their own mind during the reading process—the imprint real authors leave of themselves in the text (1983: 70–4, 138). This is important because there is no clear understanding of the historical author of the book of Job; the concept of the implied author allows interpreters to reconstruct the author and the author's perspective from the text (Powell 2010: 242).[23] Following Hauser's methodological lead,[24] the first phase of investigation is a close reading of the book of Job to show how the content and shape of the book raise the ethics of Job's God-talk as an important interpretive focus. This is done through applying literary and rhetorical analysis rooted in the works of Meir Sternberg (1987) and Robert Alter (1981), highlighting how the content and shape (i.e., structure) of the book of Job focus on Job's speech and the ethics of Job's speech as a major contribution of the book's theology.[25] Biblical texts are inherently rhetorical, shaping readers' minds and hearts (see Vanhoozer 1998: 175; Sternberg 1987: 482). This first phase is preliminary, seeking to uncover how the (implied) author shapes the reader, what Howard calls the "external" rhetoric (2008: 132–46).[26] This phase cannot and does not answer this study's question, though it lays an important foundation for the second phase of investigation.

---

author persuades readers (see Wenham 2000: 2–3); see also Powell 1990: 6–21; Corbett 1969: xxv–xxvi. Powell helpfully distinguishes between rhetorical criticism, narrative criticism, and literary criticism. He suggests that the term literary criticism be used as an umbrella term, under which narrative criticism and rhetorical criticism fall. Narrative criticism and rhetorical criticism, he suggests, are similar, yet distinct. The former is ahistorical (but not anti-historical), while the latter is historical in so far as it addresses the practical issue of what a work is attempting to accomplish in a specific historical situation (the rhetorical situation) (Powell 1990: 14–15). Thus, these are related methods, where the literary artistry of the text is the foundation for the rhetorical analysis.

23. See also Booth 1983: 20.

24. Hauser rightly argues that the literary artistry of the text needs to set the agenda, and, with adequate study of biblical narratives and texts, the critic can use this knowledge to do rhetorical criticism (Watson and Hauser 1994: 7).

25. See also Booth 1983, generally, but especially 3–4. Fox has briefly worked out some ideas regarding how the narrative of Job shapes the reader (2005: 356–8; 2011: 145–62). More methodological musings regarding this first phase are outlined at beginning of Chapter 2.

26. See n. 13 above.

The second phase of investigation applies rhetorical analysis to Job's speeches.[27] It investigates the "internal" rhetoric of the book—the rhetoric Job uses in his persuasion of God and his friends in the narrative world. The second phase of analysis is completed in three steps for each one of Job's speeches.

The first step is to identify the literary rhetorical situation.[28] What has happened that has brought about the situation to which Job must respond? What motivates him to speak? What is the goal of his discourse?[29] This means Job's speeches are analyzed in light of previous narrative action (for Job 3) and the matrix of previous speeches (for Job's subsequent speeches) to identify to what Job is responding and why. This keeps the interpretation of Job's rhetoric grounded in the literary context, showing his interactions with the friends and with God while also showing how his friends influence his discourse.

The second step is to examine the form of Job's speeches using established form-critical categories to understand the central aim of his speech.[30] This clarifies and confirms the rhetorical situation, because the

---

27. In the present work, rhetorical criticism refers to the study of how persuasion is attempted and achieved (see Bryant 1953: 401–24). As Fox writes, "The task of rhetorical criticism is…to examine and evaluate the interactions among the three constituents of the rhetorical transaction that takes place between rhetor and audience: strategies, situations, and effects (effects potential as well as real, ideal as well as actual, long-range as well as immediate)" (1980b: 4). Muilenburg's call (1969: 1–18) to go beyond form criticism is often seen as the landmark shift toward rhetoric, but the subsequent focus on rhetoric really amounted to a study of stylistics. On the application of rhetorical criticism in OT studies, see Howard 1994: 87–104.

28. See Bitzer 1992: 1–14. He notes that any work of rhetoric is pragmatic and has a goal of effecting change. This demands that rhetoric is grounded in some kind of situation that gives rise to it. This situation provides a clue as to what the aim of the rhetoric is. The situation is comprised of three components: (1) an exigency, (2) an audience, and (3) constraints. A complex rhetorical situation may have multiple exigencies, audiences, and constraints simultaneously. Yu also utilized Bitzer's theory in his rhetorical study of the book of Job. What I am calling the "literary rhetorical situation" Yu describes as the "fictive" rhetorical situation (2011: 10–11). Typically, the first step of rhetorical analysis is to delimit the literary unit under investigation (see Trible 1994: 101–6; Kennedy 1984: 33–8; Lundbom 1997: xxxiii–xliii), but every speech of Job is clearly demarcated except one, Job 26. For this speech I will defend my understanding of the rhetorical unit under investigation prior to establishing its rhetorical situation.

29. These questions are drawn from Yu (2011: 11).

30. This is not a full-scale form-critical analysis of Job's speeches. As Vanhoozer points out, right reading requires understanding the rules and following them as

form-critical categories provide a clue to the central aim of his speech (see Broyles 1989: 26). Job's speeches often combine multiple forms (*Gattungen*), so an understanding of the small units must inform the overall effect of a speech segment and even overall speech. Accordingly, the form of each clause of Job's speeches is categorized, and, from this micro-level, a macro-level form(s) for each speech is determined.[31] The forms of Job's speeches identified in this study are disputation, complaint, lament, petition, avowal of trust, hymn, wish/imprecation, avowal of innocence, and oath. Forms sometimes labeled but not included in this study are legal speech, wisdom instruction, riddle, warning, and taunt. The reason these are excluded is because they work with or comprise disputation (Murphy 1981: 176). In other words, these latter forms are used as specific elements in the broader form of disputation.

One might object to the use of form criticism in a literary-rhetorical study such as this one. Weeks' recent essay (2013: 15–25) offers a cogent warning regarding the challenges of modifying form criticism given its assumptions and origin. Nevertheless, the ubiquity of discussions regarding forms (or genres, *Gattungen*) in Joban scholarship makes the use of them in this study necessary. While I agree with Weeks' critique on the whole and understand the limitations, the use of form-critical categories as defined below—rather than a wholesale form-critical approach—is designed to understand convention and genre within this literary work. In doing so, I hope to mitigate his concerns, to some degree, with the result of illuminating the book of Job and its rhetoric in a fresh way. There is no historical emphasis in the form-critical aspect of this study.[32] The use of form criticism is designed to capture the genres of an overall speech or speech segment and from this to confirm or clarify the rhetorical situation thereby.

---

readers (1998: 335–50). Foundational for this is a proper understanding of genre, which has some kind of intent. This means that some awareness of the accepted forms (*Gattungen*) Job uses is key for understanding his goal. See also Longman 1985: 46–67, esp. 61–3; Osborne 1983: 1–27, esp. 24. Typically, rhetorical studies employ Greek rhetorical genres (i.e., deliberative, judicial, and epideictic). However, since these categories are of questionable value for OT rhetoric given their Greco-Roman roots, established form-critical genres are used.

31. A clause is defined as any unit with a verb or implied verb. In the course of each discussion of forms, these numbers will be reported. For example, in Job 6 there are seventy-seven clauses, fifty of which are disputation.

32. See n. 30 above.

The following definitions of the forms identified in this study provide the basis for the labeling (i.e., the form's distinctive elements) as well as providing the function of the form.

Disputation. Murphy (1981: 175–6) suggests that the disputation form is "an argument between two or more parties, in which differing points of view are held."[33] The function of this form is to rebut and to persuade. Many interpreters suggest this is the dominant form in the book in Job 4–27.[34] It is important to note that other forms can be used to make up disputation (Murphy 1981: 176),[35] but the purpose of these other forms is subsumed by the intention of disputing another's ideas or perspective.

Complaint. This form is marked by the use of interrogatives, specifically "why" (לָמָה), imperatives and negated jussives, and reproachful content or tone (Broyles 1989: 38–9, 46–7).[36] This form is specifically accusatory (compared to the more general lament), and often directed toward God for wronging the complainant (21, 52).[37] Complaints accuse God of passive inaction or active divine violence (38).[38] In other words, God's actions are currently perceived to be not what the complainant expects of God and

---

33. Sweeney (2008: 238) notes that disputation is often marked by an identified thesis of the disputant, a counterthesis which the new speaker will argue, and the argumentation.

34. See ibid.; Longman 2008: 108, 112; Murphy 1981: 23–36. There is not a consensus regarding the topic of dispute. Some suggestions include wisdom (Longman 2008: 108–9, 112), the source or reason for Job's suffering (Sweeney 2008: 238), or the doctrine of retribution (Murphy 1981: 16). The suggestion of this project is that the topic under dispute is ethical God-talk.

35. For example, the instruction, riddles, and rhetorical questions of Job 6 are used for disputation. Westermann, however, notes that even though the beginnings of most speeches in the book are disputation, speeches on the whole are not disputation (1981b: 17). This can probably be questioned in the sense that other forms can be used in disputation (rhetorical questions, instructions, riddles, hymns, extended topoi, etc.). The opening of each speech often indicates the whole speech is a disputation. For example, the *topos* of the fate of the wicked in the second cycle is used as a part of the disputation—it is the evidence brought to bear on the point under dispute.

36. See also Morrow 2006a: 49; Murphy 1981: 174; Gerstenberger 1988: 246; Westermann 1998: 240; Miller 1994: 70–9. The petitionary verbal forms (imperatives and negated jussives) will be labeled as petitions, despite their indication of complaint.

37. Broyles calls these "God-laments" (1989: 35–53).

38. Sin may be the root for God's active antagonism (divine affliction) and passive indifference (divine abandonment or absence), but sin may also be irrelevant (Morrow 2006a: 59). Accusation can be made in both second and third person contexts.

knows to be true of God,[39] thus indicating an appeal—a persuasive intent, usually accomplished through provocative and evocative language (14).[40] Thus it is a specific accusation, blame, rebuke, and appeal, even if the appeal is not explicitly expressed.[41]

Lament. Lament belongs to the same broad category as complaint, but a lament is more general than a complaint; "a lament focuses on a situation; the complaint focuses on the one responsible" (Broyles 1989: 40).[42] Lament, therefore, is best seen in statements that describe general expressions related to personal conditions, and expressions decrying the hostile actions of others (Miller 1994: 79–86). Like complaint, at its core a lament is also an appeal, even when the appeal is not explicit, and seeks change through provocative and evocative means. Laments attest to a situation that requires reparation.

Petition. This form can be identified by the syntactical/grammatical features of the volitional mood (imperatives and negated second person jussives) (Gerstenberger 1988: 254). As Gerstenberger notes, the petition is the "central element" of protest prayer in that all other elements support this aspect (ibid.), but it will be helpful to note specifically where these occur in order to understand their function in their respective settings in the book of Job. Petitions can also play a prominent role in disputation (e.g., Job 6), so the function of a petition is determined by context.

Avowal of Trust. This form is distinguished most clearly by its content and tone. This form expresses certainty and can be found with complaint where trust in God is expressed. This form is found in two specific passages in Job, in 16:19-21 and 19:25-27 (Westermann 1981b: 101–2). These passages are expressions of Job's faith, as this study details below in the analysis of these passages.

Hymn. The hymn form is marked notably by the participle and has a description of God's character or actions as content (Gerstenberger 1988: 249; Murphy 1981: 176; Futato 2008: 301–4). Hymns can function as expressions of order and expressions of faith (Futato 2008: 304–5), but in

---

39. Westermann (1998: 238) notes complaints "perceive a discrepancy in God"; see also Broyles 1989: 42–4.

40. See also Westermann 1998: 239; 1974: 25–6. Complaints appeal to God against God (Broyles 1989: 52).

41. On the lack of explicit appeal, see Howard's discussion on Ps. 88 (2008: 132–46). See also Morrow (2006a: 36), where he rightly notes that complaint and request for action "are two sides of the same coin. To have complained about divine action is already to have indicated the solution that is sought for."

42. On the relationship between lament and complaint, see also Miller 1994: 68–9, 382 n. 54; Morrow 2006a: 10.

the context of complaint they function as a rhetorical strategy to juxtapose what is believed about God and what is currently being experienced (Broyles 1989: 42–4). They can also be used in the context of disputation as evidence of a thesis.

Wish/Imprecation/Curse. Wish has specific linguistic markers: מִי יִתֵּן, the use of jussives, the presence of לוּ, or some other particle that indicates the optative mood. A more general wish has the function of expressing a hope or something desired, often indicating a goal of the discourse. Wishes can also play a prominent role in disputations (e.g., Job 6). One specific type of wish is imprecation; Gerstenberger defines imprecation as "[a]n element in complaints that asks for the elimination of evil that is threatening the supplicant. Functionally, imprecation is thus part of the petition" (1988: 250).[43] Jussives dominate the imprecation, and function "to achieve the supplicant's liberation and restoration" (ibid.). The function is to invoke a deity to bring about disrepute on the object of the imprecation, and its connection to complaint and petition is significant.

Avowal of Innocence. This form is "[a] statement in which one denies wrongdoing or even affirms good behavior" (Murphy 1981: 173). This form can also be used in disputation or in complaint (Westermann 1981b: 97–8; Gerstenberger 1988: 255). The function, accordingly, is subsumed under those other forms when put in the service of those forms.

Oath/Purificatory Oath. This form is a statement in the cohortative or indicative, marked by an oath formula (e.g., חַי with a divine name or חָלִילָה לִּי) that binds the one who utters it to a particular action or position (Murphy 1981: 180).[44] It can be a so-called "negative confession" in which a negative outcome is called down upon the one who utters the oath, marked by אִם or אִם לֹא (ibid.).[45] The function of this form is also connected to the larger form for which it is put into service.

Motive Clauses. This form is often marked by כִּי and provides the reason for the preceding form to which it is connected. The motive clause can play a significant role in protest prayer as it provides the basis of the petition. Miller (1993: 356–62) suggests three types of motive clauses that play a prominent rhetorical role in moving God to act: (1) those that point to God's character, (2) those that stress the situation of the sufferer, (3) and those that stress the (fractured) relationship between God and the sufferer. But the motive clause can also play a role in justifying the previous form, whether disputation, wish, or other form.

---

43. See also Kitz 2007: 615–27; Strawn 2008: 314; Murphy 1981: 174–5.
44. See also Arnold and Choi 2003: 189; Joüon §165.
45. The clearest example of this is found in Job 31.

The form(s) of Job's speeches provide(s) inroads into understanding Job's rhetorical goal. In fact, identifying both the literary rhetorical situation and the forms Job uses provides the necessary information for identifying Job's rhetorical goal. Put differently, identifying the forms Job uses can clarify and/or confirm the rhetorical situation identified in the first step.

The third step in the second phase is to analyze the strategies of Job's persuasion in light of the established rhetorical goal(s). Persuasion is analyzed by giving close attention to the structure of a text or speech, the purpose of a text or speech, the self-portrayal of the author or speaker, the language (including key terms, euphemism, metaphor, and other literary devices), and how the language is manipulated for effect (see Simons 1986: 307–9; Trible 1994: 101–6; Hart and Daughton 2005: 94; cf. Kennedy 1984: 33–8). Thus, this step involves two aspects. The first aspect is to identify the structure of the speech under investigation to identify its main points and themes. The second aspect is to analyze the strategies of Job's speech. This step is done through a close reading of the speech with attention to specific strategies Job uses to accomplish his rhetorical goals. Each clause is analyzed for syntax, form, and literary devices. Literary devices include key words, structural elements, particles, rhetorical questions, allusion, pseudosorites, hyperbole, inclusio, parallelism, and tropes.[46] Tropes refer to imagery, metaphors, similes, motifs, and personification. The allusions examined in this study are those already established in previous scholarship.[47] These strategies are identified and interpreted, specifically seeking how these strategies are working to accomplish Job's goal(s) (i.e., what are the effects of Job's language?) (see Fox 1980b: 4; Simons 1986: 283; Lundbom 1997: xxiii). This analysis is done for each of the three speech cycles and Job's final speech.

With Job's rhetoric in mind, an analysis of the speeches of Elihu and Yahweh—both of whom evaluate Job's verbal expression—is necessary. This is the third phase of investigation. After this, I will draw conclusions regarding the book's contribution to the ethics of God-talk, as well as how this fits within the book's own reconstructed rhetorical situation.

The internal rhetorical analysis is limited to Job's speeches since it is his discourse that is of main concern in the book. A rhetorical analysis of the three friends in the dialogue section of the book is not done, though an awareness of their speeches is important for understanding Job's

46. This list is adapted from Lundbom (1997: xxxiii–xliii).
47. See, e.g., Kynes 2012. For more on allusion, see pp. 54–55 n. 38 below.

rhetorical situation. The speeches of Elihu (Job 32–37) and Yahweh (Job 38–42) are analyzed for their contribution to the external rhetoric, though this necessitates a brief internal rhetorical investigation.

In sum, this study combines rhetorical, literary, and form-critical methods by first noting the rhetorical and literary emphasis regarding Job's verbal discourse and then doing a rhetorical analysis of Job's speeches. In other words, it analyzes both the external and internal rhetoric of the book of Job to answer the question of the book's contribution to ethical God-talk in the midst of innocent suffering.

The Argument of the Study

The second chapter of this study corresponds to the first phase of investigation outlined above. This chapter engages in a rhetorical study of the book of Job as a whole, and outlines the book's external rhetoric, which focuses on Job's discourse as a fundamental interpretive concern. This chapter examines the content of the book as well as its structure. The content and structure correspond to strategies from biblical poetics such as repetition of key terms and themes, narratorial assessment, gaps, the use of dialogue, and the play of perspectives. Significantly, Job's verbal expression is a concern for every major character in the book; the theme of ethical God-talk is consistently found throughout the book. This shows that Job's discourse is an important interpretive focus for the book, and, moreover, is the main vehicle through which the book makes its contribution regarding ethical God-talk.

The third chapter initiates the second phase of investigation outlined above. Beginning with Job 3, this chapter conducts an internal rhetorical analysis of each one of Job's speeches in the first speech cycle (Job 3; 6–7; 9–10; and 12–14). Chapter 4 continues the second phase of investigation by looking at Job's speeches in the second cycle (Job 16–17; 19; and 21), while the fifth chapter brings this phase to a close by examining Job's speeches in the third cycle and his final speech (Job 23–24; 26:2-4; 27; 29–31). In each of these chapters, Job's speeches are treated in canonical order. Each speech is analyzed for its literary rhetorical situation and forms to discern Job's rhetorical goal(s). Job's rhetorical strategies are identified and interpreted for each speech.

In Chapter 6 the study moves out from an internal rhetorical investigation of Job's speeches to examine how Elihu (Job 32–37) and Yahweh (Job 38–42) respond to what Job has said. Based on a brief treatment of the internal rhetoric of these characters, the chapter examines the contribution these chapters make to the external rhetoric of the book. The chapter includes a discussion of Job's final speech acts in the book, Job 40:4-5 and 42:2-6, in light of Yahweh's speeches.

The final chapter, Chapter 7, summarizes the findings of Chapters 2 through 6 and draws conclusions regarding the book's contribution to ethical God-talk. This chapter examines these conclusions in light of a reconstructed rhetorical situation for the book, arguing that the book of Job is written in response to an ethos in which protest prayer was eschewed.

The argument of this study is that Job's God-talk throughout the book is highlighted by the narrative frame and the disputation, and has particular internal rhetorical goals that are used to accomplish the (implied) author's external rhetorical goals. Job's initial complaint in Job 3 is a bold, indeed visceral, response to the suffering he endures by which he attempts to move God to act on his behalf. Job's friends are appalled and offended by his language in his opening speech and seek to convince him to pray in other ways, namely, to repent. When Job continues his defense of speaking in such ways in Job 6, the friends escalate their own rhetoric, leading to a long dialogue over the ethics of God-talk for the (innocent) sufferer. The divine assessment, in both the whirlwind speeches and the epilogue, commends protest prayer to the innocent sufferer, while also qualifying aspects of Job's verbal expression as unethical. In sum, the book seeks to encourage its readers to recognize that protest prayer is an appropriate (i.e., ethical or right) way to speak to God.

Chapter 2

"JOB DID NOT SIN WITH HIS LIPS":
THE EXTERNAL RHETORIC OF THE BOOK OF JOB—
A PRELIMINARY INVESTIGATION

Building on Gutiérrez's contention that ethical God-talk is a salient theme in the book of Job (1987: xviii, 12–13), this chapter explores the external rhetoric of the book. First, the predominance of the theme is established through an examination of the distribution of *Leitwörter* that signify the theme of ethical God-talk. Second, the external rhetoric of the major structural units of the book is analyzed in light of established devices from biblical poetics. The analysis consists of the external rhetoric of the frame narrative, the dialogue, Job 28, Job's final speech, Elihu's speeches, and Yahweh's speeches. Taken together, these two aspects of the investigation reveal that the primary way in which the book of Job accomplishes its rhetorical goals with respect to the ethics of God-talk is through Job's verbal expression. In other words, Job's internal rhetoric is the primary means by which the (implied) author accomplishes his external rhetoric regarding ethical God-talk. Before this analysis, however, some methodological considerations are in order.

Methodological Considerations

Rhetorical and Literary Foundations
As religious literature, the Bible is ideological, and as ideological, it is inherently rhetorical. Vanhoozer (1998: 175) writes, "The Bible is ideological literature insofar as it seeks, through its rhetoric, to shape readers' minds and hearts in order to bring their attitude into alignment with its own" (see also Howard 2008: 132–46). As Vanhoozer demonstrates, the Bible is a communicative speech act which has intention; the communicative act is pragmatic (see also Sternberg 1987: 1).

The question, however, is how does the Bible shape its readers? Hauser suggests that the Bible shapes its readers through its literary artistry (Watson and Hauser 1994: 4–7). He writes (7),

> Admittedly, the rhetorical critic's task is complicated by the lack of any textbooks of ancient Hebrew rhetoric, which could be used to establish what constituted literary artistry in ancient Israel... One can, however, use a sustained, extensive study of texts in the Old Testament and in associated literature as a means of obtaining a good understanding of commonly-accepted literary standards in ancient Israel. To the extent to which one can recover ancient Israelite literary models, those models should direct any attempts to understand the literary artistry of particular biblical texts.

This kind of study has been undertaken by scholars like Meir Sternberg and Robert Alter.

The Contributions of Meir Sternberg and Robert Alter

Sternberg identifies, discusses, and illustrates a number of rules or strategies in biblical literature by which a biblical narrative shapes its readers (i.e., the "poetics" of biblical narrative). Prominent among these is the omniscient narrator. Sternberg (1987: 90; cf. 80–3) writes:

> The Bible...postulates a narrator with such free movement through time and space, the public and the private arena, that he invests his dramatizations with the authority of an omniscience equivalent to God's own... And whether or not the interpreters share this belief, they cannot make proper sense of the narrative unless they take the narrator's own omniscience as an institutional fact and his demonstration of God's omniscience as an informing principle.[1]

The narrator in biblical literature knows the minds and hearts of characters and speaks with an authority that demands omniscience; as Alter reminds us, the narrator is "all-knowing and also perfectly reliable: at times he may choose to make us wonder but he never misleads us" (1981: 184). The effect of this is the establishment of "two levels of awareness," one in the narrative and one above the narrative (Sternberg 1987: 91).[2]

The second way in which biblical narrative shapes its readers is through what Sternberg calls the "play of perspectives." Biblical narratives have three basic perspectives: the narrator who tells it, the audience/reader, and

---

1. See also Alter 1981: 157.
2. Sternberg illustrates the import of the omniscient narrator using Gen. 18:10-15, but some implications of this for Job have been worked out by Fox (2005: 351–66).

the characters in the narrative (Sternberg 1987: 130). This results in three "basic relationships that constitute point of view: between the narrator and characters, narrator and reader, reader and characters" (ibid.).[3] The first relationship always remains static, with the narrator always omniscient regarding the characters. The latter two can exhibit variation: the reader may know the same or less than the narrator, while the reader may know the same or more than the characters (ibid.). In other words, the reader may enjoy a "reader-elevating" perspective (163–4).[4] In this case, the characters have an inferior perspective to the narrator and the reader, but are on the same perspective plane as one another (though each is limited by their own finitude in the narrative) (172). The narrator plays with these perspectives to accomplish his purposes, namely, that of shaping the reader, even to the point of allying the reader "with one character against another" (164).

This multiplicity of perspectives is intimately related to Alter's important contribution on the nature of dialogue, the third formative literary device. By and large, dialogue takes up more space than narration, with the latter connecting the former (Alter 1981: 65). Moreover, Alter notes that dialogue is foundational for illuminating and developing character in the biblical text (66). Speech often reveals character in the narrative (70), with the first use of dialogue having particular importance (74). Furthermore, the narrator can mirror, confirm, subvert, or focus attention on the discourse through his narration, which also plays a role in characterization (77).

Alter also highlights the significance of repetition in the biblical narrative's formative repertoire. Repetition is not superfluous, but significant, used with a purpose (89). One of the important uses of repetition is the *Leitwort* (93). *Leitwörter* cluster together to indicate themes (95). To repeat or sustain a theme is to indicate a main point of emphasis the (implied) author wishes to make and which the reader is supposed to grasp; there is a purposeful pattern to repetition (89).[5]

One of the more important formative literary devices Sternberg discusses is the use of gaps. A gap is an unexplained disparity in the narrative, a disharmony; it occurs when "the narrative juxtaposes two pieces of

---

3. Sternberg outlines four basic perspectives for narratives in general, including the author, but Sternberg argues the author/narrator are collapsed into one in the biblical narrative, so biblical narrative has only three.

4. The narrative may also elevate the characters over the reader or leave the characters and the reader on the same plane. On these see Sternberg 1987: 165–72. These are not relevant for the book of Job.

5. See also ibid.: 365–440.

reality that bear on the same context but fail to harmonize either as variants of the situation or as phases in an action. Taken at face value, event clashes with event, speech with event, speech with speech, or interior with vocal discourse" (1987: 242–3; cf. 217, 235). The narrator creates gaps (which Sternberg distinguishes from "blanks")[6] that spark interest and engagement, leading the reader to the pragmatic goal of the discourse. The reader fills these gaps to make coherence (186, 236). Gaps create interest, suspense, curiosity, and surprise, which are necessary for higher goals of persuasion and formation (259–63).

Sternberg also notes the rhetorical device of prospection (268). Prospection is foreshadowing or prediction of themes or events, and takes three forms: analogical patterning, paradigmatic summaries, and dramatic forecast (268–70). To create and preserve suspense, however, the narratives can exhibit "zigzagging" (270–1). Sternberg defines "zigzagging" as "disproportionate lingering" on an event or theme (ibid.). The suspense and focused attention become formative for the reader.

Related to prospection, Sternberg also discusses "proleptic portraits." With this device the narrator offers a portrait of a character, whether an epithet or physical description. These portraits are "direct characterization" (as opposed to indirect characterization where the narrator gives no clues and characterization is discerned through dialogue and actions) (328).[7] Moreover, as Sternberg points out, the portrait—when combined with action, especially contradictory action—brings depth in characterization (344–6). These portraits shape reader expectations and prepare readers for the plot (331, 337–8).

These rules for persuasion identified by Sternberg and Alter inform this preliminary reading of the book of Job. I identify where they occur in the structure of the book and what their effect is.[8] This poetics of biblical narrative provides insight into how the book of Job forms the reader.[9]

---

6. On the distinction, see his criteria: echoing questions, opposing juxtapositions, any threat to coherence, violation of norms (see ibid.: 235–58).

7. See also Alter 1981: 116–17. The most reliable portrait comes from the narrator, though the narrator may use actions, appearance, and other characters as well, which are less reliable.

8. Sternberg identifies a list of 15 rhetorical devices, some of which represent variations of the major techniques outlined above (1987: 476–80; on key words, see also Alter 1981: 93–5). Sternberg concludes his monograph by bringing all of these devices to bear on 1 Sam. 15, highlighting how these devices shape the reader (1987: 482–515).

9. Norman Habel has appropriated Alter's insights to the book of Job (1983: 101–11).

2. *"Job Did Not Sin with His Lips"* 25

External Rhetorical Analysis of the Book of Job

With this methodological framework in mind, this section first establishes ethical God-talk as a primary interpretive concern. Second, it explores how the shape of the book accomplishes its formative function in light of these strategies of persuasion.

The Theme of Ethical God-Talk in Job

The book highlights ethical God-talk almost immediately. Most interpreters recognize the foundational significance of the *satan*'s question in 1:9 regarding Job's disinterested righteousness.[10] Verse 11 indicates how the question of Job's righteousness will be answered: Job's verbal expression *in extremis* will indicate whether his righteousness is disinterested or not. The antiphrastic use of the word ברך and its placement at the end of 1:11 arrests the reader's attention.[11] The repetition of this root in the prologue (six occurrences), with some of the occurrences being used antiphrastically, indicates it is a key word.[12] The concept of "cursing to God's face" indicates that ethical God-talk is specifically in view. That Job closes his first words of the book with "May the name of Yahweh be blessed" (יְהִי שֵׁם יְהוָה מְבֹרָךְ) is not a coincidence: Job's first speech indicates that he blesses God rather than curses him.[13] The question of the ethics of Job's discourse is intimately related to the question of disinterested righteousness, and is thus a significant interpretive concern in the book from the outset.

The theme of ethical God-talk continues throughout the rest of the book. Several speech-related words cluster to signify this theme (e.g., nouns like אֹמֶר, בַּד, שִׂיחַ, שׁוּעַ, שָׂפָה, לָשׁוֹן, פֶּה, דָּבָר, מִלָּה and verbs like דבר, אמר, לעע, הבל, דרש, עתר, ריב, שִׂיחַ, שׁוּעַ).[14] While speech words (e.g., דָּבָר, מִלָּה, אֹמֶר, פֶּה, לָשׁוֹן, etc.) and prayer words (e.g., דרש, שִׂיחַ, תְּפִלָּה, etc.) do not necessarily relate to ethics, the context in which these words may be used can imply ethical connotations, as is the case in the book of

---

10. See, e.g., Longman 2012: 83.

11. As Cheney argues (1994: 60–7), there is no evidence to support emendation.

12. The occurrences are 1:5, 10, 11, 21; 2:5, 9. Job 1:5, 11; 2:5, and 9 are used antiphrastically.

13. The use of אמר in 1:5 probably indicates a thought rather than a speech act since Job is by himself.

14. Key words were drawn from speech ethics passages cited in two studies: Yeung 1990 and Baker 1995. Miller's list of prayer words also provided some guidance (1994: 32–48).

Job. An examination of these words reveals that speech words occur in almost every chapter of the book; those chapters where they do not occur are almost all continuations of speeches that address the theme.[15] As the following examination of the book will show, all the major characters of the book contribute to this theme. Interestingly, many of these words occur in the rhetorical questions that are asked in the book, which play a key role in providing structure to the speeches and reiterate the main theme(s) to the reader (see Magary 2005: 283–98).

The Book's Shape and the Theme of Ethical God-Talk

Having suggested that the ethics of God-talk is a significant theme in the book of Job, I now turn to inquire as to how the book uses this theme to shape the reader. In other words, how is the theme employed in the book to have its effect on the reader (i.e., the external rhetoric of the book)? The analysis falls along the lines of the major sections of the book.

The Frame Narrative

That the book of Job is set by a frame narrative has long been acknowledged.[16] Frame narratives establish the narrative world for the reader, guiding the reader into how to understand the story; they are "'aids to perception' that point to the important or high points in a text" (O'Dowd 2008: 241–5).[17] The frame is a powerful rhetorical tool for the (implied) author as he "impose[s] his fictional [or better, narrative] world upon the reader," to use Wayne Booth's phrase (1983: xiii). The prologue (Job 1–2) and the epilogue (Job 42:7-17) thus serve to establish the hermeneutical constraints for the rest of the book.[18] The narrator's

---

15. Job 17; 25; 28; 29; 32; 37; 39; and 41 do not contain the theme of speech ethics explicitly.

16. See especially Cheney 1994: 25–8, 41–8; Fox 2011: 145–62. On frame narratives within the biblical corpus and in the ancient Near East; see especially Fox 1977: 83–106. For a development and critique of Fox's work, see Bartholomew 1998: 139–71, 226–63; 2009: 61–82, 93–6.

17. Quote from 242. O'Dowd is quoting Mary Ann Caws (1985: 4). Caws argues that frames "hold the essence of a work" and "often enable the intrusion of another genre into the narrative text by appropriate means" (xi). She writes that frames "are bearers of meaning and intensity, the conveyors of revelation and insight," and "force our deeper understanding of the unity and the ultimate meaning" of the work (8).

18. Technically speaking, the frame also consists of the introduction to each speech and, in my view, Job 28. These elements of the frame will be dealt with in their respective sections below.

omniscient perspective leads the reader to read the book according to the narrator's purposes.[19]

There are two main facts that provide the hermeneutical constraints. The first is Job's character, immediately established by a string of narratorial epithets. Job's character is impeccable and the reader must keep this in mind throughout the work (1:1).[20] Moreover, Job's piety is illustrated

---

19. See Booth 1983: 3–4. The claims that the frame narrative presents a "false naivety" by which the reader is to counter-read the statements made by the narrator—that Job's character and the story are too good to be true, that God's character is different between the prose and the poetic sections, and that the theology of retribution is at odds with the rest of the book—are inaccurate with respect to the book of Job. As Fox notes, the most effective way to neutralize the frame is to read it as irony (2011: 145–6), so that is what these interpreters set out to do. The concept of "false naivety" originates with Clines (1985: 127–36), but see also Cooper 1990: 67–9; Vogels 1994: 371; Hoffman 1981: 160–70; Moore 1983: 17–31; Forrest 1988: 385–98; Brenner 1989: 37–52; Oosthuizen 1991: 295–315. As Fox aptly notes, citing Booth's work, an unreliable narrator must be unreliable through the whole work (2011: 146–7). This does not fit the facts of the book of Job because each of these alleged elements of irony are necessary for understanding the book (147). Relevant here is the fact that Job's pious character is confirmed by Yahweh (1:8; 2:3), the *satan* (whose questions imply agreement with Yahweh's assessment), and the actions of his friends (who assume Job's circumstances are a result of Job no longer acting piously); on this last point about the friends I am indebted to Fox (147). There is no indication that the narrator is unreliable at any point in the book. The knowledge (and certainty of that knowledge) of Job's character and the divine council scenes speak to an omniscience and reliability that remain consistent throughout the work. Fox aptly concludes, "The tale of Job provides stability—not existential but literary—in the form of a definitive, omniscient, authorial voice. Like a picture frame, it defines a setting that controls the way we view the picture. Without this control, the middle chapters would be a heated jumble of anger, contradiction, and ignorance" (159; Fox 2005: 351–66). See also the arguments Yu (2011: 21 n. 42) makes in response to Watts (2001: 168–80). Watts' argument proceeds along similar lines to that of those who treat the prologue as irony, namely, the use of an "unreal" setting. But as Yu points out, this does not necessarily require an unreliable narrator. Yu also argues that Watts assumes a human narrator, an unfounded assumption. I would add to this that Watts' proposed rhetoric of the omniscient character of God as a polemic against reliable narrators has little to commend it. Given Sternberg's plethora of evidence that the biblical narrator is reliable and omniscient, the burden of proof falls on those who would suggest this is not the case in Job.

20. These characteristics, taken together, indicate that Job enjoys a unique fellowship with God, embodies an ethical life, and trusts and loves God sincerely; in short, Job is the preeminent wise man (Hartley 1988: 67; Clines 1989: 11–13). See also Seow 2013: 253.

by his consistent concern for his children's speech and actions (1:5). With Yahweh's verbatim repetition of the narrator's description of Job in 1:8 and 2:3, the two most authoritative voices in biblical narrative both agree on this fundamental fact. Additionally, when Yahweh calls Job his "servant" (עֶבֶד), it testifies to a special relationship between the two (Hartley 1988: 73). This appellation occurs six times in the frame, all articulated by Yahweh (1:8; 2:3; 42:7, 8 [3×]).[21] Job's first words in the book also reveal his character. Job worships and acknowledges Yahweh's sovereignty and freedom, blessing the name of Yahweh. The frame establishes Job as a blameless worshiper of Yahweh, not only by his words, but by divine appellation and narratorial description.

The second fact established in the frame is the significance of Job's verbal expression, and, more specifically, its blamelessness. As noted above, the *satan*'s question in the first heavenly scene focuses attention on Job's words as the means by which the experiment will be resolved (1:9-11). In 1:22, after reporting that Job enters into a posture of mourning combined with God-talk, the narrator assesses Job's words: "In all this Job did not sin and he did not charge God with wrongdoing" (בְּכָל־זֹאת לֹא חָטָא אִיּוֹב וְלֹא־נָתַן תִּפְלָה לֵאלֹהִים).[22] Job 2 continues the focus on Job's verbal expression. Yahweh argues that Job's verbal expression from 1:21 indicates his disinterested righteousness by asserting that he "maintains his integrity" (וְעֹדֶנּוּ מַחֲזִיק בְּתֻמָּתוֹ). The *satan* again calls attention to Job's discourse as he intensifies the experiment, repeating the antiphrastic affirmation אִם־לֹא אֶל־פָּנֶיךָ יְבָרֲכֶךָּ in 2:5.[23] Even Job's wife recognizes Job's integrity (עֹדְךָ מַחֲזִיק בְּתֻמָּתֶךָ) and implores Job to curse God, using ברך again (2:9). The narrator confirms that Job's verbal expression is an important interpretive concern that the reader must attend to with his final assessment in 2:10: "in all this Job did not sin with his lips" (using שָׂפָה).[24]

---

21. Notably, Yahweh articulates this unique relationship to both the *satan* and the friends.

22. Hartley (1988: 78 n. 23) suggests that תִּפְלָה "has the sense of something unsavory or unseemly, an impropriety." Though its exact meaning may not be possible to determine, it is clear that it has an ethical connotation, and Job's verbal expression is considered ethically appropriate.

23. The preposition is different from 1:11, but the sense is the same. The editor of BHS does note that multiple manuscripts have the preposition עַל as in 1:11. It is likely that אֶל is original in 2:15 as the more difficult reading (with scribes making the change for consistency's sake). Either way the meaning of the verse is unchanged.

24. Some commentators, often citing rabbinic interpretations, make a distinction between the heart and the lips. In other words, the narrator is subtly pointing to the fact that Job may not have sinned when he spoke but he sinned in his heart (e.g., Seow

This is a verbatim repetition of 1:22a with the addition of the concluding prepositional phrase (בְּכָל־זֹאת לֹא־חָטָא אִיּוֹב בִּשְׂפָתָיו).²⁵

The epilogue also focuses on Job's discourse, this time looking back rather than anticipating the narrative. In Job 42:7 the narrator uses Yahweh's address to Eliphaz (and the friends) to juxtapose their discourse with Job's. The latter is considered נְכוֹנָה. This word is crucial for understanding Yahweh's assessment.²⁶ Job has spoken that which is true.²⁷ This verse looks back and provides clarity for reading Job's words in the book. Job 42:7-8 is a persuasive device for the (implied) author, as Lo points out (2003: 96). Despite what Job has said, the epilogue shapes the reader to see Job's verbal expression as true. The presence of the divine verdict in the narrative frame—the hermeneutical guide for the book—plays a significant role in shaping the reader regarding how to view the ethics of Job's verbal expression.

2013: 297; Forrest 1988: 393–4). But this assumes an irony in the prologue that is not there (see n. 19 on p. 27). Hartley has it right when he says (1988: 84), "[T]o say that Job did not sin with his lips is to state unequivocally that Job did not commit the slightest error."

25. In both 1:22 and 2:10 the demonstrative pronoun looks back to Job's speech acts in the prologue. In both cases the demonstrative comes immediately after the speech act, making Job's discourse the most natural antecedent. See Seow 2013: 262.

26. See Nam 2003: 24, 189, 191–2; cf. Seow 2011b: 70–92; Oeming 2000: 103–16. Nam suggests נְכוֹנָה means "constructively," meaning that Job's words were constructive to theological discourse because he spoke to God. But this understanding has been rightly challenged (Greenstein 2004b: n.p.). The word is better understood as "trustworthy," "true things" or "words"—in other words "truth" (*HALOT*, 464). It refers to what is established as true (see Deut. 13:15 [14]; 17:4; 1 Sam. 23:23; 26:4) or an attitude toward God the righteous possess while the unrighteous do not (see Ps. 5:10 [9], denoting true speech; Pss. 51:12 [10]; 57:8 [7]; 78:37; 108:2 [1]; 112:7, each denoting a steadfast heart). See Williams 1971: 231 n. 1. My list of references builds on and corrects mistakes from Williams' list. Walton (2012: 433) defines נְכוֹנָה as what is "sensible, logical, or verifiable." On the surface, this definition is not problematic, but, taken in conjunction with Walton's criticism of Job's verbal expression, it is. How is it that Job can speak what is sensible and verifiable, but also be wrong on so many occasions? Walton feels the tension of this, but, in my view, he does not overcome the problem; see, for example, 173–4, 230, 433.

27. This form occurs only here and in Ps. 5:10 [9], where it clearly means "truth." As Greenstein writes (2004b: n.p.), "The term *nəkônâ* has the sense of 'truth' in Ps. 5:9 [*sic*] as well, where it contrasts with *ləšônām yaḥălîqûn*, 'their tongues slide [i.e., lie].' It would seem, then, that Nam's idiosyncratic interpretation of *nəkônâ* has little basis other than his desire to find a sympathetic sense of Job 42:7."

The frame's effect on the reader is noteworthy. The frame highlights Job's words for the reader, while also providing the lens through which to view them. The focus on Job's verbal expression through the antiphrastic use of ברך, the repetition of key words, and the linking of Job's verbal expression to the issue of disinterested righteousness highlight Job's verbal expression. Together these details provide prospection for the narrative through paradigmatic summary and dramatic forecast. The epilogue provides a review of the preceding material along the same lines. The authoritative voices of the narrator and Yahweh assess Job's words, both anticipating the ensuing dialogue and reviewing it. Cheney captures the function of the frame well (1994: 69, italics original):

> The overarching question…is whether or not Job, the hero, will *speak rightly* of God or whether he will simply give up and blaspheme God… At the end of the story it is precisely the judgment of this *contest of words* which is central… In this way, the notions of blessing and cursing, indeed language about God in general, become key to the overall plot.

Furthermore, the narrator's presentation of the prologue elevates the reader over the characters of the book. The reader-elevating perspective grants the reader an authoritative stance by which to evaluate the dialogue. This is an important external rhetorical tool that constrains the reader to read the words of Job and his friends in a certain way. Confronted by Job's protests and the friends' comforting practices in the dialogue, the reader must read the dialogue in light of the prologue's narratorial epithets and summaries as well as the divine assessments. The reader must take seriously Job's character and the knowledge of his innocence when evaluating the ostensibly "correct" theology of the friends and the ostensibly "blasphemous" protests of Job. Without the frame the reader is likely to reject Job's protests outright; with the frame the reader must read Job's words in an engaged, critical, yet sympathetic, way.[28] The frame sets up Job's verbal expression as a primary interpretive issue.

---

28. Fox makes a similar point about the title character in *Uncle Remis* by Joel Chandler Harris as he illustrates how frames can work rhetorically. He writes (1977: 95), "Harris wants us to treat [Uncle Remis] seriously, so he provides a frame-narrative that treats him seriously." This point relates to the device of prospection and the narratorial epithets given in 1:1.

The Dialogue

As the dialogue begins, the omniscient narrator recedes into the background, leaving the reader to evaluate the differing perspectives on the basis of the narrative facts established by the prologue.[29] The dialogue shapes the reader by an engagement with the narrative through gaps, the play of perspectives, and focused and extended attention to the topic of ethical God-talk. Like the frame narrative, the dialogue focuses on Job's verbal expression.[30]

The foundation for the dispute is Job's opening speech in Job 3 (Beuken 1994: 41–78; Habel 1985: 102; Clines 1989: 77). The long-acknowledged juxtaposition of the prose Job and the poetic Job opens up a significant gap in the story. As noted above, gaps are elements of disharmony or ambiguity in a narrative that a reader must actively engage (i.e., fill) in order to make sense of a narrative.[31] The marked dissonance between Job's verbal expression in the prologue and his verbal expression in Job 3 arrests the reader, sparking interest, curiosity, and suspense. The gap between the Job of Job 1–2 and the Job of Job 3 is *the* central gap in the book, and it relates directly to the issue of ethical God-talk by highlighting the tension created by scathing protest prayer (note the use of קלל and פֶּה in 3:1). To fill this gap the reader must rely on knowledge from the prologue until the gap is closed in Job 42:7-8. This ambiguity necessitates active engagement from the reader; this engagement engenders "convergence" between the narrator's (i.e., the implied author's) purposes and perspective and the reader.[32] The reader is formed toward the narrator's rhetorical goals through this gap.

The dialogue also plays with perspectives without narratorial guidance, which, like gaps, engages the reader, directing the reader to evaluate the dispute. Job complains and defends his right to complain; the friends

---

29. The narrator's role in Job 3–27 is exclusively to introduce the speeches and drive the narrative forward through dialogue.

30. Longman suggests that the point of dispute is the topic of wisdom (2008: 208; see also Longman 2012: 31–2, 66), but this does not take into account the data already presented above and represented here. On why the dialogue should be viewed as a dispute, see Murphy (1981: 23–36), who suggests that every speech is a disputation. One may quibble with some of these designations, but the overall disputatious nature of the dialogue is clear.

31. See Sternberg 1987: 186–263, though see 235–63 in particular; see also Lo 2003: 81–2; Bartholomew 2009: 81–2.

32. "Convergence" is intentionally used in light of Sternberg (1987: 249).

suggest penitence rather than protest, and try to shame him as Job remains unconvinced of his need for repentance. The reader's attention is thus focused on the theme of ethical God-talk, but not in a completely polyphonic way because of the frame.[33] The narrator uses the dialogue to his own ends, as the dialogue mirrors, subverts, or confirms the narrator's assessments from the prologue. The narrator's use of character-to-character argumentation allows the reader to enter the narrative world and actively evaluate the strengths and weaknesses of the participants' perspectives (Longman 2008: 111). The questions, discord, and subsequent readerly engagement are persuasive devices.

The emerging gap in Job 3 and the play of perspectives relate to the focal point of the dialogue, the ethics of Job's words. That Job's verbal expression in protest prayer is the crux of the dispute is seen first in Eliphaz

---

33. Newsom argues the book of Job is a polyphonic work, with each section of the book providing its own perspective, without any of the voices providing *the* perspective of the book (2003: 21–31; see also Newsom 1996: 37–8). Newsom has helpfully suggested that the disparate parts of the book are a rhetorical strategy for the author (24), but there are significant problems with her argument that no one voice of the competing generic sections provides *the* perspective which the author desires for the reader to adopt. Perhaps most crucially, her suggestion that the book of Job is a polyphonic text lacks the evidence from the ancient world to be convincing. Not only is there not much by way of comparative evidence to support her contention, but there is also evidence to suggest that the book belongs better to a frame narrative genre. There are biblical books and Egyptian wisdom texts that fit this genre, both of which are more propinquitous than her suggestion (see esp. Fox 1977: 92–6). This means that the omniscience of the narrator, in accordance with other biblical texts as Sternberg has shown, should be the voice whose view the reader is to adopt, thereby precluding the view that *no* voice is championed. The friends' perspectives make sense of the knowledge, beliefs, and constraints they have. Not having the knowledge of the heavenly scenes from the prologue and believing in the retribution principle, Eliphaz, Bildad, and Zophar assume that Job has sinned and that explains his suffering. This leads them to encourage penitential prayer. They miss their own epistemological limits—something the reader quickly notices. The reader also knows Job's innocence and reads his speeches sympathetically because of that. The discordance forces the reader to consider carefully the friends' positions, most likely identifying with their ostensibly orthodox perspectives, only to have the frame narrative counteract this natural tendency. The variety of the perspectives without authoritative interjection allows for a multiplicity of solutions to and ideas about Job's problem within the narrative, but not externally (i.e., as it shapes the reader). This is risky because the reader may resist or miss the (implied) author's aims.

in Job 4–5, but the others follow suit.³⁴ As just stated, the dialogue keeps the propriety of Job's discourse at the forefront of the reader's attention, with each speech either criticizing it (the friends) or defending it (Job). In other words, on an internal level, the disputations are intended for persuasion of other characters.³⁵ After Job's complaint in Job 3, Eliphaz responds by inquiring if he can respond to Job's outrageous complaint.³⁶ As Seow notes (2013: 383), for Eliphaz, "good theology is at stake" (4:2), so he encourages penitential prayer rather than protesting prayer (5:8). Bildad and Zophar also criticize Job's verbal expression as being unwise and inappropriate God-talk and encourage him to repent with the promise of restoration through repentance (see 8:2-3, 5, 21; 11:2-4, 13-20).³⁷ They assume his guilt and instruct him toward penitential prayer rather than protest prayer. But the reader knows that advice for penitential prayer is irrelevant, even cruel, for Job. Job defends his verbal expression in 6:2-4 (see 9:25-35; 13:1-19), accusing his friends of "comforter malpractice" in 6:14-30 (see 13:4-12);³⁸ he continues his protest prayer in the latter part of each one of his speeches in the first cycle (see 7:7-21; 9:27-31; 10:1-22; 13:20-28; 14:1-22).³⁹

34. To be sure, as the speech cycles progress, there are other factors in play, but they become supplemental issues to the primary one, the ethics of Job's God-talk. As Greenstein says, "A cursory inspection of the book reveals that discourse is not only its medium but its topic" (2006: 240).

35. A number of works have now emerged to show that there is an engagement between Job and his friends throughout the book by paying attention to repetition of words and structure between speeches, primarily (though not exclusively) in the opening sections of each speech. See, e.g., Course 1994; Pyeon 2003; Yu 2011. See also Hawley (2018), where he argues for progression between speeches through the competition of conceptual metaphors.

36. Eliphaz uses the following speech words: דָּבָר, מִלָּה, קוֹל, and דרש.

37. Bildad uses the following speech words: שָׂפָה, פֶּה, מִלָּה, חנן, מלל, and אֵמֶר; Zophar uses the following speech words: דבר, אמר, לעג, בַּד, דָּבָר, and שָׂפָה.

38. See Yu 2011 for this phrase.

39. In every speech, Job is either lamenting (e.g., Job 3; 7:1-21; 10:2-22; 13:20–14:22), defending his protest prayer (e.g., 6:3, 30; 7:11; 9:35–10:1; 13:3, 6, 13, 15; 16:17; 21:4; 23:4; 27:4; using תְּפִלָּה, שִׂיחַ, פֶּה, דבר, לָשׁוֹן, לעע, יכח, רִיב, and תּוֹכַחַת), or criticizing the friends' arguments as unethical (e.g., 6:25-26, 29; 13:7; 16:3-6; 21:34; 27:4, 12; using פֶּה, דבר, ענה, הֶבֶל, הבל, עַוְלָה, רְמִיָּה, דָּבָר, מִלָּה, אֵמֶר, יכח, and שָׂפָה)—which is itself an argument in defense of his verbal expression—or some combination of the three. On the significance of Job's address to God in the second part of his speeches in the first speech cycle, see Patrick 1979: 268–77.

There is a shift in the second cycle, with the friends becoming more aggressive with their rhetoric, but the focal point of the dispute remains the ethics of Job's discourse, even if it is more subtle than in the first cycle. Though Job is not explicitly called wicked, the consistent use of the *topos* of the fate of the wicked implicitly associates Job's situation with the wicked because of past actions and his discourse.[40] This is seen clearly in Eliphaz's speech in Job 15. Eliphaz calls into question Job's wisdom because of his language, suggesting that Job's discourse hinders others in their relationship with God, is self-condemning, and will bring about Job's ruin (15:2-6, 30).[41] In 15:13 Eliphaz asks incredulously how Job can "bring (such) words out of your mouth" (וְהֹצֵאתָ מִפִּיךָ מִלִּין). Bildad and Zophar also frame their use of the fate of the wicked narrative with concerns about Job's discourse (18:2, 4; 20:3, 29).[42] Because of this, Job is forced to defend his innocence, arguing for the appropriateness of his complaint (Job 16–17; 19).[43] Job finally turns his attention to rebutting the *topos* of the fate of the wicked in Job 21.

With the third speech cycle, the disputatious nature of the dialogue has become so heated that the dialogue is breaking down.[44] The focus

---

40. Habel (1985: 251–2, 284, 314) and Yu (2011: 295–8, 309–11, 321–3) consistently note the friends' use of key words that insinuate Job's situation is caused by wickedness. See also Holbert 1981: 171–9.

41. Eliphaz uses פֶּה, לָשׁוֹן, שִׂיחָה, מִלָּה, דָּבָר, and שָׂפָה. Verse 30 is notoriously difficult, with many commentators emending פִּיו ("his mouth") to פִּרְחוֹ ("his blossom"). See Clines' discussion (1989: 344). There is no need to emend here (Seow 2013: 724). Admittedly difficult, it is at least possible that the 3ms pronominal suffix on פֶּה refers to the wicked person, who is in view in Eliphaz's extended argument. This would mean that the wicked person is turned aside by means of his own angry discourse (with the בְ-preposition indicating the means). This fits the context well in light of Eliphaz's statement that the wicked man defies God in 15:25 and his description of Job's posture earlier in the chapter. רוּחַ is used on two previous occasions in Job 15, the first time to highlight the lack of wisdom in Job's position (v. 2), the second time referring to Job's angry posture toward God (v. 13). The connection between Job, speech, and an angry spirit highlights Eliphaz's argument about Job's dangerous discourse.

42. Bildad uses the following speech words: דבר and מִלָּה (note also his use of אַף). Zophar uses the following speech words: מוּסָר and אֵמֶר (note also his use of שמע).

43. Job points to his innocent suffering as the reason his protest prayer is appropriate. See 16:17 (in light of the divine attack motif in 16:7-16) and 19:6, 21 (which form an inclusio around the divine attack and alienation motifs in 19:7-20).

44. The third cycle is notoriously difficult. A literary-rhetorical approach assumes unity to the book. But this assumption is not without warrant. First, there is no textual evidence for any of the plethora of proposals for emending this section. Second, as

remains on the ethics of Job's verbal expression in this cycle, though it is less pronounced than in the first two cycles. Nevertheless, the accusations of Eliphaz (22:2-5), the implications of Bildad's hymn (25:2-6), and Job's resistance to penitential prayer and commitment to true speech (27:2-4) relate to speech ethics. Eliphaz openly accuses Job of sin (though the reader knows there is no basis for these charges in light of the prologue), and encourages repentance (22:5-11, 21-30). Key for the accusation is 22:4, where Eliphaz sarcastically accuses that Job's "fear" (יִרְאָה) is the reason for Job's extensive suffering. Though not explicitly related to Job's words, Eliphaz's accusation likely refers to both Job's actions and words in light of the connection of Job's "fear" (יִרְאָה) and his words in 4:6 and 15:4 (cf. 4:2-11; 15:2-6). Eliphaz's advice toward penitential prayer explicitly emerges in 22:21-30; rather than Job's current mode of discourse, protest prayer, Job should repent. Job's response to Eliphaz defends his complaint (23:2-6; cf. 23:7-17). Bildad, despite being interrupted by Job, utters a hymn that is supposed to convince Job of his utterly deplorable state before God (25:2-6).[45] Job understands this hymn as an encouragement to stop protesting, accusing Bildad of cruelty and being unhelpful (26:2-4). While Zophar does not speak in the third cycle, Job maintains his innocence in the face of the accusations, taking an oath to prove it. Job insists his verbal expression is and will remain true (27:2-6), and his friends' advice is false (27:12).[46]

The attention focused on the theme of ethical God-talk is consistent throughout the dialogue. The extended, almost wearisome, treatment drives home the contribution of the book.[47] Because of the narrator's self-relegation to the background, the extended discussion over the propriety of Job's verbal expression leaves the reader in suspense despite the information already given in the prologue. The suspense creates sustained interest and forces evaluation, as the reader actively works to fill in the major gap that is opened with the juxtaposition of Job 1–2 and Job 3. The consistency of the topic of Job's God-talk in the dialogue indicates that the reader is to be engaging and evaluating this point in the dispute.

Cheney and others have pointed out, it may be that the confusion is a literary device, with the text mimicking the breakdown in the dialogue (1994: 45–6, 102, 116, 123–4; cf. Newsom 1996: 497).

45. Following Newsom (1996: 516), it seems best to see a series of interruptions. I thus see 26:5-14 as Bildad's speech, a continuation of his hymn from 25:2-6. This is developed and defended in Chapter 5.

46. See n. 39 above.

47. There is what Sternberg calls "zigzagging," a "disproportionate lingering" on an event or theme, which builds suspense for the reader (1987: 270–1).

Job 28

The narrator returns in Job 28 to give the reader an initial clue as to how to read the dialogue, to remind the reader of the facts of the prologue and provide guidance for understanding the dispute before closing the gap regarding Job's verbal expression in 42:7-8. In other words, Job 28 is a part of the frame.

There is a long history of debate regarding Job 28 and its place in the book (Lo 2003: 1–15). It is often noted that Job 28 seems out of context, and especially inconsistent with Job despite the fact that the lack of an introduction to Job 28 would initially lead one to think Job is speaking. For this reason, many scholars have suggested that Job 28 is an interlude or the words of the author/narrator.[48] Indeed, there are good reasons for seeing Job 28 as a part of the frame—the narrator's intrusion into the events of the book.[49] First, the chapter is set off by the asseverative כִּי. Ignoring the chapter divisions, the vastly different topics of 27:23 and 28:1 lead the reader to infer the function of the כִּי as asseverative. This sets off Job 28 from the preceding material. Second, the content of Job 28 is distinct from the preceding material in Job 27 and the subsequent material in Job 29. Third, Job 28 is not just different in content; it exhibits no indication that it is offered in the context of the dispute. In other words, it "is not in any way marked as addressed to the dialogue participants. Unlike much of the preceding dialogue material, this chapter does not allude to or directly participate in the previous discussion... [T]he poem is marked by a curious detachment from the heat of the debate" (Cheney 1994: 43). In fact, Job 28 is one of only six chapters in Job 4–31 which does not have a second person verb. The others—Job 23–24, 25, 29, and 31—have other indications of their role in the debate. The rhetorical questions in Job 24:25 and 25:3-6 indicate their disputatious role, while Job 29 and 31 are of a piece with Job's protest prayer in Job 30. The rhetorical questions of 28:12, 20 do not have as obvious a role in the dispute. Fourth, the narratorial introductions of 27:1 and 29:1 are identical, and yet inconsistent with the introductions to this point in the

---

48. See Cheney 1994: 43–4; Habel 1985: 391; Hartley 1988: 26–7; Newsom 1996: 528; 2003: 170; Andersen 1976: 20, 240–2; Walton 2012: 29–31, 293–6. Clines' idiosyncratic rearrangement of Job 28 to be Elihu's conclusion, while creative, has no textual evidence to be of any merit (2005: 243–53; 2006: 908–9).

49. The following arguments are adapted from Cheney 1994: 43–4. I have rearranged his arguments for better flow and added the argument of the inclusio of 28:28 and 1:1 (on which see Habel 1985: 393).

dialogue, setting Job 28 apart.[50] Fifth, the use of the divine names in 28:23 and 28:28 distinguishes the chapter from both 27 and 29.[51] Sixth, Job 28:28 alludes to Job 1:1, forming an inclusio around the dialogue section.

The conclusion that Job 28 contains the voice of the narrator meets its most significant objection in the work of Lo, who presents the most thorough case for Job 28 as Job's words. She contends that Job 28 fits within the plot development of the book in a way that is consistent with the third cycle, namely, Job's speeches exhibit contradictory juxtaposition. In each speech in the third cycle, Job exhibits a tendency to speak in a paradoxical way to rebut the arguments of his friends.[52] Job 28 is also an example of contradictory juxtaposition with Job's final speech in 29–31. According to Lo, with the dialogue collapsed, Job turns to reflect on wisdom, which in turn leads Job to become angry and return to protest prayer (2003: 56–7).[53]

Lo concludes from this analysis that Job 28 has a significant role in the rhetoric of the book as a whole. It shows the inadequacy of the friends' views (72–4), while also establishing a foundation from which Job can be criticized in the Yahweh speeches (73, 74–7).

Nevertheless, nowhere does she examine adequately the exegetical concerns just outlined.[54] Because of this, her conclusions on the rhetoric

---

50. This introduction formula occurs also at 36:1.

51. אֱלֹהִים occurs only five times outside the prologue (5:8; 20:29; 32:2; 34:9; 38:7). אָדוֹן only occurs twice in the book, here and in 3:19. Contrast this with שַׁדַּי, אֱלוֹהַּ, and אֵל occurring in Job 27 (vv. 2, 3, 8, 9, 10, 11, 13) and in Job 29 (vv. 2, 4, 5).

52. Despite the fact that Job 24:18-24, 26:5-14, and 27:13-23 are often rejected as Job's words because they are perceived to be antithetical to Job's position elsewhere in the dialogue, Lo argues these passages are intentionally juxtaposed in opposition to Job's other statements for his rhetorical purposes. Specifically, Lo argues that in these passages Job uses the friends' positions against them, forcing them into silence (2003: 96–195).

53. See also Lo 2003: 196–223. The suggestion that Job 28 is an inner reflective moment is odd in light of the interactive nature of the rest of the dispute.

54. Where she does address aspects of these arguments throughout her monograph, her criticisms are unconvincing. She does not account for the cumulative effect of the arguments presented above. Moreover, even she admits that the rhetorical questions of 28:12 and 28:20 address the audience, which throughout her monograph indicates the audience of the book (what I'm calling the external level) rather than a character in the book (the internal level) (2003: 196–7, 200). In other words, she seems to slip and suggest the questions are better seen as the narrator who addresses the audience rather than Job addressing the audience or having an inner reflective moment (56–7).

of Job 28, which on the whole are incisive and cogent, are attributed to the wrong voice. Her conclusions would be more convincing if the narrator were speaking in Job 28, showing the futility of the debate and affirming Job's superiority over the friends as it relates to wisdom. Job 28, thus, functions as the author's rhetorical device to shape the reader away from the friends' discourse that criticizes, even condemns, protest prayer as an appropriate way to approach God when suffering. Lo is right: it is an integral and significant chapter in the movement and rhetoric of the book. But, her conclusions are better warranted if the narrator is speaking the words of Job 28 rather than Job.[55]

Thus, Job 28 reveals human epistemic limits with respect to suffering as well as what wisdom is, namely, the fear of the Lord (28:28; cf. Prov. 1:7; 9:10). The connection between 28:28 and 1:1 points to Job's words as superior to the friends' words in light of his wisdom and his fear of Yahweh, giving a major, though subtle, clue to the reader as to how to understand the preceding dispute. As it relates to speech ethics, the narratorial voice emerging to the foreground as the debate collapses indicates that it is the friends who have not spoken well and that the one who is wise is Job. The friends arrogantly believe they know where wisdom is, and the poem rejects this (cf. 5:27; 8:8-10; 15:10) (Newsom 2003: 178–9). Yet, Job 28 has more to do with discrediting the friends as sages and comforters than it does with elevating Job's protests. In other words, the external rhetoric of Job 28 is to condemn the "comforter malpractice," to use Yu's phrase, of the friends, which is the foil for Job's disputations and protests. The narratorial assessment recalls the facts of the prologue, shaping the reader toward Job.

A final point can be made regarding her attribution of Job 28 to Job, namely, the connections she insightfully highlights between Job 28 and the Yahweh speeches (206–9). Given these connections, it is intriguing to see the perspectives of Yahweh and the narrator merging as a rhetorical strategy by the (implied) author.

55. Similarly, Yu contends Job 28 represents Job's words (2011: 345–56). Though not interacting with Lo explicitly, Yu concludes Job 28 provides the philosophical basis for Job's rejection of his friends' renegotiation efforts, namely, that human epistemic limits mean they have no basis from which to argue as they have. Yet despite Job 28 being Job's words, he further notes that 28:28, with its connections to 1:1 and 1:8, is "a no[t]-so-subtle reminder from the *narrator* that Job is the one with *human-appropriate* wisdom" (356, first italics mine, second italics original). So, while both Yu and Lo want to read Job 28 as Job's words, it seems that both provide readings that actually correspond better to reading Job 28 as the narrator's words.

Job's Final Speech (Job 29–31)

Job 28 provides a transition to three so-called monologues.[56] The first of these is Job's, an extended complaint, supplemented by an oath (Westermann 1981b: 38–42).[57] Beginning with his life before suffering in Job 29, Job transitions to his final protest prayer in Job 30, concluding with the oath in Job 31. Key in this speech is Job's final address to God in 30:20-23 (cf. 30:16-31). After not addressing God since 17:3-4, Job concludes where he began: with a complaint. Job describes his circumstances in a number of ways: his soul is poured out (30:16), affliction has seized him (30:16, 27), he is in pain (30:17-18, 30), he is anxious (30:27), and he is alone (30:28-29). Job mourns and weeps, utterly without joy (30:31). His complaint throughout the book culminates here because of God's silence in the face of his protest prayer (30:20), and he justifies his complaint by noting that even one on a "heap of ruins" (עִי) cries out in disaster (30:24).[58] Job, as a heap of ruins, is crying out yet receives no answer. So he takes an oath to force God to act (31:35). As Dick writes, "[I]n no more emphatic way could Eloah be made to justify himself" (1979: 49).

At the external level, Job's final speech highlights that Job's verbal discourse since his first speech in Job 3 has been about praying. It is protest prayer, to be sure—complaints uttered to bring about change—but it is prayer. He has had to defend his words to his friends throughout the dialogue, but Job's concern was to engage God in protest prayer (13:3-19). Job 29–31 represent the climax of Job's protest prayer. The

---

56. The external rhetoric of this section will only be dealt with briefly here. The internal rhetoric of this speech is treated in Chapter 5.

57. See also Clines' helpful comments that given the specific address to God, it is unlikely that this is a monologue or soliloquy (2006: 978–9). Habel (1985: 404) and Yu (2011: 357) suggest that it is a legal closing argument. See also Hartley (1985: 385), who understands Job 29–31 as an avowal of innocence, thereby laying the stress on the oath. See also Dick on the function of the oath, where he notes it is an "emphatic adjunct" (1979: 47).

58. The proposed emendation in BHS is unnecessary, though the verse is admittedly difficult. See Clines' rather unclear discussion (2006: 957). In my view, Clines' proposal that 30:25's emphasis on Job's care for the poor clarifies 30:24 is incorrect. Rather, 30:24b illuminates the challenging syntax of 30:24a, where the 3ms pronominal suffix on פִּיד indicates who the subject of שׁלח is and clarifies that the gesture of stretching out the hand is a gesture of pleading for help in complaint. ESV and NASB capture the sense: "Yet does not one in a heap of ruins stretch out his hand, and in his disaster cry for help?" (ESV); "Yet does not one in a heap of ruins stretch out *his* hand, or in his disaster therefore cry out for help?" (NASB).

narrative sequence is significant in the external rhetoric, crystallizing the seminal issue once again after the collapse of the dialogue: Job's God-talk in protest prayer. In other words, these chapters restore the question of ethical God-talk for the reader after the dialogue has dissolved, with Job's protest prayer framing the dispute about the ethics of Job's God-talk (Westermann 1981b: 4–6). This inclusio is a powerful rhetorical move by the (implied) author, highlighting the significance of the ethics of prayer in the book. The narrator closes Job 31 with the statement that "Job's words are ended" (31:40). This summary statement forces the reader to (re)consider Job's words from Job 3 through Job 31: Job's words (דְּבָרִים) are ended, recalling the main issue raised from as early as Job 1:9-11.[59]

Elihu

Following Job's final complaint, the narrator returns to introduce Elihu (32:1-5), which provides the hermeneutical lens for interpreting his speeches while also linking him to the preceding material.[60] The narrator presents Elihu as angry (32:2 [2×], 3, 5), and provides the reader with an inner view of Elihu's motivations.[61] Elihu finds the discourse of both the friends and Job problematic (32:1-3). Thus, as the narrator presents it, Job's language is also a problem for Elihu.[62]

Elihu's actual speeches also bring attention to Job's verbal expression, though his assessment of Job is to be read through the lens of his foolish anger, his comical self-description, and his responses that link him with the responses of the three friends. In Elihu's first three speeches, he disputes Job's position by specifically highlighting Job's claims through quotation or summary (33:9-11; 34:5-9; 35:2-3).[63] Elihu summarizes his

---

59. The verb in 31:40 is תמם. It is probably right to translate this as "ended"—Job's words are "complete." But the connection with key adjective תָּם used of Job (1:1, 8; 2:3; 9:21) is arresting for the reader who is keen on the issue of ethical God-talk. There is at least some ambiguity that the narrator could be saying "Job's words were blameless" (cf. Ps. 19:14). This is "loaded" terminology (see Sternberg 1987: 476).

60. The external rhetorical function of the Elihu speeches will be treated in more depth in Chapter 6 below after having investigated Job's internal rhetoric.

61. On the narrator on providing an interior character sketch, see Sternberg 1987: 121–2, 477–8. For the narrator giving Elihu's perspective, and not his own, see, e.g., Clines 2006: 712–14.

62. Wilson (2015: 156) notes that the main issue for Elihu is not Job's prior action or sin, but his verbal expression in the course of the dispute.

63. On the quotation and summary in each speech, see McCabe 1997: 47–80.

own position at the end of his second and third speeches, concluding that Job speaks unproductively and unethically (34:34-37; 35:16; cf. 33:13; 34:17; 35:9-15); he asserts that Job "multiplies words without knowledge" (בִּבְלִי־דַעַת מִלִּין יַכְבִּד). He advises Job to stop blaming God and worship the creator instead (36:22-24). This reveals Elihu's primary goals in his speeches, namely, to turn Job's impious discourse toward piety. More specifically, Elihu desires Job to eschew protest in favor of penitence (33:9-11, 26-33; 34:31-37; 35:9-12; 36:13, 19).[64] Clearly Elihu's focus is on the ethics of Job's God-talk.

That it is Job's words that Elihu highlights points again to the key interpretive question in the book: is Job's verbal expression ethical? Wilson notes (2015: 162), "Elihu reveals his view that the dispute between Job and the friends concerns how to speak rightly about God."[65] This section of the book shapes the reader by its placement in the narrative sequence. The role of the Elihu speeches at the external level is transitional: it looks back on the dialogue, showing the lack of an answer from the friends and the centrality of Job's words for the book, and preparing the way for the Yahweh speeches.[66] The Elihu speeches thus reiterate the centrality of Job's verbal expression, even if the content of Elihu's argument is undermined by the narrator's introduction, Elihu's own self-portrayal, and the analogical patterning that links Elihu with the friends.

Yahweh Speeches

After Elihu's speeches, Yahweh finally answers Job (38:1).[67] Yahweh makes two speeches (38:1; 40:6),[68] each with its own thesis, and each

---

64. See Newsom 2003: 211, 213; Clines 2006: 708, 742, 767, 775, 782, 853; Hartley 1988: 461–2, 467; Seow 2013: 100–101; Diewert 1991: 605–6.

65. See also McCabe 1997: 73–4; Wilson 1996b: 89–91.

66. On the preparation for the Yahweh speeches, see, e.g., McCabe 1997: 73–4, among others. Wilson notes that Elihu provides the necessary break so as to maintain Yahweh's freedom for the reader (1996b: 93). Wilson also stresses that Elihu's answer is given a "rival explanation" with Yahweh's speeches (2015: 157).

67. Like the Elihu speeches, the Yahweh speeches will be treated in more depth in Chapter 6 below in light of careful analysis of Job's internal rhetoric.

68. While the narratorial introduction to another Yahweh speech act occurs in 40:1, I take this as an indication of the closing of the first speech. The words of 40:2, then, reiterate the point that Yahweh was intending Job to hear. 38:1 and 40:6 are distinct from 40:1 in light of the prepositional phrase מִן סְעָרָה as well as the shared opening imperatives in 38:3 and 40:7. Nevertheless, even the content of this summary question in 40:2 points to the issue of propriety of Job's speech as Yahweh questions Job as faultfinder (יִסּוֹר) who contends (רֹב), one who argues (מוֹכִיחַ).

thesis is in the form of a rhetorical question (38:2; 40:8).⁶⁹ Both of these rhetorical questions concern Job's God-talk and the propriety thereof. In 38:2, Yahweh labels Job's words "without knowledge" (מִלִּין בְּלִי־דָעַת) (cf. 34:35; 35:16). In 40:8, Yahweh avers that Job's words condemn Yahweh and put Job in the right. Nevertheless, while Yahweh criticizes aspects of Job's words, there is no explicit condemnation of Job, accusation of sin, or call to repentance (Hartley 1988: 488; Wilson 2003: 124).

Yahweh's speeches thus also focus on Job's words and their ethics; Job has used ignorant speech. The narrative sequencing once again is a rhetorical tool, with these speeches overpowering the words of Elihu and yet bringing the book to a climax by providing the theophany Job has sought since the beginning, and providing the reader with an authoritative assessment of Job's words that shapes the reader as much as his final assessment in the epilogue (42:7-8). Job's words are emphasized again as a significant part of the (implied) author's contribution of ethical God-talk.

Summary

From this preliminary exploration of the content and shape of the book of Job, two conclusions emerge. First, each section—and every major character—of the book focuses on Job's words; this confirms and develops the work of Gutiérrez and others. Second, the narrative exhibits a number of key strategies to shape the reader, corresponding to biblical poetics. The narrator's omniscience in telling the story thrusts the reader into the narrative world of Job. The narrator shapes the reader through epithets and proleptic portraits (about Job); character voices, dialogue, neutral narration, and the play of perspectives; temporal discontinuity in the narrative; explicit narratorial assessments on actions; gaps; loaded language; the linking of characters by analogy; and the repetition of key words that indicate a theme that brings coherence to the book. Significantly, these devices are all related to the theme of the ethics of God-talk in the book of Job, even if they are not limited strictly to this theme. Putting these two points together, the following emerges: the primary way in which the (implied) author of the book of Job makes his contribution to the

---

69. While it may seem strange to think of a question being a thesis statement, rhetorical questions can be questions that make statements. Thus, there is no problem with seeing a rhetorical question as a thesis to an argument. On the function of rhetorical questions generally, see Fox 1981: 58; de Regt 1994: 362, citing Koops 1988: 418; Magary 2005: 289–92. On the connection between these two theses, see Newsom 1996: 616.

issue of ethical God-talk is through Job's verbal expression in the book. Put another way, it is Job's internal rhetoric as he protests in prayer and argues with his friends that forms the foundation for the external rhetoric of the book with respect to ethical God-talk. While this analysis does not answer the question of what the book's contribution of ethical God-talk is explicitly, it answers a preliminary question and raises a new one: what is Job's internal rhetoric?

Chapter 3

"I Will Complain in the Bitterness of My Soul": Job's Internal Rhetoric in the First Speech Cycle (Job 3–14)

The cycle begins with Job's opening speech. While Job 3 does not address the friends, it is clear that the friends (particularly Eliphaz) respond to what he says in his opening statement. So while the dialogue proper may not begin until Job 4, Job 3 belongs in the first speech cycle.

Job 3 is one of the most important chapters in the book for two reasons. First, it opens up a significant gap in the characterization of Job; how can these impatient, protesting words be uttered by the same patient, accepting person of the prologue (1:21 and 2:10)? Second, it launches the dispute between Job and his friends; it is to Job's speech act in Job 3 that Eliphaz responds (Beuken 1994: 78; see also Habel 1985: 102; Clines 1989: 77; Wilson 2015: 41–3). Eliphaz's driving concern in his response in Job 4–5 is to encourage Job to return to the kind of proper speech a sage should exhibit, recommending to Job penitential prayer over against protest prayer (5:8). In response, Job refuses this advice and justifies his complaint (6:2-4), accuses the friends of mistreatment, and sharpens his complaint against God (Job 6–7). Bildad is offended by Job's response, again encouraging penitential prayer (8:5). Job responds by entertaining ideas of God's justice, and again protests (Job 9–10). Zophar sharpens the critique from the friends in Job 11 by questioning the wisdom and propriety of Job's discourse. He also encourages penitence (11:13-14). Job dismisses his friends as "comforters" and presses his argument with God to conclude the first cycle (Job 12–14).

"Why Is Light Given to a Man Whose Way Is Hidden?": The Rhetoric of Job's Opening Speech (Job 3)[1]

Introduction

Job 3 is a scathing complaint. Job responds to his suffering with protest prayer, attempting to arrest God's attention through an extended curse on his fate and a two-part complaint.[2] Job desires rest and restoration, and feels God has "hedged him in" (3:23), an image of divine vigilance, even attack. Notably, the complaint is carefully crafted not to curse God.

The Literary Rhetorical Situation of Job 3

It is clear that the events of the prologue create Job's exigency: his suffering has led him to speak.[3] In Job 3:1 the narrator links Job's utterance with his experience (אַחֲרֵי־כֵן פָּתַח אִיּוֹב אֶת־פִּיהוּ וַיְקַלֵּל אֶת־יוֹמוֹ). Moreover, though most commentators suggest that יוֹמוֹ refers to Job's birthday,[4] it is more likely, given the other uses of this form in the book and elsewhere, that Job is cursing his fate (note יוֹמוֹ in Job 15:32; 18:20; 1 Sam. 26:10; Ezek. 21:30 [21:25]; Ps. 37:13) (Seow 2013: 338). If this is the case, then

---

1. The following analysis of Job 3 is slightly revised from the previously published article "Arresting God's Attention: The Rhetorical Intent and Strategies of Job 3," *BBR* 28, no. 1 (2018): 1–19 by William C. Pohl IV (copyright PSU Press © 2018). This article is used by permission of the Pennsylvania State University Press.

2. Claus Westermann argues that Job 3 is a "primordial lament" (1981b: 37–8, 61 n. 14). The fact that this is a primordial lament leads Westermann to suggest this is why the friends react so vehemently against it: this is no longer an acceptable form of speech (61 n. 15). Most commentators since have understood Job to be lamenting to some degree (Habel 1985: 102–3; Hartley 1988: 89, 89 n. 5, 102; Clines 1989: 104–5; Newsom 1996: 366–7, 371–2; Longman 2012: 98). Seow (2013: 336) claims that this is a subversion of lament, a "parody of [lament]."

3. Yu suggests that the "fictive" rhetorical situation of the entire dialogue is one of a sociological status renegotiation for the one who is suffering. He proposes that the context of ritual mourning envelops the work (1:20; 2:8, 11-13; 42:11) as well as appearing at key junctures within the dialogue section (16:2; 42:6). For Yu (2011: 151–96; cf. 29–150), this sociological context provides clarity for understanding the interactions of the characters of the book. This informs Yu's analysis of Job's rhetorical situation in Job 3: Job, as Yahweh's servant, is deeply grieved by the treatment he has received and "expresses [his] dissatisfaction over God's administration in the world" (197). For more on the context of ritual mourning, see Lambert 2015: 557–75.

4. See Habel 1985: 107; Hartley 1988: 91; Newsom 1996: 366; Longman 2012: 98; note Clines' tension, Clines 1989: 15, 78.

what is motivating Job to speak is the suffering that has befallen him. This is confirmed by the reasons Job gives for his words in the כִּי-clauses and especially by the short, staccato-like statements in v. 26 that portray Job as almost breathless, culminating in the final clause with the lone *wayyiqtol* of the verse: "agitation came" (וַיָּבֹא רֹגֶז).[5] The exigency helps us to locate the goal of Job's words: the alleviation of his רֹגֶז, his agitation, his suffering.[6]

Job's audience in his opening speech is initially difficult to determine because no one is specifically addressed. A number of interpreters suggest that Job's opening speech is a soliloquy, an expression of intense feelings directed at no one.[7] Yet, Yu (2011: 200) argues that the audience of Job 3

---

5. This is the fifth occurrence of בוא in Job 3 (vv. 5, 6, 24, 25, 26), corresponding to the five occurrences in 1:14-19. This lexical parallel is further evidence of a connection between Job's opening statement and his suffering in the prologue.

6. Though there is no explicit petition in Job's opening speech, a proposed solution can be implied. See Morrow 2006a: 15–17, 36.

7. See, e.g., Clines 1989: 77; Longman 2012: 98; Seow 2013: 314, 336–7. Seow bases this conclusion on the fact that Job never addresses anyone in chapter 3. That Job never accuses God directly in Job 3 is exactly the point of the following analysis. The statement is carefully crafted to avoid direct address. But this does not mean that it is not a complaint (or lament, to use Seow's term). The lack of second person address does not mean it cannot be lament; the implication in the third person address emerges clearly through the tropes and delayed reference to God, as the analysis below elucidates (and something Seow comes close to asserting on p. 336). Prayer can be done in the third person since any address to God can be considered prayer (Morrow 2006a: 17–18). Job's first words in 1:21 are worship (i.e., are prayerful), and they are in the third person. This sets a theological framework for Job's character in the narrative world. Similarly, third person prayers, though not complaints/laments, can be found in the Psalter (e.g., Pss. 103; 146–150). Admittedly, these are calls to praise, but this is nevertheless a form of prayer. Furthermore, there are examples of third person complaint. See Gen. 25:22, where Rebekah issues a complaint that does not have any specific address to God, and she goes on to inquire as to her condition; Gen. 27:46, where Rebekah's complaint is directed to Isaac but has an implied petition to God; Ruth 1:13, 20-21, where Naomi's complaint is directed to her daughters-in-law, with an implied petition; Jer. 45:3, where Baruch's complaint is not addressed to God, but is answered by God through Jeremiah in an oracle in 45:4-5. Notably, Morrow (34–5) also links Ruth with Job, albeit not Job 3. On top of all of this, it is clear from Job's own statement in 9:27 that he considers his verbal expression a complaint, something he has been doing since Job 3. And as Seow notes regarding 9:27 (2013: 568), "The term *śyḥ* is used most commonly for an audible expression of grief, often implying a plea for relief (Pss. 55:3, 18 [Eng. 2, 17]; 64:2 [1]; 77:4 [3]; 102:1[S]; 104:34; 142:3[2])."

is both Job's friends and God. He offers no textual data to validate this, but an examination of the forms Job employs indicates that Job has at least God as the intended audience.

The constraints are complex. Constraints are those things that make up the situation that might "constrain decision and action needed to modify the exigence," including "beliefs, attitudes, documents, facts, traditions, interests, [and] motives" (Bitzer 1992: 8). For Job's situation, the following may indicate important constraints: (1) the characterization of Job as set by the prologue (through narratorial epithet and divine appellation) might constrain Job's response (cf. Job 1:1, 8; 2:3; 42:7-8); (2) the severity of the suffering as depicted in the prologue and to which Job is responding provides some context for a response; (3) the possible milieu of the eschewing of protest prayer for a background of the book of Job (see Morrow 2006a: 129–46);[8] and (4) the broader canonical picture of protest prayer, which influences the proper response. Regarding point three, the milieu would constrain Job's action to the point that protest prayer is inappropriate. Nevertheless, the severity of Job's suffering, point two, and the broader canonical context, point four, would suggest that while Job cannot curse God, he can protest in prayer. In other words, these facts—Job's character and relationship with Yahweh, the severity of his suffering, and traditions and beliefs about protest prayer—are all competing forces.[9]

The Forms of Job 3

The forms Job uses confirm the exigency and indicate the audience. Job uses three forms: imprecation (3:3-9), complaint (3:11-12, 16, 20-23), and motive clause (3:10, 13-15, 17-19, 24-26).[10] Yet, three arguments point to

---

8. For more on this, see Chapter 7.

9. Lo (2003: 70–1) suggests that the dominant constraint for the characters in the book is their religious background, namely, their views of God's justice, their monotheism, the significance of the fear of Yahweh, and the causal nexus. The perspectives on prayer would also fit within this religious framework.

10. The כִּי clauses of vv. 10, 13, and 24 are best understood as giving reasons for the preceding section, the imprecation (vv. 3-9), the first complaint (vv. 11-12), and the second complaint (vv. 20-23), respectively. The כִּי of v. 25 may provide the reason of the whole poem (Seow 2013: 315; 2010: 433–6). There is no כִּי in vv. 17-19, but the flow of the speech indicates that these verses are a continuation of the themes of vv. 13-15. Perhaps the כִּי is to be understood as gapped like the לָמָּה in v. 16, but this is not certain. See Clines 1989: 76, who documents how the themes are resumed in vv. 11-19 as a whole.

complaint as the primary genre of Job 3:[11] (1) imprecation functionally relates to complaint (Gerstenberger 1988: 250),[12] (2) לָמָה plays a major role in structuring the poem,[13] and (3) there is more space devoted to the complaint than the imprecation.[14] The complaint form fits within the exigency just identified (i.e., one of suffering) since complaints are employed with the aim of persuading God to act on behalf of the sufferer.[15] This indicates that the audience, even if not explicitly noted, is God. Thus, Job's complaint is directed toward God and has persuasive intent as it relates to Job's suffering.[16]

11. Commentators are generally agreed on form-critical grounds, even if their labels do not completely match. Westermann (1981b: 60 n. 12) labels vv. 3-9 a malediction, but argues that the poet has conjoined the malediction with a lament. Hartley (1988: 89 n. 5) likewise suggests two forms have been merged, the curse and the lament. Clines (1989: 76–7) interprets the entire chapter as a complaint, made up of two forms, malediction and lament. Habel (1985: 103) identifies two genres: curse and lament. See also Murphy 1981: 22–3. Only Clines uses the term complaint in his analysis, but the others are using lament to indicate complaint.

12. He notes that imprecations are directed at persons, confirming an implied audience for Job in chapter 3. Cf. Westermann 1981b: 60 n. 12.

13. One might object that לֹא לָמָה never occurs in laments, and so this form-critical category is inappropriate for Job 3. But לֹא לָמָה does occur in a number of complaint-like, accusatory contexts (see Gen. 12:18; Num. 11:11; 22:37; 1 Sam. 15:19; 26:15; 2 Sam. 7:7; 16:17; Jer. 29:27; 1 Chron. 17:6). Most of these are human-to-human accusations, which makes Num. 11:11 stand out. In the context, Moses is certainly complaining, accusing God of mistreatment for the burden he bears leading such an obstinate people. Moses also wishes for death (11:15), a certain sign of displeasure regarding God's actions and a rhetorical strategy to appeal for change. This corresponds to other non-literal death wishes that are prophetic resignations (see the discussion of Yu in n. 47 below). In other words, לֹא לָמָה in Job 3:11, combined with the accusatory rhetoric and מַדּוּעַ in 3:12, fits within the form-critical definitions set forth in this study.

14. The complaint with its motive clauses is found in forty-two out of sixty-five clauses in Job 3 while the imprecation is twenty-three out of sixty-five. In terms of number of verses, the imprecation comprises eight verses while the complaint comprises sixteen.

15. Miller notes (1993: 356, italics original) about protest prayer, it has "*as a primary function the effort to persuade and motivate God to act in behalf of the petitioner who is in trouble and needs God's help.*" Petition need not always be explicit; lament and complaint imply a petition.

16. This is not to say that the friends are not able to overhear this complaint; they clearly do. The point here is that, given the analysis of forms, Job's primary audience is God.

The Rhetorical Strategies of Job 3

Structure

There is no consensus regarding the structure of the speech. Interpreters are divided into two main camps: some who divide the speech into two sections and some who divide it into three sections.[17] The preferable structure is to divide Job's opening speech into three parts: vv. 3-10, vv. 11-19, and vv. 20-26. This structure follows the natural breaks in the poem, with vv. 3-10 as the imprecation, and vv. 11-19 and vv. 20-26 forming two parts of a complaint, with the interrogative לָמָּה functioning as the marker of each complaint section.[18] This structure highlights Job's intent with his imprecation and complaint. As noted above, his complaint emerges to the foreground.[19] Even a cursory reading of Job 3 indicates that the imprecation and the complaint are provocative, but the imprecation as the first element is extremely provocative, serving as an opening statement of the complaint. The imprecation is intended to arrest the attention of God himself. The reason the complainer grabs God's attention is because God is the only one who can alleviate suffering (see Patrick and Diable 2008: 19–32; Miller 1994: 70–87, 130–4). The structure provides some clues as to who the intended audience is, with God being mentioned at the beginning and end (vv. 4 and 23). Additionally, Job concludes each section and the poem with his reasons for complaining, from which his goal can be deduced. The motive clauses all share a common theme: that

---

17. Fishbane (1971: 153–5), Hartley (following Fishbane) (1988: 88), Habel (1985: 103), Newsom (1996: 366), Longman (2012: 98), and Wilson (2015: 41) suggest the poem breaks into two sections (though Habel, Newsom, Longman, and Wilson see the break at v. 10 [i.e., 3-10 and 11-26] rather than at v. 13 [i.e., 3-13 and 14-26], like Fishbane and Hartley). The two-section proposal of Fishbane and Hartley that breaks the chapter at vv. 13-14 (with v. 14 starting the second main section) fails to take into account the structuring clues noted below while simultaneously ignoring the flow of the content: v. 14 needs v. 13 to provide a context for it to be understood. This division seems to be done for numerical balance (Hartley 1988: 89). Clines (1989: 76), Pyeon (2003: 72), and Fokkelman (2012: 203–4) divide the chapter into three sections. Fokkelman's divisions are vv. 3-9, 10-19, and 20-26. This fails to account for the placement and function of the כִּי in v. 10, likely forced for numerical balance. In his essay on the progression of Job's speeches, Hartley (1994: 80) has a three-part structure. Seow (2013: 315) also argues for three sections: vv. 3-10, 11-24, and 25-26.

18. Note that לָמָּה is gapped in v. 16 and in v. 23, with both of these verses looking back to the לָמָּה of the first verse of the section.

19. See n. 14 above.

of finding rest from the turmoil (see 3:10, 13-15, 17-19, and 24-26). The only one who can provide rest is God. The rhetorical situation, the forms, and the structure all emphasize Job's addressee, God, and his goal, the alleviation of his suffering.

Strategies

Imprecation. Job opens his speech with an imprecation (3:3-9).[20] Marked by a predominance of jussives, this provocative opening arrests attention, the imprecation reinforcing the complaint's appeal (Gerstenberger 1988: 250). Thus, as Job complains about his current suffering, the curse on his fate is designed to bring about relief after garnering the deity's attention. This is confirmed by Job's motive clause in 3:10. The rhetoric of the imprecation is reinforced by other strategies: Job's use of tropes, pseudosorites, and allusion.

Tropes. Job uses a number of tropes in his opening speech. The first trope is the motif of reversal (Habel 1985: 105). This comes to the foreground most clearly in his imprecation (vv. 3-9), reinforcing its rhetorical effect. The reversal Job wishes for most often is the reversal of creation itself. Interpreters have long noted the reversal of Gen. 1:3 in Job's initial words regarding the day in 3:4 (יְהִי אוֹר versus יְהִי חֹשֶׁךְ) (e.g., ibid.: 107). Reversal is related to creation where God is not to seek the day from above in 3:4 as well as the images and words for darkness that pile up in 3:4-5, where חֹשֶׁךְ is repeated (and used with צַלְמָוֶת), light is negated (וְאַל־תֹּפַע...נְהָרָה), clouds dwell (תִּשְׁכָּן־עָלָיו עֲנָנָה), and blackness terrifies (יְבַעֲתֻהוּ כִּמְרִירֵי יוֹם). Reversal of creation is evident with Job's wish on the night as well in vv. 6 and 9. In v. 6 darkness (אֹפֶל) is to claim the night, and the creation pattern of adding days to the calendar is reversed;[21] in v. 9 Job issues four clauses where the darkness of night should not end by turning to light. Reversal of creation is not the only kind of reversal Job uses. Fertility is reversed in v. 7. The reversal trope, particularly the reversal of creation as it relates to Job's day, indirectly involves God, the creator, in Job's address.

---

20. Yu (2011: 197–215) identifies only one rhetorical strategy, namely the non-literal death threat. My analysis takes this into account in the discussion of the allusion below. See n. 47 below on Yu's treatment of non-literal death threats.

21. This reading takes the emendation (or revocalization) proposed by BHS and others based on the parallelism of בוא (see Clines 1989: 70).

The second trope is the mythic imagery used in 3:8, where Job references those who are prepared to rouse Leviathan.[22] The rhetorical aim of this image is to bring about the most chaos on this one day by aligning himself with "the most clandestine powers" known to Job (Hartley 1988: 94). This image, like the previous one, works to heighten the tension in Job's already tense discourse by invoking an alliance with those who stir up the strongest creature in creation (Job 41:25 [41:33]).

The third trope Job uses is personification. Personification first occurs with the elements of darkness in 3:5 where the blackness of day is to terrify and darkness is wished to take the night in 3:6. The night is also personified, as it speaks and hopes for light, only to find nothing in Job's wish and not see dawn (3:3, 9). Night may also be personified when Job gives his reason for his wish—"it did not close the doors of [his] womb" (3:10). Most commentators take the implied subject (in the 3ms verb) as לַיְלָה, and this is probably right. Nevertheless, the fact that only God closes and opens wombs indicates that Job does not have God too far out of mind here (cf. Gen. 29:31; 30:22; 1 Sam. 1:5, 6; Gen. 16:2; 20:18, where the former four use סתר as in Job 3:10, while the latter two use עצר).[23] By ascribing the powers of God to night, Job once again uses language that arrests attention.[24]

Job also uses the arresting combination of images of Sheol and death with images of rest. This emerges in Job's statements in vv. 13-15 and vv. 17-19. Job uses the motif of rest and ease to present an alternative reality to his suffering. The preceding verses to both of these units employ

---

22. Newsom (and others—Clines, Habel, Hartley, Walton, and Longman) argues in favor of the MT because those who would curse the sea (Yam) would be those who would be working to establish creation, whereas Job's rhetorical intent in invoking these magicians is to bring about *bouleversement* (1996: 368). Thus, there is no good reason to emend in 3:8a by changing יוֹם to יָם.

23. Newsom (1996: 368) comes close when she writes, "In Israelite thought, of course, it is not night but God who opens and closes the womb. Job's poetic displacement of this function may indicate that the object of his anger is God, although he does not acknowledge this, perhaps even to himself." I would disagree with her final comments in light of the intentionality of all the strategies and structure, but I think she is right when she notes that this is intended to highlight Job's accusation against God. See also Seow (2013: 327).

24. Note also that סתר is another action Job complains about regarding night in v. 10, and this is presumably a divine action in 3:23a in light of the parallel with the explicit subject in 3:23b.

images of death at birth. This contrast leads to the effects of the alternative reality: death would bring rest and ease. Job never uses the word Sheol, instead using the imprecise adverb שָׁם as a euphemism for the place of the dead (fronted twice in v. 17). The images in these verses show that death is preferable to life for Job because, regardless of what death is, it is more peaceful than his current life. Death as a location of relief is also seen in the intensification of the images that build up in vv. 21-22. The purpose of the imagery seems to be to move God to act by its irony.[25] The death imagery is perhaps most startling with Job's wish to have been stillborn in 3:16 (see 3:11-12).

Job combines several tropes to depict his suffering as a way of justifying his complaint in an attempt to persuade God to act. First, Job describes his life as filled with turmoil (עָמָל). Job uses the term twice in Job 3, in vv. 10 and 20, both significant verses in this speech. Job's use of עָמָל to describe his whole life (cf. 7:1-6) also highlights his rhetorical aim through hyperbole.[26] Job uses images of light and darkness to depict his suffering as well (3:4-6, 9, 16, 20).[27] Moreover, Job describes his soul as bitter (3:20), and he is among those who suffer emotionally hoping for death without satisfaction (3:21-22). He suffers so intensely that it feels like food and water (3:24).[28] He experiences emotional and psychological suffering through fear (3:25), and has no rest (3:26).

The final trope is only hinted at in Job 3, but is developed in subsequent speeches, namely, divine vigilance.[29] In v. 23 Job complains against God for hedging him in (סכך). The ironic use of this word is noted by interpreters as it looks back to 1:10 (שׂוך).[30] God's actions are depicted as the cause of Job's suffering.[31] This perceived overprotection is another

---

25. A similar rhetorical use of Sheol imagery can be found in Ps. 88:11-13 [10-12].

26. On the friends' dispute of Job's use עָמָל, see Beuken 1994: 48–9; cf. Habel 1985: 109–10. It is the friends' disputation of this term that indicates Job's use of hyperbole: they rebuke Job for his over-the-top description of his condition.

27. Van Hecke (2011: 95–8) notes that these images in Job 3 are related to Job's desire for rest.

28. The simile of Job's "groanings" (שַׁאֲגָת) pouring out like water is noteworthy in light of this word as it is associated with protest prayer in Ps. 22:2 [1] and Ps. 32:3 [2].

29. This is most notably developed in 7:17-21. The trope in Job 3 is perhaps related to the divine attack imagery as well, since the hedging in of Job is a malicious action toward him (see Habel 1985: 112).

30. Clines is typical (1989: 101): "[W]hat the Satan, God, and Job once felt as protection, Job now finds a restriction."

31. This relates to the metaphor of Job's life, using a journey metaphor. See van Hecke 2011: 94–5.

provocative statement, the irony of which seems to be intended to arrest God's attention and move God to act on Job's behalf.[32]

Pseudosorites. Another persuasive strategy Job employs is a pseudosorites.[33] According to O'Connor (1987a: 240), a pseudosorites is a rhetorical device "that apes the sorites, that form of a chain of propositions that links predicate to subject, predicate to subject through its length"; it "is a negative mode, asserting 'A is not the case, and its consequent B will not follow. But in case B does follow, its consequent C will not follow.'"[34] In other words, a pseudosorites "begins by excluding an event or an outcome; it is logically irreal and grammatically counterfactual" (O'Connor 1987b: 168).

Where is a pseudosorites used in Job 3? In Job 3, the pseudosorites is: Job first nullifies his birth, but if that were to happen he would nullify his conception; Job then nullifies his gestation, but if that were to happen, he would nullify his postpartum viability. The illogical nature of these statements is clear: in both cases, if the first nullification happens, the second is unnecessary.[35]

---

32. On the role of provocative language in protest prayer, see Patrick and Diable 2008: 28–9. See also Broyles 1989: 14; cf. Alter 1985: 76–84, where he highlights the intensification of images from one line to the next.

33. This strategy is not often named as such, but is noted implicitly throughout the literature on Job 3. Clines, once again, is typical when he notes throughout his discussion that Job's wish for the reversal of past events is absurd. The fact that Job's wish is impossible indicates that he is not intending his words to be taken literally, but that they are instead intended to serve a rhetorical purpose. Clines (1989: 77–87) notes throughout his treatment that the wish is futile, "vain," "absurd," "hopeless," and "ineffectual." What is not stressed is how this device works.

34. Elsewhere O'Connor writes (1987b: 163), "The pseudosorites is a type of paradox which has some elements of the form of the sorites, but in which the negatives pattern illogically." See also Patterson 2010: 19–20. Both Patterson and O'Connor list examples of the pseudosorites, most of which are unsurprisingly found in the prophets, who use this strategy when persuading their audiences. See, e.g., Mic. 6:14-15; Hos. 5:4-6; 9:11-16.

35. O'Connor (1987a: 248–9) charts it as follows: Step 1: Conception (v. 3b); Step 2: Gestation (v. 16ab); Step 3: Birth (v. 3a); Step 4: Postpartum Viability (v. 11ab). Steps 1 and 3 correspond to each other and steps 2 and 4 correspond to each other. Both go back in time in Job's presentation (3 to 1 and 4 to 2). See also Patterson 2010: 29. Seow (2013: 319) notes that every other time הרה and ילד occur together the former precedes the latter, making this instance unique, highlighting the irreal nature of Job's statement.

The careful structuring and illogical ordering indicates Job adopts this literary device intentionally, but to what purpose? Neither O'Connor nor Patterson explore explicitly the rhetoric of the pseudosorites in Job 3. Patterson (2010: 36) concludes generally that the device elsewhere creates a "vividness" to the context, and it "arrests the reader's attention… because event B is not only unlikely and contrary to event A, the combination presents a unique paradox." If this is the way this device works generally, it makes sense that it would be working the same way in Job: the illogical extreme of the device is designed to arrest God's attention. But having God's attention implies Job's desire for God to alleviate his suffering.

Allusion. The fourth rhetorical strategy that Job uses in his opening speech is allusion. Allusion in this study refers to an implicit intentional link between two texts that is marked in some way.[36] This marking involves verbal and/or syntactical correspondence; where the correspondence involves rare lexemes or forms and/or greater frequency of correspondence, the allusion becomes more likely. When an allusion to another text has been sufficiently established, other correspondences (e.g., frequently occurring lexemes or thematic links) may also become evidence for allusion. Following Kynes, an allusion is best understood as a category that represents less explicit correspondence than a quotation, but includes an element of intentionality, unlike an echo (2012: 31).[37] Accordingly, this study will document the proposed allusion by noting the verbal and syntactical correspondence in Job to another text, noting reasons why Job is alluding to the other text (rather than the other text alluding to Job), and then interpret the internal rhetorical effect of the allusion in light of the literary rhetorical situation already discerned for each speech.[38]

---

36. See Kynes 2012: 26, 30–3, 37; Ben-Porat 1976: 105–28, esp. 107–10. See also Sommer 1998: 6–31; Schultz 1999: 211–39. While these scholars' arguments are nuanced, there is some broad overlap between their perspectives which provides the basis for my understanding of allusion in this study. Kynes' approach is most influential for my understanding.

37. The so-called "intentional fallacy" is mitigated since the text is the determining factor, as Kynes argues (2012: 33).

38. As scholars often note, it is not always clear that an allusion is present, and some readers may not find all proposed allusions entirely convincing (e.g., ibid.: 32). Nevertheless, allusion is an important rhetorical strategy for Job in his overall rhetorical situation, as this study will demonstrate (at least in part), building on the work of Kynes, Pyeon, and others. The allusions that are dealt with in this study

Interpreters have long noted the intertextual connection between Job's imprecation and Jer. 20:14-18. The connections between these two passages are both lexical and thematic.³⁹ Regarding the lexical connections, the phrase "the day on which I was born" (יוֹם אִוָּלֶד בּוֹ) in Job 3:3 alludes to "the day on which I was born" (הַיּוֹם אֲשֶׁר יֻלַּדְתִּי בּוֹ) in Jer. 20:14. The question "why did I not die in the womb, from the womb come out and expire" (לָמָּה לֹא מֵרֶחֶם אָמוּת מִבֶּטֶן יָצָאתִי וְאֶגְוָע) in Job 3:11 alludes to "because you did not kill me in the womb that my mother would have been my grave and her womb pregnant forever" (אֲשֶׁר לֹא־מוֹתְתַנִי מֵרָחֶם וַתְּהִי־לִי אִמִּי קִבְרִי וְרַחְמָה הֲרַת עוֹלָם) and "why did I come out from the womb to see trouble and sorrow" (לָמָּה זֶּה מֵרֶחֶם יָצָאתִי לִרְאוֹת עָמָל וְיָגוֹן) in Jer. 20:17-18. Job also uses עָמָל with the theme of seeing in 3:10 (עָמָל מֵעֵינָי). Thematic connections reinforce these lexical connections. They both are cursing, though the verbs are different (Job: קלל and Jeremiah: ארר).⁴⁰ Job wants his day to perish (אבד) in 3:3, while Jeremiah wants the day not to be blessed (אַל־יְהִי בָרוּךְ) in 20:14. The announcing of a male child is in both passages, though the lexemes are different (cf. Job 3:3 and Jer. 20:15). There may also be a thematic connection between Job's reversal motifs in 3:3-9 and Jeremiah's reversal motif in 20:16 (Hartley 1988: 88 n. 2). The exact direction of dependence is difficult to determine, but using Kynes' intertextual method that combines both diachronic and synchronic evaluation, it seems that Job is most likely the later text based on the criterion of coherence (2012: 17–60).⁴¹ Given Job's development of the curse formula (Hartley 1988: 88 n. 1; Greenstein 2004a: 102–3), and given that Job seems to have intentionally used Jeremiah's curse as a structuring device for his own (Habel 1985: 103), it is likely that Job is intentionally alluding to Jeremiah's similar curse. Not all scholars are willing to see dependence between these two passages, instead asserting

are those that have a) been established by prior scholarship, and b) have significant rhetorical import. Some less probable allusions are reserved for discussion in the footnotes, rather than in the body of the study.

39. Westermann provides a chart of how the passages correspond to one another. Unfortunately, he does not detail the connections explicitly (1981b: 60 n. 12). See also Hartley 1988: 88 n. 2; Pyeon 2003: 86. More recently these have been clearly arranged by Dell (2013: 108–10).

40. Technically, the narrator uses קלל. Job uses קבב and ארר in v. 8.

41. The criterion of coherence is an important step in understanding the diachronic nature of the allusion. Since many (poetic) passages in the OT are notoriously difficult to date, Kynes suggests inquiring as to which text is more likely the original based on internal and external contexts (2012: 59).

that both are adopting an independent form (Westermann 1981b: 60–1 n. 12; Hartley 1988: 88 n. 2). An allusion is likely for three reasons: (1) the point just made about Job's use of the clear lexical connections to structure his speech (i.e., the inclusio of vv. 3-9), (2) the evidence listed by Greenstein and Dell regarding allusions to Jeremiah, and Kynes regarding allusions to the Psalter and Isaiah,[42] and (3) the presence of a common source and an allusion to another text are not mutually exclusive.[43]

With this in mind, it will be helpful to clarify the rhetorical function of Jeremiah's curse as a means to understand how Job is using it. Jeremiah's curse comes at the end of his so-called confessions in chapters 11–20, a section in which there is a back-and-forth movement between, on the one hand, his proclamation of destruction and, on the other, complaint over the alienation he experiences because of his proclamation. At the conclusion of Jeremiah's dialogue with Yahweh over his alienating and suffering-producing prophetic call, Jeremiah issues the strongest complaint of the entire section. Jeremiah specifically chooses his day to focus the complaint on the extent of his pain (Dubbink 1999: 73–4). Life has become unbearable for Jeremiah because of the alienation he feels. Despite the brief hope of the positive expression of 20:11-13, Jeremiah's affliction and alienation is too great to end here; vv. 14–18 provide a perfect conclusion to his so-called confessions (80).[44]

Bruce Zuckerman agrees (1991: 125–6): Jeremiah is not rebelling. Rather, this is a "tacit appeal"; it is "a lament-of-final resort…to portray a sufferer's distress in the most nihilistic terms possible for the purpose of attracting God's attention and thus leading to the rescue of the sufferer from affliction." But Zuckerman goes in a different direction for Job 3, arguing Job's death wish is literal (126–7).[45] Three reasons justify seeing Job's death wish through allusion as "a lament-of-last resort" to "[attract] God's attention," however. First, Dell has shown that this is a re-use of a tradition rather than a parody since the original text and the alluding text have the same context (2013: 116).[46] Second, Job 3 does not bear the

---

42. See Greenstein 2004a: 98–110; Dell 2013: 106–17; Kynes 2012; 2013a: 201–13; 2013b: 94–105; 2013c: 34–48.

43. See also Pyeon 2003: 86–8, where he makes a case based on Hays' intertextual method.

44. Notably, Dubbink (1999: 80–2) concludes that Jeremiah's protest and extreme language are affirming of the place of this kind of language in the tension between faith and pain.

45. Zuckerman notes that Job's other death wishes indicate the same thing, namely, that there is no appeal for mercy, no plea for help (1991: 127–35).

46. On parody as antithetical allusion, see Kynes 2011: 276–310.

marks of a literal death wish. Yu's detailed analysis of this is thorough and convincing, showing that these are expressions of "deep dissatisfaction," appeals for God to change the circumstances of the one uttering the non-literal death threat (2011: 201–13).⁴⁷ Third, Job's use of Jer. 20:14-18 corresponds to his use of other poetic traditions, as Kynes argues. Kynes (2012) documents six psalms used by Job for rhetorical purposes in which Job appeals to God through allusion (Pss. 1; 8; 39; 73; 107; and 139).⁴⁸ Job's use of Jer. 20:14-18 reuses and affirms the tradition in his complaint for the purpose of arresting attention to obtain relief.⁴⁹

Rhetorical Questions and Delayed Disambiguation. The final rhetorical strategy that Job uses is delayed disambiguation; Job carefully crafts his words to delay the disclosure of the intended audience of his complaint. To this point, the analysis has noted that Job's complaint is directed toward God, something with which some interpreters disagree.⁵⁰ It is this rhetorical strategy that confirms Job is addressing God implicitly in Job 3, with a carefully crafted statement that does not curse God but seeks to

---

47. The quote is from p. 210. According to Yu, Abimelech (Judg. 9:54), Samson (Judg. 16:30), Saul (1 Sam. 31:4), and Jonah (Jon. 1:12) express literal death wishes, while Israel/Jacob (Gen. 46:30), the Israelites (Exod. 16:3; Num. 14:2), Elijah (1 Kings 19:4), Jonah (Jon. 4:3, 9), Jeremiah (Jer. 20:14-18), and Job express non-literal death wishes. Literal death wishes are characterized by actions of the directed party corresponding to the wish and are specific. Furthermore, with literal death wishes reasons are given in detail. These are not found in Job 3.

48. Kynes argues that Job tends to use the psalms as a way of reinforcing his faith, where he draws upon the traditional images of God rhetorically to move God to act by noting the disjunction between the traditional images of God and Job's current experience.

49. Another possible, though less plausible, allusion has been identified by Burnight (2013: 38). He points out that Job's use of the phrase דַּרְכּוֹ נִסְתָּרָה in 3:23 recalls the same phrase in Isa. 40:27. The pronominal suffixes are different and the word order is reversed in Isa. 40:27, though Burnight points out these are the only two passages with this word combination. He suggests that Job is rejecting the Isaianic comfort. While possible, it seems more likely, given how Job uses other Isaianic texts and motifs (see the discussion on Job 9 and Job 12 below), that, if Job is actually alluding to this passage, he is appealing to the tradition in which God has promised comfort to those suffering in exile. Not experiencing that comfort, Job is attempting to move God to act in accordance with the prophet's promise. The allusion, if accepted, implies a petition based on the discord between Job's knowledge of God and his experience of God in his suffering.

50. See nn. 7, 11–12.

complain with provocative language to attract God's attention with the eventual goal of seeking relief.

As noted above, the forms of imprecation and complaint are seamlessly connected here with one rhetorical goal. The complaint comes to the foreground most explicitly in six verses of Job 3: vv. 10, 11, 12, 16, 20, and 23. The latter five of these are complaint because of the presence of the interrogative (sometimes gapped). Verse 10, in providing the reason for the imprecation, is best understood as part of the complaint as well in that it describes Job's circumstances, emphasizing subtly God's role in causing his suffering.[51] This emerges plainly in Job's complaint, asking, "Why does he [i.e., God] give light to the troubled, and life to the bitter of soul?" (3:20).

These six verses are all linked through several verbal and structural connections. Verse 10 is linked to v. 20 (עָמָל); vv. 11, 12, 16, 20, and 23 are linked (לָמָּה and מַדּוּעַ and the themes of life/death, though לָמָּה is gapped in vv. 16 and 23); v. 20 is linked to v. 23 (לָמָּה יִתֵּן לְ, though gapped in v. 23); v. 23 is linked to v. 10 (סתר). The result of this is to delay the focal point of the complaint, God, who does not appear until v. 23b with אֱלוֹהַּ. The delay stresses that God is addressed implicitly at the climactic point of the complaint. This informs retroactively the prior complaints.[52] The accusations expressed through the rhetorical questions provocatively stress Job's aim for the alleviation of his suffering. Given the nature of complaint, as noted above, the address to God is designed to move him to action to bring relief.[53] The tension builds throughout the speech and it is at the end that Job finally clarifies what his previous words only hinted at: he is loudly, brashly, shockingly complaining against God.

Summary of Job 3

Job's suffering is so great that he combines arguably the most scathing imprecation (from Jeremiah) with an equally scathing complaint to accomplish his rhetorical goal. Through curse, tropes, pseudosorites, allusion to Jer. 20:14-18, rhetorical questions, and delayed disambiguation

---

51. See Miller 1993: 356–60. See also Gerstenberger 1988: 250, who stresses that imprecation implies petition and works with complaint.

52. This perhaps explains why the ambiguity is so important in v. 10: night is most likely the syntactical subject of the 3ms verb, but God is intended to be seen at that moment as well. It is also confirmed by the presence of God (אֱלוֹהַּ) in 3:4. The delayed mention of God accentuates the implicit addressee in climactic fashion.

53. As Hartley notes (1988: 89), "[Job 3] expresses Job's basic wish that God would grant him immediate relief from his suffering."

of the one toward whom his complaint is directed, Job brings together a number of rhetorical strategies to arrest God's attention. He appeals to God implicitly because God is the one who can change his circumstances; the complaint implies a petition for relief. This rhetorical reading of Job 3 reveals the foundational significance of protest prayer for Job. In the face of innocent suffering, he complains. His complaint is intentional, seeking to grab God's attention, to bring about relief.

"Is There Any Injustice on My Tongue?": The Rhetoric of Job's Second Speech (Job 6–7)

Introduction

Eliphaz responds to Job in Job 4–5. This response from Eliphaz changes the rhetorical situation in significant ways, his suffering and his friends are now two issues he must address. Thus, in Job 6–7 Job addresses both the friends and God in this new rhetorical situation. Accordingly, Job defends his right to protest in prayer to both audiences (see 6:2-4, 30; 7:11), while also continuing to protest in prayer.

The Literary Rhetorical Situation of Job 6–7

In Job 4–5 Eliphaz criticizes Job and his verbal expression in his opening complaint.[54] Beuken (1994: 48–57) shows how Eliphaz uses Job's words to rebut and reframe Job's approach.[55] Perhaps the most significant of these connections is Eliphaz's use of the word שְׁאָגָה. Job uses it in 3:24 (his "groanings" pour out like water), while Eliphaz uses the same word in 4:10 to describe the sounds of lions, who are used as an illustration of the wicked whom God rebukes (4:6-11). Beuken is hesitant to argue Eliphaz is responding to Job by so specifically linking him with the wicked at this early stage in the narrative (ibid.: 49–50). But the word only occurs seven times in the Hebrew Bible, so its infrequency testifies to its intentionality

---

54. Longman (2012: 115) is typical of interpreters when he notes that in his opening question, Eliphaz "announces his intention to challenge Job's complaint."

55. See also Course 1994: 22–3, 27–9. Habel (1985: 205) summarizes three ways in which the characters respond to one another: (1) citing specific words or summarizing the position of another, (2) isolating key motifs and developing them in a counterpoint, and (3) responding to another's speech with innuendo, key words, association, and word play. Habel illustrates this point with Zophar's speech in Job 11, but these strategies are apparent in most speeches, as the following analysis demonstrates. See also Good 1990: 220.

here (see Ezek. 19:7; Zech. 11:3; Pss. 22:2 [1]; 32:3 [2]; Job 3:24; 4:10). Eliphaz is redirecting Job away from peril, and his advice relates to prayer (5:1-8). Job's complaint places him in the camp of the אֱוִיל, as Eliphaz implies in 5:2.[56] Moreover, Job's עָמָל is not by chance, but is rooted in his own sin and he should seek (דרשׁ) God (5:6-8). Job cannot be completely innocent because Eliphaz has it by divine revelation that to be human is to err (4:12-21). By his use of the 2ms forms—thirty-nine occurrences in total—Eliphaz places Job outside the wisdom circle.[57] He also uses ambiguity to try to move Job back to his fear of God.[58] Eliphaz's statement undoubtedly is veiled in 4:10, but he considers Job's groanings misguided at best and sinful at worst. Eliphaz's low anthropology and high theology provide a foundation to reject Job's protest prayer and to encourage penitence.[59]

Eliphaz's rebuke changes the rhetorical situation for Job dramatically (Yu 2011: 230). No longer is Job simply suffering and needing to move God to relieve it; now Job must defend his speech (Fohrer 1963: 165). In other words, Job now faces two exigencies, bringing complexity to the rhetorical situation. His audience also changes in that Job will need to address both the friends and God. The constraints remain unchanged, though the intellectual milieu regarding propriety in prayer emerges more clearly in light of Eliphaz's argument.

The Forms of Job 6–7

There are a number of forms that make up Job's second speech, woven together in a complex, integrated whole. The speech consists of wish (6:2, 8-10c), motive clauses (6:3a, 4, 10c, 29d; 7:16d, 21c-e), disputation (6:4b,

---

56. Seow comments on 5:2 (2013: 415): "Eliphaz's citation of the proverb may be understood as an implicit criticism of Job's violent outburst in chapter 3. Accordingly, Job's initial response was not wise. In fact, it was dangerous."

57. Beuken notes there are fourteen 2ms forms in 4:2-6 alone (1994: 47); the remaining occurrences come in Job 5.

58. Beuken (1994: 58–9) points out the ambiguity in Eliphaz's question in 4:6, and notes that this ambiguity is disambiguated as the speech progresses, where, at the end, he questions Job's fear of God (cf. 5:8, 17, 21-22). See also Burnight 2014: 347–70.

59. Eliphaz sees Job's complaint as a "refusal to repent," and so Job "is implicitly claiming that he is more righteous than God" (Longman 2012: 120); see 4:17. On 4:17, see Whitekettle 2010: 445–8. According to Eliphaz, there is "only one solution to suffering, including Job's, and that is repentance (5:8-16)" (Longman 2012: 114). Cf. Seow 2013: 427; Yu 2011: 217; Course 1994: 29–31.

5-7, 11-23, 25-27, 30), petition (6:24, 28-29; 7:7a-b, 16c),[60] lament (7:1-2, 9-10), and complaint (7:3-6, 7c-8, 11-21b). Two significant observations emerge from a statistical analysis of the forms in this speech. First, disputation dominates Job 6 (fifty out of seventy-seven clauses), while protest prayer dominates Job 7 (with fifty-eight out of sixty-two clauses being protest prayer, comprising complaint [forty-six clauses], lament [nine clauses], and petition [three clauses]). Despite this complexity, the forms integrate well to accomplish Job's rhetorical purposes. The non-disputation clauses in Job 6 function with the disputation. For example, the wish and motive clauses of 6:2-4 provide justification of Job's complaint from Job 3. This justification is functionally disputatious in nature.[61] The wish and motive clauses in 6:8-10 also relate functionally to disputation, as Job renews his wish from Job 3 and justifies the piety of his words. Job will not back down from his position. Likewise, the petitions of 6:24, 28-29 are related to disputation, as Job appeals to his friends to consider his argument.[62] In Job 7, lament and complaint clearly dominate the chapter, with the petitions of 7:7, 16c and the motive clauses of 7:16d, 21c-e naturally serving the protest prayer. This analysis reveals two things. First, it confirms the rhetorical situation identified above, namely, one in which Job must address a friend-related exigency (the ethics of his speech) and a God-related exigency (his suffering). He predominantly uses two appropriate forms for each exigency, disputation against the friends and protest prayer toward God.[63] Second, it reveals the purposes of Job's speech in Job 6–7, namely, to justify his protest prayer and to continue protesting in prayer.[64]

---

60. The petitions (imperatives) of 6:21-22 are best understood as disputation because they are imbedded speech in a rhetorical question. Rhetorical questions are inherently disputatious.

61. This is confirmed by the use of the word בַּעַשׂ in 6:2, directly responding to Eliphaz's implication of the foolishness of Job's verbal expression in 5:2.

62. This is confirmed by the unmarked motive clause in 6:29d. See Clines 1989: 168, who suggests that 6:22-30 are disputation while also classifying 6:24, 28-29 as appeal.

63. *Pace* Hartley, Clines, and Murphy. Hartley (1988: 40–1) and Clines (1989: 168) suggest the whole speech is a lament, while Murphy (1981: 25–6) suggests the whole speech is disputation. It is both.

64. See Hartley 1988: 129–30; Newsom 1996: 384.

The Rhetorical Strategies of Job 6–7

Structure

Most interpreters are agreed that this speech has two major movements that correspond to the chapter division.[65] There is major disagreement on the identification of subunits, with almost no two proposals exactly the same. It seems best to divide Job 6 into two parts: 6:2-13 and 6:14-30. This accounts for the shift from rhetorical questions in vv. 11-13 (cf. vv. 5-6) as well as the content. The challenging 6:14 provides the transition to Job's indictment against the friends, illustrated by an extended metaphor of a dangerous wadi that is applied to them. Job 7 also divides into two main sections, 7:1-11 and 7:12-21. While most interpreters place a break between v. 10 and v. 11, it seems better to understand the interrogative *he* in both v. 1 and v. 12 providing the structural clue. The גַּם־אֲנִי in v. 11 provides an emphatic conclusion to the first section.[66] This also accounts for the shift to 2ms forms in 7:12-21.

This structural analysis reveals Job's main emphases and movements. Corresponding to the rhetorical situation and the forms, Job has two major movements in which he addresses first his friends and, secondly, God. It also provides some clues as to the emphases within these two movements. In regards to the friends, Job justifies his protest prayer and then criticizes the friends for being unhelpful. With God, Job first laments hardship in life and then accuses God of being the cause.

Strategies

Tropes. The first strategy in Job 6 is the usage of tropes.[67] There are several tropes that can be identified.

The first trope emerges in 6:2-3 involving the weighing of Job's vexation. The parallel structure of 6:2 emphasizes the image. A causal relationship is established between כַּעַשׂ and הַוָּה. Moreover, the verb שׁקל

---

65. Murphy's suggestion to place the break at 6:27 is both idiosyncratic and unsustainable (1981: 25). It makes little sense of the inclusio of הַוָּה in 6:2 (reading the *qere*) and 30 (see the discussion in Seow 2013: 468). It also ignores the connection of the plural imperatives in 6:28-30 with 6:24 (over against the singular imperatives in 7:7 and 7:16 that govern the address in Job 7) and the shift in content in 7:1.

66. Seow's proposal is also appealing; he suggests a tripartite division: 7:1-6, 7:7-16, and 7:17-21 (2013: 489). This makes good sense of the placement of the imperatives, framing the middle section, while also situating Job's key statement in 7:11 in the middle of the poem.

67. While Job 6–7 are one speech, the different rhetorical goals for each chapter (as outlined above) indicate that it is best to examine the rhetorical strategies for each chapter rather than for the entire speech.

(with the infinite absolute creating emphasis) parallels the noun מֹאזְנַיִם, while the placement of the adverb יַחַד at the end of the verse stresses Job's wish for the visual demonstration of the weight of his vexation (כַּעַשׂ) caused by his calamity (הַוָּה). But the balances imagery is not complete until the comparative in v. 3a where Job wishes that Eliphaz could see the weight of the sand of the sea juxtaposed against his vexation on the scales. Clines (1989: 170) captures the rhetorical function of this imagery: "Together [Job's calamities] form an unimaginable burden. If only that burden could be physically demonstrated on some cosmic scales, an Eliphaz would be convinced that Job's outburst is not in the least excessive." The scales imagery serves as a justification for Job's ostensibly outrageous outburst from Job 3. It also anticipates where Job will turn as his defense progresses, indicating a brewing distrust between Job and his comforters.[68]

Job also employs tropes rhetorically in Job 6 to communicate the limited knowledge and perception of Eliphaz and the friends. To do this, Job uses the imagery of taste and of his body. By focusing on the subjective and personal experience of taste and the experience and strength of one's own body (6:4, 5-7, 11-13, 30), Job rebuts Eliphaz's contention of divine revelation with an argument from personal experience. Regardless of what Eliphaz thinks he knows about Job, Job contends that he knows his experience more intimately than Eliphaz ever could. Job has discerned calamity (6:30) and knows his limited strength (6:11-13). For Job, "[s]ome experiences are intensely personal and subjective, like poison within one's body and like one's own throat knowing what is simply unpalatable" (Seow 2013: 458; cf. 88).[69] Eliphaz's pithy truisms do not work at all times; Job's language is justified in light of his discernment of his situation.

Another trope Job uses is the divine attack imagery in 6:4, 9, and 13. In 6:4 the divine attack imagery also includes body imagery, as the arrows pierce Job's body and his spirit drinks their poison. This imagery directly rebuts "Eliphaz's sanitized references to binding up wounds and healing bruises (5:18) and to the swords and famines that in Eliphaz's miraculous world leave no scars and ravages (5:19-22)" (Newsom 1996: 391). It is

---

68. See Newsom (1996: 386–7), who notes that balances "serve to establish agreement between parties who are by the nature of things inclined to mistrust each other's valuations. Job's use of the image implies that Eliphaz has underestimated the weight of his suffering."

69. Newsom captures the rhetoric (1996: 391): "No one else can tell me whenever I am hungry or thirsty or nauseated. Only I can know… Nothing is more subjective than taste."

not a coincidence that Job refers to the arrows of שַׁדַּי since שַׁדַּי was the last divine name Eliphaz used in 5:17; this is a direct rebuttal in the disputation and defense of Job's opening complaint. By contrast, Job's body is ravaged. The rhetoric of this is powerful: Job is still suffering and at the hands of God. God is not a healer but a warrior. The verse begins with a causal כִּי, indicating these are the grounds on which Job spoke and speaks. His words may have been rash (לָעַע), as Job readily admits, but Job's immense suffering—innocent suffering with God as the source—justifies his words.[70] In 6:9 the attack imagery is part of Job's wish in 6:8-10. The rhetoric of the wish will be explored more fully below, but the divine attack imagery in v. 9 builds on the imagery of v. 4. Job's hyperbolic wish asks God to finish him off so he can finally have relief. The divine attack imagery in 6:13 is more subtle, coming in the form of the divine passive (וְתֻשִׁיָּה נִדְּחָה מִמֶּנִּי). Whatever resources Job had have been driven from him by divine attack. The imagery here, in connection with the rhetorical questions of 6:11-13, also justify Job's admittedly rash words. He has no other option.

The final trope Job uses in his disputation in Job 6 is a complex one involving a number of images that come together in the extended and applied *topos* of the destructive, dry wadi. The rhetoric of this trope emerges through the opening instruction in 6:14 followed by the application in 6:21.

The exact meaning of 6:14 is debated, with three main interpretive options.[71] The first option relates the two clauses by suggesting that a friend's loyalty will protect one who is in despair from forsaking his piety; NASB captures this sense: "For the despairing man there should be kindness from his friend; so that he does not forsake the fear of the Almighty." Seow summarizes, "In this view, friendship in a time of need may help those who are discouraged not to lose faith and abandon God" (2013: 461). The second view suggests that if a friend withholds loyalty the friend himself is impious; NRSV (cf. ESV) captures this sense: "Those who withhold kindness from a friend forsake the fear of the Almighty." Seow writes, "That is, failure to live up to the expectations of friendship is tantamount to impiety; if one does not remain faithful to one's friend in times of need, then one is really not a pious person… [L]oyalty in friendship is a manifestation of piety" (462). The third option understands

---

70. Job 6:4 stands out in the structure as the lone tricolon in 6:2-7 (Habel 1985: 142), highlighting Job's justification of his verbal expression.

71. These options are organized by Seow (2013: 461–2), though see also Clines' discussion, which less clearly demarcates the different options but provides more translational options (1989: 177–8).

6:14 to say that a friend is required to demonstrate loyalty even when a despairing person forsakes his piety; NIV85 captures this sense: "A despairing man should have the devotion of his friends, even though he forsakes the fear of the Almighty." Seow elaborates, "In times of despair, when God seems utterly hostile, when faith seems impossible, true friendship that does not depend on one's confessional stance, friendship that does not depend on one's theology, may be the manifestation of grace. Friendship may be a vehicle of grace, even to one who finds it hard to believe" (ibid.).

There are three factors that determine the best option: (1) the text-critical question in 6:14a, (2) the function of the *waw* in 6:14b, and (3) the coherence with the rhetorical situation already identified. Regarding the first factor, BHS suggests reading לֹא מָאַס for לַמָּס, an emendation followed by Clines. The second option follows this emendation, but the MT is the preferred text for three reasons.[72] First, as Seow notes (2013: 476), the MT is the more difficult reading and more readily explains the proposed emendation.[73] Second, Clines' argument (1989: 160) that the MT requires emendation because the context would demand "some such sense as 'is due'" is not conclusive since a verbless clause can have a modal sense if the context demands it, as it does here.[74] Third, the loss of two *'alep*s is difficult to sustain.[75] This analysis eliminates the second interpretive option above (NRSV and ESV).

Regarding the second factor, the function of the *waw*, it is best understood as indicating result, as the NASB understands it, but perhaps it is better rendered as "otherwise" so as not to add a negation in 6:14b as the NASB translates it. Thus, the sense of the verse would be: "To the despairing one there should be lovingkindness from his friend, otherwise he will forsake the fear of the Almighty."[76] Moreover, this translation fits well within the rhetorical situation of Job 6, while the third interpretive option (NIV85) does not fit the rhetorical situation—there is no indication

---

72. The verb is likely מוס ("to melt away," used metaphorically as "discouraged" or "despairing") (Seow 2013: 476).

73. The LXX has misunderstood the Hebrew syntax and indicates a likely paraphrastic rendering to make clear what was not understood.

74. See also Joüon §154e. For verbless clauses that require a modal sense, see, e.g., Ruth 2:4, 9.

75. *Pace* Clines (1989: 160), who curiously argues that the emendation requires only the addition of "two vowel letters."

76. The word "otherwise" is not a typical translation for the conjunction, but it captures the result-oriented logic as well as the nuance of alternative ("or") of Job's instruction.

that Job *has* given up his fear of God (i.e., his faith).⁷⁷ Job is instructing Eliphaz and the friends that they are tempting him to forsake his piety through their arguments against protest prayer. Job denounces his friends' advice because they are counseling him to violate his integrity, unwittingly continuing the *satan*'s role in the test, and instructs them to be better comforters by not tempting him to violate or forfeit his piety. As Hartley writes (1988: 137, italics original), "Job accuses his friends of falling short in their expression of *loyal kindness (ḥesed)* to him in his time of affliction."

This instruction forms the foundation for the extended *topos* that follows in 6:15-29. Job abruptly shifts from instruction to a complex series of metaphors about his brothers acting treacherously, illustrated by a wadi which has become dry after the winter snow and rains disappear with the arrival of the summer heat (6:15-17). As Clines notes (1989: 178), the contrast between brothers and treacherous action is stark. The wadi imagery continues with Job describing how caravans that travel among these wadis perish; they are deceived into thinking there is respite from the heat, but the water is gone (6:18-20). Job then specifically and clearly applies this imagery to his friends in 6:21 (כִּי־עַתָּה הֱיִיתֶם לֹא)—they are deceptive (ibid.). Recognizing their fear,⁷⁸ Job continues the trope of treachery in the form of rhetorical questions. That these rhetorical questions are related to the trope is evident in the conclusion Job draws for them in 6:27: the friends' treachery includes taking advantage of Job, who depicts himself as one of the most vulnerable in society. Their words commit violence, another trope that dovetails with the trope of treachery (6:25-26).⁷⁹ After drawing this conclusion, Job concludes the extended *topos* with a series of appeals that work with the imagery of betrayal (6:28-29). Their violence with words, evident in Eliphaz's critical rebuke of Job's discourse, is an injustice (6:29b). The imagery of treachery is enclosed by instruction about friendship and a series of appeals, all of which work together in Job's rhetoric to accomplish his rhetorical goal of disputation (see Fohrer 1963: 175).

---

77. This is a point also made by Clines (1989: 178).

78. The phonological similarity of the verbs ירא and ראה also draw attention to this verse as a key verse in Job's dispute.

79. Hawley (2018: 95–8) does not see destruction in this use of metaphor, though given the destruction in view in Bildad's competitive use of the metaphor in 8:2, I am inclined to disagree. That said, Hawley's analysis of metaphor competition in speech provides some useful insights (67–108).

Through these tropes Job counters Eliphaz's argument by defending his complaint and accusing Eliphaz (and the friends) of maltreatment. In other words, Job defends the ethics of his complaint, while emphasizing the unethical treatment of his friends.

Lexical Repetition. Job also uses repetition in his persuasion of Eliphaz and the friends, using several words that Eliphaz had just used. Clearly Job is responding to Eliphaz's use of כַּעַשׂ in 5:2 when he wishes for his own כַּעַשׂ to be weighed (6:2). Eliphaz criticized Job as a fool for his complaint, but Job defends his complaint by noting his vexation is the result of his calamity. Vexation can be justified (see Deut. 32:21; 1 Kings 15:30; 21:22; 2 Kings 23:26; Pss. 6:8 [7]; 10:14; 31:10; 85:5 [4]; Job 17:7),[80] and Job makes this known. The weight of vexation relates directly to the propriety of Job's speech. Related to this point of vexation is Job's use of the divine name שַׁדַּי in 6:4. Eliphaz extols שַׁדַּי for his sovereignty in wounding and healing (5:17-26). Job responds that his vexation, his calamity, is rooted in the wounding actions of שַׁדַּי, without any trace of healing. Job's use of חֵץ in 6:4 may also recall the mention of Resheph in 5:7 (Course 1994: 37; Seow 2013: 437–8, 455). בְּעוּתֵי in 6:4 may also respond as a synonym to בהל in 4:5 (Course 1994: 37–8, esp. 38 n. 72). All of this justifies Job's complaint in the disputation.

Job also directly rebuts Eliphaz's argument when he renews his wish from Job 3 and calls it "my hope" (תִּקְוָתִי) in 6:8 (Hartley 1988: 134; Course 1994: 42). Job sees his only hope in protest prayer because of his innocence (6:10). If Job wants relief, he will have to complain and move God to act on his behalf. Job's renewed death wish continues this rebuttal by using the word דכא in 6:9, which Eliphaz had used in 4:19 and 5:4. In 4:19 Eliphaz uses it to stress his low anthropology; in 5:4 he uses it to emphasize the end of the wicked. Job's use of דכא counters both of these in light of his integrity (6:10). Likewise Job uses תֻּשִׁיָּה in 6:13, responding to 5:12. God's actions have driven "resource" from Job, another element in his attack. In the context, Job is claiming that God has attacked Job without cause; he is suffering as a wicked person despite not being wicked. Renewing his wish and using words that echo Eliphaz's arguments, Job is affirming his right to protest prayer.

Job uses lexical repetition in his accusation as well. יִרְאָה and אבד both occur in 6:14-30, picking up on 4:6 and 4:7, 9, 11, and 20, respectively. Both of these criticize Eliphaz for putting Job's fear in jeopardy; Job suggests he will perish if he accepts Eliphaz's advice. This criticism is

---

80. See Clines 1989: 169; Seow 2013: 468.

sharpened by the lexical repetition of עֵת and עלה in 6:17-18 from 5:26, which is the culmination of Eliphaz's promised restoration of peace. Also in 6:18 Job uses דֶּרֶךְ (see 4:6), where Job seems to be inferring that where his friends are leading him will result in death. In the accusatory question in 6:23 Job repeats יָד and פדה from 5:20 to reject the advice as well.[81]

The repetition of דָּבָר (see 4:2, 12; 6:3) and מִלָּה (see 4:4; 6:26) especially highlights the point of contention regarding Job's words. The latter lexical repetition also points to the integrated nature of Job's criticism of the friends' speech with his defense of his own verbal expression. Relatedly, Job rejects their reproof (יכח in 6:25), which included Eliphaz's contention that divine reproof (יכח in 5:17) was beneficial.

Emphatic Statements. Job highlights his argument with several emphatic statements, using particles to set these statements apart. The first such statement is in 6:3 in his justification of his protest prayer. Repeating כִּי־עַתָּה (see 4:5), Job concludes the weights metaphor by describing the extent of his pain, and then draws a conclusion using עַל־כֵּן. The extent of his suffering has led him to speak the way that he has. Job justifies this with the attack imagery, using כִּי in 6:4. These particles work together to make clear Job's argument regarding his verbal discourse in light of Eliphaz's critique.

Job not only uses particles in his argumentation but also in his criticism of the friends. He uses כִּי־עַתָּה again in 6:21 as he applies the deceptive wadi metaphor to the friends. Job emphasizes their lack of comfort and loyalty with the compound particle כִּי־עַתָּה emphasizing this clause.[82] The exclamatory use of מַה in 6:25 is also an emphatic statement. The exclamation condemns the friend's violence with words,[83] which he sarcastically describes as "upright" (יֹשֶׁר). The alliteration of this entire verse is striking, further drawing attention to it as a key point in Job's disputation: מַה־נִּמְרְצוּ אִמְרֵי־יֹשֶׁר וּמַה־יּוֹכִיחַ הוֹכֵחַ מִכֶּם. The particle אַף in 6:27 also emphasizes Job's accusation against the friends for their lack of kindness. Finally, the use of עַתָּה in 6:28 draws attention to Job's repeated imperatives in vv. 28-29, echoing the כִּי־עַתָּה of v. 3 and v. 21.

Allusion. Kynes, building on and critiquing the work of Cheyne, argues that Job alludes to Ps. 119:50 for rhetorical purposes in 6:10. In this significant verse, Job grounds his hope in his death wish on his integrity (note the causal כִּי). The word נֶחָמָתִי occurs only twice in the

---

81. The only other time פדה is used in the book is 33:28.
82. Though Muilenburg (1961: 138) does not list Job 6:21.
83. See the discussion below on the possible allusion to Ps. 119:103.

MT, in Job 6:10 and Ps. 119:50. This, taken together with אָמֵר and חִיל in Job 6:10 and אִמְרָה and עֳנִי in Ps. 119:50, gives Kynes reason to see an allusion, though the connection is not as strong as other allusions to the Psalter Kynes has documented elsewhere (2013a: 207; cf. 2012). Strengthening the connection, though, is the similarity between Job 6:25 and Ps. 119:103: מַה־נִּמְרְצוּ and אֵמֶר in Job 6:25 and מַה־נִּמְלְצוּ and אִמְרָה in Ps. 119:103. The "syntactical similarity" with "the aurally resonant מרץ and מלץ in the same form and the common reference to 'words'" validate the link (Kynes 2013a: 207).[84] This allusion is used against the friends in Job's accusation with Job countering the friends' arguments and advice with the psalmist's praise (ibid.). By linking himself with the righteous and lamenting psalmist in Psalm 119, Job implies the ethics of his protest prayer. Furthermore, the friends are associated with the enemies which are causing trouble for the psalmist (see 119:51). In other words, the allusion to Psalm 119 both justifies Job's protest prayer and criticizes the friends in accordance with the other strategies.

The allusion to Psalm 119 is likely not limited to the disputation. Kynes writes, "Through the evident parody, Job complains that though he has not denied God's 'words', God has violated his 'promise' to Job" (2013a: 207).[85] Kynes concludes from his study that the psalm also "adds potent rhetorical force to Job's complaint" through parody, seeking to persuade God to act on Job's behalf (210). Kynes' insightful study demonstrates Job's allusion to Psalm 119 to be a rhetorical device in his disputation with his friends and in his protest prayer.[86]

Rhetorical Questions. There are nine verses in Job's disputation that employ rhetorical questions (6:5, 6, 11, 12, 13, 22, 25b, 26, and 30).[87]

The first set of rhetorical questions in 6:5-6 work together. Job continues his defense of his opening complaint from 6:2-4 with these four rhetorical questions. Each of these questions expects a negative answer.[88]

---

84. On the relationship between paranomasia and allusion, see Kline 2016.

85. Parody is best understood as an antithetical allusion, with this example of parody best categorized as reaffirmed. For these categories, see Kynes 2011: 276–310.

86. There may be an allusion to Ps. 39:5, 8 in 6:11. See Kynes 2012: 130–2. This allusion is not as strong as the other allusions to Ps. 39, which are analyzed elsewhere in this study.

87. The use of מָה in 6:24b is the object of the imperative הָבִינוּ and so is not included in this discussion. The use of מָה in 6:25a, where it is exclamatory, is discussed in emphatic statements.

88. This is the view of most interpreters (e.g., Hartley 1988: 132; Clines 1989: 171–2), though on v. 5 see Longman 2012: 138.

The animal that is not treated properly will make his displeasure known through audible complaints (v. 5); something that is tasteless is not eaten (v. 6). As an "assertion in interrogative form" (Magary 2005: 290), Job builds on common experience with his friends, justifying the expression of his displeasure in complaint. This becomes clear in his explicit rejection in 6:7.[89]

This disputatious rhetoric continues in the rhetorical questions in 6:11–13. Related by the images of strength, Job asks five rhetorical questions to assert his lack of strength. The final clause of this section in v. 13b makes this clear, stating "resource" (תֻּשִׁיָּה) has been driven from him. He perceives himself as so weak that he cannot endure silence; he must speak (Hartley 1988: 135). These questions are intended for Eliphaz and the friends to see Job's suffering and to agree that his only recourse is protest prayer.

In accordance with the shift from justification to accusation, the next rhetorical question in 6:22a exhibits rhetoric of accusation. Job asks rhetorically if he has made certain demands from his friends, ranging from giving to bribery to deliverance from distress (6:22-23). The anticipated answer is, of course, "No." Job decries their help, their advice; he attempts to persuade his friends to cease their harmful approach through his rhetorical question. Job continues his accusatory rhetorical questions in 6:25b-26. The assertion in 6:25b is that their reproof reproves nothing (de Regt 1994: 366–7). This relates closely to 6:24, where Job sarcastically implores the friends to teach him the error of his way. He knows he is innocent (see 6:10, 30). Job senses that Eliphaz has accused him of wrongdoing, even if subtly, and argues that penitence is unnecessary. In 6:26 Job asserts that he wants them to cease what they seem intent on doing, namely, considering his words as wind.[90] Job understands Eliphaz's response as violent (v. 25).[91] Job is defending his right to protest in prayer by accusing his friends of comforter malpractice. Hartley writes (1988: 141), "Even though he is despairing (nōʾāš), his words, and especially the feelings that give rise to them, are worthy of careful attention, for in them

---

89. There is some question as to what Job is rejecting, whether his calamity at the hand of God or the arguments of the friends. For the former, see Hartley 1988: 133 and Clines 1989: 172; for the latter, see Habel 1985: 146. Perhaps the ambiguity is intentional, suggesting both.

90. NIV11 captures the sense: "Do you mean to correct what I say, and treat my desperate words as wind?" The verb חשב is gapped from 6:26a, and חשב ל means "to reckon" (see *HALOT*, 360).

91. *Pace* Clines 1989: 121, who understands Eliphaz as gentle. If Eliphaz is gentle, why would Job say this? See Burnight 2014: 347–70.

they might discern how to respond to him instructively."⁹² Job wants them to pay closer attention to his words, and not regard them as wind. He is suffering and has a right to protest.

Job closes his disputation with a rhetorical question in 6:30, a strategy that combines other elements.⁹³ Returning to the taste trope, Job asserts that he is in the best position to judge whether or not he has sinned (6:30b). The key question is "Is there injustice on my tongue?" (הֲיֵשׁ־בִּלְשׁוֹנִי עַוְלָה); using a speech term in an ethical context, Job defends powerfully through a rhetorical question the appropriateness of his complaint.

Wishes. There are two wishes in Job's speech in Job 6, 6:2-4 and 6:8-10. These have different rhetorical functions, but the effects of these wishes can be seen in light of the rhetorical situation identified above.

Introduced by the particle לוּ, the purpose of the first wish can be seen through the כִּי clauses in vv. 3-4 in connection with the rhetorical situation. Job wishes that Eliphaz could see the weight of his calamity that is rooted in divine attack as a way of justifying his opening complaint. If only Eliphaz could see the immense weight of his suffering in light of its cause, he would be persuaded to see things Job's way. As Habel (1985: 141–2) notes based on the observation of key lexical repetitions, Job's wish is a direct response to Eliphaz's implication that Job is an אֱוִיל in 5:2-7. Job knows the impossibility of his suffering being placed on cosmic scales, but the wish, the scales, and divine attack imagery combine to become a provocative rhetorical strategy to defend his protest prayer. The exasperated wish forcefully drives this point home.

The rhetoric of the second wish in 6:8-10 has been explored by Frevel. He concludes, "Der Todeswunsch scheint eher eine Form der 'Anklage an Gott, denn dadurch erbittet und ersehnt er sich das Ende der Leiden, die Gott selbst verursacht hat'" (2009: 30). The wish is a rhetorical strategy to move God to act, implicitly addressed to God (40).⁹⁴ But Frevel is also careful to note how this wish fits within the rhetorical situation regarding the friends, noting it is "ein dramatisches Stilmittel in Ijobs Verteidigung seiner Klage" (39).⁹⁵ The connection between the strategy as it relates to God and as it relates to the friends might be that, after defending his

---

92. Job will return to this in 13:5-19.
93. See the analysis of the taste trope above and the inclusio below.
94. See also Westermann 1981b: 67–70.
95. Though he sees the death wish as more a strategy directed at God than the friends, he is right to note that both audiences are intended in Job's wish.

complaint and rejecting the friends' comforting practices (6:2-7), Job demonstrates he is serious by renewing his wish from Job 3. Like the imprecation of Job 3, it does have God as an implicit addressee and serves as a provocation toward obtaining relief. But it is also a forceful retort to Eliphaz, indicating that he will not back down. He has no reason to back down (6:10c).[96] For the same reasons as the imprecation of Job 3 (its irreal modality, its provocative tone, the allusion to other poetic texts, the lack of specificity in the wish, etc.), this is not a literal death wish.[97] The rhetoric of this wish is enhanced by the allusion to Ps. 119:50. Job is desperately seeking relief from his suffering and will go to great lengths to move God to act on his behalf; Job's persistence is emphasized in each clause of 6:10 (Seow 2013: 460). The wish through its provocative nature elevates the urgency for God to act, while also functioning to defend his complaint in the disputation.

Direct Address to the Friends and Tonality. Job directly addresses the friends in Job 6 as another rhetorical strategy in his disputation. The address is limited to 6:21-29, where there is a distinct shift in tone following the applied *topos* of the deceitful wadi.[98] The shift in tone is evident from the use of the imperatives (especially of יאל) and וְעַתָּה in 6:28-29. The shift from the accusation to the imperatives represents a rhetorical strategy; "Job had reproached them as ready to treat a friend as an object, a commodity to bargain with. Now, he says, let rhetoric be put aside, and let us speak as persons" (Clines 1989: 136). Putting aside the sarcasm and reproach, Job pleads for sympathy and consideration—Job appeals to them as fellow human beings. Having shamed them through instruction, sarcasm, and accusation of poor friendship, he attempts to persuade them with a less caustic tone (Hartley 1988: 136). Job's main concern is that they no longer commit violence against him with words, something he considers to be an injustice (6:25-29).

Inclusio. Job ensures that the primary issue at stake is made clear with his use of an inclusio in 6:2 and 30 with the word הַוָּה (note the taste trope in 6:5-7 and 6:30 as well).[99] Job revisits the primary issue of his calamity

---

96. This clause stands out in 6:8-13 as the seventh line of thirteen, the lone tricolon (Habel 1985: 142).
97. Contra Clines 1989: 172. See Frevel 2009: 38–40.
98. There are twenty 2mp forms beginning with the application of the wadi metaphor in 6:21.
99. Seow notes the use of the taste trope in 6:5-7 and 6:30 (2013: 467).

as justification for his opening complaint in Job 3. Job, more than anyone, is aware of his own situation and he disputes Eliphaz's supposition that he has no right to protest in prayer because he has sinned. There is no injustice on his tongue (6:30a). In other words, he has not sinned in his speech. The inclusio provides closure to Job's disputation. With Job 7, Job returns to protest prayer, addressing God directly for the first time.

Direct Address to God. Turning to Job 7, several rhetorical strategies emerge as Job renews his complaint. The first of these is direct address. For the first time, Job addresses God, with twenty 2ms forms with God as the referent (see Fohrer 1963: 177). Beginning with the imperative זְכֹר in 7:7, Job turns to address God directly in prayer, specifically in the form of complaint. Like the psalmist in Psalm 88, Job perceives his plight as rooted in God's attack.[100] Job states that God places a guard over him (7:12), frightens him with dreams (7:13), terrifies him with visions (7:13), magnifies him (7:17), relentlessly observes him (7:17), visits him frequently (7:17), and tests him consistently with attack and relentless vigilance (7:18-19). These complaints are rooted in the current relationship Job perceives himself to have with God, and they are contrary to what he thinks he knows about God. By accusing God of malicious action, Job is putting forward the evidence for why his petitions need to be heeded. Job implores God to remember (זְכֹר) and cease (חֲדַל), and he must act now; otherwise, Job will not be around much longer (7:8-9, 21).[101]

---

100. The psalmist accuses Yahweh of no longer remembering him (88:6 [5]), placing him in the pit (88:7 [6]), directing wrath at him (88:8 [7]), afflicting him (88:8 [7]), alienating him from others (88:9 and 19 [8 and 18]), rejecting him (88:15 [14]), hiding from him (88:15 [14]), terrorizing him (88:16 [15]), assaulting him (88:17 [16]), and overpowering him (88:18 [17]). Ps. 88 readily comes to mind when one thinks of Job. In 6:4 the בְּעוּתֵי אֱלוֹהַּ brings to mind Ps. 88:17 [16] (בְּעוּתֶיךָ), since these are the only two occurrences of this term in the MT. Moreover, the alienation of the psalmist parallels Job's experience (cf. Job 19:13-19 with Ps. 88:9 and 19 [8 and 18] and the Hiphil form of the verb רחק), and both the psalmist and Job use Sheol as a rhetorical strategy to motivate God so he does not lose a worshiper (cf. Job 7:9 and Ps. 88:11-13 [10-12]). It may be hard to sustain an allusion, but the psalmist from Ps. 88 and Job are certainly comparable.

101. The petition to cease is not a rejection of God *per se* but a rejection of God as attacker (*pace* Clines 1989: 191); the imperative is a call for God not to do something, in this case attack. Noting the connection between the imperative in 7:16, the wish for death in 7:15, and the images of ephemerality, Frevel writes, "Das Ablassen zielt nicht auf ein Sterben Lassen Ijobs ('Lass ab, damit ich sterben kann'), sondern auf das Sistieren oder Beenden des als Ausdruck einer Feindschaft verstandenen Handelns

This is prayer; the censorious God-talk is put to persuasive use, as Job seeks to find relief.[102] Only God can provide relief, so Job accuses God of maleficence (i.e., he complains) and pleads for that relief.

Tropes. The tropes Job uses reinforce his other strategies. Dominating Job 7 is the imagery of suffering in life, which combines images of suffering, turmoil, ephemerality, hardship, and prolongation. Beginning in 7:1, Job describes life as צָבָא, which he further expands using the imagery of the hireling and the slave (7:1b-2).[103] Like in Job 3, Job laments his life as עָמָל (in parallel with שָׁוְא) in 7:3. The duration of his suffering is prolonged (note מָתַי, לֵילוֹת, יְרָחֵי, קִוָּה, שְׂאָף, יְמֵי, and מדד). Like the psalmist who grounds his complaint and petition in his challenging circumstances, Job describes his lack of rest in 7:4 through the image of his sleeplessness, and his physical suffering in 7:5 through imagery of his dirty and broken skin.[104] The imagery of worms and dust portray Job as corpse-like (Seow 2013: 494).[105] Job also employs a number of images that describe the suffering of life with regard to life's ephemerality. Job's days pass on without hope like a weaver's shuttle (7:6); his life is but a breath without

---

Gottes. Es zielt damit letzten Endes auf das Leben ('Lass ab, damit ich leben kann'). Weil die Lebenszeit Ijobs begrenzt ist und der im Rahmen konnektiver Gerechtigkeit erwartbare gerechte Ausgleich für das erlittene Leid und die Lebensdauer in einer Relation zueinander stehen, muss Gott schnell handeln. Für diese Lösung spricht die Begründung des Imperativs 'denn meine Tage sind ein Hauch'" (2009: 36).

102. As noted in Chapter 1, prayer is broadly defined as any communication to or with God. Certainly Job is doing that here. See Hartley 1988: 146–7 n. 6. This prayer language indicates Job's hope and faith in God are still intact, otherwise why bother addressing God at all?

103. See Hartley 1988: 144; Clines 1989: 184. Job's lament over the lot of humanity in general may also be partially directed as a refutation of Eliphaz's contention that everyone suffers (Seow 2013: 489); note עָפָר in 5:6 and 7:5 (Course 1994: 42).

104. The intensification in this poem is vertical as much as it is horizontal (on vertical intensification, see Alter 1985: 27–67). In other words, the nights of trouble in v. 3 lead quickly to a description of sleepless nights in v. 4, which leads quickly to the physical distress that causes the sleepless nights in v. 5. This kind of development continues through the chapter, where the final thought of a clause or verse is then developed further in the subsequent section (cf. v. 6 to v. 7; v. 8 to v. 9; v. 9 to v. 10; v. 16 to v. 17). The rhetorical effect of this development is a building anticipation leading to the culmination of his complaint.

105. This is noteworthy in light of Broyles' investigation of God-laments; he notes these are employed in near-death situations (1989: 84–95).

the proposition of seeing good again (7:7); God will no longer be able to find him (7:8);[106] his days will pass on like a dissolving cloud without hope for return from Sheol (7:9);[107] his comfort is fleeting and he cannot get any rest (7:13-14; cf. 7:4); he will not live forever and his life is ephemeral (7:16). Life for Job is distressing and bitter (7:11). Expressing his emotional suffering, Job would prefer death because it would bring relief (7:15-16). The represented cosmology here is another variation of this trope of hardship, reinforcing Job's rhetorical concerns. As Habel notes (1985: 154), the three cosmological spheres of earth, heaven, and Sheol undergird Job's suffering; earth is the realm of oppression, hardship, and suffering and Sheol provides relief, while the "inquisitorial ruler" resides in heaven. As in his opening complaint in Job 3 and in his wish from Job 6:8-10, the piling up of these images in Job's complaint provides the data upon which God is supposed to act. It is not a coincidence that Job closes his complaint with a כִּי, indicating his desire for rest and to be left alone (7:21). Like in Job 3, the images of relentless restlessness highlight what Job is seeking to escape. Job wants his suffering-sated experience to end and for relief and restoration to come, also indicated by the use of the word צֵל in 7:2. The repeated words that indicate duration of time "create an image of prolonged intense suffering" (Course 1994: 45). The futility and ephemerality establish urgency (Habel 1985: 147). The appeals to remember and desist in 7:7 and 7:16 are rooted in Job's present misery and ongoing, and seemingly ceaseless, suffering.

Another trope, which also brings to mind Job 3, is Job's use of mythological imagery. In 3:8 Job used a reference to Leviathan as a means to arrest God's attention and provoke God to act. In 7:12 Job draws a comparison between himself and Yam and Tannin.[108] He argues through a rhetorical question that God is mistreating him by besieging him like he would a chaos creature. The imagery here reinforces Job's complaint through accusation regarding God's relentless surveillance and divine attack.[109]

---

106. The alliteration of לֹא־תְשׁוּרֵנִי עֵין רֹאִי עֵינֶיךָ בִּי וְאֵינֶנִּי draws attention to this verse, highlighting the urgency.

107. The mention of Sheol brings to mind Job 3 and combines the transient nature of life with the imagery of death and Sheol (cf. 7:15).

108. It seems Leviathan, Yam, and Tannin are the same chaos creature. See Averbeck 2004: 340–1.

109. See Diewert 1987: 203–15; though see also Janzen's important response (1989: 109–14).

The vigilance and attack tropes are significant in Job's rhetoric as well. Job complains of God's personal attack through besiegement (7:12), through psychological disturbances and nightmares (7:14; cf. 7:4),[110] and through physical harm as an archer (7:20; cf. 6:4). Job complains of God's ceaseless surveillance through consistent observation and testing (7:17-18) and through the disproportionate punishment of wrongdoing (7:21). He emphasizes this vigilance through the image of God's interminable attention (Job cannot swallow his spit)[111] and the epithet נֹצֵר הָאָדָם in 7:19-20. These images, combined with the reproachful, condemnatory tone, are persuasive strategies to move God to act. Blame and rebuke emerge to the forefront here, and serve persuasive (i.e., rhetorical) goals.

Emphatic Statement. One of Job's persuasive strategies involves declaring an emphatic statement of his intentions and resolve to complain in 7:11. As Fohrer puts it (1963: 179), "Daher will er sich an Gott wenden, wie Eliphas geraten hat (5,8)—aber in anderer Weise!" Closing the first major section of Job 7, which is dominated by tropes detailing Job's suffering condition, this statement serves to justify his preceding general lament and initial direct address to God in 7:7. It is marked by the emphatic particle גַּם followed by an independent personal pronoun, which draws attention to this particular statement.[112] The three verbs of the verse relate directly to Job's speech: he will not restrain his mouth (חשׂך + פֶּה), he will speak (דבר), and he will complain (שׂיח). The latter two verbs are modified by prepositional phrases that ground his intentions according to his distress, with בְּמַר נַפְשִׁי recalling Job's complaint in Job 3 (cf. 3:20). While the first of the three verbs is a *yiqtol*, the latter two are cohortatives, indicating Job's resolve to protest in prayer.[113] This emphatic statement, marked as such by גַּם־אָנִי, speaks directly to the concern of the ethics of Job's speech. Job is aware that his complaints are troublesome, but, as he indicated in 6:2-4, the weight of his suffering requires him to speak. He is passionate in his defense of his right to protest in prayer (to both the friends and God); this protest prayer testifies to his clinging to

---

110. The chiasm of 7:14 heightens the rhetorical effect of God's attack with the verbs enclosing the objects. Newsom writes (1996: 395), "The image is an aggressive, invasive one, a psychic counterpart to the physical image of piercing arrows in 6:4."

111. On the sense of the idiom "swallowing one's spit," see Hartley 1988: 152 n. 9.

112. Regarding גַּם Waltke and O'Connor write, "[גַּם] generally has more distinctly logical force than אַף, though it can be used as an emphatic, often with a pronoun following. It can signal a final climax in an exposition and is the only Hebrew adverb that marks a discourse ending—all others mark beginnings or middles" (§39.3.4d).

113. See Hartley 1988: 147 n. 1.

God in hope and faith—he will not give up.[114] It provides a transition to the next section (7:12-21) as Job increases the complaint rhetoric with his rhetorical questions and accusation.

Rhetorical Questions. As is typical of protest prayer, Job's protest prayer in Job 7 employs several rhetorical questions, through which he attempts to modify his exigency. The first rhetorical question in 7:1 anticipates an affirmative answer, making an assertion that life for a person is one of hardship. Job highlights with this question the continuity between humanity in general and his current experience (7:1-6; see also 3:10, 20).

The remaining rhetorical questions function similarly as reproachful accusations against God. Beginning with 7:12, Job turns to accuse God of improper conduct, specifically divine attack and hyper-vigilance. Combined with the mythic imagery, the question in 7:12 is an accusation of mistreatment. In the allusion to Psalm 8 in 7:17-18, Job builds on 7:12 by accusing God of relentless and disproportionate attention. There is an implied plea for relief in these accusations. In fact, in 7:19 the interrogative כַּמָּה combined with the verb שעה and the imagery of swallowing spit highlights the urgency of Job's implied plea (see also Pss. 35:17; 119:84). The accusation resumes with three rhetorical questions in 7:20. Though typically understood as an unmarked conditional, the first clause of 7:20 (חָטָאתִי) is best understood as an unmarked interrogative.[115] In accordance with the accusations of mistreatment, through the rhetorical questions of 7:20 Job affirms he has not sinned and is therefore undeserving of the

---

114. This point about faith is important. Job's faith is evident through his engagement with God. If Job really believed that God's character were in accordance with the accusations, he would cease dealing with the deity all together. It is not surprising that Job seems to preface some of his most scathing God-talk with statements that emphasize his distress and his perception of God's attack. This point is also made by Yu (2011: 187–92). Hartley notes (1988: 148–9), "He who laments freely has the hope that his words will touch God's compassion, moving God to deliver him."

115. There are a number of unmarked interrogatives in Job, as de Regt (1994: 362–3) and Magary (2005: 284) point out. Magary includes 7:20 in his list of unmarked interrogatives. Though most interpreters and translations do not understand it this way (cf. ASV, ESV, GW, HCSB, JPS, KJV, NCV, NIV85, NIV11, NRSV, RSV, LXX, Andersen, Habel, Clines, Hartley, Newsom, Seow), it is at least possible, if not likely, given the heavy use of interrogatives in 7:17-21. Perhaps it is unmarked (i.e., the interrogative *he* is absent) because the interrogative *he* only occurs twice in this chapter, both marking the major units (as noted above). The NASB is the only major English translation that understands this as an unmarked interrogative (though see the SCH2000). It is definitely not a confession since this neither fits the rhetorical situation or the context of the book (*pace* Andersen 1976: 150).

treatment he has received (7:20b-d). The final question in 7:21 builds on this accusation; Clines notes (1989: 195), "The emphasis...lies not upon any admission of guilt...but upon Job's plea for toleration." The rhetorical questions culminate here, indicating his accusations through rhetorical questions imply a petition for relief. This coheres with his imperatives in 7:7 and 7:16 as well as the other persuasive strategies outlined in Job 7.

Allusion. The intertextual connection between Job 7:17-18 and Ps. 8:5 has long been acknowledged.[116] Yet it is Kynes' exceptional treatment of this allusion that provides a window into understanding its internal rhetorical effect (2012: 63–79).[117] Kynes establishes the connection by pointing out the correspondences between the two passages: the rhetorical question מָה־אֱנוֹשׁ; the use of פקד in Job 7:18 and Ps. 8:5, especially with energic *nun* (the only two places where פקד has an energic *nun* in the MT); the similar structure; the use of גדל in Job 7:17 and the imagery of Ps. 8:6-9; and the similarity between the sense of זכר in Ps. 8:5 and תָּשִׁית אֵלָיו לִבֶּךָ in Job 7:17. Given that it is less likely that the psalmist would take Job's bitter complaint and turn it into praise than it is that Job would take a praise psalm and turn it into a bitter complaint, it is almost certain that Job is alluding to Psalm 8 (69). Kynes argues persuasively that the use of Psalm 8 is "as an argumentative device against God"; Job appeals to God against God (70–1).[118] Regarding complainants, Kynes remarks, "These sufferers consistently cling to God who causes their suffering because this God is the only one who can end it. Their accusations are neither condemnations nor objective theological declarations but appeals intended to cause change... [The use of Ps. 8 is] intended for rhetorical effect" (2012: 71).

This analysis coheres with the rhetorical situation identified in this study. Job, in his suffering, has complained bitterly in Job 3, only to be rebuked by Eliphaz for his inappropriate language. Job now must defend his language while still complaining in faith to move God to act on his behalf. One of the ways in which he does this is by parodying Psalm 8 in his complaint, appealing to the traditional view of God in order to move

---

116. See, e.g., Clines 1989: 192; Fishbane 1992: 86–98; Kynes 2012: 1–2. For an alternative view, see Van Leeuwen 2001: 205–15. For Kynes' cogent critique of Van Leeuwen, see Kynes 2012: 65, 67. Note also that Ps. 144:3 has similar language. On this, see ibid.: 67.

117. Kynes shows that both Job and the friends allude to this psalm (2012: 71–5). Beyond 7:17-18, Ps. 8 is alluded to in 15:14-16, 19:9, and 25:5-6.

118. This comports well with Broyles' understanding of God-laments (1989: 224–5); see also Westermann 1998: 233–41.

God to act on his behalf. This is a reaffirming parody where Job is not disputing the psalm but God's actions, and in so doing affirms the psalm's theology (Kynes 2011: 303–6). Job's use of other biblical material further evinces his faith, already evident in the act of protest prayer. Job is using whatever means possible to move God to act on his behalf and alleviate his suffering.[119]

Summary of Job 6–7

This analysis of Job 6–7 highlights that Job has two main objectives after Eliphaz finishes speaking. First, Job now needs to defend his complaint from Job 3, which he does in Job 6. Second, Job needs to continue to protest in prayer to seek relief and restoration, which Job does in Job 7. This latter objective is continued from Job's opening speech, though in chapter 7 Job will adopt a new strategy, this time speaking directly to God throughout the chapter. Using tropes, lexical repetition to rebut Eliphaz, allusion, rhetorical questions, tonality, inclusio, direct address to the friends and God, and emphatic statements, Job accomplishes his goals. Job's use of God-talk in this speech is evident in light of his rhetoric. He decries God's attack and surveillance to justify his complaint (6:4) and in his complaint (7:12, 14, 17-21). His direct address to God in 7:7, 8, 12, 14, 16, and 17-21 takes on a reproachful tone that characterizes protest prayer. Overall, it is clear that Job uses his God-talk (whether third person or second person) in his rhetoric to accomplish the goals he has in light of his (literary) rhetorical situation.

"I Will Speak in the Bitterness of My Soul":
The Rhetoric of Job's Third Speech (Job 9–10)

Introduction

Bildad responds to Job's second speech by arguing that Job's words are harmful, even dangerous. He argues further that God does not pervert justice, encouraging repentance and promising restoration. Job rebuts

---

119. Allusions to two other psalms may be present in Job's address to God. The first is in 7:6-8 where Job appears to allude to Ps. 39:5 [4], 8 [7] and 7:16, 19 where Job appears to allude to Ps. 39:14 [13]. See Kynes 2012: 132–5. The allusion to this psalm coheres with Job's use of Ps. 8, and in the context implies Job's petition for relief. The second possible allusion in Job's address to God occurs in 7:18 where Job's use of לִבְקָרִים recalls Ps. 73:14. See ibid.: 166–7. Appealing to a psalm in which the psalmist struggles over the apparent injustice of righteous suffering also strengthens his appeal.

Bildad's argument with a disputation regarding God's justice, and explores possible ways in which to engage God, closing by outlining a complaint. Job asserts he has no other recourse but to continue his protest prayer (9:27-28, 35; 10:1).

The Literary Rhetorical Situation of Job 9–10

Bildad responds to Job's arguments and continued protest prayer with an argument of his own, which includes two rhetorical questions that communicate his disapproval of Job's speech and his thesis that God does not pervert justice (8:2-3). Bildad also includes an exhortation toward repentance with a promise of restoration that is rooted in the sapiential traditions of the elders (8:5-10, 20-22), and an extended *topos* of two plants designed to motivate Job to accept his advice (8:11-19; cf. 8:13). Bildad is clearly responding to Job's previous speech (Course 1994: 49–50).

While Job's speech has not altered the rhetorical situation much, Bildad is forced to reply (Clines 1989: 202; Yu 2011: 247). Bildad perceives Job's protest prayer to question implicitly God's justice, so he must intervene. Noting that Job has not actually stated God has perverted justice, Westermann writes (1981b: 21), "Bildad has made a theoretical proposition out of the lament which Job has directed to God in his burning agony. To be sure, it is the proper logical deduction from what Job has said—of this there can be no doubt. However, it abstracts from the lamentlike character of the words of Job." Like Eliphaz previously, Bildad draws upon his low anthropology, theology of transcendence, and retribution—that humans are inherently sinful, reaping what they sow, and God is inherently just—to encourage Job to consider his sin, and repent (8:5-6).[120] The use of the independent personal pronouns in 8:5-6 heightens the impact of the advice. That Job's verbal expression, and its (un)ethical nature, is a concern for Bildad is immediately clear as Bildad answers Job's question from 6:26: he does consider Job's words wind (repeating both רוּחַ and אֵמֶר [cf. 8:2]). He considers Job's words dangerous (רוּחַ כַּבִּיר) (Seow 2013: 515; Hawley 2018: 98–9). Not only does a reference to Job's verbal expression open the speech, it closes the speech as well, forming an inclusio. The dangerous "words of [Job's] mouth" (אִמְרֵי־פִיךָ) in v. 2 need to be replaced with repentance, which will lead God to replace

---

120. Clines writes (1989: 204), "Bildad nowhere in this speech expressly says that Job is a sinner, but what else can be inferred from his doctrine?" Repentance is key to Bildad's advice in v. 5 (ibid.). On the similarities between Eliphaz and Bildad, see Pyeon's comparison of ideas (2003: 149).

Job's current verbal expression with one of joy in v. 21 (יְמַלֵּה שְׂחוֹק פִּיךָ וּשְׂפָתֶיךָ תְרוּעָה). In 8:5 and 8:10, Bildad also indicates that it is the ethics of Job's speech that is of preeminent concern, encouraging the cessation of protest for penitence, noting that the words of the previous generation will provide Job with more adequate words. Hartley notes that Bildad is "vigorously objecting to Job's lamenting" in v. 20 (1988: 163). This clarifies that the doctrine of retribution, so often noted as the principal point of Bildad's speech (e.g., Clines 1989: 201), is actually employed in service of correcting Job's verbal expression. The rhetorical questions, exhortations, tradition, *topos* of the two plants, and the explicit juxtaposition of the godly and the wicked are inherently connected to this end. Over against Job's protest prayer, Bildad promises joy if Job were to take his advice.

With this in mind, Job's literary rhetorical situation emerges. It remains largely unchanged from the situation Job faced after Eliphaz's first speech. In response to Bildad's thesis that God does not pervert justice, Job must continue to defend his protest prayer in light of this new argument. He will do this through exploiting the legal metaphor Bildad introduces (Habel 1985: 174). Because God has not yet brought about restoration, Job's rhetorical situation vis-à-vis his suffering remains unchanged. In fact, the stress of the literary rhetorical situation can probably be seen as intensifying—the longer God waits to respond and the more Job has to deal with his "comforters," the more Job seeks God's attention and the restoration only God can provide. In sum, Job's literary rhetorical situation still involves two exigencies, and, therefore, two audiences.[121] In this speech, however, the audiences are merged, as the following discussion of the forms and structure demonstrates. The constraints of the rhetorical situation also remain unchanged.

The Forms of Job 9–10

The forms of Job 9–10 confirm the rhetorical situation just identified, one in which Job is disputing the arguments against him that intend to silence his protest prayer as well as continuing to move God to act on his behalf. The speech begins with sixty-seven consecutive clauses of disputation, with thirteen of the sixty-seven comprising the hymn used

---

121. Yu (2011: 253) notes that Job has two goals: (1) to continue his provocation of the deity, and (2) to dispute Bildad's use of the legal metaphor. I agree with Yu in general, but in light of the criticism of Job's verbal expression in Bildad's speech, it seems that, as before, Job is best seen as justifying his protest prayer rather than strictly disputing Bildad's legal metaphor. Job exploits the legal metaphor to do this.

in disputation (9:2-24). The disputation is evident immediately, with the presence of the particle אָמְנָם, which introduces the summary of Bildad's argument and sets Job up to provide his own thesis in 9:2c-3 (Yu 2011: 256). The rhetorical question of 9:3 presents in question form Job's own thesis for which the rest of the speech argues. In 9:4-24 Job presents the evidence for his thesis. The hymn form of 9:5-10 is used in service of the dispute. Job piles up evidence for his thesis by arguing for God's power, hiddenness, and injustice, drawing implications in 9:14 and 9:22-24 using logical connecting particles (אַף־כִּי, עַל־כֵּן, and אִם־לֹא אֵפוֹא). The description of his suffering condition in 9:25, coupled with the 2ms address with reproachful tone and the interrogative לָמָּה, indicates a shift in form to protest prayer in 9:25-33, with 9:34 being petition (two clauses) and 9:35 returning with disputation (three clauses). In 9:25-33 there are fourteen clauses of lament (9:25-28b, 32), two clauses of wish (9:33), and seven clauses of complaint (9:28c-31). In Job 10:1-22 Job continues the disputation with four clauses of disputation in 10:1-2a, but the remainder of the speech is dominated by the complaint form with forty-seven clauses of complaint (10:3-8, 9b-15e, 16a-20a). The speech closes with six clauses of lament (10:21-22), with eight clauses of petition interwoven into the complaint (10:2b-d, 9a, 15f, 20b-d).[122] Given the interrelationship between complaint, lament, and petition, 10:2b-22 is best seen as protest prayer at first glance. Nevertheless, the entire section is embedded speech, thus indicating that it is serving the disputation with which 10:1-2a begins (which builds on Job 9).

In sum, there are seventy-four clauses of disputation and eighty-six clauses of protest prayer (including the complaint, lament, wish, and petition) in a fully integrated speech.[123] The protest prayer serves the

---

122. This analysis takes the verbal form in 10:15f (וּרְאֵה) as an imperative (though see Seow [2013: 590] for a defense of this verbal form as an infinitive).

123. Murphy (1981: 28) understands this entire speech as a disputation speech, with other forms such as hymn and complaint being interwoven. Hartley (1988: 40–1) considers most of 9:2-24 as a lawsuit, with 9:5-13 being a hymn and 9:17-18, 21-24 complaint; he suggests most of Job 10 is lament or complaint (10:1-7, 13-17), with a hymn form used in 10:8-12 and a petition for relief in 10:18-22. Hartley does not take into account that disputation can be made up of a number of forms, though he helpfully points out that 9:17-18 have an underlying complaint function, even if the logical connectors indicate this is disputation. Clines (1989: 224) does not parse out the details, suggesting that the entire speech in Job 9–10 is a combination of legal controversy, hymn, and appeal. Clines' attention to the hypothetical nature of the speech helps clarify that this is not exactly a legal speech, but a consideration of one, which points to it being a disputation. Westermann (1981b: 73–4) takes 9:4-13 and

disputation to demonstrate Job's rebuttal to Bildad while also serving as prayer. Even though Job speaks primarily to Bildad, he intends his words to be heard by God as well. This is confirmed when one notes the abrupt, yet seamless, shifts in address and the lack of a distinct structure in the speech as a whole. The disputation argues that Bildad's argument regarding divine injustice is flawed. Job must protest in prayer: "Wie soll der Mensch dann im Leide verhalten? Es bleibt nur die Anklage gegen Gott" (Fohrer 1963: 201). In other words, Job defends his protest prayer in disputation and then uses protest prayer in his disputation by renewing and developing his previous complaints.

The Rhetorical Strategies of Job 9–10

Structure

There is little consensus regarding the structure of Job's third speech, and understandably so. Seow remarks (2013: 542), "[T]here are admittedly no clear linguistic markers of transition from one stanza to another, no closural cues."[124] Nevertheless, Habel notes (1985: 185), "The design and rhetoric of this speech becomes apparent when we recognize its integrated thought progression," moving from the futility of litigation to other possibilities.

The different structural proposals are the result of looking at the speech from different perspectives. Following Clines (1989: 239), there is a structural shift with 9:25, noting that 9:24 is the only tricolon of 9:2-24. Job closes his first section with the climactic rhetorical question that directly rebuts Bildad's argument from Job 8: "If not he, then who?" But viewed from another perspective, the hypothetical progression in the speech as it relates to options for God-talk reveals a certain structure as well. In other words, taking into account the use of אם in Job 9 with speaking verbs, there emerges a progression of thought in Job's argument. Beginning with the first conditional in 9:3, Job suggests that an equal give-and-take

---

10:8-12 as a hymn, 9:21 and 29 are an avowal of innocence (97), 9:17-31 and 10:1-22 are lament (31), and 9:34-35 and 10:18-20 are wish (67–8). This lack of consensus on the form of Job's speech indicates the difficulty of determining the forms precisely.

124. Seow suggests a structure of 9:2-10, 11-24, 25-35; 10:1, 2-17, 18-22 (2013: 542, 576). Clines (1989: 223) divides the speech into two parts based on the markers of address: 9:2-24 and 9:25–10:22. Hartley (1988: 165), Yu (2011: 254), and Wilson (2015: 67) also see two major units, but see the division along the chapter division. Habel's (1985: 186–7) structural proposal is quite detailed: 9:2-4, 5-13, 14-24, 25-35; 10:1-7, 8-17, 18-22. As Yu notes (2011: 254 n. 484), the markers of address cannot be used to determine structure in this particular case. It seems to me that the abrupt shift in address is to show that Job intends to address both audiences at the same time.

between God and a person is impossible.¹²⁵ In 9:16 Job progresses to consider the second option of the ambiguous 9:3 with more specificity, namely, if Job calls to God he does not believe God will hear it. Job, then, in 9:27 considers another hypothetical speech-act, one in which he declares that he forgets his complaint and puts on a happy face.¹²⁶ He quickly concludes this will prove ineffective as well. So another option arises, of undergoing some kind of purity ritual, perhaps an oath (9:30).¹²⁷ This he quickly dismisses as well, contending that his only recourse is to complain in protest prayer despite the risks (9:35–10:1). Then, in 10:2-22, he reports exactly what he will say in light of his limited options.¹²⁸ The statements expressing despair of life (9:21, 35; 10:1) provide some structure as well at the beginnings and ends of major units, prefacing or reiterating Job's disbelief in what he is saying (see Yu 2011: 190–2).

Thus, Job first begins his disputation by arguing God is unjust (9:2-24). Next, Job addresses God directly (9:25-34), and concludes with his conviction that he might as well continue to complain, which he then outlines (9:35–10:22).¹²⁹ Scheindlin (1998: 74) captures the sentiment of

---

125. There is some uncertainty as to whether or not God will not answer a person "one in a thousand" or if a person will not be able to answer God "one in a thousand." As Hartley (1988: 167) and Seow (2013: 544) point out, the latter is expressed in 9:14 and the former in 9:16. In light of v. 14 providing a conclusion to the first movement of the argument and v. 16 as the next conditional, it seems that in 9:3 Job is saying a person cannot answer God.

126. On the verb עזב in 9:27, see Hartley 1988: 178 n. 3.

127. This could be taken metaphorically as an oath (see Clines 1989: 241) or literally; cf. Seow 2013: 551.

128. On the progression of the speaking verbs, see Habel 1985: 186.

129. This proposal captures the major movements, following Hartley, Habel, and Seow at most points despite their attention to smaller units. Hartley (1988: 92) summarizes the progression of chapters 9–10: (1) there is no possibility for litigation, (2) there is no possibility for demonstration of innocence, (3) there is no arbiter, (4), so lament is the only possibility. Habel (1985: 186–7) notes the progression from "conviction about the futility of litigation" (9:2-4) to "characterization of the adversary at law" (9:5-13) to "considering the difficulties of litigation" (9:14-20) to "considering a charge against God" (9:21-24) to "considering other alternatives" (9:25-35) to "rehearsing a case against God" (10:1-17) to a "closing complaint and plea" (10:18-22). Habel's proposal has much to commend it, though seeing 9:2-24 as a whole unit with subunits is preferable given the integrated nature of the content and the tricolon in 9:24. Cf. Seow 2013: 542, 576. It seems preferable to see 10:1-17 as a full unit (*pace* Seow) because of the tight flow of thought from 10:1 to 10:2. There is a clear shift as a subunit in 10:18, as all three point out. This subunit as a complaint and plea is the capstone to Job's protest prayer in this speech.

10:1 well: "I might as well complain with all abandon." What Job affirms in 9:35–10:1 summarizes his argument to Bildad. The cohortative form of דבר establishes the outer component of a chiasm around Job's statements of emotional distress:

   A "I will speak"
      B "I will not fear him"
         C "I am not so with myself"
         C' "I loathe my life"
      B' "I will let loose my complaint"
  A' "I will speak in the bitterness of my soul."

This chiasm highlights Job's resolve to protest in prayer.

This discussion reveals Job's emphases in this speech. First, he is primarily concerned with rebutting Bildad's argument that God does not pervert justice (8:3). This relates to the second emphasis, namely, that in light of God's injustice Job will defend his protest prayer. Job will use his complaint as a part of his rebuttal, with the complaint intended to be heard by both Bildad and God. This defense of protest prayer counters Bildad's advice in 8:5. This analysis coheres with the rhetorical situation and the discussion of the forms noted above. It confirms that the primary audience of Job's third speech is Bildad, with the grammatical markers of address to God in Job 10:2-22 intended as a rebuttal. Nevertheless, it is clear from Job's abrupt shift in form and addressee in 9:25-34 that Job addresses God in this speech as well. The seamless shifts indicate that Job 9:25-34 are intended to be overheard by Bildad (and the friends) and that 10:2-22 are intended to be overheard by God.[130]

---

130. Clines (1989: 244) notes that there are forty grammatical markers of address in 10:2-17, with three more in 10:18-22. In light of this, it is hard to see how Longman (2012: 182) can say that Job does not address God at all in this speech, using this to argue that Job is different from the psalmist who accuses God in protest prayer (and whose speech Longman considers ethical). Even if one rejects the notion that 10:2-22 are intended be overheard, there is a clear grammatical address in 9:28-35 (in the 2ms forms in 9:28 and 9:31, the 1cp forms which include God in 9:32-33, and the third person jussives in 9:34). Furthermore, the echo of so many themes from his first two speeches indicates God is intended to be understood as a part of the audience. Perhaps the most persuasive of these is the reprise of 3:11-12 in 10:18. Job intimates in 9:27-28 that he has understood himself to be complaining (i.e., protesting in prayer) since his opening speech. Job addresses God directly in 9:25-35 and in a mediated manner in 10:2-22.

Strategies

Hypothetical Thinking and Inclusio. One of the foundational rhetorical strategies Job uses in his third speech is a series of hypotheticals.[131] These hypotheticals, initiated with 9:3, directly rebut Bildad's invocation of the legal metaphor. In light of Bildad's argument that God does not pervert justice (which, according to Bildad, Job's complaints have insinuated), Job outlines several hypotheticals to consider other possibilities of seeking engagement with God.[132] In the end, Job rejects other modes of engagement in favor of continued protest prayer.

The major movements in the hypothetical thinking relate to the litigation trope.[133] Job begins generally with the hypothetical notion of a human desiring to contend with God. Initially rejecting it in 9:3-4,[134] Job explicitly rejects this option in 9:14-15 in light of God's (destructive) power (9:5-10, 13), hiddenness (9:11), and injustice (9:12). Job considers a more specific hypothetical in 9:16: "If I called and he answered me." But this too is impossible in light of God's (destructive) power (9:17-19b) and injustice (9:19c-20, 22-24). That God would use his power for destruction and that he would be hidden and unjust clearly relate to Bildad's contention that God does not pervert justice. The forensic metaphor is flawed.[135]

---

131. אִם occurs fourteen times in Job 9–10, with only two occurrences in 10:4-5 indicating a question. The rest are hypotheticals. As Clines writes, this speech exhibits a "marked impression of experimentation" (1989: 224).

132. That Job is seeking engagement with God is clear from the five-fold repetition of ענה in 9:3, 14, 15, 16, and 32.

133. This is significant. Roberts (1973: 162), Seow (2013: 544), and Newsom (1996: 410) take Job's lawsuit to be literal (i.e., not rhetorical). Roberts (1973: 161) notes that this would be something humans elsewhere want to, or are warned to, avoid. But see Jer. 12:1 (which also has themes of injustice). How can Jeremiah's dispute with God be rhetorical, while Job's is not (especially when Job is "reusing," not parodying, Jeremiah's material [see Dell 2013: 106–17])? Much as Job's imprecation in Job 3 was rhetorical, like Jeremiah's in 20:14-18, so also is this legal dispute. The frequency of אִם in this speech also indicates that Job's legal dispute is a rhetorical strategy. Certainly, there are risks, as Isa. 45:9 makes clear (to which Job alludes), but Job recognizes these and makes his case for why he has no other recourse. The futility and danger noted by Roberts, Seow, and Newsom are also expressed by Job.

134. On v. 4, see Seow's suggestion that קשה is best taken as a comparative term of the Aramaic verb meaning "to argue against, dispute" (2013: 555). On the lexical repetition of שלם in 9:4 and 8:6, see below.

135. As Clines notes, the book reveals "it is not exactly a forensic process that will lead to the desired end but persistent address to God" (1989: 227). See also Yu 2011: 262.

In light of Bildad's advice that Job should pursue penitential prayer in light of God's justice, Job responds by saying that his only recourse in a legal dispute would be to plead (חנן) with God (i.e., to plead with God for mercy), which would require Job to admit to wrongdoing which he has not committed.[136] Job responds by reiterating his innocence (9:20-21), indicating Bildad's advice is nonsensical for Job's situation.

Job outlines two other options. The first of these in 9:27 involves hypothetically resolving to change his posture from protest prayer to joy. Job rejects this option, noting that he would still fear pain and be pronounced guilty (9:28-29). So Job offers a second option in 9:30, either to literally or metaphorically purify himself.[137] This option is also rejected as impossible (9:31). Given the flawed nature of Bildad's use of the legal metaphor, Job wishes there was a מוֹכִיחַ that could bring relief (9:33-34).[138] Job desires someone who would advocate for him before God. This seems impossible, so complain he must (9:35). If Bildad argues that God does not pervert justice with the conclusion that Job must repent, then Job argues God does pervert justice, and there is no possibility for legitimate legal recourse (Job 9); he needs to complain, and he will outline an example (Job 10).

Job's point is clear: he has no other recourse, and he rejects the friends' advice. The hypothetical thinking contributes to Job's argument. Job concludes he must complain, and complain without restraint (9:35–10:1). The inclusio of the particle כִּי in 9:2 and 9:35 provides closure, and highlights the resolve communicated in 9:35 with the cohortative: Job will speak boldly in protest prayer, without fear, despite the risks. In 10:1, Job is "justifying his complaint in that God has made his soul...bitter"

---

136. Seow's translation of 9:15 is helpful (2013: 539): "Whom, even if I were in the right, I could not answer, I could (only) make a plea to my adversary for mercy." Job expresses that his only recourse is to act as if he were guilty, even if he is not: "Job imagines himself in such a legal setting, where he will nevertheless have to plead for mercy, as if he were guilty" (548). This would violate his integrity, and thus prove his righteousness is not disinterested.

137. Clines notes this may be a metaphor for an oath, another form of engagement with God (1989: 241).

138. This reading takes the variant. This is not the normal construction for saying something does not exist, which would use אֵין. Clines points out this would be the only occurrence of לֹא יֵשׁ (ibid.: 220). On the meaning of מוֹכִיחַ, see Ticciati 2005: 119–35. Though I disagree with her exegesis on some points, her discussion on the function of a מוֹכִיחַ clarifies what Job is looking for in 9:33.

(Hartley 1988: 183).[139] His physical and emotional condition provides the justification for his complaint (cf. 3:20; 7:11). He then reports what his complaint would be (and is) in 10:2-22.[140]

Tropes. The dominant trope in this speech is that of litigation. As Seow notes (2013: 541; cf. Habel 1985: 188–9), this speech teems with legal terminology.[141] This legal terminology establishes the metaphorical context of the court room, which Job contemplates as an effective means of obtaining restoration. Job then employs a series of tropes in Job 9 in the legal context to demonstrate the anticipated futility of such a course of action. First, Job uses images of strength in 9:4 and 19 (cf. 9:10). Affirming that God is powerful, Job draws the conclusion that he is so powerful he cannot be pressed into litigation where Job and God can engage one another on equal grounds. This relates to the second trope used to demonstrate the futility of litigation, the creation imagery in 9:5-9 (cf. v. 10). God's power—demonstrated in his reversal of creation by overturning mountains, causing earthquakes, and darkening astronomical phenomena—is such that he creates chaos. The imagery is hyperbolic. Job emphasizes God's exhibition of unjust power in 9:13, used with the mythological trope, mentioning the cowering helpers of Rahab. Images

---

139. See also Yu 2011: 262; Seow 2013: 553. What he wants is the ability to complain freely to persuade God to act on his behalf.

140. Patterson (2010: 22) suggests there is a pseudosorites in 9:13-17. It seems better, however, to see the conditional of 9:16 as a part of the development of Job's hypothetical considerations. Yet Patterson is right to note that the use of this conditional is a part of Job's argument that God is not just (23), a direct rebuttal of Bildad's thesis from Job 8. Patterson also suggests that Job uses a pseudosorites in Job 10:15 (23). While Job does use the formal conditional אִם, this is not a strict pseudosorites where the second half assumes or builds on what was already excluded or negated. In 10:15 Job considers two mutually exclusive options, and considers himself in a lose–lose situation. This is certainly a rhetorical device, and, like the pseudosorites, is attention-grabbing. Through this hypothetical Job asserts his innocence over against God's perceived injustice. To both Bildad (as well as the friends) and God, Job is justifying his protest prayer, a justification that is fundamentally related to his innocence and his experience. To Bildad, this justification is intended to refute his contention that God does not pervert justice. To God, this justification carries an implicit plea that God should modify his approach toward Job and bring relief (i.e., "You are not acting like what I know to be true of you!").

141. The following terms occur in Job 9: מִשְׁפָּטִי, יעד, מִשְׁפָּט, רִיב, שֹׁפְטִים, מוֹכִיחַ, צדק, רֶשַׁע, תָּם, נָקִי, נקה, עֲנֵה, and כֵּן. Legal terminology is not limited to Job 9, however. Job 10 includes רֶשַׁע, רִיב, צדק, נקה, and עֵד (Seow 2013: 576). The litigation trope thus comes to the foreground in 9:2-4, 14-16, 19-21, 28-29, 32-34; 10:2-3, 7, 14-15.

of injustice emerge in 9:12 and 9:22-24, which make clear Job's point in response to Bildad: God does pervert justice.[142] The rhetoric highlights Job's perceived injustice personally, but Job extends his assertion of divine injustice to include the rest of creation.[143] God's injustice is documented through the trope of divine absence as well in 9:11 and the images of attack in 9:12, 17-18, 23, 31, and 34. Job has used divine attack imagery in the previous speeches, but it is at this point that he highlights explicitly the issue of justice as he responds to Bildad's argument in 8:3. God snatches without the possibility of recourse (9:12); if Job could gain a hearing (9:16), God would crush him and multiply bruises relentlessly (9:17-18).[144] Job depicts God as unjust in his attack, in the way that he mocks those who despair of his slaying scourges (9:23). In 9:34 Job demonstrates God's injustice and the futility of litigation by appealing for God to remove his rod, used here as an image of attack, and for God's wrath to cease terrifying him. Job's purification ritual would also be ruined by God's attack as he plunges Job back into a pit to soil his clothes, which are personified as abhorring Job (9:30-31). The imagery of purification, divine attack, and the trope of personification thus emphasize his point of the futility of the legal metaphor in a strictly forensic sense. God is unjust, Job avers. The trope of the ephemerality of Job's life—using the images of speed from the land (the runner), the water (the skiffs), and the air (the eagle)—establishes urgency and demonstrates the need for his continued complaints (9:25-26).[145] Job's physical and emotional turmoil, represented by images of uneasiness and bitterness in 9:35–10:1, justify his argument for continued protest prayer as well (9:18, 21, 28-29).

Many of these tropes are also used in Job's complaint, in conjunction with some unique tropes as well. As in the previous speeches, Job uses the tropes of divine attack and vigilance in his complaint in Job 9–10. Job accuses God of unethical treatment toward him in 10:3, where God oppresses (עשׁק) and rejects (מאס) his own creation. But the attack imagery

---

142. Job's conclusion in 9:22-24 refutes the statements of Eliphaz and Bildad in 5:19-22 and 8:20, respectively. See Seow 2013: 549; Hartley 1988: 177.

143. The personal focus emerges in the repetition of 1cs forms in 9:17-20. The global focus emerges in 9:22-24, especially in v. 24 with the divine passive and 3ms verb. Scholars note this is the pinnacle of Job's assertion of divine injustice. See Clines 1989: 236–7; Longman 2012: 173; Seow 2013: 550.

144. Seow (2013: 548) notes that v. 18a-b respond to Eliphaz's statement in 5:18, while v. 18c responds to Bildad in 8:21.

145. The observation of the three spheres of the earth is found in a number of commentators, and seems to go back to Fohrer (1963: 210; Clines 1989: 240; Seow 2013: 551).

occurs in accusations with other verbs as well: בלע ("to destroy") in 10:8,[146] נתק ("to pour out") and קפא ("to congeal") in 10:10, צוד ("to hunt") in 10:16, and חדש ("to renew") and רבה ("to multiply") with the objects עֵדִים ("witnesses") and צָבָא/כַּעַשׂ ("vexation"/"troops"), respectively, in 10:17. The attack imagery is also implied in 10:11-13. Vigilance appears in the accusations regarding the relentless search for Job's sin in 10:6 and 14.[147] These accusations are inherently tied to Job's perceived injustice as it relates to the creation imagery, which dominates his complaint in Job 10. Job views himself as the "labor of [God's] hands" (יְגִיעַ כַּפֶּיךָ) in 10:3,[148] one who was fashioned carefully by God's hands (יָד with עשׂה and עצב) in 10:8-9.[149] The imagery of gestation in v. 10 is also creation imagery. The creation imagery sets up the accusation in v. 13, as Job depicts the intimate creative work of God in clothing him with skin and flesh and knitting him together with bones and sinew in v. 11. Job describes his suffering as well. The trope of ephemerality in 10:9 and 20-21—where Job reminds God that God will return Job to the dust and that his days are few—heightens the urgency of the petitions to leave Job alone. Job grounds his pleas by describing his suffering with images of human frailty in 10:9 and images of affliction and shame in 10:15. Job closes his complaint with a reprise of images from his opening speech, with the trope of death at birth in 10:18-19 and the trope of darkness. The words for darkness pile up in 10:21-22,[150] emphasizing the urgency of Job's plea for relief; the goal is to move God to action. The repetition of the adverb מְעַט in 10:20 (bracketing the verse) and the temporal adverb בְּטֶרֶם in 10:21 are the clues to the use of these images. Job is essentially saying, "Do something before I am in a place where there is no possibility of relief and restoration." These tropes are combined to point to God's injustice toward Job personally, with the tropes of injustice occurring explicitly in 10:3 and 7. God is depicted as treating Job unethically, as well as committing injustice, by favoring the wicked. In fact, the trope of injustice reaches its apogee in v. 7, when Job exclaims that God is acting in a way that violates what he knows to be true

---

146. This echoes 2:3, especially so in light of the use of the word חִנָּם in 9:17.

147. The chiasm of v. 6 reinforces the imagery of unyielding vigilance.

148. Collocated with מאס following the verb עשׁק, Hartley comments (2013: 539), "[B]y turning this metaphor inside out, Job scathingly charges that God has rejected or renounced (mā'as; cf. Job 9:21; 42:6) this bond [of creator to created]. He heightens the sarcasm of his question with the words *oppress* and *toil*." Job uses the phonologically similar verb עקשׁ to describe God's injustice in 9:20.

149. עשׂה also occurs in 10:9, heightening the rhetoric of the petition.

150. Note עֵיפָה, צַלְמָוֶת, חֹשֶׁךְ, and אֹפֶל. The poetic articulation of darkness shining (וַתֹּפַע כְּמוֹ־אֹפֶל) is provocative as well.

of Job, namely, that he is not guilty. It is this perceived injustice that drives Job's complaint and informs the rhetorical effect of the other tropes.[151] The tropes together rebut Bildad's contention about divine injustice.

Allusions. There are a number of allusions to other poetic texts in this speech. Job alludes to several passages in Isaiah 40–55 in chapter 9.[152] Brinks Rea (2010: 167; cf. 137–44; see also Kynes 2013b: 94–105) has documented five connections between Job 9:2-12 and Isaiah 40–55. In 9:4b Job describes God as אַמִּיץ כֹּחַ, alluding to Isa. 40:26. In 9:8a Job describes God as נֹטֶה שָׁמַיִם לְבַדּוֹ, alluding to Isa. 44:24. In 9:10a Job uses the phrase אֵין חֵקֶר, echoing Isa. 40:28. In 9:12b Job emphasizes God's freedom with the question מִי יְשִׁיבֶנּוּ, alluding to Isa. 43:13. And in 9:12d Job asks rhetorically about the possibility of saying to God מַה־תַּעֲשֶׂה, alluding to Isa. 45:9.

Each of these allusions highlights divine transcendence and sovereignty. Job and Bildad agree on this point (Seow 2013: 544). But Job experiences this negatively rather than as comfort, as in the Isaianic context,[153] and uses latent ambiguity in the textual tradition to argue against Bildad (Brinks Rea 2010: 169). Job uses these traditions to lay a foundation to move toward his conclusion in 9:22-24: God's power and transcendence do not eliminate the possibility of injustice. Job recognizes the trouble in engaging God legally (9:4), highlighting the futility of the legal metaphor. The allusions in 9:8, 10 reflect Job turning the praise of God into a dispute over God's justice, also alluding to Eliphaz's statement from 5:9.[154] Pulling from Eliphaz's characterization of God, Job refutes Bildad's views with Eliphaz's words (Seow 2013: 545). God as the great

151. On the personification of God in 10:4-5, see the discussion of the rhetorical questions below.

152. The following analysis is indebted to Brinks Rea's data (2010) and Kynes' subsequent article (2013b: 94–105). Brinks Rea, who is, on the whole, critical of seeing a connection between Isa. 40–55 and Job, considers Job 9:2-12 to be one of the two places in which an allusion is likely (2010: 164, 167, 237). The other is Job 12:7-25. Kynes argues that Isaiah is likely the earlier text, noting that "allusions to Job's speeches [by Isaiah] would undercut the message of Isa 40–55 altogether" (2013b: 98); see also Brinks Rea 2010: 170. Moreover, Kynes also notes that the author of Job uses the Isaiah texts in different ways through the different characters; if Isaiah were using Job, which perspective would he be using (2013b: 104)?

153. The two questions in 9:12 are used "to present God's transcendence, as he is currently experiencing it, as threatening… Job could be using this phrase from Isa. 40–55 to accuse God of not acting in such a way in his life" (Kynes 2013b: 103).

154. Kynes suggests that in 9:10 Job is "turning praise into accusation" (ibid.: 101).

Creator is absent and acting unjustly toward Job (9:11-12) and Job has few options remaining (9:12d; cf. 9:14-16). It is noteworthy that Isa. 45:9, to which Job alludes in 9:12d, is one of the few passages in which a human considers bringing a *rîb* against God. Isaiah 45:9 suggests this is fraught with risk. Job, in this speech, recognizes this risk and argues that complaint is his only option anyway (9:35–10:1).

Kynes (2013b: 105) argues that Job uses the Isaiah passages in a parodic fashion to accuse God, implying a petition. This analysis is insightful, though it does not take into account the context of the dispute, which the previous discussion of the rhetorical situation, forms, and structure established. Given the dual audience in this speech, both effects—refutation of Bildad and accusation against God—are possible. If this is the case, Job's allusions to Isaiah 40–55 in Job 9 both dispute Bildad's arguments and advice and imply a petition for God to act as the soteriological traditions of Isaiah 40–55 portray. In other words, that these allusions are functioning as protest prayer in some sense, as Kynes argues, is not out of the question, though the primary effect of these allusions is to appeal to other biblical traditions and to emphasize the negative aspects of God's sovereign rule in order to portray divine injustice, a refutation of Bildad's main argument.

Another allusion in this speech is to Psalm 139 in Job 10. Kynes (2012: 102) documents the connections between Job 10:8-12 and Ps. 139:13-16: the clustering of סכך, עשׂה, and עֶצֶם/עָצְם, with the verb סכך being the strongest link since it only occurs in these two passages, with both forms as *yiqtols* with a 1cs suffix and in the same thematic context.[155] The way Job uses the image of knitting together in such a scathing complaint makes it unlikely that the psalmist would use it after Job (ibid.: 106–7). Job combines the expression of worship in Psalm 139 with complaint; adoration becomes accusation (107). He uses "the psalmist's rhetoric to further his case against God" (Brown 2000: 117), parodying the psalm

---

155. Beyond the explicit verbal links, there is an abundance of thematic links. See Kynes 2012: 108–12. See also Brown 2000: 107–24. Brown concludes there is "intertextual dependence" (117). Beyond the connections to this speech, Ps. 139 is alluded to elsewhere. As Kynes notes, Zophar also uses Ps. 139 in Job 11:7-9 (2012: 112–15); Job reuses it in Job 23:8-10 (115–17). These strengthen the case for an allusion, especially with Zophar picking up what Job has said in the next speech. There may also be an allusion to Ps. 119:73, with the collocation of יָדֶיךָ with the verb עָשׂה; Kynes writes, "The lexical and syntactical similarity between these verses is striking, and so, if this is not a formulaic way of expressing divine involvement in personal creation, then dependence is likely" (103).

3. *"I Will Complain in the Bitterness of My Soul"* 93

for rhetorical effect in his accusation (Kynes 2012: 111; cf. 118).[156] Job uses the psalm to assert, and complain about, the injustice of the creator. The function of the allusion to Psalm 139 is to attract attention, ultimately to motivate God to act on Job's behalf—to bring about relief from his suffering (106). Job's words and those of the psalmist are different "in tone and tenor" but seeking the same rhetorical goal: relief from their suffering (Brown 2000: 108).

Job also alludes to Psalm 39 in Job 10. In 10:20-21, Job alludes to Ps. 39:14 [13]: מִמֶּנִּי, וְאַבְלִיגָה, and בְּטֶרֶם אֵלֵךְ (Kynes 2012: 123–35).[157] There is some question about the text of Job 10:20-21, however, so some examination of the text-critical issues in Job 10:20 is necessary. Kynes adopts the LXX and Peshitta readings (following the BHS proposal) to make the first clause of 10:20 read "are not the days of my duration/life [חֶלְדִי] few?" He writes (124),

> By reading the *kethib*, moving the *yod* at the beginning of יְשִׁית back to the end of חדל/חלד, and removing the extra *yod* at the beginning of the word, the text becomes הֲלֹא־מְעַט יָמַי חֶדְלִי שִׁית מִמֶּנִּי ("are not the days of my life few? Withdraw from me"). This version, proposed by the editors of BHS (with the more common spelling חֶלְדִי), makes more sense than the possibilities in the MT and only involves removing a single *yod*.

The result of this is really strong agreement with Ps. 39:14 [13]. Yet, Seow argues that the LXX and Peshitta represent an easier reading, so the MT is to be preferred. If so, the *kethib/qere* can be resolved by recognizing the discrepancy is probably a mistaken *waw/yod* issue—an orthographic error rather than needing to remove a consonant from the Hebrew text (Seow 2013: 592). Thus, there is good reason to follow the MT, reading the *qere*. Even adopting this reading, there remains a strong link between Job 10:20-21 and Ps. 39:14 [13].

---

156. See also Brown 2000: 124; cf. 116.

157. Kynes also outlines a number of superficial similarities between the two texts (2012: 122). Ps. 39 may be first alluded to in Job 6:8-11 by Job and again in 7:6-8. Job also brings it back up in 13:28–14:6 (130–6). These other allusions strengthen the connection between Job and the psalm. Kynes makes the obvious point that Job is the only one to allude to this psalm; if the friends were to allude to Ps. 39 it would "undercut their argument" (138–9). Though he admits dependence could work either way, he notes that Job is likely later because of Job's development of the lament, making it unlikely that the psalmist could soften the image presented by Job (127–30). Moreover, because the book of Job is clearly later than the other psalms discussed in Kynes' study, it is likely true with Ps. 39 too.

As in the other allusions, Job's use of Psalm 39 is consonant with the intent of the psalmist, namely, "to motivate God to intervene" (Kynes 2012: 130). Kynes writes, "Job's threat is slightly more forceful than the psalmist's, and by superseding the complaint of one of the most despairing psalms in the Psalter, one of the few laments that does not end in praise, Job demonstrates the extreme depths of his sorrow" (ibid.). He concludes, "[Job's] choice of Psalm 39 is significant because it is one of the bleakest songs in the Psalter… By exceeding even this psalm's dismal presentation of relationship with God, Job suggests to God that his suffering is beyond anything to which God has previously subjected his people" (137).[158]

Job also alludes to Psalm 1 in 10:3. The phrase עֲצַת רְשָׁעִים only occurs in this psalm and the book of Job (cf. 10:3; 21:16; 22:18). Job's use of Psalm 1 in 10:3 responds to Bildad's argument in 8:3 as well as to Eliphaz's statements from 5:13-14 (where he also alludes to Ps. 1), while also accusing God of wrongdoing. In stark contrast to Bildad, Job unambiguously asserts God has treated him unjustly (Kynes 2012: 152–3).[159] With these words, Job juxtaposes God with the wise men of the psalm; Kynes (ibid.) notes that this is not to reject the psalm but to use it against God rhetorically (see also Seow 2013: 579).[160] As elsewhere, Job is using other biblical traditions in his rhetoric to show that his experience is contrary to what he knows to be true of God, justifying his complaint and intending to motivate God to respond to his protest prayer. Seow's comment on the use of biblical traditions in the hymn of 9:5-10 is apt for all of these allusions: "God is not who the tradition claims God to be"—at least as Job perceives it, and this is why he continues to protest in prayer (545).[161]

Rhetorical Questions. Job also uses rhetorical questions in his argumentation. After conceding Bildad's point, Job raises the question in 9:2 in order to set up his thesis regarding the impossibility of engaging God in litigation. Job issues his thesis in 9:3, and then emphasizes this thesis through rhetorical questions in 9:4, 12, and 19. Each question affirms the futility of litigation by means of the legal metaphor. Job asserts in 9:4 through his question that no one has contended with God and succeeded.[162] In 9:12, through allusions to Isa. 43:13 and 45:9, Job asserts that God's

---

158. He calls this "intensification of lament."
159. Kynes does not connect this with the rhetorical situation and Job's response to Bildad.
160. On parody, see Kynes 2011: 276–310.
161. There may also be an allusion to Ps. 73 in 9:29-31; see Kynes 2012: 167–8.
162. On the verb קשה, see Seow 2013: 555.

transcendence and freedom are such that a human cannot force him into litigation. In 9:19 Job underscores the impossibility of summoning God. The reason for the futility is God's injustice; Job builds his case for this point throughout 9:4-24, culminating in the rhetorical question אִם־לֹא אֵפוֹא מִי־הוּא. In response to Bildad's scathing rhetorical question in 8:3, "Does God pervert justice?"—the obvious and expected answer being, "No, of course not"—Job concludes, "Yes, he does."[163] Job communicates his exasperation over the futility of options for engaging God in 9:29.

In Job's complaint in 10:2-22 there are six verses in which Job articulates ten questions, and all but one is an accusation. Job asks three accusatory questions in 10:3, asserting the unethical treatment of God toward Job as a creature and toward the righteous in general.[164] This complaint accuses God of injustice while also refuting Bildad's argument. Though it is reported speech, Job intends for God to overhear this protest prayer. The accusations continue in 10:4-6, where Job asks God rhetorically if God has human characteristics as he pursues Job's sin. This personification heightens the rhetorical impact of these accusations of mistreatment. Seow captures it well: "To Job, though, it is only a human who can be short-sighted… God should know Job's innocence. Yet Job is treated as if he were guilty, as if God cannot see as God ought to see… God certainly cannot use the excuse of finitude" (2013: 579–80).[165] The accusations of mistreatment become even more pronounced in 10:10.[166] As noted in the treatment on allusion and in the tropes of creation, Job perceives God's injustice as God violates his inherent covenant with one of his creatures. The rhetoric of accusation comes to its culmination in Job's complaint that God brought Job into the world in 10:18. These accusations carry with them an implied petition. As in chapter 3, Job is seeking relief, where the grave would provide relief from the suffering he experiences. The petition to bring relief is urgent, as the final rhetorical question in 10:20 affirms.

---

163. The question of 9:24 is clearly a response to Bildad—a direct refutation—on the internal level. On the external level, the reader is forced to wrestle with Job's words in light of what is known from the prologue and Yahweh's admission of injustice when he harmed Job "without cause." Yahweh's speeches in Job 38–41 will help the reader navigate this gap; see Chapter 6 below.

164. Yu suggests that Job's questions in 10:3 could be either insults or implicit appeals (2011: 263). It seems best to read the illocution as an accusation, and thus as an implicit appeal, given the form (complaint).

165. Seow points out this may respond to Bildad's point in 8:18.

166. As Magary notes (2005: 290), the הֲלֹא anticipates an affirmative answer.

Emphatic Statements. Job also uses particles to make key points throughout this speech. Some of these have been treated above (e.g., the use of אִם and the hypothetical progression in the speech). But a closer look at key particles such as אָמְנָם, אַף כִּי, אֵפוֹא, and הֵן reveals some of Job's pivotal statements. Job begins his speech with the particle אָמְנָם, which seems to indicate that Job agrees with Bildad (9:2a). But this apparent agreement is intended to set up the disagreement between Job and Bildad, as Job rejects Bildad's argument with the rhetorical question, begun with a contrastive *waw*, in 9:2b. Job further refutes some of Bildad's key statements with his double use of the particle הֵן in 9:11-12. Bildad had also used this particle to introduce consecutive verses in 8:19-20 as he concludes the defense of his thesis and his advice. Job, in no uncertain terms, rejects the thesis and the advice in 9:11-12: God has rejected him, a blameless man (9:20-21). Job uses the particle אַף כִּי in 9:14 to assert the futility of litigation, a key statement in his defense of his protest prayer. Another emphatic statement, with the fronted prepositional phrase עַל דַּעְתְּךָ כִּי־לֹא אֶרְשָׁע, occurs in 10:7. With this statement, Job directly accuses God of injustice by condemning him despite his knowledge of the contrary. Each of these emphatic statements works to refute Bildad's argument and exhortation toward penitential prayer, and to justify Job's protest prayer.

Lexical Repetition. There are twenty-eight shared lexemes between Job's third speech and Bildad's speech in Job 8, indicating a tight connection between the two speeches. As previously noted, Job uses the double occurrence of הֵן in 9:11-12 to respond to Bildad's statements in 8:19-20. But there are other direct rebuttals regarding God's justice through lexical repetition. Job uses חנן in 9:15 to reject Bildad's advice from 8:5-6. Job uses both תָּם and מאס, which Bildad had used together in 8:20 to encourage Job to take his advice, to assert that God has rejected him despite his blamelessness (10:3; cf. 9:20-21). Job argues that God has perverted justice both individually and generally, using the verb צדק in response to Bildad's use of the nominal form צֶדֶק (cf. 8:3, 6; 9:2, 15, 20; 10:15). Job affirms he is righteous (cf. 9:20-21), and, by repeating Bildad's words in this context, directly refutes Bildad's contention that God does not pervert justice. Despite Job's righteousness he is treated as if he were unrighteous. Job also uses מִשְׁפָּט in 9:19 and 32 (cf. לְמִשְׁפָּטִי in 9:15 as well) after Bildad had used it, with צֶדֶק, in 8:3. Also related to God's perversion of justice is Job's use of רָשָׁע in 9:22, 24, and 10:3. Bildad concludes his speech with the assertion that the tent of the wicked will be no more (וְאֹהֶל רְשָׁעִים אֵינֶנּוּ).[167] Job intends to refute Bildad's assertion from 8:3 by pointing out both cosmic and personal injustice.

---

167. See also מְרֵעִים in 8:20.

3. *"I Will Complain in the Bitterness of My Soul"*

Job is not only refuting Bildad's argument regarding God's justice, but also intends to defend his protest prayer as an appropriate means of speech, given his circumstances. Job accomplishes this with a few significant lexical repetitions from Bildad's speech. The word קוט in 10:1 echoes both 8:14,[168] where Bildad used it, and Ps. 139:21.[169] Kynes points out that perhaps Job recognizes the paradoxical nature of using Psalm 139 in a way that would ostensibly be in opposition to the psalmist's approach to those who "rise up against [God]" (Ps. 139:21). Kynes writes (2012: 109–10),

> Job's allusion to this verse right before he begins his case against God may represent an internal tension to Job himself. The psalmist indicates his piety most prominently by his hatred and loathing of any who oppose God, but Job is attempting to maintain his piety at the same time he opposes God, and even to establish it by that opposition. Because of Job's rare situation as a pious opponent of God, he must reject God even as he worships God and loathe himself as he defends his life and innocence.[170]

Job's response to Bildad articulates his recognition of the risks involved in pursuing this kind of protest prayer, but also communicates Job's conviction in his argument. Moreover, by repeating the word פֶּה in 9:20 to express the futility of litigation, Job defends his protest prayer. Bildad had used the word in 8:2 and 21, forming an inclusio around his argument to stress the importance of Job modifying his verbal expression. Job clearly rejects Bildad's suggestion (9:35–10:1). Moreover, while Bildad had claimed that if Job modified his approach to penitence his abode would be restored (שׁלם) in 8:6, Job responds in 9:4 by asserting that no one has ever engaged in litigation with God and succeeded (שׁלם) (Course 1994: 62). Job's only recourse, he contends, is to continue protesting in prayer.

---

168. There is some dispute over this verb in 8:14. As Clines notes (1989: 200), the proposals of קָרֵי קַיִט or קִשְׁרֵי קַיִט (meaning "threads of summer" or "bands of summer") lack warrant. The proposal of קטט has more merit, but remains unnecessary. While the syntax is challenging (with the parallelism suggesting יָקוֹט should be a noun, as Clines notes [199]), the text is not impossible and emendation is unnecessary. The meaning of the verse seems to be that the godless' confidence is revolting (קוט) to others; see *HALOT*, 1083.

169. The root occurs only eight times in the MT: Ezek. 6:9; 20:43; 36:31; Pss. 95:10; 119:158; 139:21; Job 8:14; 10:1. The link to Job 8:14 is obvious—the same word is used in consecutive speeches. Ps. 139 stands out because of the other allusions to this psalm.

170. This apparent internal struggle in Job is evident elsewhere (9:21, 35).

Direct Address to God (Accusation and Appeal). Job addresses God in this speech as well, another significant strategy to accomplish his rhetorical goals. Job directly addresses God in 9:28-31 as he contemplates other options to litigation. Job accuses God that even if he were to forsake his complaint, God would not declare him innocent (9:28). He also accuses God that if Job were to purify himself, God would sully him again anyway (9:31). In both of these cases, Job uses 2ms forms to address God.[171] This indicates that Job is addressing both Bildad (i.e., the friends) and God in this speech, and denotes the interrelated nature of Job's complaint and his defense of his protest prayer in the face of the friends' criticism.

This dynamic of dual addressees is evident in Job 10:2-22, where Job states explicitly what his complaint would be. On one level, 10:2-22 function in the dispute over Job's verbal expression: Job is saying, "I have no other recourse, so let me tell you exactly what I will say in my protest prayer." But, on another level, it is likely that Job intends God to "overhear" these words as well. Like 6:8-10, Job addresses God as a part of his disputation. Throughout 10:2-22 Job accuses God of violating their relationship;[172] this is personal—as indicated by repetition of 1cs forms in 10:2-22. These accusations are shocking and attention-seeking—in a word, provocative. As is true of complaint generally, by accusing God of improper conduct (cf. 10:3), Job is seeking to move God to act on his behalf.[173] The appeal is implicit in the accusations, especially in light of the allusion to other biblical traditions.

But there is also explicit appeal in Job 10:2-22. Job's first appeal is for God not to condemn him (10:2). Quickly following this appeal, Job implores God to make known why he contends against him (10:2). Job then issues four other imperatives: "remember" (זְכֹר) his frailty and humanity in 10:9, "look" upon his affliction (רְאֵה) in 10:15, and "cease" (חֲדַל), following the *qere*, and "leave [him] alone" (שִׁית) in 10:20.[174] It

---

171. Address of God is also indicated by the 1cp forms in 9:33.

172. God oppresses and rejects his creation (10:3), refuses to see Job's situation (10:5), relentlessly pursues Job's sin (10:6), violates justice (10:7, 14), destroys his creation (10:8, 10), stores up negative actions (10:13), and hunts and harms Job (10:16-17). This is especially clear in the creation imagery and the allusions to the psalms passages, as noted above.

173. Ps. 88 again comes to mind: the psalmist accuses God of mistreatment as a persuasive strategy in seeking relief. See Howard's list (2008: 141).

174. Wilson (2015: 74) draws attention to the significance of these imperatives in connection with other speeches in the first cycle: "It seems significant that the call on God to remember Job occurs in chapters 7, 10, and 14. Thus, in the midst of the darkest laments in Job and in each speech in the first cycle, Job is still concerned to have his relationship with God restored by having God remember him."

is clear that Job is seeking relief from his suffering; these are pleas for a reprieve from God's onslaughts, which have been outlined throughout the address.[175]

The mediated nature of this direct address in 10:2-22 is intriguing. Given that this is "the most severe accusation against God in the entire Main Dialogue" (Yu 2011: 264), it is noteworthy that Job hedges his rhetoric with three statements articulating his discomfort (9:21, 35; 10:1) as well as by stating his complaint in 10:2-22 as what he would say. He does not address this complaint directly to God. It seems Job recognizes the riskiness of articulating such strong accusations, especially as regards divine justice, in his protest prayer and in defense of his protest prayer.

Job's purpose in direct address is "not to reject God, but to force God to show up" (ibid.). Job is seeking relief from his suffering, and only God can bring such relief. Job uses direct address and mediated direct address to accomplish this, while also defending his protest prayer to his critical friends.

Tonality. While Job's overall tone in this speech could be described as one of despair (Hartley 1988: 165; Clines 1989: 225), there is also an element of anger and bitterness toward both God and the friends. But in examining the details, one specific stark shift in tone stands out. In a move similar to Job's address to the friends in the previous speech, Job changes his tone in his address to God in 10:11-13. In Job 6, Job had used a strongly accusing tone toward the friends, and then changed his tone in his pleas for them to consider his plight. In Job's address to God in 10:2-22, Job begins with the accusations, but adopts what appears to be a softer tone in 10:11-12. Recalling the positive images of God's personal involvement in Job's genesis and "life" (חַיִּים), "loving-kindness" (חֶסֶד), and careful preservation (פְּקֻדָּתְךָ), Job's softer tone becomes evident. The strong disjunctive and adversative *waw* at the beginning of v. 13, however, indicates the sharp and quick return to the caustic, accusatory tone which otherwise dominates the speech: "but these things you hid in your heart" (וְאֵלֶּה צָפַנְתָּ בִלְבָבֶךָ), with the implied referent of אֵלֶּה being God's unjust and destructive actions. The shift in tone accentuates the accusation, while also heightening the implied petition for relief. By softening the tone and recalling the positive images, Job sets up the change in tone to draw God's attention and to remind God of how antithetical his actions are toward Job. The shift in tonality is connected to the strategy of allusion

---

175. See also the implied petition for relief in 9:34. As Hartley (1988: 181) notes on 9:34, this is "a search for vindication," "a search for God to make himself known."

and the creation imagery that implies a covenant between the creator and the creature. Job's shift in tone works with the appeal to other biblical traditions, especially Psalm 139. There is also clearly hyperbole in these statements, which also creates the effect of establishing urgency in the implied appeal.

Summary of Job 9–10

In this speech, Job has two main goals: (1) to obtain relief from God—the only one who can provide relief from his suffering—by protesting in prayer, that is, by arresting God's attention and appealing to him (whether explicitly or implicitly), and (2) to defend his protest prayer in light of the arguments and advice provided by Bildad. Job accomplishes these two goals through a number of strategies: hypothetical thinking, inclusio, tropes, allusion, rhetorical questions, emphatic statements, lexical repetition, direct address to God, and tonality. What emerges consistently throughout these strategies is the recurrence of statements regarding God's injustice (sometimes explicit, sometimes implicit). This relates to the thesis proffered by Bildad in 8:3. Job argues for personal and cosmic injustice based on observation, other biblical traditions, and personal experience. He acknowledges the risks involved in articulating such things (9:21, 35; 10:1), but feels constrained to do so given his rhetorical situation. This kind of God-talk escalates the rhetorical situation for the friends, as Zophar's response will demonstrate. But this God-talk is also important in light of how Yahweh will respond in his speeches. Job's rhetoric is inextricably bound to his rhetorical situation—using the blatant statements regarding God's injustice, destruction, and cruelty in verses such as 9:17-18, 9:22-24, and 10:3 to refute Bildad and motivate God to act. Job's speech to God is provocative and accusatory, supplementing the explicit appeals for relief.

"All the Days of My Hardship
I Will Wait Until My Renewal Comes":
The Rhetoric of Job's Fourth Speech (Job 12–14)

Introduction

Zophar refutes Job's contention of innocence in his speech in Job 11, and, like the other friends, suggests Job try penitence to find restoration. Job responds with his longest speech of the dialogue to close this first cycle, arguing that his protest prayer is both appropriate and wise, while also addressing God again in protest prayer.

The Literary Rhetorical Situation of Job 12–14

Zophar's speech in Job 11 exhibits clear signs of escalating tension. A disputation intended to convince Job of his guilt and "move him from his convictions" (Murphy 1981: 29), Zophar's speech is directly refuting Job's verbal discourse.[176] Zophar's pointing out Job's sin implies Job has no right to complain. According to Zophar, Job needs to repent not protest. Zophar opens his speech with rhetorical questions that assert his compulsion to respond to, and his criticism of, Job's verbal expression (11:2-3). Job's discourse is harmful—a mockery (לַעַג)—and he needs to be shamed. After summarizing his view of what Job has said (11:4), Zophar issues a wish and his thesis regarding God's response to Job's verbal expression: If God were to speak to Job, Job would be forced to reckon with his guilt (11:5-6). The repetition of שְׂפָתַיִם in 11:2 and 5 juxtaposes Job's speech (which is impious) with God's speech (which is true). Zophar then emphasizes God's transcendence, refuting Job's presumptuous claim of innocence (11:7-12). Zophar clearly responds to Job in 11:10 with the verbatim use of 9:12: מִי יְשִׁיבֶנּוּ (see Habel 1985: 205). As discussed above, this is an allusion to Isa. 43:13. While Job used the allusion in his rhetoric for disputation (and possibly complaint), Zophar uses it as a threat (Kynes 2013b: 103). God does not make mistakes, and Job's suffering is evidence of his guilt. As the unmarked rhetorical question in 11:11 indicates, when God sees iniquity, he acts.[177] According to Zophar, if Job wants restoration, penitential prayer—not protest prayer—is the only available means (11:13-19).[178] To refuse this advice is to follow the way of the wicked, whose expiration is their only hope (11:20). The expiration of the breath of the wicked in 11:20 is a powerful way to finish and serves as a warning to Job. Overall, "[t]o Zophar, Job had forgotten his finitude and stepped beyond the bounds of what is appropriate language of theological discourse" (Seow 2013: 601–2).

---

176. Many scholars have documented links between these two speeches. See, e.g., Course 1994: 65–7; cf. Habel 1985: 205–6; Hartley 1988: 195; Clines 1989: 262; Newsom 1996: 420; Pyeon 2003: 184; and esp. Seow 2013: 601–8.

177. On the unmarked rhetorical question, see de Regt 1994: 362.

178. While Zophar never uses a term for repentance or for prayer, his description of the actions communicate the concept of repentance. Particularly noteworthy is the action of "establishing your heart" (הֲכִינוֹתָ לִבֶּךָ), an action associated with repentance in 1 Sam. 7:3. Moreover, he clearly sees Job as guilty of sin (11:6c-d). While many interpreters see an encouragement toward repentance (e.g., Hartley 1988: 199; Newsom 1996: 421; Yu 2011: 265–6; Longman 2012: 186; Walton 2012: 183), they do not note the contrast between the penitential prayer and protest prayer.

Despite the escalating tension, Zophar's speech does not change the literary rhetorical situation. His goal was to shame Job (explicitly acknowledged in 11:3) and turn Job from his impious and inappropriate speech.[179] Job, thus, still faces two exigencies: (1) his suffering, and (2) the dispute over the ethics of his discourse.[180] The audience of Job's speech thus also remains the same as in the previous speeches. The constraints also remain constant.

The Forms of Job 12–14

There is some consensus regarding the forms of Job's fourth speech. There is agreement regarding the hymn form of 12:13-25. Disputation and legal speech are common labels for sections of Job 12–13 as well, but there is some divergence of opinion regarding the exact identification of each verse or section.[181] Moreover, interpreters agree that the speech of Job 14 is protest prayer (some term it lament, others complaint).[182] A close analysis of the forms confirms the general consensus.

The significance of the shift in addressee in 13:20 encourages an examination of the forms of the two major movements of the speech. An examination of the forms in 12:2–13:19 indicates that sixty-one of the 108 clauses are disputation (12:2-6, 7b, 7d, 8b-12; 13:1-4, 7-12, 14-16a, 18-19).[183] These clauses exhibit the disagreement over the stated positions

---

179. That it is Job's speech that is in view here emerges in the piling up of speech-related words: רֹב דְּבָרִים and אִישׁ שְׂפָתַיִם in 11:2 and בַּדִּים and the verb לָעַג in 11:3.

180. This corresponds with Yu's (2011: 274) analysis in which he suggests Job has two goals in this speech: (1) to silence his friends and (2) to move God to appear.

181. See, e.g., Murphy 1981: 30; Habel 1985: 215, 226; Hartley 1988: 40–1; Clines 1989: 286–7.

182. See Westermann 1981b: 31; Murphy 1981: 30; Hartley 1988: 40–1. Clines (1989: 288) understands Job 14 as an elegy, made up of wisdom instruction, appeal/lament, and wish; he summarizes the whole second movement of this speech (13:20–14:22) as disputation with God. But the consensus just noted, the lack of disputation elements, and the dominance of protest prayer elements (e.g., interrogatives, petitions, accusations, reproachful tone, and descriptions of suffering) confirm the second movement is best understood as protest prayer. Furthermore, is not a disputation with God better understood as a lament/complaint (i.e., protest prayer)?

183. It is possible that nine of these clauses should be identified as lament (12:4-6). As Clines notes (1989: 287–8), the vocabulary of these clauses fits more naturally in the lament (he uses the label appeal) form. But in the context it is clear from the disputation that surrounds these forms that this is not a context for protest prayer, but address to the friends (note the 2mp forms in 12:2-3). Because of the context, it seems

of the friends (or Zophar, specifically) and Job's argument. The clauses of 12:7-12 that use imperatives indicate the petition form, though there is a consensus that 12:7-12 as a whole are wisdom instruction, a subset of disputation. Petition makes up ten clauses (of 108) in 12:2–13:19. Three of these are 12:7a, c, 8a. The other petition clauses are 13:6, 13, 17a-b. There are thirty-four clauses of the hymn form (12:13-25). The rhetorical questions of 13:7-12 indicate disputation. Additionally, there are two clauses of wish (13:5), and one motive clause (13:16b).

What emerges from this analysis is that disputation is the dominant form. Moreover, and significantly, each of these other forms is used in service of the disputation. The hymn form is being put to the service of the disputation as it relates to God's wisdom (cf. 11:7-11). The key particles אָמְנָם and אוּלָם (see 12:2, 7; 13:3-4) make clear that Job is arguing, that is, disputing.[184] Clines (1989: 288) is right to see this first half of the fourth speech (12:2–13:19) as a disputation speech against the friends.

The form of 13:20–14:22, as noted above, is generally acknowledged to be lament or complaint (i.e., protest prayer).[185] In this movement of the speech, there are twelve clauses of petition (13:20-22, 23b; 14:6), twenty-seven clauses of complaint (13:23a, 24-27; 14:3-5, 18-20), thirty-seven clauses of lament (13:28–14:2, 7-12, 14a-b, 21-22), and fourteen clauses of wish (14:13, 14c-17).[186] With lament, complaint, and petition comprising seventy-six of ninety clauses, it is clear that protest prayer is the dominant element of this second major movement—and wish has a petitionary force (Westermann 1981b: 68).

Overall, this analysis confirms the rhetorical situation outlined above, namely, that Job still faces two exigencies and two audiences. He addresses both in this speech. He addresses the friends in disputation (12:2–13:19) and then turns to protest in prayer (13:20–14:22).

---

best to identify these nine clauses as disputation, part of Job's argumentation with his friends. Hartley takes 12:2-6 and 13:1-3 as complaint against the friends (1988: 40), but a complaint against the friends is a disputation (as in Job 6:14-30).

184. Note also the particle הֵן in 12:14-15; 13:1, 15 (cf. 13:18). Note also גַּם in 12:3; 13:2, 16.

185. See n. 182 above.

186. Westermann suggests that 13:21-22 and 14:6 are wish (1981b: 68). But the imperatives and negative jussives indicate petition. That said, Westermann treats wish and petition together since they are often inherently linked.

The Rhetorical Strategies of Job 12–14

Structure

As hinted at in the foregoing analysis, the structure of this speech is best seen in two movements, with the change in address in 13:20 marking the beginning of the second major movement (see Clines 1989: 285).[187] There are five subsections in the first movement: 12:2-6; 12:7-12; 12:13-25; 13:1-4; and 13:5-19. The first section is delimited by the tricolon in 12:6 and the use of וְאוּלָם in v. 7. This section (12:2-6) is Job's opening disputation regarding wisdom, which Zophar introduced in his speech in Job 11. Job avers the friends' lack of wisdom and his superior wisdom, and mocks their perspective regarding his suffering with regard to his character. Job's next section is a didactic section in which he advances his argument regarding wisdom and his suffering (12:7-12). The exhortation to consider the observable natural world is in contradistinction to Zophar's understanding of God's wisdom that is utterly unknowable (cf. 11:7-11). The significant rhetorical question "Who does not know this among all these things, that the hand of Yahweh has done this?" sits in the middle of this section, with seven clauses preceding the question and six following it. Job affirms his experience in 12:11 and mocks the friends' position in 12:12. Following the exhortation to acquire wisdom, Job moves into the hymn (12:13-25), in which he outlines God's "dark ways" (Clines 1989: 302). Job articulates this hymn in dispute over how he experiences God.[188] God's destructive acts in creation and society play an important role in Job's criticism of the friends' wisdom and his defense of his position.

Job returns to his main point in 13:1-4. The conclusion offered in 13:1 (signaled by הֵן) asserts Job's experience of the hymn's description of God. The repetition of לֹא נֹפֵל אָנֹכִי מִכֶּם in 13:2 returns Job to his main

---

187. Good (1990: 234) suggests placing the break at 13:19a based on address. Hartley (1988: 205) and Yu (2011: 275) also suggest two major movements in the speech, but break the movements at 13:17, with 13:18 initiating the second movement. I would suggest that vv. 17-19 are better seen as the conclusion of Job's address to his friends, with the verb חרשׁ functioning as a closural clue (note the use of the finite verb and infinitive absolute in 13:5). The particle אַךְ in v. 20 marks the start of the next unit, along with the 2ms verbal forms. Moreover, both 13:20 and 14:22 begin with the particle אַךְ, creating an inclusio for the second major movement. Habel's (1985: 215) proposal that there are three movements (12:2–13:5; 13:6-28; 14:1-22) misses the shift in address.

188. See Seow (2013: 624), who labels this section as "Different Experiences."

point after the digression of the hymn. Job then presents his thesis in 13:3-4.[189] The repetition of אוּלָם links these verses and clarifies Job's two exigencies. Job first states his commitment to protest prayer in v. 3 and then articulates his assessment of the arguments and exhortations of the friends in v. 4. The final subsection of the first movement is 13:5-19, where the verb חרש frames an inclusio. Job's wish is for the friends to be silent. This verb also occurs in 13:13 as an imperative. The call to be silent is reiterated by the imperatives to listen (שמע in 13:6 and 13:17 and קשב in 13:6). The repetition of the imperatival mode provides structure to this section, and the call for silence is a criticism of their verbal expression.[190] As in his second speech, Job's justification of his own language involves a criticism of the friends' language (cf. 6:14-30).

The first movement reveals the following key points based on this structural analysis. First, Job disputes the friends' wisdom and asserts his own. Second, he teaches them about the cause of his suffering. Third, he provides a hymn to document God's potentially destructive ways. Fourth, Job asserts his commitment to protest prayer. And, fifth, he calls for them to be silent while criticizing their approach. These key points relate to Job's exigency regarding the friends' criticism of his verbal expression.

The second movement (13:20–14:22) also divides into five subsections that help reveal Job's major emphases. The first, 13:20-28, is Job's initial address to God. This section reveals Job's main complaint and accusation against God in this speech (Westermann 1981b: 53–4). Job's accusations against God concerning mistreatment in the complaint proper in 13:23-27 imply a plea for change; this is confirmed by the petitions of 13:20-21. Job stresses the urgency of this plea in 13:28, which also forms a bridge to the general lament regarding the suffering of humanity in the second unit, 14:1-6. The general description is preparation for Job to apply the problem of suffering to himself, and closes with a petition for relief in v. 6 (cf. 7:16; 10:20).[191] The grounds for the petition are given in the third section, 14:7-12, which is demarcated by the inclusio of tricola in v. 7 and v. 12 (Seow 2013: 674). The nature tropes give the reason for Job's

---

189. Clines (1989: 288) suggests 13:3 is the nodal verse. See also van Hecke (2003: 120), who links 13:3 with 42:7-8.

190. They speak (דבר) injustice and deceit (13:7); they show favoritism and argue for God (13:8, 10); their sayings are worthless ("maxims of ashes" [זִכְרֹנֵכֶם מִשְׁלֵי־אֵפֶר] and "defenses of clay" [לְגַבֵּי חֹמֶר גַּבֵּיכֶם]) (13:12).

191. This interpretation reads two imperatives in 14:6: שְׁעֵה and וַחֲדָל. This reading is attested by one manuscript, though is admittedly the easier reading.

petitions in v. 6, establishing the urgency of the petition for relief. Job's wish in 14:13-17, the fourth section, also relates to a plea for relief as he envisions being hidden from God's wrath until the relationship can be restored. The jarring adversative וְאוּלָם in v. 18 brings Job back to reality as he reiterates his complaint of mistreatment in his final unit (14:18-22). The closing of mourning implies a plea for relief.[192] These subunits of the second movement correspond to Job's other exigency, namely, his continued suffering.

Strategies

Lexical Repetition and Direct Address to the Friends. It is clear that Job is responding to the friends collectively, and Zophar's speech in particular, in light of the number of lexical repetitions between Job's fourth speech and Zophar's speech in Job 11. There are forty-five individual lexemes that are shared between these two speeches, some of which are significant rhetorically. Zophar was critical of Job's speech, linking it with foolishness (11:2-6). In response Job uses חָכְמָה four times in his disputation (12:2, 12, 13; 13:5), mocking the wisdom of the friends (12:2, 12; 13:5) and arguing that wisdom resides only with God (12:13). Job uses לֵבָב in 12:3 to respond to Zophar's riddle and exhortation in 11:12-13.[193] Job also repeats the concept of security that Zophar had promised in 11:18. Job maintains in 12:6 that those who have security are actually those who agitate God. This repetition implicitly impugns God's justice while also contradicting Zophar's promise of restoration for repentance. Where Zophar emphasized God's transcendence and wisdom in 11:7-11, Job employs a number of the same words Zophar used in 11:7-11 to reframe God's transcendence in his instruction and hymn.[194] These links confirm that 12:7-12 are a direct rebuttal of Zophar's argument in 11:7-11. Job retorts even nature can instruct the friends as to what is going on in Job's life. That the disputation centers around the ethics of Job's speech is

---

192. Seow notes the "complete story" Job 14 tells as it moves from *'alep* to *taw* in twenty-two verses (2010: 445–6; 2013: 669).

193. As Hartley notes (1988: 206), "With these words Job forthrightly rejects any personal application of Zophar's proverb."

194. Note יָד, יָם, אֶרֶץ, ידע נגד, שָׁמַיִם, and עָמֹק. Both אֶרֶץ and ידע occur elsewhere in Job's fourth speech (cf. 13:2, 18, 23; 14:21 for ידע and 12:15, 24; 14:8, 19 for אֶרֶץ). Though not an exact lexical match אֹרֶךְ occurs in 12:12 and the adjectival form אָרֹךְ occurs in 11:9. While עָמֹק occurs in the hymn (12:22) and not the wisdom instruction, these are the only two occurrences of this word in Job, which indicates a likely connection. See also the nominal and verbal forms of the root חקר in 11:7 and 13:9.

indicated by the repetition of שָׂפָה (cf. 11:2, 5; 12:20; 13:6), דבר (cf. 11:5; 13:3, 7, 13, 22), חרשׁ (cf. 11:3; 13:5, 13, 19), מִי־יִתֵּן (cf. 11:5; 13:5), and אוּלָם (cf. 11:5; 12:7; 13:3, 4). Zophar considers Job's speech unethical and wants God to rebuke Job for his sin, so Job can see he has no right to protest (11:2-3, 5-6); he introduces his wish and thesis in vv. 5–6 with the particle אוּלָם. Job will use these same words in his emphatic statements, introducing them with אוּלָם, and his wish. He suggests that it is his lips (שָׂפָה) that will provide instruction to the friends (13:5-6), and affirms his commitment to his current verbal expression (דבר; cf. 13:3-4). In sum, Job's use of some of Zophar's words indicates that Job is responding directly to Zophar in disputation to defend his verbal expression.

The number of second person forms as direct address to Job's friends also confirms the disputatious nature of the first movement in 12:2–13:19. There are thirty-three second person forms, most of which are plural, indicating he is addressing them collectively.[195]

By directly addressing his friends, Job is seeking to persuade the friends to act and think differently. Job criticizes their wisdom in 12:2-6, culminating in the strong refutation of their understanding of God's justice in 12:6 where those who oppose God prosper and are secure.[196] His address to the friends also shows the bankruptcy of their arguments by

---

195. Of the thirty-three second person forms, six are singular (two imperatives and four pronominal suffixes), all in 12:7-8. On שִׂיחַ in 12:8, see Seow 2013: 632–3. These 2ms forms have led to different solutions. Clines (1989: 292–3), following Gordis, suggests that Job is citing the friends' advice to him. There are problems with this interpretation. Clines bases this designation predominantly on the fact that this would be the only place Job addresses the friends with a singular form, an argument that does not stand up to close scrutiny. As Ho points out (2009: 708–9), Job addresses the friends in 21:3 and 26:2-4 with second person singular forms. See also Fox 1980a: 427, 429. Moreover, Yu notes that the quotation would be inexact (2011: 278 n. 517). Rather, it seems Job is directly addressing them in a parodic manner, using the style and tone of the friends in 12:7-8, with the purpose of refuting Zophar's perspective on God's utter transcendence (11:7-11). On this see Newsom 1996: 427; Ho 2009: 708–9. Job's address takes on a mocking tone in his disputation to suggest that God's actions here are knowable: even the creation knows what God has done (12:9).

196. The enigmatic 12:6c can be taken a couple of ways. It could be that Job is referring to idolaters, those who "take their god in their hand," or, he could be suggesting that God actually sustains the wicked in their prosperity and security. On this latter interpretation, see Seow 2013: 623. Seow's translation is probably correct, with the parallel ל preposition in each clause of 12:6 indicating the focal point of injustice: for destroyers there is prosperity, for those who agitate God and those whom God brings by the hand there is security (see also 632). Whatever the meaning of this

using expressions and arguments from one friend against another.[197] Job summarizes his point that the friends are speaking unwisely and acting inappropriately in 13:2, 4, grounding his argument in their common experience: "according to your knowledge I also know" (כְּדַעְתְּכֶם יָדַעְתִּי גַם־אָנִי). Job highlights that his perspective regarding protest prayer is not formed on a different theological or sapiential foundation (Seow 2013: 642). This leads seamlessly into Job's explicit call for silence because of their unwise and inappropriate speech in 13:5-19. Though there are a number of other strategies employed in this section (including tonality and rhetorical questions), Job's persuasive goals are clearly indicated in the repetition of the imperatives. He implores the friends to listen (שמע and קשב) and to be silent (חרש). Silence for them would be wisdom (13:5); Job's words will provide instruction (13:6, 13, 17).[198] They need to learn how to speak well of God and to God by listening to the arguments Job will present to God (vv. 17-18) (Clines 1989: 307). The imperatives provide a strong conclusion to Job's rhetoric toward the friends in the first cycle: their wisdom is insufficient and what would be wisdom would be to listen and not to speak.

This strategy reveals that Job's disputation is intended to persuade the friends to agree with him regarding protest prayer. Job calls for their silence and attention while shaming their wisdom and actions, the latter of which he accuses of being unethical. Job explicitly accuses the friends of having unethical speech in 13:7 (Seow 2013: 644). Their words are unethical; his wisdom disputation is intended to instruct them in wisdom, which will lead them to better speech ethics. This is akin to Job's rhetoric in 6:14-30.

Tonality and Characterization. Intimately related to Job's strategy of direct address is his tone and characterization of the friends. Clines (1989: 288) summarizes the variation in tone, noting that it moves from sarcasm to anger in Job's address to the friends. Newsom agrees (1996: 424),

---

verse, Hartley (1988: 208) is right in saying, "With this description of the wicked, Job refutes the teaching of the friends." See 5:8, 17-26; 8:5-6, 20-22; 11:13-20. This anticipates the fate of the wicked, the significant *topos* used in the second cycle (Newsom 1996: 427).

197. E.g., the repetition of שְׁאַל־נָא (cf. 12:7 and 8:8) uses Bildad's expression in the refutation of Zophar (see Seow 2013: 623).

198. Speech words dominate these verses: תּוֹכַחְתִּי ("my reproofs"), רִבוֹת שְׂפָתַי ("contentions of my lips"), וַאֲדַבְּרָה־אָנִי ("let me speak"), מִלָּתִי ("my words"), וְאַחְוָתִי ("my declaration").

writing, "Savage parody is Job's chosen weapon in this part of the speech, introduced by his mocking compliment to the friends' wisdom (vv. 2-3)." The sarcasm comes through in Job's opening words in 12:2, and continues in 12:3, where he uses exaggeration, of the friends and of himself (426).[199] The sarcasm combined with the exaggeration is a compelling strategy in disputation concerning wisdom: Job, the humble one, is the sage. Related to tone in this opening section of 12:2-6 is Job's characterization of himself as a joke (שְׂחוֹק) despite being righteous and blameless (צַדִּיק and תָּמִים), which implies their characterization as unethical comforters, something made explicit in 13:4, 12 (Seow 2013: 621). There is great irony in Job's self-characterization. Job's tone of sarcasm, irony, and exaggeration lay the foundation for 12:7-12 and the hymn of 12:13-25.

Job's exhortation to consider creation in 12:7 parodies the tone of the friends, rebuking them. Job "mimics the way the friends talk, exaggerating the use of wisdom figures, proverbs, traditional sayings, and hymnic forms" (Newsom 1996: 431; cf. Habel 1985: 219). One effect of this parody is to show their bankruptcy as counselors (comforter malpractice), and thereby to defend his position regarding the appropriateness of protest prayer. Job issues another sarcastic jab in 12:12 by summarizing their position. From this summary Job transitions into the hymn to refute their perspective that "with the aged is wisdom, and length of days is understanding."[200] Wisdom is not with the friends or their traditions, but wisdom resides with God—and in potentially destructive ways—as the hymn details.[201] The use of sarcasm and parody shames the friends, with the goal of persuading them to change their approach and adopt Job's perspective.

Job leaves sarcasm behind with 13:2 (Newsom 1996: 424). Job's tone turns to an amalgamation of earnestness (as seen in the use of a wish, imperatives, and rhetorical questions) and anger (as seen in the characterization of the friends). Job labels the friends as "smearers of lies" (טֹפְלֵי־שָׁקֶר) and "worthless healers" (רֹפְאֵי אֱלִל) and labels their

---

199. Clines (1989: 289) rightly calls this a litotes. While Job may simply claim to be not inferior, what he actually means is that he knows better. His superior knowledge is rooted in his experience as the man who suffers despite being blameless and upright (289–90).

200. Hartley (1988: 210 nn. 1–2) suggests that בִּישִׁישִׁים is a reference to the "Aged One" (i.e., God). But as Seow points out (2013: 633), this word is used only of humans.

201. The twice fronted prepositional phrase עִמּוֹ in 12:13 and 12:16 juxtaposes the friends' (or their traditions') wisdom with God's.

words "proverbs of ashes" (מִשְׁלֵי־אֵפֶר) and "defenses of clay" (גַּבֵּי־חֹמֶר). Seow captures Job's point and rhetorical goal with this characterization (2013: 643): "Their theological platitudes are as unreliable as deceitful and useless idols… Platitudinous theology is idolatrous." The use of the second person independent pronoun (אַתֶּם) in 13:4 highlights the harshness of Job's tone (cf. 12:2).

Through a sarcastic, exaggerated tone, and the variation of that tone to anger and earnestness, Job is seeking to dispute the friends' position on wisdom and protest prayer. His words are ethical while theirs are not; they embody poor speech ethics while he embodies proper speech ethics.

Rhetorical Questions to the Friends. Job uses eleven rhetorical questions in his disputation that are seamlessly integrated with his address and tone. Job's question in 12:3 affirms his knowledge and wisdom in light of Zophar's speech. He builds on this in 12:9 when he asserts through his rhetorical question that Yahweh is the one who has caused his suffering.[202] If even creatures in nature or the earth itself can know this fact, then it should be obvious to Job's friends as well. Building on this, in 12:11 Job reprises the trope of taste from his second speech when he asserts by the rhetorical question that he knows God is the source of his suffering through his own personal experience. The effect of this is to show that his friends' position regarding God's wisdom is bankrupt. Job is thereby defending his God-talk because God is the root cause of his suffering. Taken together in the context of Job's argument in 12:7-12, these two rhetorical questions justify Job's position as a wise sage who protests in prayer.[203]

In 13:7-9 Job issues a series of rhetorical questions that function as a criticism of and a warning for his friends. Job views their speech as a defense of God, showing favoritism toward God over against Job; this he considers unethical. The final question asserts that their approach will not end well because humans cannot deceive God (Hartley 1988: 220). The question in 13:11 has a similar illocution: the fact that God cannot be boxed in and explained with simple platitudes is, for Job, a thing that

---

202. As Newsom notes (1996: 428), the reference to the hand of God in v. 9 echoes v. 6; together indicating that "[a]ll that one needs to know, Job suggests, is that God is ultimately responsible."

203. Both Eliphaz and Zophar have questioned Job's wisdom in respect of his verbal expression. See 5:2-8, 27 and 11:2-12. The issues of wisdom and the ethics of God-talk in this context are intimately related.

should give the friends pause.²⁰⁴ They need to stop and learn what it means to submit and fear an awesome, free God. The question in 13:14 is an exasperated exclamation.²⁰⁵ Job recognizes that there is danger in what he is doing but asserts he must proceed and accept whatever consequences come (13:13). Job's final rhetorical question to the friends in 13:19 functions as a summary of his argument and is a taunt in question form. Affirming his own position, he asserts that there is no one who can argue successfully with him regarding his verbal expression.

The Hymn and Allusion. Job's use of the hymn, rhetorically speaking, is intimately related to the strategy of allusion. As Clines notes (1989: 296), the hymn is not intended for praise; this is evinced by the lack of a call to praise, and so the hymn as a form is functioning rhetorically in the broader context of the dispute.²⁰⁶ Job is disputing the friends' arguments related to God's wisdom and justice. Like in the previous speech, Job is highlighting the opposite side of the tradition to substantiate the cause of his suffering (see 12:9). That God is destructive in the cosmos indicates by implication that God acts this way toward Job too. Thus, by the hymn, Job is defending his protest prayer in light of God's destructive acts.

A number of interpreters have noted the allusion to Psalm 107 in the hymn.²⁰⁷ Job 12:21a and 12:24b are identical to Ps. 107:40 (see Kynes 2012: 81).²⁰⁸ This is "the closest textual parallel with the Psalms in the

---

204. See Magary 2005: 290 n. 11, who notes that this question implies an affirmative answer.

205. The MT is the preferred text, with the LXX representing haplography rather than the MT exhibiting dittography, given the lack of widespread attestation of this variant.

206. Clines does not use the word "disputation," but notes that the hymn's function is "to convey Job's 'wisdom.'" Seow calls the hymn an "antidoxology" (2013: 626).

207. E.g, Clines 1989: 296–7. Clines calls Ps. 107 a "source" for Job (297). Kynes' treatment is the most thorough (2012: 80–97).

208. There is a slight change in the orthography of the participle שׁוֹפֵךְ, with the Job text reflecting a *plene* spelling and the psalm text reflecting a defective spelling. There are also a number of other connections throughout 12:13-25. Cf. Job 12:14 // Ps. 107:16; Job 12:15 // Ps. 107:33-37; Job 12:17-20 // Ps. 107:14; Job 12:22 // Ps. 107:14; Job 12:22 // Ps. 107:10, 14; Job 12:23 // Ps. 107:38-41; Job 12:25 // Ps. 107:10-14. For a discussion of these parallels, see Kynes 2012: 89–91. Kynes concludes from the several parallels between the hymn in Job 12:13-25 and Ps. 107 that Ps. 107 is "a subtext" for Job's hymn by which Job counters "Eliphaz's positive version of its reversals by emphasizing their negative aspect. This view accords with his experience, what he has seen and heard" (91). Kynes points out that it is unlikely

book of Job" (80). In response to Eliphaz's use of Ps. 107:17 in Job 5:2-5, Job alludes to the same psalm in his argumentation (87–9). Job stresses the psalm's negative imagery to the exclusion of its positive imagery, in contradistinction to Eliphaz who had excluded the negative imagery to focus on the positive imagery (89–91).[209] Where Eliphaz's rhetoric excludes "room for lament," Job uses the psalm to defend his protest prayer (94). Yet there is more to the rhetoric; Job may also be using the psalm as an accusation against God by highlighting the dissonance between what Job experiences and how God is presented in the psalm; the psalm is used to challenge God to act according to what the psalm indicates about who God is (94). Kynes concludes, "Job's challenge expresses implicit faith in the psalm's accurate presentation of how God interacts with his people. To accuse God of straying from the norm, he must believe that it exists, and his argument for a change in God's behavior requires that a return to that standard is possible" (96).

Another possible allusion in the hymn occurs in 12:17, where Job appears to use language from Isa. 44:25 in response to Eliphaz's apparent allusion in 5:12-13 (Kynes 2013b: 103–4).[210] Job 5:12-13 and Isa. 44:25 are only two places where מֵפֵר occurs, and in both cases חֲכָמִים occurs as well. Furthermore, Isa. 44:25 and Job 12:17 both use the rare Polel form of the verb הלל. The rhetorical effect of this allusion is to dispute Eliphaz's contention about God's wisdom and justice, which Job is not experiencing. Eliphaz had used Isaiah as a threat. Job replaces the objects of the verbs used in Isaiah 44 and Job 5, and thereby portrays arbitrary divine power in accordance with his own experience (at least as he perceives it), suffering he hopes will end. This suggests that Job is using the allusion rhetorically to motivate God to cease such destruction and deliver him from his affliction (104). According to this interpretation, the allusion plays a role in the disputation and as an implied petition.[211]

---

that the psalmist would allude to Job in his praise of God given the negative portrayal of God in the Joban context (84–5). Furthermore, given the fact that two characters use the psalm (note Eliphaz's use of Ps. 107:42 in Job 5:16 and 22:19), the psalmist would have a hard time distinguishing which context he is alluding to (86). Thus, it is more likely that Job is using the psalm than the psalmist using Job.

209. See also Clines 1989: 296–7; Westermann 1981b: 73.

210. See especially there nn. 36 and 37. Kynes admits this allusion is not as strong, but it is at least possible in light of the other connections to Isa. 40–55 already outlined.

211. There may also be an allusion in the hymn to Prov. 8:14-16. See Habel 1985: 216; Newsom 1996: 429. Newsom highlights the overlapping words: תּוּשִׁיָּה, עֵצָה, שֹׁפְטִים and נָדִיב, מֶלֶךְ, גְּבוּרָה, בִּינָה.

In addition to allusions in the hymn, there are other possible allusions in the disputation. One that has been noted is an allusion to Jer. 20:7 with the word שְׂחֹק in 12:4 (Dell 2013: 110–11).[212] Given that Job has already alluded to Jeremiah 20 in his first speech, it is plausible to suggest that this word is used here intentionally to bring to mind Jeremiah. Through this allusion, Job links himself with Jeremiah and his complaints, particularly the scathing imprecation in 20:14-18 (Pyeon 2003: 204–5).[213] By intentionally linking himself with Jeremiah, one who was rejected by God and a righteous sufferer, Job rebuts his friends, defends his protest prayer, and implies a petition for God to act on his behalf.

The rhetorical question in 12:9 likely alludes to Isa. 41:20 (Brinks Rea 2010: 172–4).[214] Job once again alludes to another text to heighten the contrast between his experience and what the tradition affirms about God. In Isaiah the hand of Yahweh reverses the fortunes of the people and the cosmos. In Job the hand of Yahweh is used to afflict Job. Seow writes (2013: 624), "[T]he fact that we have a precise parallel in Isa. 41:20b is important, for there the expression refers to the power of God as the sovereign of history, the one who comes through for 'my servant' (Isa. 41:8; cf. 'my servant' in Job 1:8; 2:3; 42:7, 8), the one who redeems sufferers (Isa. 41:14). It is precisely this God who has done 'this' (v. 9b) which is well known among all 'these' (v. 9a)." The disputatious nature of this allusion becomes evident in this contrast, namely, that Job again parodies a text by appealing to its opposite sense, outlining the discrepancy between his experience and the affirmed tradition. But there is also an implicit appeal in this as well, as Job emphasizes the difference between his experience and what the tradition affirms in order to motivate God to act.

In addition to the allusion to Psalm 107, there are other psalms which scholars have identified to which Job may be alluding in his disputation. Kynes, following Cheyne, notes a possible allusion in Job 13:4 to Ps. 119:69. In both cases טפל occurs with שֶׁקֶר. The effect of this allusion would be to link Job with the righteous psalmist and the friends with the enemies of the psalmist (Kynes 2013a: 208). In doing this, Job defends his righteous cause to protest in prayer, something which the lamenting psalmist in Psalm 119 is doing (210).

---

212. Possibly also Lam. 3:14. See the discussion of allusions to Lamentations in Chapter 4 below.

213. This is not a parodic allusion like many of the previously discussed allusions. This is, as Dell argues, a "re-use" (2013: 115–17).

214. *Pace* Clines 1989: 293–4.

Clearly, Job uses allusion rhetorically in his disputation. Many of the allusions are in the hymn, with Psalm 107 being the main text which Job uses in his argument. This indicates that the hymn and allusion function together rhetorically in Job's disputation and defense of his position and wisdom. The friends had argued for a similarly one-sided view of God's wisdom and transcendence; Job responds with the other side. Job also highlights divine freedom, something which the friends have limited by their arguments. In the context of Job's rhetorical situation, it seems reasonable to suggest that Job is subverting these materials as a defense for his protest prayer ("God has done these things to me, and we know he does these things as the sovereign Lord of history, so I should protest and move him to act according to the traditions"), while also implying a petition ("God, you know you are not acting as you should; so come and prove you are as the traditions affirm"). That God does these things in the cosmos implies God does them to Job too—something explicitly asserted in 12:9 and its allusion to Isa. 41:20. Allusion to other biblical texts in his argument demonstrates that Job's faith is present and his assertions of injustice and destruction are rhetorical strategies. He believes the traditions, but Job's experience does not cohere. Job uses these traditions to try to move God to act on his behalf.

Emphatic Statements. Job uses a number of particles in his disputation to emphasize and summarize his argument. He opens his speech in 12:2 with אָמְנָם to stress the disputation immediately. Having had his wisdom questioned by Zophar in the previous speech, Job responds quickly and sarcastically to reverse Zophar's association: Zophar and the friends are the ones who are destroying wisdom. In 12:3 Job quickly adds to his opening refutation another emphatic statement using גַּם. Together 12:2-3 affirm Job's superior wisdom in direct response to Zophar's criticism in Job 11. Job highlights his next key statement with וְאוּלָם in 12:7. Using it to transition the argument, this particle introduces the entire movement in 12:7-12 to emphasize that even the tangible created order knows that "the hand of Yahweh has done this." Wisdom is not with the traditions of the friends, but with God (12:12-13). Job also uses the focusing particle הֵן in 12:14-15 in his hymn to emphasize God's freedom and destructive nature. Job seems to recognize that the friends' theology implies a restricted deity rather than a free deity. But Job also uses the images of destruction to stress his own personal experience. After the hymn, Job uses הֵן again in 13:1 to stress this point: Job has experienced the things he describes in the hymn. Following the fronted prepositional phrase in 13:2, Job uses גַּם again to add to this conclusion, repeating 12:3. These particles all indicate

Job's salient points: he is not unwise, the friends are; moreover, God has acted destructively, causing Job's suffering. Together these arguments work within the rhetorical situation to defend his protest prayer.

Job's theses emerge clearly with the double use of אוּלָם in 13:3-4. Both of these theses relate directly to his two exigencies: (1) Job will continue to protest in prayer by speaking to the Almighty (אֶל־שַׁדַּי אֲדַבֵּר), and (2) Job defends his position by characterizing the friends as liars and quacks. These emphatic statements reveal that "Job is saying that he will pursue a course far different from the one that the friends have recommended. Instead of appealing to God for mercy, as they have exhorted, he will reason or argue with God" (Hartley 1988: 219).

In 13:15 Job uses הֵן again to stress one of his most important points. This verse is an interpretive crux in the book, so a more detailed analysis is necessary. The initial issue relates to the *kethib/qere* on 13:15a. BHS notes there are multiple manuscripts that reflect the *qere*, though most interpreters prefer the *kethib*.[215] The rejection of the *qere* seems to be rooted in its alleged overly pious reading, which seems out of context.[216] Clines (1989: 312–13) thinks that the context does not indicate Job has any hope, but if Job is protesting in prayer throughout this cycle, as this study contends, Job's faith is implicit, undergirding the act of protest prayer. Moreover, if evaluated according to standard text-critical protocol, there is no reason to dismiss the *qere*.[217] Seow (2013: 660) suggests that the *kethib* is the easier reading.

---

215. See Habel 1985: 224–5; Hartley 1988: 221 n. 2, 223; Clines 1989: 312–13; Newsom 1996: 434–5 (though she does not make a decision in favor of either reading); see the thorough discussion of versions and interpretations in Seow 2013: 659–60. There is even less agreement among the interpreters regarding how to understand this verse. For example, Hartley prefers the *kethib*, but still takes the verse to indicate the statement to reflect hope and faith (1988: 223). Yet Seow, noting the ambiguity in the *qere*, writes, "One may understand that Job, believing that God is intent on killing him, is nevertheless confessing faith in the trustworthiness of God… Perhaps, however, Job is being defiant. He believes that God is trying to slay him, and he, wanting to end his misery, says he is waiting for God to do just that" (2013: 659). As for the translations, they favor the *qere*; see ESV, KJV, NKJV, NASB, NIV85, NIV11, TNIV, RVR1995, SCH2000, SG21. The following translations, however, reflect the *kethib*: ASV, JPS, RSV, NRSV, NVI.

216. See the discussion in Hartley 1988: 221 n. 2; Clines 1989: 312–13; Newsom 1996: 434–5; Seow 2013: 660.

217. In fact, Newsom argues both readings are defensible (1996: 435).

Thus, reading the *qere* and interpreting the *yiqtol* of קטל in a modal sense, the first two clauses of 13:15 reflect the following sense: "Behold, he may slay me, but I will hope in him." The next emphatic particle comes in 13:15c with אַךְ. This particle is not meaningless (so Clines 1989: 312), but reflects the terseness of the poetry. Assumed in the entire statement is Job's recognition of his suffering, God's involvement, and the risk of his approach. To all of this, Job says, "Nevertheless, I will argue my ways before him." The emphatic statement in 13:15, indicated by the use of both הֵן and אַךְ, summarizes Job's position regarding his protest prayer: he will not give it up no matter what happens. His protest prayer reflects an underlying faith and hope in God, as all protest prayer does. This coheres with the context in which Job demands the friends' silence to listen and learn from what he will say to God (13:5-6), while also recalling his thesis in 13:3-4. Moreover, this fits within the more immediate context, looking back to 13:13-14: Job had just asserted that he will speak no matter what comes upon him, recognizing the danger of this act.[218] Job uses another emphatic particle in 13:16, גַּם, to continue emphasizing this point. The independent personal pronoun הוּא is ambiguous, possibly referring to God or to "it," his protest prayer. With this Job affirms his hope again by stating that either God or his protest prayer—which implies a hope in God who acts—will be his salvation. Job concludes these emphatic statements by justifying them: "for the godless do not come before him." This causal כִּי grounds this whole sequence. It echoes Eliphaz's statement from 4:6-7, suggesting that Job recognizes that he rightly protests in prayer as a righteous sufferer. Job's hope and faith emerge clearly in these verses, and his integrity gives him confidence in his argument. He can approach God boldly since he is not godless (12:4). This causal clause—this whole sequence—is a direct refutation of the friends' position and justifies his protest prayer.

Job's final use of an emphatic particle is in 13:18, using הִנֵּה to mark the conclusion of his disputation. This provides a summary of his argument: he has arranged his case. He builds on this by affirming he is right and asserting no one can successfully refute him (13:18-19). His defense of his status as wise and as one who rightly protests is certain.

Tropes to the Friends. Job uses a number of tropes in his disputation to heighten the rhetorical effect of his argument. To defend his wisdom against accusations that he misdiagnoses the cause of his suffering, Job

---

218. Job's use of the cohortative form in 13:13, following the imperative demanding silence, indicates Job's resolve; cf. 9:35–10:1.

reprises the image of injustice from the previous speech in 12:6 to stress that God acts unjustly: God preserves those who destroy and agitate.[219] The image of security in 12:6 not only reinforces the injustice, but also responds directly to Zophar's contention that it is the repentant and humble that experience security (cf. 11:18), as noted above. Job's hymn also incorporates images of injustice in 12:16 by portraying the divine preservation of the one who errs and the one who misleads. This image is imbedded in the images of divine destruction in 12:13-25. God destroys without the possibility of rebuilding and closes without the possibility of opening (12:14); God restrains water to create drought and sends deluges to destroy the earth (12:15); God humiliates and overturns leaders and nations (12:17-25; cf. 9:22-24). Job also reapplies the trope of darkness, though this time in a different way. The images of darkness in 12:22 relate to divine destructive actions rather than to Job's impending death (cf. 10:21-22).

Job also defends his wisdom and the appropriateness of his approach with animal images and images from the natural world in 12:7-8, listing beasts, birds, the earth, and fish as sources of wisdom. These images from nature are personified in that they are portrayed as being able to teach (ירה), declare (נגד), and recount (ספר). This combination of animal images and personification culminates in the personification of the hand of Yahweh in 12:9, which acts unjustly in creation, and, by implication, Job's life. Job defends his personal epistemology with the trope of taste in 12:11;[220] the body trope relates to the trope of taste clearly in 12:11 with the parallelism of the ear (אֹזֶן) and palate (חֵךְ). The body trope communicates the same certainty in 13:1, where אֹזֶן is repeated and placed in parallel with Job's eyes (עֵינִי). Job also uses images of friend attack to characterize the friends. According to Job, the friends' actions and words are unethical because of their mockery, falsehood, and platitudinous nature (see 12:4; 13:4, 12).

Job returns to the litigation metaphor from the previous speech. The litigation trope emerges in 13:3 (with יכח), 6 (with תּוֹכַחַת), and 17-19 (with אַחֲוֶה, מִשְׁפָּט, צדק, and רִיב) (Seow 2013: 640). In the previous

---

219. That images of injustice are used in argumentation (i.e., rhetorically) and do not reflect Job's actual beliefs is seen in 13:10, when Job communicates his conviction that God will justly reprimand the friends for their unethical demonstration of favoritism. The images of injustice reflect Job's rhetorical attempt to refute half-truths uttered by the friends.

220. As Seow notes (2013: 625; cf. 642), Job rejects their arguments, having heard them and tasted them.

speech, Job dismissed the strictly forensic litigation trope introduced by Bildad in Job 8 as flawed. Here Job re-appropriates the litigation trope as a point of comparison for his protest prayer, reframing the metaphor. Job sees himself as arguing with God (see 13:3, 15). These are the only two occurrences in the MT of יכח used with the preposition אֶל. In Job 13:3, it is in parallel with דבר אֶל, which informs how to understand יכח אֶל. The latter means "to argue with" (*HALOT*, 410), and given the object of the preposition אֶל (in parallel with שַׁדַּי), it places the argumentation in the context of prayer. The implications of this are profound for how one understands the litigation trope in this context, namely, that it is a metaphor employed to elucidate the kind of protest prayer Job intends. *He is arguing with God.* This relates well to what complaint, by its nature, is (Morrow 2006a: 1–2). Job acknowledges the risks involved in such a move, as is evident by the gruesome trope of death and savage animal imagery in 13:14 (Seow 2013: 646). But speak out he will (13:13).

Tropes to God. Job's other goal in this fourth speech relates to his exigency with God, namely, his continued suffering. To modify this exigency Job uses numerous tropes to make his rhetoric vivid and to move God to act; every clause in 13:20–14:22 employs a trope that draws attention to Job's goal or his suffering.

Job's goal emerges from the outset when he uses imagery of hiddenness in 13:20 (cf. 13:24). His goal is also evident in what he hopes for in 14:14 as he uses imagery of renewal in parallel with a term for struggle (חֲלִיפָה // צָבָא). Together his experience of divine hiddenness and a hope for renewal point to Job's desire for restoration and the alleviation of his suffering.

Job's suffering is portrayed through a number of tropes. From the beginning of his address to God Job uses divine attack imagery. In 13:20-21a the negated jussive and the imperative for God to cease action and to remove his hands from Job implies attack, especially in parallel with another negated jussive in 13:21b not to allow God's wrath to terrify Job. The attack imagery emerges to the forefront of Job's complaint in 13:24-27. In 13:24 divine attack emerges in the word "enemy" (אוֹיֵב), and continues in 13:25 as Job portrays God's attack as a pursuit of worthless chaff or a dried leaf. In 13:26 Job portrays God inscribing bitterness on him and overwhelming him by causing him to inherit the consequences of youthful iniquities. God's attack is portrayed in the protest prayer as he shackles Job (13:27). Job's self-portrayal as nothing is starkly juxtaposed to God's attack, making God look like a overpowering, brutish bully.[221]

---

221. So also Clines (1989: 320): God is depicted here as "preposterous and grotesque."

Job connects a series of tropes together as he closes his speech, all of which relate to divine attack. In 14:18-19 Job brings mountain and rock imagery together with water imagery to portray the destructive, eroding power of water, and explicitly applies this imagery to God's actions toward mankind: he destroys hope. It is notable that the nature imagery moves from plants (weak) to mountains and rocks (strong) over the course of the poem (Habel 1985: 237). This escalation highlights Job's perceived overpowering attack when Job states baldly in 14:19: "but the hope of mankind you cause to perish." Seow (2013: 679) notes that these images portray a passage of time, and the duration of God's attack illuminates the magnitude of Job's perceived suffering. In the end, Job is overcome by God's power, beaten to dust, much as water erodes a rock over time. Job summarizes God's attack by linking himself with humanity broadly, articulating that he has been overpowered and altered by God (14:20).[222] These attack images portray God's destructive power.[223] Relatedly, Job portrays God as acting unjustly in 14:21. As provocative tropes, these images combine to depict the cause and extent of Job's suffering in an attempt to move God to respond to his prayer.

The divine attack imagery in 13:27 is also related to divine vigilance.[224] God's shackling of Job includes unceasing surveillance. These images recall similar images in 3:23 and 7:12-21, where God hedges Job in and scrutinizes his every move. In 14:5-6 Job first applies divine vigilance to mankind generally, and then exhorts God to turn away, showing that Job seeks to motivate God to cease such surveillance. This coheres with Job's rhetorical goal in relation to God, and is confirmed by the opposite sense of this image in Job's wish in 14:16. Thus, the trope of divine vigilance is used in two different, but integrated, ways. It portrays God in a negative

---

222. Job 14:20 corresponds to the overpowering imagery of 13:25-26. The adverbial לָנֶצַח heightens the rhetoric by portraying the relentless nature of God's destructive acts. The participle מְשַׁנֶּה in the third clause of the verse modifies וַתְּשַׁלְּחֵהוּ by indicating the circumstances of the main verb: "having changed his face, you send him away." Fohrer (1963: 260) interprets this verse to indicate rigor mortis, thus bringing in death imagery as well.

223. The destructive nature of relentlessly pounding water also brings to mind Ps. 88:17-18 [16-17] as the psalmist accuses God of surrounding him with waves, though an allusion is difficult to establish.

224. The syntax and parallelism of 13:27 emphasize the significance of this verse in Job's complaint. It is a tricolon, setting it apart from the rest of the section; it is also chiastically arranged with verbs in the first and last position related to feet (רַגְלַי), highlighting the middle colon—"and you guard all my paths" (וְתִשְׁמוֹר כָּל־אָרְחוֹתָי)—and the trope of divine vigilance.

light as a relentless spy, as well as being used in Job's expressed hope for when this vigilance will no longer happen.

Contrasting use of the same trope in this speech is also found in the creator imagery used in 13:21 and 14:15 and the sin imagery in 13:23, 26, and 14:16-17. God as creator is exhorted to remove his hands from Job in 13:21, while in 14:15 Job expresses in his wish that God as creator would desire Job. Job thinks he is being punished for hypothetical sins, as articulated in 13:23 and 13:26. Job's wish, however, is to have these sins sealed and erased to bring about restoration in his relationship with God (14:16-17).

Job portrays his suffering in other ways. He uses images of frailty, ephemerality, hardship, and inconsequentiality in 13:25, 28, 14:1-2, 14, and 22. Job links his lot with the lot of humanity by using the word רֹגֶז in 14:1 (cf. 3:17, 26); Job is sated (שׂבע) with רֹגֶז. Elsewhere Job had described himself as sated with tossing (7:4), bitterness (9:18), and shame (10:15). He is brimming over with turmoil. He uses imagery of Sheol in 14:13 and death in 14:14 to highlight the extent of his suffering.[225] In 14:22 Job concludes this speech with references to his pain (כאב) and mourning (אבל). Given the futility of his current relationship with God—where his hope for relief is thwarted by God's attack, injustice, and surveillance—Job returns to lament. Job's dramatic portrayal of his suffering also provides the grounds upon which his complaints are based. Job uses the threat of death and mourning again to motivate God to act on his behalf. He desires rest and uses these vivid and intricate images to motivate God to act.

To stress this point Job uses an extended, complex trope of a tree in 14:7-12.[226] The image of a cut-down tree is compared to the death of a person. The former will sprout anew with the return of water and thus has hope; the latter will not return from sleep and thus has no hope. The euphemism of sleep is attention-grabbing here since מות is applied to the stem of the tree in 14:8. For the tree, whose expiration is not permanent, it is described as death. Yet, for the person, whose expiration is permanent, it is described using sleep terms: שׁכב and שֵׁנָה (note קיץ and עוּר). It is also worth noting that the water imagery in 14:9 is a renewing force, whereas water elsewhere in this speech is a destructive force (see 14:11, 19). The application of such a provocative metaphor articulates Job's lack

---

225. The imagery of death in 14:14 is through the euphemism of sleep imagery.
226. There is also water and death imagery as well as personification used in this trope. See Newsom 1996: 441.

of hope and seems to be intended to arrest God's attention. It portrays his helplessness in the face of his suffering. When juxtaposed with his wish in 14:13-17, its effect is to move God to act on Job's behalf—to grant Job's wish for renewal and rest.

The litigation metaphor plays a role in Job's address to God as well. In 13:22-23 the images of call and response and the demand to know his alleged sins (i.e., his crimes) portrays Job as one who is in litigation (Chin 1994: 96–7). But the metaphor prefaces the complaint in 13:24-27, highlighting its rhetorical intention. Although he avoids articulating outright God's injustice, Job portrays God as being unjust (101).[227] In the context of a complaint with the legal metaphor providing the background, Job emphasizes that God is acting in a way that does not cohere with what Job thinks he knows. Job's belief in God's justice is what allows the rhetoric to have its effect. The effect is an implicit appeal for relief, for God to act on Job's behalf. This rhetorical intention is clarified in 14:3 as Job uses the metaphor again. Since God has seen the lot of humanity (14:3a), it should be no problem for the two of them to engage one another in judgment (14:3b). This is Job's expressed hope in 14:15, where the legal metaphor again works to stress Job's goal: there will be a renewed engagement; God will no longer be hidden.

Direct Address to God. While Job did not address God explicitly in Job 3 (though his discourse is intended for God, as the delayed disambiguation makes clear), Job has addressed God in both his second and third speeches. In his fourth speech, beginning with 13:20, Job again addresses God directly.[228] Job's initial address is a negated jussive in 13:20 as he implores God to stop two things in order to establish some common ground. The parallel line indicates the desired result: Job will no longer be hidden from God. The imperatives that follow reveal Job's goals in his protest prayer. He desires relief from God's attack, as evidenced by the imperative to "remove your hands far from me" (כַּפְּךָ מֵעָלַי הַרְחַק) and not

---

227. Chin notes that this part of the speech is a "masterpiece of insinuation." Her treatment of the images in this movement cogently demonstrates that the negative portrayal of God justifies Job's protest prayer. But the use of this imagery also implies a petition for change.

228. There are forty-two 2ms forms in 13:20–14:22. Clines (1989: 316) counts thirty-nine, but does not list them. On the emendation of the second imperative in 14:6, see n. 191 above. Job also uses thirty-three 1cs forms, reflecting the personal nature of his suffering.

to allow "your wrath to terrify me" (וְאֵמָתְךָ אַל־תְּבַעֲתַנִּי). Job also desires an open dialogue, a restoration of the relationship between himself and God, as seen in the imperatives of "call" (וּקְרָא) and "respond to me" (וַהֲשִׁיבֵנִי) in 13:22. Job also demands that God make known to Job the reasons for God's negative actions toward him in 13:23 (הֹדִיעֵנִי).[229] The final two volitional forms in 14:6 confirm that Job is seeking relief and restoration. Job issues two imperatives: "turn away" (שְׁעֵה) and "cease" (חֲדָל). Job addresses God and uses bold command and prohibitive forms in order to move God to act.

But the direct address is not merely related to explicit petitions. The remainder of the direct address forms are more subtle rhetorically, as they combine with other rhetorical strategies. But the direct address sets these strategies in an important framework: Job is boldly addressing God, in prayer, and seeking to influence God's actions directly. Job describes directly to God his attack, vigilance, and injustice in 13:24, 25, 26, 27; 14:19, 20. The most provocative of these verbal forms, however, is Job's bold statement to God that "you cause the hope of mankind to perish" (וְתִקְוַת אֱנוֹשׁ הֶאֱבַדְתָּ). The use of אבד and תִּקְוָה in such close proximity is noteworthy here in light of Zophar's conclusion that the only hope for the wicked is expiration (11:20). This lexical repetition, though directed at God, also is a sharp rebuttal of Zophar's position. This coheres with the analysis of Job's disputation with lexical repetition discussed above. The verb stresses God's unjust and destructive actions. Job's provocative address to God reaches its crescendo here in this speech. Taken together with the explicit calls for relief, these accusations in direct address imply a petition for God to cease treating Job like this.

That Job intends to move God to act becomes clear by how Job addresses God in 14:13-17. The rhetoric of the wish is explored more fully below, but the verbal forms in this section point toward a renewed relationship, as is evident from Job's expressed desire for being hidden from God's anger and being remembered (14:13), for renewed communication (14:15a-b), for revitalized affection (14:15c), and for a different approach to Job's "sin" (14:16-17). The imperatives and accusations that fill up this movement of Job's fourth speech are interrelated with this wish, as Job seeks to make this seemingly impossible wish a reality.

---

229. Referring to the series of exhortations in 13:20-23, Westermann (1981b: 54) notes that the "extensive introduction to this preliminary inquiry of God shows that 13:23-27 is meant to be particularly emphasized." In other words, these petitions emphasize the complaint proper in 13:23-27.

Rhetorical Questions to God. Job's address to God in 13:20–14:22 includes rhetorical questions that have the same effect of moving God to act on his behalf. Job asks six questions, five of which are rhetorical. His first question in 13:23a, while not a rhetorical question, initiates a series of three questions through 13:25.[230] He reproaches God in each of these questions, making clear his position that he has not sinned and therefore does not deserve this kind of treatment in which God hides himself and treats Job as an enemy (13:23-24) (Clines 1989: 319). It is noteworthy that Job is the only one in the dialogue to use the interrogative לָמָה (highlighting the complaint-nature of his speech), and that it occurs in this first cycle in each speech (3:11, 20; 7:20; 9:29; 10:18).[231] In each case this question is directed at God. The rhetorical question of 13:25 increases the reproachful tone by combining the rhetorical question with the divine attack imagery. As noted above, the juxtaposition of Job's self-portrayal as something as insignificant as a dry leaf or chaff with God's relentless pursuit creates a stark contrast, which should have the effect of motivating God to act on Job's behalf. In other words, Job is asserting through the question: "Stop pursuing me and treating me like this; this is not who I know you to be." These questions are complaints that imply petition for relief and restoration.

The rhetorical question in 14:4 is also reproachful. This is one of two occasions in the book in which a speaker answers his own rhetorical question (Magary 2005: 289–90). This is not about sinfulness but about opposites (Seow 2013: 673). Job portrays God and himself in antithetical terms to reproach God to move him to act in accordance with what Job stated in 14:3, namely, to look upon his affliction and respond to Job's complaint. Job heightens the effect of the rhetoric when he disambiguates the answer to the question.

The final two rhetorical questions in 14:10 and 14:14 both work together to assert Job's perceived lack of hope. Working with the trope of the tree, the question וְאַיּוֹ asserts that when a man dies he is in Sheol. The implication is that he is of no use to God (cf. Ps. 88:11-13 [10-12]), and the effect is to motivate God to act by the urgency of the situation.[232] The question in 14:14, הֲיִחְיֶה, also implies finality in death and establishes an urgency for God to act in accordance with Job's expressed wish in 14:13-17.

---

230. Magary (2005: 288) identifies this question as one of the twenty-three information-seeking questions in the dialogue, which is confirmed by the immediately following imperative in 13:23b.

231. See also 3:16, 23, where the interrogative is gapped.

232. See Hartley 1988: 234, who points out that this question emphasizes finality.

Emphatic Statements to God. As in his address to his friends, Job uses particles to emphasize salient statements in his address to God.²³³ He bookends his address to God with an inclusio of the particle אָז in 13:20 and 14:22. More than demarcating this as a unit, this inclusio draws attention to Job's desired ends: given his pain and his suffering, he desires God to act. The negated jussive in 13:20 highlights his desired action, while the description of his suffering and mourning establishes urgency for God's actions. To be sure, 14:22 is in the third person rather than the first, but this fits poetically with the movement of all of Job 14, which began with a description of the suffering of humanity. The seamless way in which Job moves from this description of all of humanity to his own suffering reveals he includes himself in humanity's experience. This is confirmed by the use of אָז in 13:20b, which provides a clue as to Job's desired result: that God would no longer be hidden. By introducing and closing his address to God with such clear statements using these particles, Job sets a context in which to understand his protest prayer.

Job also uses אַף in 14:3 to make an emphatic statement.²³⁴ Given the ephemerality of human life, Job uses the particle to draw attention to the tension between the fact that God has seen human suffering, and yet he still does nothing. Job's use of this particle, combined tropes of vigilance and litigation, creates urgency for and illuminates the goal of Job's complaint. This statement implies a petition. God has witnessed the turmoil and frailty of human life, including Job's, and should be willing to act to bring relief.

The final particle Job uses in 13:20–14:22 is אוּלָם in 14:18. This particle sets off the final movement of his address to God from the preceding wish, creating a stark contrast between what he hopes for (his rhetorical goal) and his perceived reality. This statement combines the destructive imagery with the provocative accusation discussed above that "the hope of mankind [God causes] to perish." As noted above, this accusation also implies a petition.

---

233. Aside from the particles noted here, Job's use of כִּי is significant in this speech. Though כִּי does not mark an emphatic statement, Job uses it three times to provide the basis for his complaint. Cf. 13:26-27; 14:7, 16.

234. Clines (1989: 277), Hartley (1988: 229, 231), and a number of translations take this as introducing a question, but this seems unlikely (see, e.g., ESV, NIV11, JPS). Waltke and O'Connor suggest that אַף often "[serves] as a correlative, lining up the situation of its clause with that of the previous clause" (WO §39.3.4d), which seems to fit exactly how it functions in 14:3. Even if this is understood as a rhetorical question, the particle emphasizes the illocution outlined here.

Allusion. There may be allusion in Job's rhetorical question of 13:25. The words עָלֶה ("leaf") and נדף ("to drive away") both occur in Ps. 1:3-4. These are the only two passages in which עָלֶה occurs with a word for chaff (קַשׁ or מֹץ). With נדף only occurring nine times, a case can be made for an allusion (Kynes 2012: 154).[235] Once again Job draws attention to the dissonance between what he experiences and what the tradition teaches (153–4). In accordance with other allusions, Job uses the psalm against God: Job is righteous and so should be like a tree planted by water, but is, instead, blown about and treated as an enemy. The effect is to show God that he is acting in opposition to what other biblical traditions affirm; the illocution is an implied petition for relief. This analysis corresponds to the analysis above regarding the rhetorical question and the divine attack imagery of 13:25.[236]

Wish. Job also uses a wish in his rhetoric as he addresses God in prayer. The wish, 14:13-17, is marked by מִי יִתֵּן, which is used as a fixed expression to articulate desire nine times in the book, with eight of these nine occurrences expressed by Job. Of these eight occurrences, six convey Job's craving for God's intervention (Magary 2005: 286).[237] This illuminates the relationship between Job's wish and what he is seeking in his address to God. The wish in 14:13-17 reveals Job's hoped-for rhetorical goal, the end toward which his rhetoric is intended. In the context of the prayer, it should illuminate for God what Job desires from him (so also Wilson 2015: 89–90).

The goal of Job's words is to induce restoration and alleviation of his suffering. There are four reasons for this conclusion. First, Job addresses God directly by expressing his goal of being hidden from God's anger until it abates (תַּסְתִּירֵנִי עַד־שׁוּב אַפֶּךָ). Job portrays God's anger as the reason for his suffering, and if he can be hidden from this anger, he will experience a reprieve. Second, and related, Job desires that God would remember him (וְתִזְכְּרֵנִי). This points to Job's hope of restoration, a return to the kind of relationship Job previously experienced with God. This is confirmed by what Job expresses in 14:15, where he reveals what this relationship should be: an open communication between the two of them,

---

235. Though the allusion here is relatively weak, its likelihood is increased by the other allusions to this psalm (see the discussion on 10:3 above).

236. Job may also be alluding to Ps. 39 again in 13:28 and 14:6. See Kynes 2012: 136–7. With this allusion Job again links himself with the complaining psalmist and implies a petition for God to act; Job is "motivated by an underlying hope that his psalmic allusions will draw God out of hiding to act on his behalf" (137).

237. Magary cites only five. Cf. 6:8; 14:14; 19:23; 23:3; 29:2; 31:35.

a relationship where God desires the work of his hands (לְמַעֲשֵׂה יָדֶיךָ תִכְסֹף). Third, Job expresses his desire for his sin to be erased—sealed and smeared (14:16-17). Job is seeking a complete reversal of the relational dynamic between himself and God as he currently experiences it (13:23); divine vigilance would not lead to relentless surveillance of Job's sin (14:16). The final reason relates to 14:14. The three clauses that make up 14:14 are the only clauses not governed by the מִי יִתֵּן of 14:13 in this section.[238] Job links his wish with the tree trope of 14:7-12 through the finality of death (14:14a). But in the midst of this wish, Job expresses his conviction in 14:14b-c: "all the days of my hardship I will hope until my renewal comes" (כָּל־יְמֵי צְבָאִי אֲיַחֵל עַד־בּוֹא חֲלִיפָתִי).[239] This conviction echoes Job's faith in 13:15-16. In 14:14 Job expresses his faith in God to act and bring about renewal (חֲלִיפָה). This word indicates clearly that Job's desire is the alleviation of his suffering and a restoration to his previous life. All of the rhetorical strategies in Job's address to God in 13:20–14:22 need to be read in the context of Job's wish, since it expresses most clearly his rhetorical goal.

Summary of Job 12–14

The analysis of Job's fourth speech reveals that Job continues to face two exigencies in light of the friends' ongoing criticism of his speech and his continued suffering. To address these exigencies, Job first addresses the friends, using a number of strategies to dispute their contention that Job's speech indicates he is unwise, which arises most specifically in Zophar's speech in Job 11 (see also Job 4–5). These include: lexical repetition, direct address, tonality, characterization, rhetorical questions, hymn, allusion, emphatic statements, and tropes. Seow writes (2013: 652–3):

> [Job's] judgment of his friends is harsh. He sees them offering neither consolation nor counsel but deception or, worse, theological distortions. For Job, theology that does not take the plight of human beings in suffering with adequate seriousness is tantamount to unfaith. The miscreance of the friends is evident in their secret bias in favor of God and against sufferers. Such a stance…is in fact a lack of faith… They speak *about* God, but Job insists on speaking truthfully to God. Indeed, it is in this forthright speaking that one has victory (*yəšûʿâ*).

---

238. The presence of אִם in 14:14 takes this clause out of the wish context governed by מִי יִתֵּן.

239. On צְבָא, see 7:1 and 10:17. This word is a significant word for Job's description of his suffering.

Job's arguments expose the bankruptcy of their theology and advice.

Job closes the first cycle by escalating his rhetoric toward his friends, becoming more critical of them in the defense of his protest prayer. While Job had been critical of his friends in 6:14-30, he also pleaded with them to consider him (6:27-29). The criticisms in this speech are clear accusations of mistreatment, not mediated through the complex trope of a deceptive wadi. Their pious platitudes do more harm than good; Job's complaint is justified in light of his innocent suffering. This alters the rhetorical situation when the second cycle begins with Eliphaz's speech in Job 15.

Job then turns to address God, also employing a number of strategies to move God to act on his behalf: tropes, direct address, rhetorical questions, emphatic statements, allusion, and wish. Through these strategies Job hopes to secure a restored relationship. His suffering, and God's persistent silence in the midst of that suffering, has led Job to protest in prayer as a way of seeking the alleviation of his suffering and obtaining that restored relationship. Job's descriptions of divine attack, vigilance, and injustice serve to appeal to God, especially in the context of the other petitions and wish.

Summary of the First Speech Cycle

Each speech in the first cycle negotiates speech about God and to God. Job opens the cycle in Job 3 with his complaint implicitly addressed to God. The literary rhetorical situation, the forms, and, especially, the strategy of delayed disambiguation that reveals an intentional lexical and structural shaping indicate Job's audience is God. The entire speech is protest prayer as Job seeks to move God to alleviate his suffering. This God-talk offended the friends, as Eliphaz (Job 4–5), Bildad (Job 8), and Zophar (Job 11) each respond to Job with major concerns regarding the ethics of such God-talk. Their disputation over the propriety of his discourse creates a new exigency which Job must address, namely, the defense of his protest prayer. In Job's second (Job 6–7), third (Job 9–10), and fourth (Job 12–14) speeches, Job addresses this exigency with a disputation of his own. The ethics of Job's verbal expression is the primary issue under debate in Job 4–14. Notably, however, each one of these speeches also contains explicit address to God—more protest prayer. This address to God always comes after an initial disputation and makes up a second movement in each of the final three speeches of the first cycle (Patrick 1979: 268–82). In other words, *in the first cycle Job is either protesting in prayer (talk to God) or defending his protest prayer to his friends (talk about God)*.

This is confirmed by Job's particular use of forms (i.e., genres). A statistical tabulation of the forms and the number of clauses in which Job is addressing either the friends, God, or both simultaneously confirms the equal emphasis on protest prayer and disputation. In the first cycle, the number of clauses comprising protest prayer (complaint, lament, imprecation, petition, wish, and motive clauses) in the first cycle is 313 out of 562. In other words, more than half of this speech cycle is protest prayer. As for disputation, including other forms put to use with disputation, there are 320 clauses, out of 562 in the entire cycle. There are 249 clauses in which Job is addressing the friends, 242 clauses in which he is addressing God in prayer, and seventy-one clauses in which he is addressing both simultaneously. These seventy-one clauses are intended primarily for the friends, with God as the intended secondary audience. These seventy-one clauses are also used in disputation, accounting for the overlap in numbers. Overall, in the first speech cycle Job addresses God 43% of the time, the friends 44% of the time, and both of them together 13% of the time.

One pregnant observation from this first speech cycle relates to Job's use of verbal modes. Job uses twelve cohortatives in the first speech cycle (6:10; 7:11 [2×]; 9:14, 27 [3×], 35; 10:1 [2×], 20; 13:13). Each one of these cohortatives reflects Job's resolve to protest prayer.[240] Only the cohortative of 7:11 is in the midst of protest prayer; all other occurrences are directed at the friends as Job determines to continue to engage in his chosen method of prayer. Job's use of other volitional moods is also notable. Job uses twelve imperatives in protest prayer, coupled with twenty-six jussives.[241] Fifteen of these thirty-eight verbal forms are addressed specifically to God, asking him variously to remember or look upon Job in his suffering (7:7, 16; 10:9, 15), cease from certain actions (10:2, 20 [2×]; 13:20, 21 [2×]; 14:6), interact with him in dialogue (13:22 [2×]), or make known his sin (10:2; 13:23). This confirms Job's prayer is for relief and a restored relationship with God, intended to move God to act on his behalf. Job's use of petition is a significant part of his prayer, while Job's statements of resolve are seminal in his disputation, and relate primarily to protest prayer.

---

240. דבר/דָּבָר occur in five of these (7:11; 9:14, 35; 10:1; 13:13), while שִׂיחַ/שִׂיחַ occur in three others (7:11; 9:27; 10:1).

241. For the imperatives, see 7:7, 16; 10:2, 9, 15, 20 (2×); 13:21, 22 (2×), 23; 14:6. For the jussives, see 3:3, 4 (3×), 5 (3×), 6 (3×), 7 (2×), 8, 9 (3×); 9:33, 34 (2×); 10:2, 16, 17; 13:20, 21.

Looking more specifically at Job's God-talk, there are 128 clauses in which Job talks about God, referring to God in the third person. Thirteen of these 128 instances of talk about God occur in protest prayer in the first cycle.[242] In the other 115 clauses Job's talk about God tends toward portraying God in a negative light, though not exclusively. Job portrays divine attack (6:4, 13; 9:17-18; 12:9), divine destruction (9:5-7; 12:14-15, 17-25), divine injustice (9:12, 20, 22-24; 12:6, 9), divine absence (9:11), and unflinching divine anger (9:13). Job's description of God's wisdom and power is also pejorative in his rhetoric (9:8-10, 19; 12:10, 13, 16). He talks about God as he asserts his inability to engage God because of divine absence and divine power (9:2-4, 14-16). Yet he balances this with a commitment to protest prayer (13:3). Furthermore, he balances his emphasis on divine injustice with instruction about God's justice (13:7-11). Moreover, Job reveals his faith and hope in God in his talk about God in the declaration in 13:15-16.

While the negative portrayal of God in Job's talk about God is more prominent than his positive portrayal in this first cycle, it is noteworthy how significant this God-talk is in Job's disputatious rhetoric. The above summary reveals that Job uses this God-talk to defend his protest prayer: God has attacked him (e.g., 6:4, 13), and is acting unjustly (e.g., 12:9), so Job must protest in prayer (e.g., 13:3). Job not only portrays this injustice and destruction personally, but also globally (e.g., 9:22-24; 12:13-25). The imagery of divine injustice, divine destruction, and divine absence occur almost exclusively in Job's address to the friends.

As for Job's talk to God, there is also a variation in what Job says. Job accuses God of attack (3:23; 7:12, 20; 9:30-31; 10:8, 10-13, 16-17; 13:24-27; 14:19), absence (13:24), hyper-vigilance (3:23; 7:17-19), and injustice (9:28-29; 10:2-7, 14; 13:23; 14:3-4). Job reinforces this protest prayer with descriptions of his suffering (3:20; 7:1-6, 8-10, 15-16, 21; 9:25-26, 29; 10:18-19, 21-22; 13:28; 14:1-2, 5-12, 18, 20-22).

There are a few tropes that are either exclusively or almost exclusively used in Job's address to God. These tropes include imagery of divine attack, imagery of divine vigilance, death imagery, Sheol imagery, light and dark imagery, mythic imagery, imagery of rest and ease, images of suffering, and sin imagery. The two most frequent tropes Job uses in his talk to God are suffering imagery and divine attack imagery. These two tropes occur in every speech in the first cycle. Job describes his life as without rest (3:26; 7:4, 13-14), as full of turmoil (3:20, 26; 7:3; 14:1), affliction (10:15), bitterness (3:20; 7:11), distress (7:11), and fear (3:25;

---

242. See 3:4, 10 (2×), 20, 23 (2×); 6:8, 9 (4×); 9:34 (2×).

9:28). Noting the frailty of human life (10:9; 13:28–14:1), Job describes life as arduous (7:1-2; 9:29; 14:14). He articulates emotional suffering (3:21-22; 7:15-16; 10:15; 14:22), and describes his suffering in prolonged terms (7:1-4). The most frequent trope as it relates to Job's suffering is the ephemeral nature of life (7:6-10, 16; 9:25-26; 10:9, 20-21; 14:1-2, 7-12). Together, these tropes point to Job's current condition. Through hyperbole and vividness, this image-laden language is intended to move God to act, implying a petition for relief.

The divine attack imagery works the same way, vividly and provocatively attributing this suffering to God. The divine attack occurs in protest prayer without direct address in 3:23 and 6:9. The former is the climax of Job's opening complaint; the latter is a part of Job's wish as he seeks relief, portraying God as letting loose his hand and finishing Job off to give him the rest he desperately seeks. Both of these imply petitions for relief. Other statements imply attack, often occurring with imperatives or negated jussives (see 7:4, 16; 9:34; 10:20; 13:20-21; 14:6). Job portrays God's attack in numerous ways in direct accusation, describing mythological imagery (7:12), nightmares (7:14), relentless vigilance (7:17-21), and physical harm (9:31; 10:3, 8, 13, 16, 17; 13:24-27; 14:19-20). As noted in the investigation of the rhetoric above, the use of this trope implies a petition for relief, a petition made explicit in the clauses in which a volitional form implies attack.

The imagery for death and Sheol also occurs in each of the four speeches. The wish for death in Job's first two speeches changes in the third and fourth speeches. In the former speeches, death is a place of rest, something Job desperately desires and the goal toward which his rhetoric in talk to God is directed. In the latter two speeches of the first cycle, Job uses the death imagery in his complaint, accusing God of mistreatment (10:18-19) and to portray the finality of death (14:8, 12, 14). These occurrences of the death imagery also imply a petition, employed rhetorically to heighten the urgency of Job's complaint (cf. 10:20-22). These tropes relate closely to the trope of rest (cf. 3:13-15, 17-19). The significance of the wish in 14:13-17 emerges in light of its placement at the end of the first cycle. Balancing the imprecation and the imagery of rest from Job 3, the inclusio highlights the ultimate goal of Job's protest prayer throughout the first cycle. This comports with protest prayer in general, as Job describes his suffering, uses death or near-death images to describe his condition, and accuses God of inappropriate action.[243] As noted

---

243. See Broyles 1989: 55–131, esp. 84–95 on death imagery and the accusations of God's active participation in the suffering in individual laments documented on pp. 116–20.

throughout this chapter, Job uses this imagery as a rhetorical strategy to move God to act. It is not surprising that Job also uses the imagery of rest and ease exclusively in his talk to God. This reveals his rhetorical goal: relief and restoration.[244]

In sum, facing two exigencies in this first cycle, Job protests in prayer to inspire God to act, and disputes with the friends to defend his protest prayer against their arguments and advice. As this discussion elucidates, Job's talk about God in his disputation has certain emphases (e.g., divine injustice and destruction), while Job's talk to God reveals other foci (e.g., divine attack and his suffering), bringing clarity to how Job argues and how he prays.

---

244. Furthermore, the illocution of every petition and wish clause is the relief from Job's suffering (Job 3:3-9 [cf. 3:13-15, 17-19, 24-26]; 6:8-10; 7:7, 16; 9:33-34; 10:2, 9, 15, 20; 13:20-21, 22-23; 14:6, 13-17).

Chapter 4

"Why Do You Pursue Me Like God?": Job's Internal Rhetoric in the Second Speech Cycle (Job 15–21)

In the second speech cycle, the rhetorical situation changes. With Job having rejected his friends as comforters by characterizing them as liars and as worthless (13:4), by intentionally choosing to maintain his current mode of discourse (i.e., one of protest prayer) (13:3), and by calling for their silence (13:5), the friends must change their strategy. They each apply the *topos* of the fate of the wicked in their speech to move Job from his dangerous and theology-threatening position (Westermann 1981b: 81). They seek to have Job see himself as the wicked person whose end is near and certain. Job's responses in this second cycle take into account their rhetorical strategy. He disputes their utilization of the *topos* as it relates to him in his fifth and sixth speeches, while in the seventh speech he refutes their arguments generally.

"To God My Eye Leaks":
The Rhetoric of Job's Fifth Speech (Job 16–17)

Introduction

Eliphaz begins the second cycle by arguing that Job's words are dangerous and destructive, both in terms of theology and praxis. He applies to Job the *topos* of the fate of the wicked after rebuking Job for his verbal expression, hoping to persuade Job to cease his impious discourse. In his fifth speech, Job does two things. First, he disputes the applicability of the *topos*; Job is suffering, he admits, but innocently, not in accordance with the retribution theology that undergirds Eliphaz's argument. Second, Job complains to God.

The Literary Rhetorical Situation of Job 16–17

When Job closes his disputation in the first cycle by characterizing his friends as liars and as worthless, calling for their silence, and reaffirming his commitment to protest prayer, the rhetorical situation for the friends changes (Yu 2011: 287). They must modify their rhetoric if they are to persuade Job to cease speaking unethically. Eliphaz's speech in Job 15 provides a template for the other comforters to follow.

Eliphaz's speech in Job 15 is one of the clearest instances in the dialogue of the friends' discomfort with Job's words (Habel 1985: 252; Hartley 1988: 245; Clines 1989: 247, 351, 366; Good 1990: 242; Newsom 1996: 449; Yu 2011: 291; Seow 2013: 708–9). Eliphaz clearly finds Job's words unethical. They are worthless and dangerous (15:2; cf. 8:2),[1] useless and unprofitable (15:3), theologically problematic and leading to poor religion (15:4), crafty (15:5), and self-condemning (15:6; cf. 9:20). Eliphaz's use of שִׂיחָה in 15:4 is notable. This is a variation of שִׂיחַ, which Job has employed to describe his own protest prayer (see 7:11 for the verb, and 7:13, 9:27, 10:1 for the noun; cf. 21:4 and 23:2). Job's protest prayer is hindering others from meditation before God, according to Eliphaz. All of this points towards Job's lack of wisdom (15:7-11). Job's words demonstrate his anger toward God (15:12-13; cf. v. 25), which will lead him ultimately to ruin (15:30). To modify Job's unethical approach, Eliphaz employs two theological truths: (1) mankind is inherently sinful, so Job's suffering cannot be innocent (15:14-16; cf. 4:17-21), and (2) retribution for the wicked person, with whom Eliphaz links Job by implication, is certain (15:20-35) (Habel 1985: 251–2). The two major movements of his speech work together to persuade Job to drop his protest prayer by disputing the ethics of his verbal expression (vv. 2-16) and portraying what will happen if he does not heed his advice (vv. 17-35). The implication is that Job needs to repent rather than protest in prayer, since his suffering is rooted in sin.[2]

This unyielding criticism of Job's words and the intentional association of Job with the wicked person changes the rhetorical situation for Job. While in the first cycle, Job had to defend his words to the friends, the use of the *topos* of the fate of the wicked forces Job to defend himself against this charge. Job must consider a new argument and offer new arguments in response. This changes his exigency, and thus changes Job's

---

1. On the metaphor of "wind" and the "east wind," see Seow 2013: 698–9; Hawley 2018: 100–101.
2. See Hartley 1988: 242, who draws out the implication of repentance in the friends' use of the *topos* of the fate of the wicked.

purpose in argumentation. He must now defend his innocence, though this is intimately related to a defense of his protest prayer in that it is the innocent sufferer who should protest rather than repent. Job is still suffering, so his exigency as it relates to God remains. Job's primary exigency is, however, with his companions, and they become the primary addressees. The introduction of the fate of the wicked also modifies the constraints by adding a new element which shapes the rhetorical goals.

The Forms of Job 16–17

There is little scholarly agreement regarding the forms of Job's fifth speech, though Job's opening strophe in 16:2-6 is generally interpreted as a disputation.[3] The opening disputation sets the trajectory for the rest of the speech. In response to Eliphaz's disputation in Job 15, Job responds in kind. Job's fifth speech is comprised of ninety-four clauses, sixty-nine of which are disputation (16:2-7a, 8c-17; 17:5-9, 10c-16). Many of these clauses appear in the lament or complaint form, and this is how most interpreters identify them. Nevertheless, the logical particles in key locations in this speech indicate that the "laments as description of suffering" and the "complaint against God" (to use Hartley's classifications) are the evidence which Job uses to rebut Eliphaz's application of the *topos* of the fate of the wicked (note אַךְ־עַתָּה in v. 7a; עַל in v. 17a; אוּלָם in 17:10; אִם in 17:13; אֵפוֹ in 17:15). As Eliphaz used the form of an appeal to tradition as evidence for his argument, Job responds with the forms of complaint and lament as evidence in his argument. Complaint and lament do occur in this speech, as Job briefly addresses God with complaint in 16:7b-8b (three clauses) and with lament in 17:1-2, 3b-4 (eight clauses). There is one petition offered to God in the midst of the lament in 17:3a. Job also addresses the friends with petition as a part of his disputation (17:10a-b). Job employs two wish clauses in 16:18, followed by six clauses of avowal of trust in 16:19-21. The avowal of trust is followed by three motive clauses (16:22).

This analysis confirms Clines' overall assessment that this speech is a disputation speech (1989: 376). This analysis also confirms the rhetorical situation identified above, namely, that Job is addressing a new exigency as it relates to his suffering. He uses his suffering as evidence in his argument to defend his innocence. This ultimately defends the appropriateness of his protest prayer. Job addresses God directly with three verbal forms (16:7b, 8a; 17:3a). This confirms that Job has not forgotten

---

3. See, e.g., Murphy 1981: 32; Westermann 1981b: 42–59, 101–2; Hartley 1988: 40–1; Clines 1989: 376–7.

about his exigency related to his suffering. Nevertheless, Job's primary rhetorical focus in this speech is his defense against being associated with the wicked.

The Rhetorical Strategies of Job 16–17

Structure

There is a general consensus regarding the structure of this speech.[4] The units of Job 16 can be discerned through address, common topics, and the presence of אַךְ־עַתָּה in v. 7 (balanced by עַל in v. 17). A slightly different structure for Job 17 than suggested by the consensus can be discerned by noting the closural effect of עַל־כֵּן in 17:4 and the disjunctive nature of וְאוּלָם in 17:10. Thus, Job 17 divides into three units: 17:1-4, 5-9, and 10-16. Despite these six major units, Job's fifth speech is a coherent movement from beginning to end, with Job addressing both the friends and God simultaneously (though predominantly, the friends). Job begins by addressing the friends (16:2-7a), addresses God briefly (16:7b-8a), and returns to address the friends (16:8b-22). Job addresses God in 17:1-4 and concludes the speech by addressing the friends in 17:5-16.[5]

This movement reveals Job's emphasis, namely, the exigency he faces with respect to the friends. Nevertheless, the few statements directed to God in this speech reveal that Job desires God at least to overhear his arguments to the friends, especially considering the seamless way in which he turns to address God in 16:7b-8a. One can almost imagine Job looking directly into the friends' eyes to focus on them, and then in 16:7b turning his head skyward as he addresses God. This indicates that Job continues to complain to God, attempting to provoke him into action, but is primarily concerned with "persuading the comforters to stop talking" (Yu 2011: 300, esp. n. 549) and convincing them that his speech is in fact ethical.

---

4. The consensus is 16:2-6, 16:7-17, 16:18-22; 17:1-5, 17:6-10, and 17:11-16. See Clines 1989: 375–6; Newsom 1996: 457–63; Seow 2013: 730, 753. Hartley (1988: 256) suggests all of Job 17 is a long unit. Habel (1985: 267), whom Yu follows (2011: 300), divides the speech slightly differently, suggesting 16:2-5, 16:6-17, 16:18–17:1, 17:2-10, and 17:10-16.

5. The markers of address do not indicate the structure of this speech as they did in Job's second and fourth speeches. Yu (2011: 300 n. 548) rightly notes that to focus on the addressee "splinters the speech into unrelated sections." Hartley argues that 16:7–17:16 is addressed to God (1988: 256, 258), but this is difficult to sustain in light of 17:10 and the 2mp forms. Rather, God is an implicit addressee in 16:7-22, 17:11-16.

Strategies

Direct Address to the Friends, Characterization, and Lexical Repetition.
The disputatious nature of this speech emerges in light of Job's explicit address to the friends, his use of characterization, and the lexical repetition from Eliphaz's speech in Job 15.

Job wastes no time in disputing Eliphaz's argument, stressing he is aware of such "commonplace" ideas regarding the fate of the wicked (Seow 2013: 731; cf. Clines 1989: 378).[6] Recognizing the application of this *topos* is an implicit call for repentance, Job characterizes the friends' collectively as מְנַחֲמֵי עָמָל. Their self-proclaimed gentle consolations (15:11) only serve to proliferate Job's hardship (note עָמָל in 15:35) (Hartley 1988: 257; Clines 1989: 378; Seow 2013: 732). Job quotes the friends' words back to them in 16:3 to accentuate this characterization (Clines 1989: 379; Seow 2013: 732).[7] Job reinforces the characterization through contrast in 16:4-5. The modality of the verbs is significant: "[w]hat he *could* do is not what he *would* do" (Clines 1989: 379, italics original). In v. 6 Job defends the necessity of continuing to speak (Hartley 1988: 258; Seow 2013: 733–4). This is a pivotal verse: Job captures his predicament about speaking. He sees both speaking and refraining as losing outcomes. He is constrained to speak (cf. 6:3; 7:1; 9:35–10:1; 13:3, 13-15). Each of these texts leads Job into a bold speech about God's attacks (6:4; 7:12-19; 10:2-17; 13:20-28 [cf. 14:18-22]). Job's laments and accusations against God are (understood by him to be) the only recourse for reestablishing their relationship. Job continues to speak because he must; it is his only recourse. This demonstrates that Job's criticism of the friends' speech is integrally related to the defense of his own. The concentration of speech words in this opening section indicates that the primary issue at stake is

---

6. Eliphaz implores Job to hear (שמע) things which Job has heard (שמע) (cf. 15:17; 16:2). Despite the putative wisdom of Eliphaz's teaching (חָכָם in 15:18), Job refuses to attribute to them wisdom (חָכָם in 17:10). Job rejects the accusation regarding self-violence (חמס), having committed no violence (חָמָס) (cf. 15:33; 16:17). The use of מִסְפָּר and שָׁנָה in 15:20 (also connected with the רְשָׁעִים) is reversed in 16:22 as Job rejects the application of the *topos* to himself. What is stored (צפן) is not the end of the wicked, but insight from his comforters (17:4; cf. 15:20).

7. See also Greenstein 2006: 247; Ho 2009: 705 n. 9. The chief reason for this interpretation is the use of 2ms suffixes in a context in which 2mp suffixes abound (six times). The 2ms form marks the quotation in this case because of the close connection between 16:3 together with 15:2 (the preceding speech) and 8:2 (note the use of רוּחַ). This contrasts with the use of the 2ms forms in 12:7-8, where there is little correspondence with what the friends have said; see Fox 1980a: 422–3, 429.

Job's discourse.[8] He defends it in response to their criticism, addressing them directly (note the six occurrences of the 2mp pronominal suffix in 16:2-6).

Job continues his characterization in the enigmatic 17:5, which seems best taken as a warning.[9] The movement from those who strike Job reproachfully in 16:10-11 to the mockers that surround him in 17:2 reaches a climax in this warning, clarifying that Job has the friends in mind throughout as he describes the treachery he experiences. The warning is developed when Job uses ethical terms to characterize himself and the friends in 17:6-9. Job begins by noting again his alienation and suffering at the hands of God (17:6-7), and quickly turns this into an accusation of their lack of loyalty. The plural יְשָׁרִים in 17:8a and the collective singular נָקִי in 17:8b contrasts with the singular חָנֵף in 17:8b and the singular צַדִּיק and טְהָר־יָדַיִם in 17:9. Job ironically applies "upright" and "innocent" to the friends and "godless" (חָנֵף) to himself.[10] The ironic characterization drives home the warning of 17:5, and leads seamlessly to Job's final direct address to the friends in 17:10. A mocking taunt, Job implores them to keep issuing arguments, but insists he will not find them wise. They should therefore remain silent (13:5). The enigmatic 17:12 also relates to this as Job jabs at their advice. They are trying to turn Job's suffering (night) into relief (day) through their pious platitudes that provide no comfort at all.[11]

---

8. Note: דָּבָר, ענה, מִלָּה, פֶּה, שָׂפָה. Almost all of these words occur in Eliphaz's speech as well (for שָׂפָה see 15:6; for פֶּה see 15:5, 6, 13, 30; for מִלָּה see 15:3, 13; for ענה see 15:2, 6; for דָּבָר see 15:3, 11). See also the use of יכח in 16:21 (cf. 15:3).

9. The referent of the impersonal 3ms verb could be taken as God or the friends. If God, then 17:5 belongs with 17:1-4. If the friends, then it begins Job's new section as he addresses the friends again (note the closural clue of עַל־כֵּן). Hartley interprets 17:5 as a warning (1988: 268–9). This "proverb" matches the sense of 6:14 as it leads into Job's criticism of the friends in 6:15-30. Notably both 6:14 and 17:5 begin with a prepositional phrase. This seems to confirm the use of 17:5 as a topic sentence, which Job will expound in 17:6-9, and which prepares for his mocking taunt in 17:10. Hartley notes on 17:10, "[T]hese lines serve as a searing incrimination of the three companions" (270). It also corresponds to Eliphaz's use of נגד in 15:18 as he introduces the fate of the wicked (note רְשָׁעִים in 15:20 and 16:11).

10. Their failing is an act of omission (they were appalled at his suffering and did nothing) and commission (they roused themselves against him). That Job refers to himself facetiously as the godless one goes back to Eliphaz's use of חָנֵף in 15:34 (cf. 8:13). *Pace* Clines 1989: 396. Note the use of עֵדָה in 15:34 and 16:7, which strengthens this connection. Good (1990: 251) describes 17:8-10 as sarcastic.

11. *Pace* Seow 2013: 757–8.

Job thus addresses the friends directly, accusing them of comforter malpractice and a lack of wisdom, and warns them to be silent. Through the address, characterization, and use of key lexemes, he casts a vision of their unethical actions to show they do not have the moral highground to criticize and correct his verbal expression.

Tropes. Job vivifies his argument through tropes, which can be combined in different groups for analysis. The first group of tropes Job employs are friend violence and treachery. These tropes first emerged in Job's second speech (Job 6–7), but are revisited in this speech with renewed vigor in light of Eliphaz's heightened rhetoric. The epithet מְנַחֲמֵי עָמָל in 16:2 characterizes the friends in a way that portrays them as causing more suffering. This act of treachery is an act of violence with words, as the parodic quotation of 16:3 makes evident. Job continues the characterization of the friends' infidelity by contrasting his approach in 16:4-5. Job would not be cruel with his words; their rhetoric has been ineffective (Hawley 2018: 85–7). The characterization of the friends who are treacherous and commit acts of violence with words emerges again in 17:2, where Job prays for God's aid in confronting them, in 17:8, where their being appalled at Job's condition implies treachery, and in 17:12, where he cites their bad advice. The tropes occur together also in 17:5 as Job warns them (cf. 6:14). The treachery and violence tropes are also found in 16:10. Though the friends are not explicitly mentioned in 16:10, it is difficult not to see Job implicating them in his general description of those who "amass themselves against him" and "strike his cheek with reproach." This statement describes physical violence, seemingly using physical violence as an image for the violence with words Job has continually accused the friends of committing.

The most important group of tropes includes the complex integration of the tropes of divine attack, personification, animals, body, suffering, and rest and ease. Job mentions his suffering in 16:6. He is suffering—innocently—at the hands of God. The divine attack trope comes to the fore in 16:7-9 and continues in 16:11-14 and 17:6. Addressing both the friends in disputation (note אַף־עַתָּה) and God in protest prayer (note the direct address in 16:7b and 8a), Job describes God's actions in causing his suffering using a number of vivid images.[12] God has worn Job out

---

12. For an insightful discussion of the use of metaphor in 16:7-14, see Jimenez 2013: 49–70. Newsom describes this as "thoroughly traditional language," while also suggesting that "Job disrupts the form" (1996: 457–8). But Jimenez disputes this, concluding, "[B]eneath the seemingly blasphemous, and irreverent surface, lays a language in harmony with ancient Israelite approaches to the Divine" (51), adding,

(16:7), alienated him (16:7; 17:6a), shriveled him (16:8), torn him (16:9), hated him (16:9), gnashed his teeth at him (16:9), sharpened his eyes at him (16:9). God gives him up to others who mistreat him (16:11; 17:6b),[13] split him (16:12), seized him (16:12), shattered him (16:12), erected him as a target (16:12; cf. 7:20). God then surrounds him with archers (16:13), splits open his organs (16:13), pours his gall on the ground (16:13), besieges him (16:14),[14] and attacks him as a warrior (16:14).[15] These images of divine attack integrate animal imagery (16:9 describes a ferocious beast),[16] body imagery (16:8, 9, 12, and 13),[17] personification (16:8, 9), and suffering (16:7, 8, 10, 12, 13, 15,[18] 16 [cf. v. 20]; 17:6, 7, 8).[19] The narrativity of 16:7-14 is arresting. The verbs work with the images to create a narrative-like movement.[20] Alter captures this (1985: 40): "[O]ne might describe these lines as a continuous series of interlinear semantic parallelisms, one image of assault piled onto another, with a unifying metaphor of tearing or rupture… [I]t is important to note that the process

---

"Thus to argue that Job is blasphemous, or irreverent, in the way that he laments, is to overlook the fact that the motivational basis for the way he addresses God, and argues with him, is mediated by the socio-religious context, the same elements that make up the metaphors" (2013: 70).

13. The words עָוִיל and רְשָׁעִים in v. 11 are the subject of the impersonal 3cp verb in v. 10. The inclusio in v. 11 places the verbs around the subjects, drawing attention to God's actions.

14. The alliteration draws attention to Job's battered state: יִפְרְצֵנִי פֶרֶץ עַל־פְּנֵי־פָרֶץ. This imagery recalls Pss. 80:13 [12] and 89:41 [40].

15. On the provocative reversal of the image of the divine warrior, see Clines 1989: 385. Divine attack is implied also by the reference to blood in 16:18.

16. See Jimenez 2013: 62–3; cf. Hartley 1988: 260; Seow 2013: 745; Hawley 2018: 134–6.

17. Body imagery also occurs in 16:15, 16, 20, and 17:7. While not explicitly linked with the divine attack, the use of body imagery as reinforcing his suffering implies a connection to the divine attack. Body imagery also occurs in 16:10, at the hands of wicked men who strike Job's cheek. Since God instigates these men (v. 11), one could say this body imagery relates to divine attack as well.

18. Newsom's (1996: 459) attention to the rhetoric of the imagery in 16:15 is perceptive.

19. These verses of suffering portray his emotional (16:15-16, 20; 17:7) and physical (16:7, 8, 10, 12, 13, 15; 17:7) suffering. They also depict his ephemerality (17:7) and alienation (16:7; 17:6, 8). All of this is "without pity" (16:13); that is, his suffering is prolonged.

20. The narrativity is indicated by the use of the *wayyiqtols*. The flurry of activity in quick succession ascribed to God in these verses mirrors the quick calamity that befell Job in Job 1.

of intensification here is projected onto a temporal axis, which is to say it becomes narrative."[21] Notably, Job is at the center stage of this treatment.[22]

The combination of these images provides a provocative justification for Job's protest prayer. Yu (2011: 302–3) describes this as a "pathos argument," noting how suitable Job's response is to Eliphaz's description of Job's suffering that links Job with the wicked.[23] The divine attack and the personal suffering Job describes in this speech are the evidence which justifies his protest prayer: not only is his suffering immense (the so-called I-lament of 16:15-16 and 17:6-7, 11), but also this suffering is caused by God (the so-called enemy-lament of 16:7-14 and 17:6). Job is not among the wicked who has received his just recompense of wrong-doing; Job is unjustly suffering, and therefore defends his protest prayer. Given how Job concludes 16:7-17, where he notes that these images are true despite his innocence (16:17), it is clear that Job is also rebutting Eliphaz's application of the *topos* of the wicked.

The suffering of Job's body in Job 16 gives way to the suffering of his spirit in Job 17. This movement of tropes portrays the imminence of death, emphasized by the reference to graves in 17:1 (Seow 2013: 753–4, 756). Contrast this with the use of the image of rest and ease in 16:12 and then combine it with the image of the ephemerality of life in 16:22 and 17:11 and it becomes clear that Job's suffering is used in his dispute and in his petition for relief.[24]

Death and Sheol imagery play a role in Job's rhetoric as well. Death imagery emerges in connection with the צַלְמָוֶת that overcomes Job's eyes in 16:16 and then again in 16:22 as Job prepares for the transition of his broken spirit to the grave in 17:1. As just noted, death is imminent and Job's need is urgent.[25] Related to the death imagery is Job's use of Sheol imagery in 17:13-16. This imagery is intimately related to Job's use of hypotheticals and rhetorical questions. As Seow points out (2013: 759),

---

21. He likens this to a "cinematic illusion" of "overlapping stills," which creates the impression of quick, successive actions without interruption.

22. Job employs thirty-three 1cs forms in 16:7-17. Only three of these 1cs forms are verbs (16:12 and 15 [2×]). The rest are pronominal suffixes, twenty-four of which depict him as the object of divine or friend attack.

23. Perhaps further linking Job's disputation of the *topos* of the fate of the wicked is the lack of interrogatives in both sections. See Magary 2005: 297.

24. Seow (2013: 753) notes that the syntax of 17:1 and 11 poetically captures the disintegrating nature of Job's life: short, staccato-like clauses, culminating in verbless clauses.

25. There is an implicit petition for God to act in the use of this imagery (Hartley 1988: 265).

the use of Sheol imagery emphasizes Job's perceived alienation and lack of hope.[26] The implication in the context of the dispute is that Job must continue to complain. It is his only recourse.

The combination of light and dark imagery plays an important rhetorical role in Job's fifth speech. The first occurrence of darkness imagery was just noted in the discussion of death in 16:16, and it reemerges in a similar context in 17:7: Job's eyes are failing.[27] This coheres with Job's statement using a light metaphor to describe his suffering in 17:1: "my days are extinguished."[28] The images of light and dark are used differently in 17:12, where Job parodies the friends again, criticizing their approach to him. Integrating the images of light and darkness with treachery, Job suggests that their advice regarding his suffering (darkness) and their desire to give him hope (light) are unethical.

Job also uses a legal metaphor with the trope of injustice in this speech. Both tropes are found in 16:8 when he suggests God's attack has caused his suffering condition to testify against him.[29] Divine injustice is also related to divine attack in 16:10-11, when God gives Job over to the עֲוִיל and the רְשָׁעִים for mistreatment. The metaphors work together again in 17:3-4, with the legal metaphor in 17:3 leading into the accusation of injustice in 17:4.[30] The tropes also complement each other in Job's emphatic statements in 16:17 (injustice) and 16:19-21 (legal metaphor) and Job's wish in 16:18 (injustice implied), where earth is also personified. Job uses this combination of tropes in his disputation to defend his protest prayer (16:8, 10-11, 17-21) and in his petition for relief (17:3-4; cf. 16:17-21).

Direct Address to God. In the midst of his God-attack narrative, Job briefly turns his attention heavenward in 16:7b-8a. The two verbal forms in these verses (הֲשִׁמּוֹתָ and וַתִּקְמְטֵנִי) demonstrate that the description of divine attack not only serves as a justification of his complaint-laden

---

26. Seow notes how Job's use of family metaphors for Sheol in 17:14 indicates his alienation. The personification of Sheol in 17:14 further emphasizes this.

27. The progression Job portrays of his eyes is notable here: deep darkness comes over his eyelids in 16:16, his eyes weep in protest prayer to God in 16:20, fixate on the friends' provocation in 17:2, and fail from vexation (17:7). The suffering he experiences at the hands of God and the friends leads him to darkness, death.

28. On this metaphor, see van Hecke 2011: 97–8.

29. Seow (2013: 734) notes the syntax of 16:8 mimics Job's personal disintegration.

30. The accusation of injustice in 17:4 includes a petition for relief. Job accuses God of having hidden understanding from the friends and then concludes (עַל־כֵּן): "you *must not* let them be exalted" (i.e., triumph in the debate). See Seow 2013: 755. Hartley (1988: 268) notes the underlying faith in this accusation.

language, but also itself serves as complaint. It thus implies a petition for relief.[31] Job uses the provocative language, at home in the context of protest prayer, to accuse God reproachfully and move him to respond. This is confirmed in Job's lone petition to God in this speech in 17:3.[32] Job desires God to take his side and bring relief from his suffering and from his friends. Hartley writes (1988: 268), "In light of the hostility of his mockers, Job pleads for God to put up a pledge with himself for his servant… There is no one to whom Job can turn as his guarantor…save God himself." Job's faith emerges plainly in this petition (ibid.). Job has not forgotten his exigency related to his suffering, but now with the friends causing additional suffering (cf. 16:2), Job must appeal to God to cease his actions toward Job, as well as to vindicate him in the face of his friends' accusations.[33] Since the friends' lack of understanding is rooted in God's actions, God must do something (17:4).[34]

Emphatic Statements. As in the first cycle, Job uses particles to highlight key statements in his argument. The first emphatic statement occurs in Job's opening disputation in 16:4. Marked by גַּם, Job highlights the direct address and characterization in 16:4-5. Job's direct address to the friends and his characterization of them as poor and unethical comforters is a seminal rhetorical move in this speech. This is confirmed by the emphatic statement in 17:2, marked by אִם־לֹא. In this verse, Job is praying to God (note the direct address to God in 17:3-4), but the friends are obviously listening to his words. He stresses their role as mockers (הֲתֻלִים) who provoke him with their rebelliousness (וּבְהַמְּרוֹתָם). This is certain (אִם־לֹא). This is the evidence Job presents to move God to act on his behalf, as indicated by the petition in 17:3 and the conclusion he draws with עַל־כֵּן in 17:4b. This compound particle introduces Job's petition for God not to allow the friends to triumph over him in this dispute. Also marking an

31. Both Seow (2013: 730) and Hartley (1988: 256) take these two forms to indicate that Job addresses God throughout 16:7-17.

32. This reading is based on the emendation of the imperative עָרְבֵנִי to a nominal form as suggested by BHS and followed by a number of commentators (e.g., Hartley 1988: 266 n. 9; Seow 2013: 761).

33. It is important to note that Job's limited address in this speech is not rooted in any kind of loss of an ability to pray (Patrick 1979: 270–1); rather, Job's new exigency forces him to address the friends in more detail in this speech. The address to God relates to his suffering (16:7-17; 17:1-4), suffering caused by both God and the friends. Job is seeking to have this suffering alleviated in these brief diversions into protest prayer in the midst of the disputation.

34. Job 17:4b is best understood as a *yiqtol* denoting obligation ("must"), and therefore a petition.

emphatic statement regarding his disputation is his use of וְאוּלָם in 17:10 to mark his taunt. Job draws attention to their malpractice and character, criticizing his friends with these statements marked for emphasis.

Job employs other particles in his disputation that relate more directly to his defense of protest prayer. Job draws attention to his evidence using אַךְ־עַתָּה in 16:7. His evidence is the divine attack that has caused him great suffering.[35] As noted above in the discussion of this complex use of tropes, this is a direct refutation of the *topos* of the fate of the wicked. Job's suffering is not rooted in sin and his protest prayer is not inappropriate, as Eliphaz had maintained in Job 15. This is confirmed by the use of עַל to emphasize a key statement at the end of this unit: "even though there is no violence on my hands and my prayer is pure" (עַל לֹא־חָמָס בְּכַפָּי וּתְפִלָּתִי זַכָּה).[36] Clines (1989: 387) contends this is best understood as indicating the reason for Job's suffering. This is an astute suggestion: the reason Job's suffering is so immense is that there is no violence in his hand and his prayer is pure. This reading has Job making an ironic statement that matches the prologue: Job is suffering *on account of* his blamelessness—which is exactly what the reader knows from the prologue. Job is speaking the truth! Job's protest prayer has not caused further suffering, as Eliphaz had suggested (cf. 15:2-6, 13, 30); Job's protest prayer is pure in motive and in ethics.[37]

The most important emphatic statement occurs in Job 16:19-21, marked by גַּם־עַתָּה. Job has argued that the friends' arguments are wrong and that he has no recourse but to complain (16:2-6), validated his argument with evidence (16:7-17), and wished for his unjust experience not to be suppressed (16:18). The avowal of trust of 16:19-21 is linked to this sequence through the compound particle גַּם־עַתָּה. Job accentuates that he has a witness to his unjust suffering in heaven who will help him navigate his two exigencies.[38] The identity of this "witness" is an interpretive crux. Clines (1989: 389), Yu (2011: 303–4), and Seow (2013: 738–9) understand the witness to be Job's "cry." Others suggest that

---

35. In other words, it seems likely that the אַךְ־עַתָּה governs all of 16:7-16—all of his evidence.

36. The exact nuance of עַל here remains somewhat unclear. It could be an abbreviation for עַל־אֲשֶׁר, as Hartley suggests (1988: 259 n. 12; cf. GKC §104b, 160c). Note the same expression in Isa. 53:9.

37. This verse may be a counterpoint to Eliphaz's statement in 15:14, connecting the root זַךְ/זכה (Seow 2013: 737). Cf. Hartley 1988: 262.

38. The two cola of 16:21 relate to these two exigencies: "let him argue for a man with God, and [let him argue] between a man and his friend." The verb is gapped in the second colon, and the preposition בֵּין should probably be read instead of בֶּן ("son") as suggested by BHS. See Seow 2013: 750.

Job's witness is a celestial being, perhaps in the divine council (Curtis 1983: 549–62; Habel 1985: 275–6; Newsom 1996: 460–1; Walton 2012: 214–15).[39] Hartley (1988: 263) suggests that Job's witness is God himself based on the fact that throughout the book Job considers his argument to be with God.[40] There seem to be two related arguments most often suggested against this third option: (1) that Job has nowhere to this point demonstrated any trust in God, and so this more "pious" interpretation makes Job appear at odds with himself, and (2) that it makes little sense that God is both Job's enemy and Job's defender (how can God appeal to God against God?).[41]

Regarding the first objection, Job's faith is evident throughout the book, implicitly in his protest prayer and explicitly in his emphatic statements in 13:15-16 (cf. 14:14). Broyles' analysis of protest prayer in the Psalter is insightful regarding the second objection. Broyles, differentiating between psalms of plea and psalms of complaint (God-laments), concludes God-laments appeal to God against God (1989: 24–5). That Job's statements to this point in the book comprise God-lament can be seen in his depictions of God's active violence (see 7:17-21; 10:2-17; 13:23-27; 16:7-16), the incongruity of God's actions with Job's current experience (see the allusions and hymns), non-specific and negated jussive petitions (7:7, 16; 13:20-21), descriptions of God's anger (16:9), divine rejection (16:10-11), divine forgetfulness and hiddenness (7:7; 10:9; 13:20; 14:3), the imminence of death (3:3-26; 7:21; 10:21-22), and the description of weariness (16:7; 17:7) (cf. ibid., 35–131). Moreover, the notion of God-against-God is also found outside of biblical laments. Muffs (1992: 9–41) shows how the prophet "stands in the breach" between the people of Israel and God, and in doing so appeals to God against God.[42] Ticciati (2005: 119–37) has developed this insight to understand the development of the מוֹכִיחַ figure from 9:33 to the witness in 16:21.[43] Job moves from

---

39. Wilson (1996a: 243–52; 2015: 98) suggests a variation on this view, that this is a hypothetical being, an imaginary figure to whom Job is appealing for help.

40. This is the view of a number of other interpreters; see Seow 2013: 738–9.

41. This is captured most clearly in Clines 1989: 389–91. Seow reasons similarly (2013: 738; cf. 739, 748–9). Walton (2012: 214) considers the concept of God defending Job against God a "kangaroo court." Wilson (1996a: 246), Newsom (1996: 460), and Longman (2012: 239) concur.

42. This tension is also found within the book at 27:2 (Gordis 1978: 527).

43. Though I disagree with Ticciati's exegesis of 9:33, particularly her reading of the text-critical issue regarding the particle and that she identifies the figure in view as a human intermediary, her insights on the role of the מוֹכִיחַ are astute for understanding how God can be against himself.

wishing he had a מוֹכִיחַ to recognizing he has God who will be his witness in his predicament with his friends. These lines of reasoning all point to the fact that if Job's witness is God there is no conflict, whether internally with Job or externally with God. As Gordis notes (1978: 526–7), to suppose this figure is someone other than God is to force "Western categories of logic" on the text.

Furthermore, there is good reason in the context to see God as the witness. The phrases "in heaven" (בַּשָּׁמַיִם) and "on high" (בַּמְּרוֹמִים) naturally lead in this direction, even if not conclusive on their own. Moreover, the second colon of 16:20 explicitly mentions God: "to God my eye weeps" (אֶל־אֱלוֹהַּ דָּלְפָה עֵינִי), with the prepositional phrase fronted to stress the addressee of Job's prayer. This coheres with Job's address to God in 17:1-4. One sticking point is the plural pointing of the elements of the verbless clause in 16:20a, but there is good reason to emend the pointing here to read "my intercessor is my friend."[44] All of this suggests that God is to be identified as the witness, while the two major objections to this view are not as conclusive as supposed by the consensus.

With this in mind, Job's use of this emphatic statement coheres with the rhetorical situation identified above. Having offered evidence of his suffering and wishing for his injustice not to be covered, Job declares emphatically his faith and trust in God that he (1) will not let the friends triumph, which he will make clear in a petition in 17:4, and (2) will hear his affirmation of trust and respond in accordance with what Job knows to be true of God, even if his experience does not match what he believes. Fohrer notes that Job brings up God as a witness to remind God to fulfill his duties (1963: 291). In other words, the affirmation of faith is an emphatic statement that both functions in the disputation and implies a petition for God to act (cf. 13:15-16; 14:14)—a warning and a plea. Through these words Job appeals to God in risky and bold faith, while also confident that God will vindicate him. Job is confident: God, as Job's witness, is Job's defender and friend, and will argue for Job against himself (God) and the friends (16:19-21).

Wish. There are three wishes in this speech. The first is marked by the particle לוּ in 16:4b. This irreal wish is intended to grab the attention of the friends in Job's disputation as he wishes he could switch places with

---

44. This would be the only occurrence of the Hiphil participle of ליץ (Hartley 1988: 263 n. 6; cf. Habel 1985: 265–6; Clines 1989: 371; Seow 2013: 748–9). With מֵלִיץ also occurring in Job 33:23, there is strong reason to read the lexeme here, too (cf. Gen. 43:23; Isa. 43:27; 2 Chron. 32:31). This is not to emend the consonantal text, but merely the pointing.

them. This wish prepares for Job's rhetorical maneuver discussed above as he contrasts their approach (v. 4c-d) with his own (v. 5). The wish thus works with the characterization and direct address as Job criticizes the friends and offers his apology for his own verbal expression (v. 6). He simply must speak.

The second wish is marked by the negated jussive in 16:18. After describing in vivid detail God's attack despite Job's innocence (16:7-17), Job utters this wish that the earth would not cover his blood and that his cry might not be silenced. The reference to blood is striking given the violence just depicted. Job's wish further implies injustice.[45] Job's statement in v. 18 is intimately tied to the rhetoric of the emphatic statement of 16:17, where Job reveals his conviction of innocence by calling on the earth as a witness. It is also tied closely with Job's emphatic statement, the avowal of trust in 16:19-21, as Job moves from the earth to heaven. Job's rhetoric reveals his confidence in his argument as he disputes the comforters' suggestions while also implying a petition for relief.[46] The injustice is Job's evidence for both rhetorical goals, evidence he wishes to be made plain.

The third wish occurs in 16:21 with the use of the jussive form וְיוֹכַח. This jussive makes clear the implied petition of the entire section by describing Job's hoped-for outcome (cf. 17:3-4). Notably, this wish relates to both of Job's exigencies: he desires someone to mediate between himself and God (16:21a; cf. 9:34) and between himself and the comforters (16:21b). Job's faith emerges as he defends his protest prayer by issuing bold wishes that also imply petition.

Rhetorical Questions and Hypotheticals. While Job's use of rhetorical questions is not as prominent in this speech as in the previous speeches, they do occur.[47] His rhetorical questions work in conjunction with other rhetorical strategies, whether functioning with petition (direct address to God) or as the apodoses of hypothetical scenarios. Job uses two hypothetical scenarios in his fifth speech, and both function as an apology for his protest prayer, and in both cases the apodosis is given in a rhetorical question. The first rhetorical question closing a hypothetical is found in 16:6d. Through the question Job argues that he must complain. His complaint

---

45. See Gen. 4:10; Isa. 26:21; Ezek. 24:7-8; see Seow 2013: 738.
46. Hartley (1988: 264) suggests this cry is a desire for God "to avenge [Job] before it is too late."
47. On the rhetorical question in 16:3, see the analysis above under "characterization."

prayer is the only means by which he can reestablish his relationship with God and find the restoration he is seeking.

The second hypothetical is found at the end of the speech in 17:13-16. After issuing his taunt (17:10), describing his suffering (17:11), and characterizing the friends' advice (17:12), Job rebuts their advice by presenting a hypothetical scenario. Hope emerges as a key factor in his hypothetical (17:13a, 15a, 15b), after being implicit in 16:6. He questions what hope he would have if he were to give up his course of action and die without restoration. Through the apodosis and rhetorical questions in 17:15-16 (with the questions in 17:16 unmarked), Job implies he will continue to complain.

The rhetorical question in 17:3 functions within Job's protest prayer of 17:1-4. Following his petition in 17:3, Job substantiates his need for divine response to this petition through the rhetorical question. If God will not come to his aid, Job avers there is no one else who can help him. The rhetorical question in 17:3, then, implies a petition. It also reveals Job's hope in God—a notion that we have seen explicitly in 13:15 and implicitly throughout the first cycle in his protest prayer.

Allusion. There are a number of possible allusions in this speech that Job may be employing for rhetorical goals.[48] Job appears to allude again to

---

48. In addition to the allusions discussed, there may be an allusion to Ps. 39:2, 9 in 16:10-11 and 17:2, 6, thematically linked by the wicked surrounding the sufferer. See Kynes 2012: 122. This allusion reiterates Job's characterization of the friends as the wicked. There may also be an allusion to Ps. 24:4 in Job 16:17, also thematic regarding blamelessness (Hartley 1988: 262). By alluding to this psalm Job links himself with the purity of the worshipper who can ascend Yahweh's holy hill (cf. Ps. 24:3), and prepares for his statement of confidence in vindication (24:5). Job's allusion to this psalm disputes the friends' arguments and association of Job with the wicked; he is blameless. Job may also allude to Ps. 119 in two places in this speech. The verb דלף in 16:20 recalls Ps. 119:28 (Kynes 2013a: 208). Strengthening this allusion is the link between Ps. 119:121-122 and 17:3 (Hartley 1988: 268). The verb ערב occurs only sixteen times and the root only in these two places in the Psalter and the book of Job (though the Job text has the nominal form). The psalmist petitions for God's surety amidst the attack of the insolent (זֵדִים); Job appeals to God for the same reason (note the use of הֲתָלִים in 17:2 and רְשָׁעִים in 16:11). Hartley writes, "This parallel passage makes it clear that Job is now pleading to God for immediate relief from his suffering… This plea offers evidence that Job's faith in God remains firm and that God is the witness spoken of in 16:19" (ibid.). There may also be an allusion to Pss. 35:16 and 37:12 in Job 16:9 with regard to the image of the gnashing of teeth, but Kynes considers this more likely to be an example of formulaic expression linking the texts (2012: 41–2).

Isaiah 40–55, a phenomenon also seen in Job's third and fourth speeches. Bastiaens (1997: 423–7) has identified the links: Job 16:10 // Isa. 50:6; Job 16:17 // Isa. 53:9; Job 17:6 // Isa. 50:6; 53:3; Job 17:8 // Isa. 52:14.[49] The first pair is linked by the words נכה and לְחָיִי, while the second is linked by the phrase עַל לֹא־חָמָס (and the thematically similar pure prayer and lack of deceit). The third pair exhibits the similar images of spitting and alienation, while the fourth connection is found in the use of שמם עַל. These allusions link Job with the Servant figure of Isaiah 40–55, who suffers at the hands of enemies in the third and fourth songs yet remains steadfast in his commitment to Yahweh, even entrusting himself to Yahweh (Isa. 50:4-9; 52:14–53:12).[50] In the context of Job's rhetorical situation, these allusions reinforce the characterization of the friends as wicked and himself as blameless, thereby further criticizing them and justifying his protest prayer. As in his associations with Jeremiah, Job links himself with the suffering Servant as a way of disproving the association with the wicked, as the friends had proposed. This allusion is a fitting response to Eliphaz's arguments.

The strongest allusion in this speech is to the book of Lamentations. Job's description of God's attack has numerous parallels to Lamentations.[51] Seow writes (2013: 737), "The many affinities between this stanza and Lamentations prompt one to read the passage in light of Lamentations. God is the enemy in both cases," yet in Lamentations the enmity is rooted in the sin of the people, whereas Job is innocent. This contrast is

49. He also finds parallels between Job 16:19/Isa. 49:4 and Job 16:21/Isa. 50:7-9, though these are not as strong. See also Brinks Rea 2010: 146–7, 183–4. Though she acknowledges the strength of the connection between Job 16:17 and Isa. 53:9, she remains convinced that the connections between Job and Isa. 40–55 are mostly tenuous. Even in spite of her conclusion, she admits that this specific link establishes some association between Job and the Servant. A reuse rather than a parody, she argues persuasively for Job's dependence on Isa. 40–55 (184–8). It seems that the strength of this link encourages the interpreter to consider the other weaker connections noted by other interpreters.

50. Oswalt writes of the third song (1998: 326), "The Servant is confident that, with the help of his defense attorney, no prosecuting attorney would even have a case... [A]lthough the Servant's adversaries might think he had deserved the humiliation and abuse he received (see 53:4), God would be the Servant's witness that no such charges could be justified." This intriguing picture of the Servant may illumine further Job's confidence over against the friends if this allusion is accepted. Confident of God's vindication, Job stands firm in his arguments against the friends (cf. 16:19-21). Job's friends, like the Servant's enemies, will not prevail.

51. These have been documented most fully by Seow (2013: 737), though see also Mettinger 1993: 273.

significant: the lamenting voice of Lamentations still accuses God of attack knowing full well the judgment is deserved, while Job knows full well his suffering is undeserved. By alluding to Lamentations, Job highlights "the acute incongruousness of [his] situation... By means of this intertextual strategy the poet places added emphasis on Job's guiltlessness. His is a suffering that is even more paradoxical than the sufferings of devastated Zion" (Mettinger 1993: 274).[52]

Job's use of these allusions stresses his justification for protest prayer by reiterating the incongruity of the application of the *topos* of the fate of the wicked to him. He is innocent, and his prayer is ethical (16:17).

Summary of Job 16–17

With Eliphaz accusing Job of being wicked and implying a call to repentance through an explicit condemnation of his verbal expression, Job is forced to defend himself against this charge. To do so, Job sustains one of the harshest descriptions of God's actions in the book, combining imagery, allusion, and emphatic statements to rebut Eliphaz. Job addresses the friends, characterizing them as "comforters of trouble" (16:2), to gain their attention and appeal to them to cease their rhetoric. Despite the shocking language about God, Job also accentuates his faith in God through emphatic statements and his protest prayer. He petitions God implicitly and explicitly for relief and vindication.[53]

"Be Afraid of the Sword":
The Rhetoric of Job's Sixth Speech (Job 19)

Introduction

In Job 18 Bildad continues the trajectory set by Eliphaz with his speech. Job's response in Job 19 thus mirrors his response in Job 16–17. The application of the *topos* of the fate of the wicked is again set in the context of criticism of Job's verbal expression. Job disputes this criticism in order to defend his protest prayer.

---

52. Mettinger's conclusion relates to what this study calls the external rhetoric as he notes the poet's use of this allusion. Job's allusion in the narrative world, the internal rhetoric, is the same.

53. Westermann (1981b: 45) draws attention to the significance of the avowal of trust in Job 16, noting that it is "precisely where Job utters the sharpest and most dangerous words against God [that] he also speaks the words which nevertheless most clearly show him holding fast to God."

The Literary Rhetorical Situation of Job 19

Bildad responds to Job's speech with the same rhetorical strategy as Eliphaz. Since Job did not dispute the veracity of the *topos* of the fate of the wicked, but tried to defend his protest prayer by pointing to God's involvement in his suffering, Bildad chooses to employ it as well (Yu 2011: 307; cf. Hartley 1988: 273). Bildad's goal remains the same as Eliphaz's—to modify Job's verbal expression—even though his goal is not as explicitly stated. This is seen in his opening section in 18:2-4. Job's words (מִלִּין) are problematic, and his contention that the friends lack wisdom disturbs Bildad. Both interrogatives (עַד־אָנָה and מַדּוּעַ) signify rebuke of Job's speech (Seow 2013: 771; cf. Newsom 1996: 468). Job's position threatens the created order, and Bildad uses the rhetorical questions of 18:4 to draw attention to the problems of Job's argument. Bildad's repetition of טרף and אַף in 18:4 (cf. 16:7) stresses that God is not the enemy; Job is his own enemy. The use of אַף to describe Job's position is conspicuous in light of Eliphaz's criticism of Job's angry disposition in 15:12-13 (cf. 15:4-6, 30). Bildad reiterates that Job's suffering is self-inflicted in two other ways: (1) through his insinuation of Job's lack of wisdom in 18:7, where the wicked person is cast aside by his own "counsel" (עֵצָה), and (2) by articulating that the wicked person's own feet ensnare him in 18:8. Bildad's focus is on the conduct of the wicked, and given the book's emphasis on speech ethics, it is Job's conduct in terms of his verbal expression that is in view. Similar to Eliphaz, Bildad argues Job's words are doing him (more) harm. This criticism is the context for understanding the fate of the wicked, described in 18:5-21.[54]

Bildad intends Job to see himself as the wicked person in an attempt to persuade Job to turn from his protest prayer (Hartley 1988: 281; Clines 1989: 408; Seow 2013: 778). Habel (1985: 284–5) and Yu (2011: 309–11), following Holbert (1981: 171–9), have noted the use of specific lexemes and themes that make the implicit association of Job with the wicked clear (see also Seow 2013: 770–1, 777). Bildad's argument is that Job's continued angry verbal expression is unbecoming and places him firmly in the camp of the wicked, whose end is sure. Job is one who "knows not God." Job's suffering is not innocent and his current approach will lead to a certain unpleasant end. This speech is a warning, and the implication is a call to repentance (Hartley 1988: 281).

---

54. In addition to these observations, it is significant that Bildad concludes his argument with a summary statement that is marked by אַךְ, the same particle Job used to mark his extended trope on God's attack in 16:7. Moreover, Job had lamented his plans being "torn" (נתק) in 17:11, to which Bildad replies this is characteristic of the wicked (18:14).

This analysis illuminates Job's rhetorical situation. It has not changed since his previous speech: he must continue to defend his protest prayer (so also Yu 2011: 311–12). As in the previous speech, defending the ethics of his verbal expression is the primary exigency given the seriousness of the charge that he is wicked. The audience for Job's sixth speech is thus primarily the friends, though the provocative imagery may also be intended to move God to act. The constraints remain unchanged.

The Forms of Job 19

Job's sixth speech is a disputation in response to Bildad's arguments and application of the *topos* of the fate of the wicked to Job.[55] This is confirmed by looking at the number of clauses of each form in this speech. There are four forms that comprise this speech: disputation, wish, avowal of trust, and petition. Of the sixty-nine clauses in this speech, fifty-seven clauses are disputation (19:2-20, 21c-22, 28-29). The direct address and the use of particles to mark the argument confirm this identification. There are three clauses of wish (19:23-24), marked by מִי־יִתֵּן, seven clauses of avowal of trust (19:25-27), marked by tone and content, and two clauses of petition (19:21a-b), marked by the plural imperative.[56] These latter three forms all work together with the disputation. The lament-like character of 19:7-20 is not a complaint or a lament, but is evidence used in Job's disputation. This is confirmed by noting the statements that surround these verses in 19:6 and 21: in both cases, Job emphasizes that his suffering is caused by God (so also Clines 1989: 435–7, 469–70; Yu 2011: 314–15).

This analysis confirms the rhetorical situation above. Job responds to Bildad's argument, specifically that Job is one who "knows not God" and is suffering deservedly, through a disputation that presents his arguments of divine attack and social alienation. Clines (1989: 437) notes that the speech, as a disputation, is "a demonstration to [his companions] that

---

55. There is little agreement on the forms that make up this speech. Hartley (1988: 40–1) identifies seven forms: complaint against the friends (19:2-6), complaint against God (19:7-12), lament as a description of suffering (19:13-20), petition to the friends (19:21-22), petition for vindication (19:23-24), affirmation of trust (19:25-27), and a warning to the friends (19:28-29). Westermann (1981b: 31, 68, 101) identifies 19:7-20, 23, and 27 as lament, 19:23-24 as a wish for an advocate, and 19:25-27 as an avowal of trust. Murphy (1981: 33) understands Job 19 as a disputation speech, with elements of complaint in 19:7-20, and a closing warning in 19:28-29. Clines (1989: 436–7) notes that this entire speech is a disputation speech, though it is comprised of rhetorical questions, lament, wish, desire, and conviction.

56. The imperatives in v. 6a and v. 29a are best seen as disputation since they do not appeal for anything. They are rather instructions or warnings.

Job's apparent guilt is something imposed on him by God (v. 6a), he himself being wholly innocent and bound to be vindicated ultimately (vv. 25-26a)." Yet in the context of the book regarding the ethics of Job's speech, it is important to note that Job's argument—that God has caused his suffering and that he is innocent—is intimately related to his defense of his protest prayer. The innocent sufferer is the one who has the right to complain.

The Rhetorical Strategies of Job 19

Structure

There is little agreement on the structure of Job 19.[57] It seems best to divide it into three movements: (1) 19:2-6 comprise an opening rebuke in disputation, (2) the הֵן marks the second movement, which provides the evidence for Job's thesis in 19:6, and (3) the double imperative in 19:21 demarcates the third movement as Job returns to address the friends, again in rebuke, disputation, and warning.[58] The shifts in content and the inclusio of direct address to the friends in vv. 2-6 and vv. 21-29 provide the clues to Job's major emphases. Job insists that God is the one who has wronged him (19:6, 21). This latter emphasis is illustrated by the middle section, and pertains to Job's defense of his speech. Because he is suffering innocently, he has a right to protest in prayer. These emphases confirm the analysis above regarding the rhetorical situation and the use of lament-like language in 19:7-20.

---

57. Habel (1985: 294) divides the speech into the following sections: 19:2-5, 6-12, 13-20, 21-29. Clines (1989: 435) divides the poem into five sections: 19:2-6, 7-20, 21-22, 23-27, 28-29. Hartley (1988: 282) divides the speech into five different sections: 19:2-6, 7-12, 13-20, 21-27, 28-29. Seow (2013: 793–4) suggests yet another five-section division: 19:2-5, 6-12, 13-22, 23-27, 28-29. Longman (2012: 255) suggests three sections: 19:2-3, 4-22, 23-29.

58. To break the first movement at v. 5 makes little sense of the connection with v. 6 as the apodosis, as Habel and Seow do—אֵפוֹ concludes the movement begun in v. 5 with אִם־אָמְנָם. Furthermore, to divide vv. 7-20 into two sections (vv. 7-12 and vv. 13-20) does not account for the seamless connection between Job's description of divine attack and social ostracism. The final 3ms verb (הִרְחִיק) referring to God in 19:13 provides the final element in Job's description of divine attack, providing a clean transition into the description of his alienation. This shows that vv. 7-20 comprise a unit. Lastly, the inclusio around vv. 21-29 (the imperatives and the use of רדף), noted by Habel (1985: 296–7) and Clines (1989: 436), suggests this to be a unit (cf. Balentine 1999b: 271–2).

Strategies

Direct Address to the Friends, Inclusio, and Lexical Repetition.
Confirming that this speech is a disputation speech is the primacy of Job's direct address to the friends in Job 19. Not only does direct address provide structure to the speech (Clines 1989: 435–6), but Job uses seventeen 2mp forms in eight verses (19:2 [2×], 3 [3×], 5 [2×], 6, 21 [3×], 22 [2×], 28, 29 [3×]). Job charges the friends with comforter malpractice—violence with words (19:2-3)—which leads to his thesis in 19:5-6: if they continue to vaunt themselves over him in their argumentation they need to know that it is God who has perverted justice and wronged him. After developing his argument in 19:7-20, Job returns to address the friends in 19:21 to reiterate his thesis: "the hand of God has done this" (19:21). This is the reason why Job pleads for their pity. The double imperative coupled with the independent personal pronoun as a vocative creates urgency in Job's request. The request, however, is ironic. Job characterizes his comforters as "friends," though they are not acting as such. The illocution of the double imperative is not, then, for them to pity him, but to get them to cease their arguments, their violence with words (so also Clines 1989: 453).[59] Job's reiterated thesis provides the grounds for his appeal (note the causal כִּי). This double petition in v. 21 leads Job to address the friends with a scathing complaint in the rhetorical question in 19:22. Job closes his sixth speech where he began, with a didactic imperative grounded by a characterization of their violence with words, with the imperative further stressed by לָכֶם in 19:28-29. The כִּי of 19:28 is causal, indicating the reason for the imperative in 19:29 (so also Seow 2013: 792 and Hartley 1988: 298).[60] Because they continue to harm him with their words, they should fear the sword. Job's purpose, again, is to get them to cease their verbal violence by pointing to the result of noncompliance: "so that you might know judgment." Job's final imperative in 19:29 is thus linked with his first in 19:6 through the verb ידע. Job addresses the friends to implore them to cease their comforter malpractice.

---

59. The illocution of the call for mercy makes perfect sense in this rhetorical situation given Job's companions' behavior; it is not a parody of traditional piety (*pace* Newsom 1996: 477; Seow 2013: 802).

60. Clines interprets the כִּי as temporal (1989: 428), which is also plausible: "when you verbalize acts of violence fear the sword." Job had offered a similar warning of divine judgment in 13:5-19. As in that context, this context accuses the friends of perjury (Seow 2013: 809).

The inclusio of direct address around this entire speech, seen especially in the didactic imperatives of 19:6 and 19:29, highlights the rhetoric of direct address in Job's disputation. The imperatives in 19:21 and 19:29 and the repetition of רדף in 19:22 and 19:28 also form an inclusio, demarcating Job's final movement in this speech and reiterating the macro-level inclusio of 19:2-6 and 19:28-29.[61]

Job's rhetoric of direct address is an unambiguous response to Bildad's argument from Job 18, though he addresses the friends together. This is confirmed by the lexemes that are shared between the two speeches. As many have noted, Job's opening rhetorical question echoes both of Bildad's speeches (19:2; 18:2; cf. 8:2) (e.g., Hartley 1988: 282; Course 1994: 115; Seow 2013: 794–5). But Job repeats other lexemes to rebut Bildad's argument. He uses נֶפֶשׁ in 19:2 in response to Bildad's use of the word in 18:4. Job counters Bildad's supposition that Job destroys himself by stressing that the friends' violence with words is what destroys his נֶפֶשׁ (so also Course 1994: 116). The repetition of מִלָּה (cf. 18:2; 19:2) keeps the issue of speech ethics at the forefront of the discussion. Job's thesis relates to his justification of his verbal expression, using ידע in 19:6. Job instructs the friends to "know" that God has harmed Job, in response to Bildad's insinuation that Job does not "know" God.[62] Though not from Bildad's second speech, Job recalls Bildad's first speech with עות in 19:6 (cf. 8:3). The verb is used elsewhere in the book of Job only at 34:12. Job's modification of the object makes clear his argument: God has perverted "me" and, therefore, has perverted justice.[63] Job twice uses סָבִיב, in 19:10 and 12, to stress the thoroughness of divine attack. This word has only occurred three previous times in the book, and one of these is in Job 18:11, where Bildad describes the terrors that surround the wicked. Job recasts the image to show that divine attack has surrounded him, directly rebutting Bildad's insinuation that Job's terrors indicate that he is among the wicked. Job uses אַף in a similar way in 16:11, namely, to rebut Bildad's use in 18:4. Continuing the argument regarding anger from 16:9, Bildad had claimed that it is not divine anger, but self-inflicted anger that was Job's problem. To this, Job replies that the problem is God arousing his anger. To refute Bildad's contention that the snares inevitably capture the wicked (18:8-10), Job explicitly notes that God has enclosed

---

61. Habel (1985: 296–7) and Clines (1989: 436) suggest that the latter inclusio is a part of a chiasm that focuses attention on Job's wish and conviction in 19:23-27.

62. This is admittedly precarious, given the frequency with which ידע occurs. The root also occurs in 19:13, 14, and 25.

63. Course also makes this connection (1994: 116).

him with his net (מָצוּד) in 19:6.⁶⁴ Further rebutting Bildad's argument that associates Job with the wicked is his use of אֹהֶל. Bildad had used this word three times (18:6, 14, and 15) to stress the fate of the wicked; Job replies by using this term to stress God's attack hyperbolically in 19:12 (so also Fohrer 1963: 314). Finally, Job uses עוֹר in 19:20 and 26 in response to Bildad's use of the word in 18:13. Bildad had claimed that the wicked person's skin is devoured by the Firstborn of Death; Job replies that his skin has been flayed by his enemies, the friends.⁶⁵ With these lexical repetitions, Job recasts Bildad's argument regarding the wicked and further stresses his own contention regarding his innocence.

In sum, Job's rhetoric of direct address is intended to convince the friends to discontinue the violent attacks of their words. He reinforces his disputation with an inclusio and lexical repetition. His argument is that God has harmed him (19:6, 21); the implication is that Job is innocent. This refutes the friends' implication that Job is among the wicked while also justifying his protest prayer.

Tropes. The tropes of Job 19, as in the previous speeches, abound and reinforce the other rhetorical strategies. Job opens and closes the speech with the trope of friend violence with words. Job uses six verbs to portray the friends' arguments as attack: יגה, דכא, כלם, הכר, גדל, and יכח.⁶⁶ Their attack is verbal, as indicated by the use of מִלָּה in 19:2 and the final verb יכח. The attack imagery is provocative and accusatory, with the goal of silencing his comforters. Working with this trope is the imagery of error or sin in 19:4. His error is not obvious to them or they would argue with

---

64. מָצוּד is not one of the six terms Bildad uses in 18:8-10, but the similarity of imagery is hard to miss. See Hartley 1988: 284; Course 1994: 117.

65. Seow proposes possibly reading the 3cp *qatal* form in 19:26 as a reference to the friends (2013: 808). This intriguing reading may also provide some insight on the timing of Job's vision of God, a crux for interpreters. Job's use of אַחֲרוֹן and אַחַר in 19:25-26 echoes Bildad's use of these words in 18:20 and 18:2, respectively. Job's condition appalls those in the west (אַחֲרֹנִים); after (אַחַר) Job ceases arguing, the friends will speak. (אַחֲרֹנִים only occurs twice in the book, while אַחַר occurs twenty times, though the only previous occurrences of the preposition are 3:1; 8:19; and 18:2.) Perhaps the timing of Job's vision of God has nothing to do with ante-mortem or post-mortem questions, but refers to after the dispute, the ordeal with the friends during which they have committed acts of verbal violence, is completed. After the friends have flayed Job's skin, Job will see God and be vindicated.

66. The verb בוש in 19:3 functions as a hendiadys with the verb הכר to emphasize the main verb. See Hartley 1988: 284 n. 2; GKC §120c. See ESV, NIV11, JPS, and NASB.

specificity (Seow 2013: 795); he uses this to justify further his implied call for silence. Their attack is further portrayed as persecution in 19:22 and 19:28. In 19:22 the persecution is modified by the prepositional phrase "like God" (כְמוֹ־אֵל), which links Job's friends with the divine attack previously described (19:6-13, 21). This provocatively captures the extent of their attack. The persecution is explicitly linked with words in 19:28 where Job characterizes the friends with a quotation.[67] This trope characterizes the friends as enemies and attackers whose harmful words need to stop.

As in Job 16, Job uses a complex trope centered around divine attack to substantiate his argument that God has wronged him. The divine attack trope emerges with 19:6, balanced by 19:21, where Job states plainly that God has wronged Job, enclosed him with a net, and struck him with his hand.[68] These unambiguous statements are elaborated in the narrative-like description of divine attack in 19:7-13.[69] Divine violence is implied in 19:7, but is explicit in the verbs of 19:8-13. There are eleven verbs depicting divine violence in this section,[70] with the passive in 19:7 indicating God's silence. There are an additional five possessive suffixes that indicate that God is attacking Job (19:6, 11 [3×], 12). This description is provocative—as it was in Job 16—and intended to shock Job's friends to help them see that God has done this (Hartley 1988: 285). Further reinforcing the trope is Job's six-fold use of the preposition עַל and double use of סָבִיב to portray the extent of divine attack against Job (Habel 1985: 295).[71] Further reinforcing the extent of Job's suffering at God's hand is the hyperbolic reference to his tent in 19:12. Seow (2004: 694) connects God's troops with the friends, writing, "There is obvious caricature in the depiction [of the besiegement], for these troops act as if they are attacking

---

67. This characterizing quote is stark in that it portrays the friends as admitting that they are persecuting Job, another subtle rhetorical move on Job's part to convince the friends to stop talking. He portrays the friends as asking how they can continue to persecute him when the "root of the matter is found in him." This reading adopts the variant (Hartley 1988: 298 n. 1; Clines 1989: 466; cf. NIV11, ESV, JPS), though see also Seow's argument regarding the MT as the more difficult text (2013: 827).

68. On the divine warrior motif, see Seow 2013: 796.

69. This is similar to Job 16:7-16. Clines also highlights the narrative dimension of 19:7-12 (1989: 445).

70. עוּת, נקף, גדר, שׂים, פשט, סור, נתץ, נסע, and רחק. There are also חרה with the subject אַפּוֹ and חשב with the prepositional phrase כְּצָרָיו; on the theme of adversaries see 16:9.

71. The thoroughgoing nature of the attack is also stressed by Job's use of the adverb יַחַד in 19:12.

a massive walled city instead of one individual in his tent."[72] The trope of darkness (19:8), the imagery of death (19:10), and the tree imagery (19:10; cf. 14:19) all reinforce the divine attack portrayed by Job. The divine violence trope is conjoined with images of divine injustice as well in 19:6-7: Job cries violence, but "there is no justice" (וְאֵין מִשְׁפָּט). This statement refutes the theological positions of the friends, whose God does not pervert justice (8:3) and whose paradigm makes no room for someone to suffer innocently, without cause. The provocative God-talk suits Job's disputation as he defends his innocence and right to protest in prayer.

Job also follows the paradigm set in Job 16 by commenting on his suffering following his description of divine attack. He joins the two images, indicating that the divine attack is the cause of his suffering, his alienation.[73] Job describes his marginalization in 19:13-19. He has been ostracized from all his relationships—family, employer/employee, and civic. Ultimately, though, Job's suffering is emotional, as the culmination of the section in 19:20 makes clear. Clines notes the inversion of normal order in Job's image that his bones are so weak they cling to the skin, the effect of which bespeaks Job's weakened emotional and mental state. The body imagery in 19:20 is a trope for his emotional suffering (Clines 1989: 451–2; Erickson 2013: 313).[74]

Job reuses body imagery in 19:22 to heighten the rhetoric of his depiction of the violence of his friends. By noting their insatiable appetite for his flesh, he accuses the friends of being savage animals, though he may be accusing the friends of slander in his accusation (Seow 2013: 802). This savagery may be further depicted in 19:26, if one takes the implied subject of נִקְּפוּ as the friends.[75] Despite their attack, Job assures them of his confidence that his mangled body will survive and see God. His emotional exhaustion is reiterated with body imagery in 19:27 as well.

Job also employs writing imagery in his wish. Job depicts writing media of increasing degrees of permanence to emphasize his wish for documentation (Balentine 1999b: 273; cf. Good 1990: 257). Job desires that his words are engraved into rock, not merely recorded on a scroll.

Job's final trope in this speech is his use of sword imagery to warn the friends of the consequences of their attack. The sword imagery responds to Eliphaz's imagery of the sword in 15:22, where the wicked person is

---

72. See also Clines 1989: 444; Hartley 1988: 286.

73. The 3ms form הִרְחִיק in 19:13 is not to be emended, but refers to the final action of God depicted in Job's sequence.

74. On the image of Job's escape "by the skin of teeth," see Newsom (1996: 477), where she suggests that Job means "I have escaped with nothing."

75. See n. 65 above.

destined for the sword.⁷⁶ Job turns the tables on the friends, indicating they are destined for the sword, not him. His speech is defensible; theirs is not.

These tropes work with Job's other rhetorical strategies, enhancing their provocative nature as a means toward convincing the friends that God—not his wickedness—is the cause of his suffering, which ultimately justifies his protest prayer.

Rhetorical Questions. Job uses two rhetorical questions in the rhetoric of his sixth speech.⁷⁷ Job opens his speech with a question in 19:2. The question initiates Job's direct address in 19:2-6, asserting through the rhetorical question that the friends have committed verbal violence. The interrogative "how long" (עַד־אָנָה) not only connects Job's speech with Bildad's, but indicates the urgency of Job's desired rhetorical goal. This interrogative implies that the attack has been ongoing while also implying a petition for it to cease. The second rhetorical question builds on Job's opening accusation. In 19:22 Job uses לָמָּה to accuse further the friends of committing acts of persecution (רדף). It is not merely an accusation of the friends' violence but also an implied petition for them to cease. In this way, it functions in his disputation in the same way as a complaint,⁷⁸ and builds on Job's direct address in 19:21.

Allusion. Previous interpreters have suggested a number of different allusions to other biblical texts in Job 19. In Job 19:7, with the collocation of חָמָס with צעק/זעק, Job alludes to Jer. 20:8 (Dell 2013: 111; Seow 2013: 797; cf. Greenstein 2004a: 100). While the lexical similarity between these two texts is not as strong as other allusions discussed in this study, the fact that Job has already alluded to this passage in Jeremiah in his opening complaint makes it more likely Job is again drawing attention to this text. Job is portraying himself as the quintessential sufferer, linking himself with Jeremiah (Greenstein 2004a: 100). The injustice Jeremiah protests, Job also experiences—and protests. In the context of his rhetorical situation Job uses Jer. 20:8 to counter the narrative formed for him

---

76. See also 5:15, 20, where Eliphaz had promised Job's ultimate protection from the sword if he would repent. The insinuation of 15:22 is the same: the sword is Job's end if he does not repent.

77. The rhetorical question of 19:28 is a hypothetical question of the friends which Job uses for characterization. See the analysis of 19:28 above in direct address and the trope of friend violence.

78. See Morrow (2006a: 15), where he highlights the similar rhetorical dynamics of human-to-human and human-to-divine complaint.

by his friends. He is not suffering as a wicked person, but as a righteous person. Like Jeremiah, Job has reason to complain. The thematic overlap regarding the social marginalization for both Job and Jeremiah is noted by Greenstein (99–100). This reinforces the lexical connection that is made.

The second allusion, suggested by a number of scholars, occurs in 19:8, to Lamentations 3.[79] The verb גדר, used in 19:8 and Lam. 3:7 and 9, is the strongest link given its relatively infrequent use (ten occurrences in the MT). Other shared lexemes further substantiate the link between this section of Job 19 and Lam. 3:7-9: זעק/צעק, שוע, דֶּרֶךְ, עָוֹה/עָוֹת and נְתִיבָה (Hartley 1988: 285 n. 5). The verb נקף occurs in Job 19:6 and Lam. 3:5, and חֹשֶׁךְ occurs in Job 19:8 and Lam. 3:2 (cf. Lam. 3:6).[80] Job thus reprises an allusion from Job 16 with the same effect: it is a refutation of the friends' application of the *topos* of the fate of the wicked.[81] The irony of being innocent yet treated like guilty Zion is provocative and incisive.

Another reprised allusion occurs in Job 19:9, with the כָּבוֹד and עֲטֶרֶת alluding to Ps. 8:6 (Kynes 2012: 73).[82] Kynes suggests, "For Job to accuse God of tearing the crown from his head, he must assume that this is where it intrinsically belongs, and thus, though he parodies the psalm, a conviction of the worth of humankind, which Psalm 8 declares, motivates his lament and accusation of God" (74). While this interpretation of the allusion relates to Job's protest prayer, the rhetorical situation here is more likely, or primarily, a refutation of Eliphaz's use of the psalm, which Kynes also suggests. Eliphaz upends the meaning of Psalm 8 with his allusion in Job 15:14-16, "twisting it into its opposite [meaning] in order to support his argument," the argument of the fate of the wicked (72). In a situation where Job has Psalm 8 applied to him to modify

---

79. See, e.g., Westermann 1981b: 66 n. 75; Hartley 1988: 285 n. 5; Mettinger 1993: 272–3, and Aitken 2013: 208–9; for an argument that there is no allusion, see Clines 1989: 442. Aitken (2013: 210), after outlining many of the connections, ends up agreeing with Clines. Even if these are stock images, the number of connections between Lamentations and Job 16 and 19 makes allusion likely; Mettinger argues similarly (1993: 273). Westermann suggests a number of parallels to Lamentations in Job 19: 19:8a // Lam. 3:7; 19:8b // Lam. 3:2, 6; 19:7 // Lam. 3:8; 19:9 // Lam. 3:14; 19:11 // Lam. 3:43; 19:9 // Lam. 5:16; 19:10 // Lam. 2:2; 19:11 // Lam. 2:4-5. One could add to this list the thematic overlap between Job 19:20 and Lam. 3:4 (physical deformation) and Job 19:12 and Lam. 3:5 (besiegement). Not all of Westermann's parallels are convincing as allusions, but, taken as a whole, it is clear there is some connection between how Job portrays himself and the city of Zion in Lamentations.

80. On the link with חֹשֶׁךְ, see Aitken 2013: 209; Mettinger 1993: 272.

81. See the Mettinger quote at n. 52 above.

82. The reuse of the psalm is likely given the allusion to the psalm in Job 7 and Job 15.

his perspective on protest prayer, Job reprises the psalm to defend his innocence and protest prayer. Kynes suggests that Job's faith is evident and that he remains committed to the idea that the psalmist's theology is correct (ibid.). This commitment to the psalmist's anthropology—that Job is a divine image bearer and thus has a right to protest his innocent suffering to move God to act in accordance with what Job knows to be true—counters the friends'. There is possibly an implied petition for God to act in accordance with the psalm—Kynes' interpretation—but Job is arguing against the friends in this speech. These two interpretations are not necessarily mutually exclusive. Job, as a human, is not too low to engage God in honest dialogue.

The final allusion occurs in Job 19:25-27. Kynes notes that וַאֲנִי, אַחַר, לִי, and כלה occur "in the same order and roughly the same distance apart" in Ps. 73:23-26 (2012: 170).⁸³ Since this psalm is used in each of the friends' applications of the fate of the wicked to Job (cf. 15:27; 18:3, 11, 14; 20:8), it becomes clear that Job alludes to this psalm to refute their arguments (168–9). His avowal of trust expressing his faith and hope in God bringing vindication links him with the psalmist, who becomes assured of vindication after his sanctuary encounter (Ps. 73:17-28). This rhetorical move undermines the friends' argument and use of the fate of the wicked *topos*.⁸⁴

83. Kynes admits the lexical links are not strong, but notes the thematic, stylistic, and structural similarity. Furthermore, this psalm is alluded to in other contexts, further substantiating the allusion here. See 2012: 162–79. See also Luyten 1990: 77–80, upon whom Kynes is building.

84. Bastiaens also suggests an allusion in Job 19 to the fourth Servant Song (1997: 427–9). He notes the use of the verb דכא in 19:2 and Isa. 53:5, 10 as well as the shared experience of social alienation. The links he suggests are weaker than some of the other allusions discussed here. For a helpful list of the alleged connections between Job and the Servant Songs, see Brinks Rea 2010: 183–4. The strongest link between Job 19 and Isa. 52:13–53:12 is probably the overlap of the verb נגע in Job 19:21 and Isa. 53:4. With the connection having been established in Job 16, it is possible that Job reprises this allusion. But Brinks Rea is right to suggest that the stronger links with the Servant figure appear in Job 16 (185–6). If there is an allusion to the fourth Servant Song in Job 19 it functions the same way rhetorically as the allusion in Job 16, namely, to provide a clue as to Job's confidence in vindication, a condemnation of the friends' arguments. Furthermore, Hartley suggests a connection between Job 19:13 and Ps. 88:9 [8], 19 [18] (1988: 12). The link is intriguing—see p. 73 n. 100 above—but the frequency of this verb and the lack of other verbal links makes it unlikely to be an allusion. If this allusion is accepted, however, it seems that, by alluding to this psalm, and identifying himself with the psalmist of the darkest psalm of the Psalter, Job subtly substantiates his protest prayer.

Wish. Following Job's rhetorical question in 19:22 where he accuses the friends of persecution, Job issues a wish, marked by a double מִי־יִתֵּן in 19:23-24. The wish expresses Job's desire for a permanent recording of his words, with Job expressing increasing permanence in three modes of writing: written, inscribed in a scroll, and hewn into a rock with an iron pen and lead (Balentine 1999b: 273; cf. Good 1990: 257). While the exact referent of Job's words is uncertain, Hartley (1988: 291) suggests that Job has in mind his protest prayer. This coheres well with Job's rhetoric throughout the book: he has disputed the friends' contention that he cannot and should not protest in prayer. As the rhetoric has intensified from the friends, Job issues these wishes to reiterate his position. Far from being convinced of their position, Job desires that his protest prayer would be an enduring monument of lament (294 n. 14). Such a monument would stand in opposition to the friends' call for repentance in the second cycle, while also providing a constant plea to God. Following his implied petition for the friends to cease their current comforter malpractice (19:21-22), Job reiterates his main argument. He stands by his conviction that he has every right to protest despite their criticisms and insinuations.

Emphatic Statements. Job uses a number of particles to draw attention to key statements in his dispute in Job 19. The first of these is the combination אַף־אָמְנָם in 19:4. This draws attention to Job's argument regarding the inappropriateness of their general arguments. If Job were truly guilty of wickedness, as the friends claim, this would be obvious (Seow 2013: 795). Building on this emphatic statement, Job further disputes their comforter malpractice with an emphatic statement, his thesis in 19:5-6. The protasis (אִם־אָמְנָם) presents the friends' actions; the apodosis (אֵפוֹ) suggests Job's thesis that the friends need to learn. If they are to continue vaunting themselves over him (19:5), neglecting proper comforter ethics, he will continue to point out that he is innocent, that God has done this (19:6). To substantiate his thesis, Job uses הֵן to mark God's actions as evidence in 19:7-20.[85] Job further uses particles in an inclusio to stress his social alienation, with אַךְ in 19:13 and גַּם in 19:18. These particles emphasize Job's key arguments against his friends' insinuations by underscoring the cause and effects of his suffering.

Job also makes emphatic statements at the end of his speech, using other means than particles. Job's urging that they cease their violence in 19:21 is a key statement, marked by the double imperative and independent personal pronoun. Both Job's clear articulations of his thesis in 19:6 and

---

85. The הֵן governs all of 19:7-20 as אַךְ־עַתָּה governs all of 16:7-16.

21 are emphasized in his rhetoric. Job's final imperative in 19:29 emerges as a marked statement with the use of the seemingly superfluous לָכֶם, highlighting his final warning and threat.

One of Job's most significant emphatic statements is an interpretive crux in Job 19, namely, his avowal of trust in 19:25-27. Marked by the disjunctive *waw* in 19:25, the independent personal pronouns in 19:25 and 27, and by its location at the center of a chiasm, Job uses his conviction rhetorically to build on his wish and as a bridge to his final warning in 19:29. Two interpretive questions need to be addressed in order to understand 19:25-27 in Job's rhetorical context: (1) who is Job's redeemer, and (2) what does Job envision from this redeemer?

The question of Job's redeemer remains unresolved. The same basic positions regarding the identity of Job's witness are given when dealing the identity of Job's redeemer.[86] Accordingly, the same logic is often applied for why Job's redeemer cannot be God. Habel is typical (1985: 305–6):

> His God is his accuser, adversary, enemy, spy, destroyer, hunter, and siege commander. Against this opponent Job needs a *gō'ēl*, one who will take up his case and bring it before the court of heaven for public resolution. That this *gō'ēl* would be one and the same person as his cruel opponent seems quite illogical, inconsistent, and, from Job's perspective, intolerable… Job has portrayed God consistently as his attacker not his defender, his enemy not his friend, his adversary at law not his advocate, his hunter not his healer, his spy not his savior, an intimidating terror not an impartial judge.[87]

As argued above in the discussion of the identity of Job's witness, the putative illogical conclusion is largely alleviated when one considers the inherent tension in biblical protest prayer. More positively, the context—even if challenging—provides a number of clues for seeing Job's redeemer as God. First, as other interpreters have pointed out, גאל

---

86. Seow (2013: 823) outlines the different options for the identity of Job's redeemer : (1) God, (2) a third party as (a) an arbiter and witness, (b) a member of the divine council, (c) Baal, (d) a personal deity, (e) a human, (f) Job's cry, (g) an accuser of God, (h) a demigod opposed to God, and (3) a hypothetical being. Habel (1985: 306), Newsom (1996: 478), and Balentine (1999b: 274) consider Job's redeemer as a celestial being, while Clines (1989: 459) argues Job's redeemer is his personified cry. Wilson suggests Job's redeemer is a hypothetical being (1996a: 243–52). Longman (2012: 260), Hartley (1988: 293–5), and Seow (2013: 804–6) interpret the redeemer as God, though Seow thinks Job's reference to God is ironic. See also Pinker 2015: 18–19.

87. See also Clines 1989: 459.

is a common epithet for God (Pss. 19:15 [14]; 78:35; Isa. 41:14; 43:14; 44:6, 24; 47:4; 48:17; 49:7, 26; 54:5, 8; 59:20; 60:16; 63:16; Jer. 50:34).[88] Depicting God as the גֹּאֵל, rooted in the monotheism found throughout the book of Job, Job draws powerfully on the background of deliverance from Egyptian bondage and God's defense against personal attacks (Ps. 119:154; Prov. 23:11) (Gordis 1978: 206). Seow (2013: 806) captures Israel's understanding of God as redeemer: he saves (Hos. 13:14; Ps. 103:4), rescues (Pss. 69:19 [18]; 106:10; Mic. 4:10), frees (Exod. 6:6; 15:13; Isa. 43:1; 44:22-23; 48:20; 52:9; Ps. 77:16 [15]), and defends the afflicted (Lam. 3:58; Ps. 119:154). Particularly relevant for this point is the connection between Job and Isaiah 40–55. Even more specifically, Isa. 44:6, which also uses אַחֲרוֹן as a divine epithet, provides an important clue to identifying Job's redeemer. Second, Job describes his redeemer as living (חַי). Seow notes this brings to mind the "living God" (Deut. 5:26; Josh. 3:10; 1 Sam. 17:26, 36; 2 Kings 19:4, 16; Isa. 37:4, 17; Jer. 10:10; 23:36; Hos. 2:1 [1:10]; Pss. 42:3 [2]; 84:3 [2]; Dan. 6:21, 27 [20, 26]) (ibid.; cf. Hartley 1988: 294). Many of these texts are in the context of God's deliverance from various exigencies involving enemies.

So, what does Job expect God, as redeemer, to do? Simply, "the Last" (אַחֲרוֹן) will rise over the friends, vindicating Job in the process (19:25).[89] Job's conviction, then, is that God will vindicate him against the friends and he plainly communicates this expectation in hopes that it will accomplish his rhetorical goals: to get them to cease their malpractice and to defend his right to protest in prayer. But there is also an implied petition in this statement. Hartley writes (1988: 295), "Job is beseeching the God in whom he has faith to help him against the God who is punishing him." Though Seow may reject the notion of faith, he concurs regarding the implied petition. He suggests that by bringing God into the discussion Job "remind[s] God of a role abandoned that must be taken up again" (2013: 806). In his summary of the passage, Seow expands on this comment: "Job seems implicitly to accuse God of abandoning the responsibility of redemption that tradition has affirmed," but like his allusions, this is intended to move God to action. "One might indeed see Job's words as a desperate longing, a bold challenge for God to be God" (809). This

---

88. This analysis leans heavily upon Seow 2013: 804–6 and Hartley 1988: 293–5. Job is not referring to God as redeemer in an ironic way, *pace* Seow.

89. On this interpretation, see Seow 2013: 806–8. Seow includes Ps. 44:24-27 [23-26] in his discussion: the "call is for a dormant deity to rise and act" (807; see Pss. 7:2-3 [1-2]; 35:22-24). Hartley notes that the lack of the article on אַחֲרוֹן indicates it is best understood as an adverb (1988: 294 n. 15), but Seow counters that this word is a noun.

is the same logic as we find in Job's parody of the psalms and other biblical traditions, as articulated, for example, in the work of Kynes and documented throughout this study. In the midst of condemning the friends with his confidence in vindication, this statement calls on God to act in accordance with this conviction. This truly is an expression of "genuine faith" (Hartley 1988: 295).

Job's conviction is emphasized with his confidence of seeing God. The twice-repeated חזה with ראה and the 1cs forms that occur twelve times in 19:25-27 reinforce Job's proposition of the friends' eventual judgment.[90] Despite the friends' flaying of his flesh, Job states with confidence that he will see God, that his relationship with God will be restored. This analysis and the analysis of the allusion to Ps. 73:23-26 are mutually reinforcing. Job's use of Psalm 73 in this section directly refutes the friends' interpretation of Psalm 73 in their application of the *topos* of the fate of the wicked in their second cycle speeches. Indeed, this conviction of vindication implies Job's confidence in the appropriateness and effectiveness of his protest prayer. Job 19:25-27, as an emphatic statement of confidence, serves as a bridge between Job's accusation in 19:21-22 and wish for a permanent monument of his protest prayer in 19:23-24 and his warning to his friends in 19:28-29 by highlighting (and calling upon) God's role as redeemer.

Summary of Job 19

In Job's sixth speech Job continues to face the exigency of the friends' criticism of his language as Bildad insinuates that Job's fate is that of the wicked. In order to refute this and defend his protest prayer, Job again attempts to document his innocent suffering by elaborating the divine attack and alienation motifs. He wishes for a permanent documentation of his protest prayer and warns the friends of the consequences of their comforter malpractice. He is confident that he will be vindicated, which he articulates through his conviction regarding a redeemer. Job's faith in God keeps him from repenting of sin he has not committed in order to receive blessing, as his friends urge him to do (Hartley 1988: 299). His faith plays a major role in his argumentation, even as he describes God's attack.

---

90. As both Clines (1989: 462–3) and Seow (2013: 810) point out, this is exactly what happens at the end of the book (42:7-9). This is best seen as a foreshadowing of the conclusion of the book rather than an interpretive insight that develops only in a rereading of the book.

"Treachery Remains of Your Answers": The Rhetoric of Job's Seventh Speech (Job 21)

Introduction

After Job's strong rebuke and warning, Zophar responds with his second speech. In this speech, almost exclusively an elaboration of the *topos* of the fate of the wicked, Zophar brings the friends' rhetoric in the second cycle to a climax. Job, however, responds differently than in his other speeches in the second cycle. In Job 21 Job deals with the *topos* of the fate of the wicked more generally, rather than disputing its specific application to him.

The Literary Rhetorical Situation of Job 21

Zophar's second speech in Job 20 follows the trajectory set by Eliphaz and Bildad. He makes clear at the beginning that Job's speech has insulted him, a fact Zophar uses to justify his response to Job (20:2-3). After this brief opening justification, Zophar elaborates the demise of the wicked person in 20:4-29. Like Eliphaz and Bildad before him, Zophar uses the demise of the wicked person to associate Job with the wicked with the goal of modifying his behavior.[91] More specifically, Zophar wants to modify Job's speech. Clines (1989: 481) notes that the function of Zophar's speech is "to encourage Job into a change of life that will prevent him suffering the fate of the evildoer here depicted." While not explicitly stated, it seems best to understand this in the sense of Zophar desiring Job to repent. This is evident in 20:2-3 and 20:29. Zophar asserts his "disquieting thoughts" (שְׂעִפַּי) compel him to respond to Job (20:2); a "spirit from [his] understanding" (רוּחַ מִבִּינָתִי) leads him to address Job (20:3). Furthermore, "instruction" (מוּסַר) has insulted him (כְּלִמָּה). Though there is less explicit focus on Job's words than in other speeches, taken together these clauses indicate that Job's words have created Zophar's disquieting thoughts and offended him. Clines writes (483), "In calling Job's speech an 'instruction', Zophar intellectualizes Job's words as he did in 11:4, when he called them 'doctrine,' as well as criticizes Job for taking a superior position"; Zophar calls into question Job's presumption to teach. Such God-talk offends Zophar, so he continues the disputation.

---

91. The insinuation is made apparent through the number of words and motifs Zophar uses that echo Job's words, which has also been a strategy of Eliphaz and Bildad. On these connections, see Holbert 1981: 171–9. Cf. Habel 1985: 314–15 and Yu 2011: 322–3.

Zophar's summation also draws attention to Job's words. Most interpreters understand 20:29b to refer to the judgment decreed by God.[92] But a better reading of the clause might be: "the inheritance of his speech from God." The issue involves the word אִמְרוֹ.[93] The question is whether the pronominal suffix is best understood as an objective genitive (i.e., "the inheritance of the word or decree for him, the wicked person, by God") or as a possessive (i.e., "his speech"). The latter interpretation reads the parallelism more straightforwardly and fits the context of the disputation throughout the book to this point. The friends each have made Job's words the focal point of their dispute (4:2-6; 8:2-6; 11:2-6; 15:2-6; 18:2-4). The word is used a number of times in the book of Job (6:10, 25, 26; 8:2; 22:22; 23:12; 32:12, 14; 33:3; 34:37). Each of these occurrences refers to "words," with the referent being Job's words specifically in 6:26, 8:2, 32:12, and 34:37. Further support can be found in some ancient versions: the Targum, Vulgate, and Peshitta support this reading (see Seow 2013: 862–3). Understood this way, Zophar's point is that Job's verbal expression is the root cause of his sin, and thus his suffering. The inheritance of Job's speech is the fate described in 20:4-28. Zophar's speech is intended to encourage Job to cease his "impious rants of a wicked man" (Yu 2011: 319–20).

This clarifies the literary rhetorical situation for Job's seventh speech. As in the previous speeches he continues to face the exigency from his "comforters," as they challenge the ethics of his speech. Like the other speeches in the second cycle, the narrative of the fate of the wicked is used to turn Job from his lamentation (or defense of lament) to repentance—even if by implication. Job still faces the exigency of his suffering but the primary exigency is the one created by his friends. Accordingly, the audience of Job 21 is best seen as the friends. The goal of Job's speech is to refute their narrative, and the implication that he is wicked and that his speech will cause his demise. He needs to subvert this narrative and defend his discourse.

---

92. E.g., Seow (2013: 834): "His designated lot from God"; Clines (1989: 472): "such [is] the inheritance appointed him by God"; Hartley (1988: 304): "even the heritage decreed for him by God"; NASB: "even the heritage decreed to him by God"; NIV11: "the heritage appointed for them by God"; ESV: "the heritage decreed for him by God"; JPS: "the lot God has ordained for him."

93. Clines (1989: 480) writes of אֶמֶר that it "hardly seems like the appropriate word; but no convincing emendation has been offered," though the following analysis proposes how it might be considered appropriate. Seow notes that this word in the singular is unattested in the MT (2013: 862), though this in itself need not be problematic.

The Forms of Job 21

Interpreters are in agreement that the form of Job's seventh speech is disputation (e.g., Murphy 1981: 34; Westermann 1981b: 87–90; Hartley 1988: 41; Clines 2006: 520). The speech consists of arguments, most of which can be seen as direct refutations of the friends' arguments (Westermann 1981b: 87). There are a number of disputatious elements: the direct address, the presentation of theses, summaries of other positions, and rhetorical questions. There are seventy-six clauses of disputation in Job 21, with the five plural imperatives in 21:2-3, 5 indicating petition. These clauses of petition work with the disputation by calling for attention and silence, so that Job's argument may be heard.

The Rhetorical Strategies of Job 21

Structure

There is no consensus among scholars regarding the structure of Job 21, though there is some broad agreement. There are three major proposals: those who divide the speech into two major movements with a summary statement (e.g., Murphy 1981: 33–4; Hartley 1988: 310; Clines 2006: 517; Yu 2011: 325), those who suggest a four-fold division with a summary statement (Habel 1985: 324), and others who divide the poem into five movements with a summary statement (Newsom 1996: 491; Seow 2013: 866).[94] Seow's observation of the motif of death bringing closure to each stanza suggests the following structure: vv. 2-6, vv. 7-13, vv. 14-21, vv. 22-26, vv. 27-34 (ibid.).[95]

This structure reveals Job's emphases. Appealing for their attention (21:2-3), Job opens his speech with a disputation in which he sets forth his thesis that his complaint is not with people, but with God (21:4). He knows they will be appalled at his argument, but he will refute their narrative of the fate of the wicked anyway (21:5-6). In the second movement, Job describes the wicked person's prosperity, security, and joy (21:7-13). Despite their godlessness (21:14-16), the wicked do not experience

---

94. Longman's (2012: 274–5) division is idiosyncratic: vv. 2-3, vv. 4-5, vv. 6-17, vv. 18-21, vv. 22-26, and vv. 27-34.

95. Other factors help identify the structure as well. Job 21:2-6 is dominated by direct address. The second movement is marked by the interrogative מַדּוּעַ in v. 7 and is unified by the themes of the prosperity, security, and joy of the wicked. The third movement is framed by the root חפץ in vv. 14 (in verbal form) and 21 (in nominal form). The interrogative in v. 22 shifts the discourse. The particle הֵן coupled with the direct address in v. 27 initiates Job's conclusion, with v. 34 providing an inclusio with v. 2. On the inclusio, see Habel 1985: 325 and Seow 2013: 866.

retribution (21:17-18a); Job calls for appropriate judgment (21:18b-21). Job criticizes the doctrine of retribution in 21:22-26, suggesting there is no distinction between the wicked and anyone else. Job closes his seventh speech with the argument that the wicked are even spared in judgment and experience a good death (21:27-33), thereby articulating that the friends' arguments are false and harmful (21:34).

These emphases cohere with the literary rhetorical situation identified above. Job's argument consists of three main points: (1) his complaint is justified (21:4), (2) the narrative of the wicked as depicted by the friends is false (21:7-33), and (3) the friends are unethical comforters (21:2-3, 34).

Strategies

Direct Address to the Friends, Characterization, Inclusio, and Lexical Repetition. Four strategies are intimately related: Job's direct address to the friends, his characterization of them as violent comforters, inclusio, and his use of key terms that reflect his refutation of their use of the *topos* of the fate of the wicked. The direct address occurs at the beginning and end of the speech, forming an inclusio around the main argumentation. Job opens his speech with five imperatives that implore the friends to consider his argument in silence. Clearly Job does not think the friends are listening to his argument (21:2-3; cf. 13:17). Job uses the first two imperatives (שִׁמְעוּ and שָׁאוּנִי) to draw attention to his argument that his complaint is with God (21:4). The friends have inserted themselves into a dispute that does not concern them. Appealing for sensitivity (21:5a), he anticipates that they will be appalled at his argument (21:5b-c) (Westermann 1981b: 88; Hartley 1988: 310 n. 3; Newsom 1996: 491). Seow captures the point of 21:5a (2013: 869): "He wants them to see him as a human face and not just as an occasion for theological talk. The friends have been talking theology, while he has been complaining of personal suffering." He made a similar appeal in 6:28. After Job has laid out his arguments, he sarcastically grants the friends permission to mock on (21:3).

This is the first instance of characterization in this speech: Job portrays himself as an innocent sufferer and the friends as mocking enemies (Seow 2013: 869). At the end of the speech, Job builds on this characterization when he returns to direct address in 21:27. He anticipates that they will continue to commit acts of verbal violence (21:27) (so also Yu 2011: 328). Job's direct address incorporates characterization also in 21:28, when he cites a hypothetical quotation of their argument. In response, Job marshals evidence from those who are well-traveled (21:29-30). He concludes his speech by portraying the friends as treacherous and unfaithful (21:34). The friends' words are "vacuous and unreliable," even "idolatrous" (Seow 2013: 876). This characterization reinforces Job's disputation. The inclusio of the trope of the friends' treachery (21:2-3, 27-28, 34) reinforces the oft-noted inclusio of the root נחם, with the noun תַּנְחוּם in 21:2 and the verb in 21:34. The effect of the inclusio is to situate the narrative of the wicked within the dispute over words—Job's words and the friends' responses. The friends consider their words to be comforting words (cf. 15:11); Job considers them mockery (21:3), empty (21:34a), and treacherous (21:34b). The inclusio reveals that undermining the friends' narrative of the wicked is a means to an end. Their practices are unethical (note the use of מַעַל in 21:34). By this, Job implies that his speech is and has been ethical. Thus, Job's criticism of his friends' comforting practices is implicitly related to his defense of his protest prayer (cf. 6:2-30; 21:4). Not only is the friends' argument regarding the fate of the wicked false, but they lack the moral character to make an argument at all. This characterization establishes an inclusio around Job's speeches in the second cycle (see 16:2) (Habel 1985: 326), indicating a major point of emphasis in Job's rhetoric in the second cycle. Their lack of compassion for him as a sufferer undermines their argument. Job sees no reason why he should concede their call to repentance, affirming implicitly his right to protest in prayer.

While Job's disputation begins and ends with direct address to the friends in his effort to persuade them of the irrelevance and insidiousness of their use of the narrative of the wicked, Job's argument proper—that the doctrine of retribution is false—uses key terms and themes from the friends' speeches. Several lexemes link Job's seventh speech with Zophar's immediately preceding speech in Job 20. One of Job's main points is made through his rhetorical question in 21:7, asking why the wicked live (cf. 21:16, 17, 28). The use of רְשָׁעִים counters the narrative expounded by Zophar in 20:5, 29. When Job elaborates this thesis with a series of images, he uses a number of lexemes from Zophar's speech to recast the narrative. The wealth (חַיִל) of the wicked increases, Job contends (21:7); it neither poisons nor lacks joy (20:15, 18). Moreover, the house (בַּיִת) of the wicked experiences peace, not dread (21:9; cf. 21:11-13, 28), a point that recasts Zophar's contention that the wicked's house is destroyed in judgment (20:28). Contrary to Zophar's contention of the momentary joy (שִׂמְחָה) of the godless (20:5), Job portrays the wicked's joy (שׂמח) in 21:12 (Habel 1985: 325). Zophar had contended that the joy of the wicked was ephemeral, עֲדֵי־רָגַע, in 20:5; Job suggests the death of the wicked is quick and painless, בְּרֶגַע, in 21:13. It is not coincidental that 20:5 is a verse from which Job draws a number of lexemes given its prominence in Zophar's argument. Job describes the prosperity of the wicked (21:13,

16) in response to Zophar's assertion in 20:21 that the prosperity (טוֹב/טוּב) of the wicked does not last (so also Clines 2006: 527–8). Job uses a series of words to recast Zophar's contention of deserved retributive justice for the wicked: אַף in 21:17 (cf. 20:23, 28), where Job contends that the wicked are not judged;[96] אֹהֶל in 21:28 (cf. 20:26), where Job sets up his hypothetical quote by using a word that Zophar had used, only to refute it with evidence from others in 21:29-30; and יוֹם in 21:30, where Job articulates the lack of divine retribution (cf. 20:28). Job argues that the wicked do not experience the judgment Zophar so confidently asserted in 20:26-28. Job also uses several lexemes to dispute Zophar's portrayal of the wicked in 20:11-12. Rather than having bones full of vigor, using עֶצֶם and מלא, for only a moment before he lies down in the dust, using עָפָר and שׁכב, Job highlights the inadequacy of Zophar's argument by showing that there is no distinction between the wicked and any other person (21:23-26): all will lie in the dust (יַחַד עַל־עָפָר יִשְׁכָּבוּ וְרִמָּה תְּכַסֶּה עֲלֵיהֶם), whether strong and virile or bitter of soul (using עֶצֶם and מלא).[97] Further linking Job's speech with 20:11-12 is his contention that death is sweet (using מתק) for the wicked rather than a source of poison as Zophar suggested in 20:12-14 (Seow 2013: 876). Summing up these lexical connections is the shared lexeme שָׁלֵו (cf. 21:23; 20:20): Zophar portrays the wicked as one who does not experience ease, whereas Job suggests the opposite.

But the lexical and thematic connections are not limited to Zophar's speech, as a number of interpreters have noted. Habel (1985: 325) suggests that Job is responding to Bildad's speech, 18:5-6 in particular, in 21:17-26; Seow (2013: 866) concurs though he limits the response to 21:17-18. This is confirmed by the lexical connection of דעך and the very similar אוֹר רְשָׁעִים in 18:5 and נֵר־רְשָׁעִים in 21:17. Habel (1985: 325) suggests 21:27-34 responds to ideas from each of the friends (cf. 15:28, 34; 18:15-21; 20:26-28). Seow (2013: 866) associates Job's argument in 21:7-13 with Eliphaz's second speech.

These general analyses are confirmed by the shared lexemes between Job's seventh speech and the speeches of the friends in the second cycle. In 21:2 Job uses "consolations" (תַּנְחוּמוֹת) in response to Eliphaz's use in 15:11. This lexical link "repudiates what the friends say are divine consolations" (Seow 2013: 868). Acknowledging the truth of the accusation of his anger, using רוּחַ (cf. 15:12-13, 30; 18:4), Job argues that he has a

---

96. Habel (1985: 325) also considers 21:17 a retort to 20:28-29. On the rhetorical question, see below.

97. On the connection between 21:23-24 and 20:11-12, see Seow 2013: 874, and on the connection between 21:26 and 20:11, see Clines 2006: 531.

right to be angry and his complaint is not with the friends, but with God (21:4). This assumes his portrayal of divine violence from his previous two speeches and reflects Job's contention that he has a right to protest in prayer.

Not only does Job justify his protest prayer, but he uses words from the friends' description of the wicked to refute the narrative as well. Job's portrayal of secure houses, free of fear, in 21:9 contradicts the portrayal of the wicked's house from Eliphaz in 15:21 (cf. 15:20-27) (Habel 1985: 325).[98] Imagery of the abode of the wicked has played a major role in the friends' narrative of the wicked (cf. 15:28, 34; 18:6, 14-15; 20:26, 28), all of which Job refutes in his portrayal of their security (Clines 2006: 526). Eliphaz had promised Job a proliferation of posterity if he were to repent (5:25), and described the wicked as barren (15:34; cf. 18:19) (Clines 2006: 525; Seow 2013: 870). Job counters by describing the fate of the wicked as not barren but bountiful (21:8). Eliphaz had portrayed the distress of the wicked in 15:20-24 (cf. 5:5, and Zophar in 20:11, 15-18) (Hartley 1988: 313 [cf. 313 n. 8]; Seow 2013: 870); Job's thesis in 21:7, elaborated by the entire speech, portrays the opposite. The wicked live; not only do they live but they thrive in life and death. Moreover, the sound (קוֹל) of the wicked is not dreadful (15:21), but joyous (21:12) (Habel 1985: 325).

In sum, the direct address to the friends sets the table rhetorically for Job's attempt to convince the friends of (a) his right to protest because his issue is with God not man (21:4), (b) the fallacious nature of the *topos* of the fate of the wicked, accomplished through lexical repetition throughout the speech, and (c) their comforter malpractice, accomplished through characterization (21:3, 27, 28, 34).

Tropes. The imagery Job uses in his seventh speech reinforces the rhetoric of his disputation. Given Job's use of lexical repetition, it is no surprise to see the dominant trope of Job 21 to be the fate of the wicked. A number of tropes are amalgamated into a complex narrative that depicts not the judgment of the wicked but their prosperity, joy, and security.

The trope makes up almost all of the speech, covering vv. 7-26 and vv. 28-33. Job depicts the wealth, lineage, and security of the wicked person in 21:7-13. Regarding their wealth, Job first states generally that it increases (21:7), but then illustrates his point with the animal imagery in 21:10-11, concluding that their prosperity is certain in 21:13 and 16.[99] The

---

98. Seow (2013: 870), Clines (2006: 526), and Hartley (1988: 314) cite 5:24 as well.

99. Note also Job contrasts the wicked's wealth with others in 21:25.

fecundity of the livestock not only preserves wealth, it propagates it. That their descendants are "established before them" indicates the "security of lineage" for the wicked (21:8) (Seow 2013: 880). Their homes are secure, even at ease (21:9a; cf. vv. 23-24). The reason why, Job explains, is that divine justice has not been executed (21:9b). The imagery of security and divine injustice undermines the narrative of the retribution principle espoused by the friends by providing a counternarrative. Divine injustice is further elaborated later in the speech (21:17-20).[100] Job questions divine justice in 21:17-19a, which utilizes light and chaff imagery, and then calls for divine justice in 21:19b-20. The use of jussives in 21:19b-20 makes the imagery of divine injustice even more provocative by providing an implicit appeal for God to reveal himself as just. The rhetorical nature of this imagery is seen when Job returns to the trope of divine justice in 21:22b, as he mocks the friends for their dogmatism.[101]

Job also depicts the wicked as experiencing joy (21:12); Hartley (1988: 314) writes of the image of dancing, "This picture represents idyllic happiness." There is no indication of fleeting joy given Job's use of death imagery (20:5). The wicked are depicted as dying without complications in their prosperity (21:13), as not caring about the judgment that may come after (21:21), as experiencing the same lot as those whose life is full of hardship (21:26), and—most provocatively as the rhetoric builds throughout the poem—as having their grave watched, with death being sweet (21:32-33). The strength of the wicked is illustrated in 21:23-24, as Job describes the vigor of the wicked even in death; they reproduce without complications and are full of strength and stamina: "his testicles are full of milk and the marrow of his bones is moist."[102] While the wicked person is implied to have strength, others experience bitterness and lack prosperity (21:25). The juxtaposition of these images forms a contrast that serves Job's rhetorical purposes as he attempts to undermine the narrative the friends have expounded.

---

100. Some interpreters and translations understand 21:19a to be a quotation from the friends (e.g., Habel 1985: 328; Hartley 1988: 316–17; cf. the table in Ho 2009: 707; cf. NASB; ESV; NIV11; JPS). But the friends have said nothing like this. In fact, Bildad espoused the opposite view in 8:4. Fox rightly points out that with this statement Job is impugning God's injustice (Fox 1980a: 429).

101. Job 22:22 is another statement often interpreted as an unmarked quotation (see Fox 1980a: 429–30; Ho 2009: 707). But this is unlikely (Fox 1980a: 429–30; cf. Clines 2006: 530; Hartley 1988: 318).

102. On the understanding that עֲטִינָיו refers to testicles, and therefore to reproductive powers, see Seow 2013: 889.

Job uses another literary device in this speech: characterization through hypothetical quotes. He characterizes the wicked in his argument in 21:14-15. He depicts their blatant rejection of God through a quotation. The juxtaposition of this rejection with the idyllic life and death Job depicts throughout vividly refutes the friends' narrative. Job also uses characterization in 21:29-30 when he imagines a group of travelers and involves them in his dispute. They would provide evidence that corroborates the narrative he has told of the wicked: "in the time of calamity the wicked are spared; in the time of wrath they are delivered" (21:30; cf. 21:31). This implies divine injustice, returning to this pervasive trope. In order to subvert the friends' *topos*, Job is driven to impugn God's justice again.

Job also uses the trope of treachery, that is, friend violence with words, in this speech. The use of this motif is tied intimately to his characterization of the friends. It emerges in 21:2-3, 27-28, and 34. Their teaching is false (21:34).[103] The friends have committed violence, Job contends, by applying the fate of the wicked to him. They have failed to accomplish their comforting goal (cf. 2:11).

While Job combines a number of tropes in this speech, the dominant trope in Job 21 is the fate of the wicked, a trope that utilizes a number of images. What Seow writes of 21:7-13 is accurate for the entire speech (2013: 871): "The portrayal of the life of the wicked in this stanza (vv. 7-13) is thus entirely blissful, contrary to what the friends have argued." Job's speech "makes nonsense out of the *topos* that [the] comforters have used repeatedly, thereby removing it from the comforters' cache" (Yu 2011: 325). Nevertheless, the narrative of the wicked Job expounds is set within the context of the dispute over the friends' comforting practices as the inclusio of the trope of friend violence indicates, a dispute that is bound up with Job's words. This confirms that Job's argument in this speech concerns a justification of his discourse. The subversion of the narrative of the fate of the wicked is thus put in the service of justifying his speech. Because their narrative is false and because their verbal expression is unethical, Job is implicitly arguing for his innocence and that his God-talk is ethical.

Rhetorical Questions. Job asks twelve rhetorical questions in this speech.[104] The first two questions are in 21:4, where Job asserts a thesis

---

103. On the metaphorical nature of הֶבֶל, see Fredericks 1997: 1005.

104. Additional questions are asked in this speech in 21:15, where Job reports the reproachful questions of the wicked person in their rejection of God, and in 21:28, where Job entertains a hypothetical question from the friends to set up his argument

that his problem is with God and that he has every right to be impatient (Hartley 1988: 311). This refutes the arguments marshaled against Job regarding his angry speech (15:12-13, 30; 18:4). Job's suffering has been caused by God and therefore he has a right to be impatient and protest in prayer. The first question is emphasized by the fronted independent personal pronoun, marking it as an important point Job is making in this speech. Job reminds the friends of his exigency in relation to God.[105] The point of the question is to defend his right to protest in prayer.

The next question in 21:7 provides another thesis, namely, Job's position regarding the fate of the wicked.[106] Job argues through his question that the fate of the wicked as narrated by the friends simply cannot be true, because they not only live but prosper. As Clines notes (2006: 524), "Even a single case of a prosperous wicked man would destroy the friends' dogma." Job introduces his own narrative with this question, undermining the doctrine of retribution as espoused by his friends.

Job's next questions are found in 21:17-18, with four questions asked with one interrogative. The interrogative כַּמָּה in v. 17 governs five clauses, being gapped in 21:17b-18. The lexical link with 18:5-6 points to the argumentative nature of these questions. These questions assert that retribution does not happen (i.e., it is not often that the lamp of the wicked is extinguished, faces calamity or divine judgment, or experiences the fate of the wicked as depicted in Ps. 1, to which he alludes). Divine injustice is asserted in these questions, refuting the narrative of the friends.

The question of divine justice continues with the rhetorical question in 21:21, which forms the conclusion of Job's argument in 21:19-21. Job asserts in question form that delayed justice is immaterial. God may mete out justice on the wicked's posterity, but this is inconsequential,

---

in 21:29-30. There is some debate about whether or not a question is unmarked in 21:16a. See de Regt 1994: 368; cf. NRSV; ESV. Nevertheless, Seow makes the case that הֵן לֹא in 21:16a is the equivalent of an emphatic particle (2013: 884). Whether one takes it as an unmarked question or an emphatic statement, the point is the same: the wicked prosper.

105. Seow notes the ambiguity in 21:4a (2013: 869). שִׂיחַ לְ could refer to complaint against God or a complaint about God. Nevertheless, as he notes, "Either way, God is the issue. God is either the addressee of Job's complaints (so the first view), the problem about which he complains (so the second view), or both (see 7:11, 13; 9:27; 10:1; 12:8)" (869).

106. Clines (2006: 521) understands 21:7 as the node of the speech. Yu (2011: 327) suggests that Job's main argument occurs in 21:7-13, with the rest of the speech supplementing this main argument.

since the wicked person does not have to face any consequences for his wickedness. The lack of justice undermines the rigid formulation of the retributive principle affirmed by the friends.

Job turns his attention to this principle with his rhetorical question in 21:22. Clines (2006: 530), noting that the friends' theological system has taken precedence over God, writes this is Job's "own defense of God against the purely human doctrine of retribution."[107] This question is thus an accusation regarding their hubris and limiting of God by their theology. The accusation contributes to Job's goal of subverting their narrative of the wicked. The rhetorical question in 21:29-30 further stresses that their doctrine of retribution is untenable. Job documents the hypothetical testimony of the travelers, using the question to impugn the viability of the friends' narrative.[108] The rhetorical question in 21:31 also reflects the problems of the doctrine of retribution, the friends' narrative, and implies divine injustice. The wicked, as a tyrant, is unopposed; there is no accountability. In the context of the argument, this reinforces Job's thesis that the narrative of the fate of the wicked, as suggested by the friends, is false. Job protests this lack of accountability, using it in his argument, and perhaps also implying a petition for God to right the wrong (note the use of the jussive in 21:19b-20).

The final rhetorical question, in 21:34, is Job's climactic question in this speech, driving home his dispute over the unethical treatment he has experienced at the hands of the friends. Introduced by וְאֵיךְ, the interrogative indicates a reproachful question (*HALOT*, 39). The implied answer is that they cannot comfort Job with these vacuous consolations and arguments. But just in case they miss the point of the rhetorical question, Job states clearly, "treachery remains of your answers."

Each of these rhetorical questions relates to Job's three arguments; they are used to assert his position regarding his protest prayer (21:4), subvert the fate of the wicked as narrated by the friends (21:7, 17-18, 21, 22, 29-30, 31), and accuse the friends of comforter malpractice (21:34).

Allusion. Job also uses allusion rhetorically in Job 21. Kynes cites four allusions to various psalms in Job 21. In Job 21:11 the phrase כַּצֹּאן likely alludes to Ps. 107:41. While this phrase occurs eighteen times in the MT, Kynes points out that these are the only two occurrences of this phrase with reference to families (2012: 92). Since this psalm has played an

---

107. See also Fox 1980a: 430; Hartley 1988: 320–1; Seow 2013: 874.
108. On the virtual quotation, see Fox 1980a: 430–1.

important role in the dialogue elsewhere (cf. Job 5; 12:21, 24; 12:13–13:2; 15:24; 22:19),[109] the probability of the allusion increases. Notably, Eliphaz in 15:24 had alluded to this psalm in his use of the *topos* of the fate of the wicked (cf. Ps. 107:6, 13, 19, 28).[110] The allusion to Ps. 107:41 in Job 21:11 rebuts Eliphaz's use of the psalm. In 15:24 Eliphaz, exploiting the positive elements of the psalm to argue for retributive justice against the wicked, "uses [the psalm] with an antagonistic intent to silence Job's complaint by associating him with the wicked in the psalm and affirming a doctrine of retribution that allows no room for lament" (94; cf. 92). Job, on the other hand, depicts the wicked experiencing joy where the psalm uses this imagery to depict God's deliverance of the afflicted. This parody, then, depicts those who should not see deliverance and joy, the wicked, as those who experience just that, thereby refuting the retribution principle and emphasizing divine injustice.[111] This allusion also counters Eliphaz's attempt to silence his protest prayer. Beyond the disputatious rhetoric, Kynes also suggests a likely implied petition in this allusion (94). Job's parody is intended not only to refute the friends' narrative of the fate of the wicked, but also to provoke God to act in accordance with what the psalm affirms: for God to meet the afflicted and bring deliverance.

The other three allusions to the psalms are mutually reinforcing. In 21:14 Job alludes to Ps. 73:11, with the characterization of the wicked.[112] In 21:16 Job alludes to Ps. 1:1, with the phrase עֲצַת רְשָׁעִים, a phrase that only occurs in Ps. 1:1 and Job 10:3; 21:16; 22:18. In 21:18 Job again alludes to Psalm 1, this time v. 4 (Kynes 2012: 145–7).[113] Job alludes to these psalms elsewhere, strengthening the probability of allusion here. The allusion to Psalm 73 coheres with Job's use of other strategies to refute the friends' narrative of the fate of the wicked. The friends each

---

109. For a discussion of these allusions, see Kynes 2012: 87–93.

110. The noun מְצוּקָה occurs only seven times in the MT, with five of the occurrences in the refrain of Ps. 107 or Job 15:24 (ibid.: 92 n. 70).

111. As Kynes puts it, "[T]he wicked get the procreative blessing promised to the needy (21:11; cf. Ps 107:41)" (ibid.: 94). Notably, Eliphaz will respond with another allusion to Ps. 107 in 22:19; see Kynes' discussion (93).

112. The lexical links include אמר, אֵל, and דַּעַת, with strong thematic links. See ibid.: 171–2.

113. Kynes points out that 21:18 has other parallels (see Pss. 35:5; 83:14 [13]; Isa. 17:13), and that the use of language from Ps. 1 in such close proximity and other expressions from Ps. 1 indicate an allusion to Ps. 1 is likely. Kynes further suggests Job is in a sense parodying all of these passages for rhetorical effect in his disputation (ibid.: 147).

employ allusions to Psalm 73 (168–9). When Job depicts the prosperity of the wicked despite their rejection of God (21:7-21), he exposes his comforters' simplistic and naïve use of the psalm. But he also uses the allusion to Psalm 73 to set up his allusion to Psalm 1. After characterizing the wicked, he states emphatically that he has no association with them (21:16). Then he questions whether the retribution they deserve according to the psalm—to be treated like chaff (מֹץ)—actually occurs (21:18). In light of the friends' use of Psalm 1 in their argumentation (see 5:13-14; 8:11-13; 18:16, with 22:18 as a response to this speech) Job's rhetoric emerges.[114] As Wilson writes (2007: 229), "Job is contesting a naïve reading of the psalm in light of his own experience." This illuminates the allusion in 21:16, where Job uses Psalm 1 as "an affirmation of [his] righteousness. The prosperity of the wicked…indicates that things are the opposite way the psalm depicts them" (Kynes 2012: 150). By associating himself with the psalmist he furthers his rhetoric of using the psalm to refute the use of the psalm. Confirming this interpretation is Eliphaz's use of the psalm in 22:18 (155). Job is innocent—not like the wicked depicted in 21:14-15—despite his suffering. Like the allusion to Psalm 107, the allusion to Psalm 1 creates an implied appeal to God to act in accordance with the theology of the psalm. In this way these allusions further defend his protest prayer by being implied protest prayer while also subverting the arguments of the friends.

These four allusions have the same effect.[115] First, they are primarily used to refute the narrative of the wicked advanced by the friends: their narrative exploits Psalm 107 to silence Job's protest prayer (21:11), yet the reality of life calls into question their naïve and simplistic reading of Psalms 1 and 73 (21:14, 16, 18). Second, the allusions become provocative appeals for God to act in accordance with the theology inherent in the psalms.

---

114. On these allusions, see ibid.: 149–57.

115. In addition to these four allusions, Greenstein and Dell suggest an allusion in 21:7 to Jer. 12:1. See Greenstein 2004a: 103–4; Dell 2013: 114. This is possible, especially given the allusions to Jeremiah's other so-called confessions. But the lexical links are not as strong as with the other allusions. Greenstein accounts for the slight variations between Jer. 12:1 and Job 21:7 by noting that other lexemes from the Jeremiah text can be found in Job 21:8 and 23 (Greenstein 2004a: 104). If there is an allusion here, the internal rhetoric would be to refute the narrative of the wicked as advanced by the friends. Furthermore, by linking himself with Jeremiah, a righteous sufferer, Job substantiates asking such a question.

Emphatic Statements. There are two uses of particles in Job 21 that mark emphatic statements. Job uses הֵן לֹא in 21:16. Though sometimes interpreted as an unmarked rhetorical question,[116] Seow (2013: 884) suggests that הֵן לֹא is an emphatic statement that has its origins in an oath formula.[117] The compound particle stresses Job's conclusion regarding the prosperity of the wicked and his self-distancing from their community. Hartley is attuned to the rhetorical situation when he writes (1988: 315),

> He affirms his own integrity and faith in God even in the midst of lament over the good that befalls those who reject God. Thus he is arguing against the position of Zophar on two levels: (1) since there are wicked men who prosper and live to an old age, his own suffering does not automatically put him into the category of the wicked; (2) since he wholeheartedly rejects the counsel of the wicked, he cannot be categorically identified with them.

By emphasizing 21:16b, the allusion to Psalm 1 is stressed. Job uses הֵן again in 21:27 as he brings his dispute to a close. This particle emphasizes Job's characterization of the friends as violent comforters who he anticipates will still argue with him. These particles, therefore, mark key statements in Job's argument, emphasizing the fallacious nature of the *topos* and their treachery in using it.

Summary of Job 21

After repeatedly being associated with the wicked as a threat and an attempt to silence Job's protest prayer in this second cycle, Job changes his rhetorical approach. He attempted to document his innocent suffering in Job 16–17 and Job 19, but in Job 21 Job transitions to take on the *topos* of the fate of the wicked in general. The entire speech is an argument against the friends' narrative. He addresses them directly in order to silence them, characterizing them as unethical and harmful comforters, using an inclusio to frame his narrative of the fate of the wicked; he re-uses their own words to undermine their arguments; he uses rhetorical questions

---

116. See n. 104 above.

117. There is clearly difficulty in reading the negative particle given Job's argument in the context. See Clines 2006: 509–10 for an exhaustive list of the possibilities. Whether one interprets this difficult clause as an unmarked question or as an emphatic affirmative, the illocution of 21:16a is the same: Job is accentuating the wicked's prosperity. Another interpretation is to understand Job as saying the wicked have no control over their prosperity (see NIV11; JPS). This interpretation, however, does not fit the rhetorical situation as well because this is not the focus of the speech or the arguments Job is refuting.

and emphatic statements to advance his own argument; he alludes to the same psalms as they do to recast their narrative; he advances a new narrative through his collection of tropes to depict the joy, security, and prosperity of the wicked. The argumentation is designed to subvert their narrative, but the underlying goal is to silence them as comforters and thus to justify his speech. Job's justification of his protest prayer, however, is not entirely implied. It emerges clearly in his rhetorical question in 21:4. Job's dismantling of the viability of the *topos* brings the second cycle to a close, causing a change in the rhetorical situation, which in turn leads Eliphaz to heighten his rhetoric in the third cycle.

Summary of the Second Speech Cycle

There is a major shift in emphases and strategies in the second cycle for each of the participants in the dispute. With Job's rejection of the comforters in his fourth speech, the friends escalate their rhetoric, employing the *topos* of the fate of the wicked. Their goal with this *topos* is to encourage Job to see himself in their narrative (through insinuation) and to silence his theologically dangerous protest prayer. Their speeches are, thus, calls to repentance. Calling Job to repent is a repudiation of Job's chosen path to God-talk, protest prayer (13:3-4). Facing an altered exigency in relation to the friends, Job's speeches exhibit less explicit protest prayer in this cycle (only twelve of 244 clauses are protest prayer) and more disputation (232 clauses are addressed to the friends, 202 of which are disputation). Job seeks to dispute the comforting practices of the friends in Job 16–17, justifying his speech with a provocative narrative of divine attack. In this speech, Job also appeals to God—both implicitly and explicitly—to alleviate Job's suffering, including the added suffering caused by the friends' comforting strategies. In Job 19 Job maintains these goals: to dispute the comforting practices of the friends and to justify his protest prayer. When he sees that his attempts at proving that he is suffering innocently have fallen on deaf ears, Job subverts their cherished narrative with his disputation in Job 21. Each of the friends have used the *topos* of the fate of the wicked as an ethical critique of Job's discourse (15:2-6; 18:2-4; 20:2-3, 29). Their main concern is Job's God-talk. In response Job continues to use provocative God-talk to defend himself and his protest prayer.

As was the case in the first speech cycle, Job's use of the volitional mood in this cycle demonstrates his concern to defend his protest prayer. Job uses twelve imperatives in this cycle, only one of which is a petition to God to act on his behalf (17:3), though there is a petitionary illocution in 17:4 too. The request is for deliverance from his friends' "comfort." On the other hand, ten imperatives are addressed to the friends.[118] The illocution of these imperatives is of two kinds: (1) instruction (19:6, 29) and (2) pleading for the friends to discontinue their criticism (17:10; 19:21; 21:2-3, 5). These imperatives reflect Job's desperation to have his discourse, his God-talk, no longer rebuked and censured. Job's direct plea with the friends implicitly defends his discourse. Job's use of cohortatives in the second cycle accomplishes the same thing, relating to his pleas for the friends to dispense with their criticism. Five of the six cohortatives in this cycle criticize the friends' approach and juxtapose what Job would do (16:4-6). His point is that he would not act as they are doing; they need to cease expounding such narratives. Job's characterization of them as poor comforters defends his verbal expression by emphasizing that their verbal violence is unnecessary and harmful.

Certain strategies stand out as Job attempts to persuade his friends of the appropriateness of his protest prayer and the harmfulness of their arguments and advice. Job's re-use of lexemes from the friends in his argumentation occurs in 20% of the clauses (fifty out of 244 clauses) in this speech cycle, an astounding number that reveals his concern with disputing their arguments, with almost half of the lexical repetitions (twenty-two out of the fifty clauses) occurring in Job 21 as Job reutilizes and recasts words and images from the friends' speeches to demonstrate how untenable the *topos* of the fate of the wicked is. Direct address to the friends occurs in thirty-eight out of 244 clauses (16%), but of more significance is how Job addresses the friends, in that he combines direct address with other rhetorical strategies. Seven clauses use direct address and rhetorical questions (19:2, 22; 21:29, 34). Each of these rhetorical questions plays a major role in Job's argumentation as he appeals for the friends to stop their harmful speech (19:2, 22; 21:34) and to present evidence that contradicts their narrative of the wicked (21:29). Twenty-five of the thirty-eight clauses of direct address include the trope of violence with words (16:2, 4-5; 17:10; 19:2-3, 5, 22, 28; 21:2-3, 27-28, 34). These twenty-five clauses that combine direct address with the trope of violence with words occur in each speech, are found at significant structure junctures in each speech, and reveal one of Job's main concerns in this cycle. Job 19:22 is emblematic of this concern in the second cycle, emphasized by its integration of one of the frequent tropes of the cycle (violence with words) with three rhetorical strategies (rhetorical question, direct address

---

118. There is one additional singular imperative in this cycle, in 21:14, where Job characterizes the wicked who demand that God turn from them.

to the friends, and inclusio): "Why do you persecute me like God, and from my flesh are not satisfied?" In the context, Job has just articulated his divinely caused suffering for a second time (19:6-21), and immediately transitions and compares the friends' comforting practices with God's actions. This question captures Job's two arguments: (1) God has attacked him and he should seek relief through protest prayer, and (2) the friends are causing more harm and should be silent.[119]

An analysis of Job's use of tropes over the whole cycle indicates Job's preference for a few tropes, with five tropes dominating Job's rhetoric in the second cycle. The most frequently used trope is the fate of the wicked, found exclusively in Job 21:7-33. Furthermore, Job frequently describes his suffering (16:2, 6-8, 10, 12-13, 15-16, 20, 22; 17:1, 6-8, 11, 14; 19:13-20) and divine attack (16:7-9, 11-14, 18; 17:6; 19:6-13). These tropes occur exclusively in Job's fifth and sixth speeches, and establish vividly the connection between his suffering and divine attack. Together these tropes stress the severity of Job's plight and document his right to protest prayer; the attack and his suffering occurred despite his prayer being pure (16:17). Accordingly, Job articulates divine injustice through various images (16:8, 10-11, 17-18; 17:4; 19:6-7).[120] Another prominent trope Job uses in the second cycle is the trope of violence with words, by which he criticizes the friends' ethics (16:2-5, 10; 17:2, 5, 10; 19:2-3, 5, 22, 26, 28; 21:27-28, 34). By applying the narrative of the fate of the wicked to Job they have committed more harm, caused more suffering.

Looking more specifically at Job's use of God-talk, it is evident that Job's discourse directed to God is less frequent than in the first cycle. But it is noteworthy that Job uses the same tropes as in the protest prayer of the first cycle. In the twelve clauses of protest prayer, Job describes his suffering (17:1-2) and portrays divine attack (16:7b-8b). God's attacks, portrayed in 16:7-8, lead to his near-death experience, described in 17:1. Job is seeking relief, with the depiction of divine actions used to move God to cease such antagonism and with his suffering designed to motivate God to act quickly to bring relief and restoration. The one imperative in Job's protest prayer, 17:3, emerges as a clear expression of Job's goal: "offer a pledge for me." As in the first cycle, he uses his talk to God to try to motivate God to act on his behalf, bringing relief, especially as his friends proliferate his suffering.

---

119. Another significant rhetorical question occurs in 21:4, and relates to Job's two exigencies.

120. Divine injustice is an inherent part of Job's use of the fate of the wicked narrative as well.

Job talks about God in this cycle more than to God, in accordance with his modified rhetorical situation. Job talks about God almost exclusively using imagery. The most common trope is divine attack (16:7, 9, 11-14; 17:6; 19:6, 8-13, 21). The prevalence of this trope is stark. Job's talk about God stresses his innocent suffering at the hands of God, defending his protest prayer.[121]

Job's talk about God does not focus solely on divine attack, however. Job describes God's injustice explicitly in 16:11; 19:6; 21:9, 17-20, while his use of the fate of the wicked narrative in Job 21:7-33 implies divine injustice. But, as in the first cycle, these statements of divine injustice are balanced by other statements of divine justice. Job affirms divine justice as it relates to the friends explicitly in 21:22; they will be judged for their poor theology. Moreover, Job's talk about God includes his avowals of trust (16:19-21; 19:25-27). Job uses these expressions of hope and faith to remind the friends of his conviction of vindication and justice; they will face the sword (19:29). Job's talk about God, therefore, is rhetorically driven; what he says about God is contextually anchored, and needs to be interpreted within that context. Job uses his talk about God to defend his protest prayer and to silence the friends' arguments. Because Job is able to refute the narrative of the fate of the wicked and defend his protest prayer to some degree, the friends will take up a new strategy in the third speech cycle.

---

121. Job's description of divine attack is frequently marked for emphasis in some way. Forty-four of the 110 clauses (40%) of emphatic statements utilize divine attack imagery (16:7-9, 11-14; 19:6-13, 21). Relatedly, 33 of 110 (30%) use suffering imagery, whether physical or emotional, social alienation, or ephemerality (16:7-8, 10, 12-13, 15-16, 20; 19:13-20). For Job, divine attack and his suffering are significant aspects of his defense of protest prayer and are emphasized accordingly.

Chapter 5

"Even Today My Complaint Is Bitter":
Job's Internal Rhetoric in the
Third Speech Cycle (Job 22–27)
and His Final Speech (Job 29–31)

With Job subverting the *topos* of the fate of the wicked, the third cycle manifests an initial escalation in the friends' rhetoric with Eliphaz's speech in Job 22 and a subsequent breakdown of the dialogue. Job maintains his position regarding his integrity and his speech and continues to reject the friends' arguments. There is unmarked interruption and the use of mockery to caricature ideas that bring the dispute over Job's verbal expression to an end. Despite the scholarly conjecture regarding the loss, dislocation, and misidentification of speakers in the third cycle, this study regards the text's difficulties to be a literary device that portrays the breakdown of the dialogue.[1] Each of the speeches in this cycle are thus interpreted in accordance with the form of the text as we have it now. With the dialogue coming to a close, Job issues his final speech in Job 29–31, an extended prayer of protest with an oath that intends to force God to act.

---

1. This assumption is in part rooted in the method of this study, with a literary-rhetorical approach requiring a unified text. Nevertheless, the notion that the literary artistry of the text indicates the breakdown in the dialogue has been suggested by other scholars. See, e.g., Newsom 1996: 496–7; Seow 2013: 26–39, esp. 29–30. Despite the ingenious reconstructive work done by scholars, there is no textual evidence that supports any other form of the book than as it stands now. For a summary of the arguments against cohesion in the third cycle and a plausible response, see Long 2012: 113–25.

"I Am Not Destroyed before Darkness":
The Rhetoric of Job's Eighth Speech (Job 23–24)

Introduction

No longer having the fate of the wicked as a rhetorical strategy, Eliphaz escalates his rhetoric, falsely accusing Job of committing specific sins. Job responds by maintaining his integrity and refuting the theological foundation that led Eliphaz to accuse him of sin.

The Literary Rhetorical Situation of Job 23–24

Job's speech in Job 21 creates a change in the rhetorical situation (Yu 2011: 355). The friends can no longer employ the *topos* of the fate of the wicked to insinuate that Job is wicked and thereby encourage repentance. Still desiring to correct Job, however, Eliphaz changes his strategy—he "[adjusts] the facts to the theory" (Gordis 1978: 238). His speech opens with an accusation of Job's sin, asserting through a rhetorical question that, indeed, Job's sin is great (22:5). Job's verbal expression remains a problem for Eliphaz, who accuses Job of justifying himself and making himself blameless through his arguments (22:3). Through the sarcastic rhetorical question in 22:4, Eliphaz avers that Job's piety is not what he thinks it is; his impiety in both speech and action have resulted in God's judgment. In case Job missed the point, he summarizes his opening movement in the final clause: "there is no end to your iniquities" (22:5). Eliphaz turns, in v. 6, to enumerate Job's sins for him, using a series of images that portray Job as one who harms the marginalized (22:6-9). From this, Eliphaz draws a conclusion about Job (22:10-11): Job's suffering is rooted in his sin. Reprising a strategy from the use of the narrative of the wicked, he further insinuates that Job's suffering is the cause of his sin by using key words that Job has used to describe his suffering (cf. 19:6 for פַּח; cf. 7:14; 21:6 for בהל; cf. 3:25; 21:9 for פַּחַד; cf. 3:4-5; 7:9; 10:19, 21-22; 17:13; 19:8 for חֹשֶׁךְ; cf. 14:19 for מַיִם). Eliphaz argues that God judges the wicked justly—among whom Job can count himself (22:12-20).

Eliphaz uses allusion rhetorically. Following Job's allusions to Psalms 1, 73, and 107, Eliphaz uses allusions to these psalms in 22:19 (cf. Ps. 107:42), 22:18 (cf. Ps. 1:1), and 22:13-14 (cf. Ps. 73:11). With each of these allusions Eliphaz insinuates that Job is wicked and rejects God; Eliphaz and the friends will rejoice at the wicked person's end (see Kynes 2012: 93, 155, 166, 173). Eliphaz rebukes Job for his characterization of God as unjust—accomplished by misrepresenting Job's words in 22:13-14 (Fox 1980a: 429–30). Job had accused the friends of untrue speech; Eliphaz now returns the favor. Eliphaz's speech reaches a climax with his call to repentance in 22:21-30. The imperatives of 22:21 reveal his ultimate goal: for Job to "agree with God" through repentance, using שׁוּב (22:23). This reveals once again that Eliphaz's problem with Job is rooted in Job's God-talk. If Job will take Eliphaz's advice, Eliphaz promises Job complete restoration. Simply put: restoration for Job can only be accomplished through penitence because he is a grave sinner (Hartley 1988: 330).[2]

Eliphaz's main arguments—Job is a great sinner, has been judged justly, and needs to repent—illuminate Job's literary rhetorical situation for his eighth speech. He must continue to resist the call to repentance and defend his protest prayer. The audience of his speech is the friends. Nevertheless, because Job's suffering remains, his exigency in relation to God remains, even if only in the background. The constraints have not changed.

The Forms of Job 23–24

There is little scholarly consensus regarding the form(s) of Job's eighth speech.[3] There are three forms in this speech: disputation (23:2, 4-9, 23:13–24:25), wish (23:3), and avowal of innocence (23:10-12).[4] The disputation is not marked by direct address in this speech, the first time Job speaks without a second person form since Job 3. This does not indicate that the speech is a soliloquy, as Clines contends (2006: 591).[5] The presence of rhetorical questions—especially the quite confrontational 24:25—confirms this speech is directed at the friends (cf. 23:6).

Other factors in interpreting this speech as a disputation are (1) the large sections of argumentation developing individual theses, (2) the citations of viewpoints (24:18-20, 24), and (3) the use of logical particles (23:2, 6, 8, 15, 17; 24:5). Regarding the first factor, the opening verse of

---

2. With the knowledge that Eliphaz has entirely fabricated his list of sins, Yu (2011: 338) notes that with this speech, the narrator brings his critique of comforter malpractice to an apogee; cf. Wilson 2015: 117–19.

3. For example, Hartley (1988: 40–1) lists six different forms: lament (23:2, 15-17), lawsuit as a wish (23:3-7), affirmation of trust in God (23:6-7), hymn (23:8-9, 13-14), avowal of innocence (23:10-12), and disputation (24:1-25). Westermann (1981b: 67–9, 56–9) labels 23:2-13 as a wish and 23:13-17 as a lament. Clines (2006: 591–2) argues this speech is a complaint, albeit one made up of other forms: wish, rhetorical questions, and disputation, while Murphy (1981: 35) categorizes this speech as a disputation, noting 23:10-12 is avowal of innocence and 24:1-17 is a complaint.

4. The totals are as follows: 102 disputation clauses (of 113 clauses in the speech), three wish clauses, and eight avowal of innocence clauses.

5. Clines admits that 24:25 is addressed to the friends (2006: 589).

the speech in 23:2 does use lament-like language (e.g., שִׂיחַ), but it is not a lament about Job's situation. It is a thesis rejecting the call to repentance in 22:21-30. The cohortative forms that follow in 23:4-5 develop the thesis, stating Job's resolve. The question of 24:1 indicates a thesis which is elaborated by the extended tropes in 24:2-17 and is a response to Eliphaz's arguments in 22:12-20. Regarding the second factor, Job seems to be citing his friends' views in 24:18-20, 24.[6] By citing arguments of his friends, Job is able to refute their theses with counter-arguments in 24:21-23, 25. Finally, regarding the third factor, Job highlights arguments and draws conclusions throughout this speech using particles, namely, גַּם in 23:2, הֵן in 23:8 and 24:5, עַל־כֵּן in 23:15, and כִּי־לֹא in 23:17. The wish, marked by מִי־יִתֵּן, works with the disputation form by drawing attention to Job's exigency with God—part of the justification for his protest prayer. Likewise, the avowal of innocence works within the disputation framework.

The Rhetorical Strategies of Job 23–24

Structure

This speech has two major movements, corresponding to the chapter division.[7] These major movements can be further subdivided to identify Job's major themes. Job's first stanza, 23:2-7, is marked by its similar content, the closural clue of the rhetorical question and an answer in 23:7, and the use of הֵן in 23:8 to initiate the second stanza. Job's first stanza is an affirmation that his complaint has yet to be answered (23:2), a wish to find God, so he can resolve his exigency (23:3), a declaration of resolve to continue to argue in prayer (23:4-5), and a rhetorical question (23:6a), with an answer of confidence that God will respond to him (23:6b-c). These verses thus affirm his protest prayer and reject the call to repentance from Eliphaz in 22:21-30. The second stanza, 23:8-12, builds on the first movement by pointing to the futility of finding an

---

6. This interpretation is debated, with a number of different perspectives taken (see below for details). This point is defended and developed below.

7. So also Hartley 1988: 336; Clines 2006: 589; Wilson 2015: 120. Comparing different structural proposals of commentators is challenging for this speech because of the myriad of proposals about 24:18-24. While Hartley (1988: 342) considers Job the speaker, he does rearrange parts of 24:1-17. Clines (2006: 547–8, 661, 667–73) moves 24:18-25, arguing it is a part of Zophar's speech in Job 27. Habel (1985: 358) considers Job 24 to be unified but attributes the entirety of Job 24 to Zophar. Longman's (2012: 293–304) division is 23:2-7, 8-10, 11-12, 13-17; 24:1-17, 18-25. Newsom (1996: 507–13) divides the speech into two major movements, with eight subsections: 23:2-7, 8-12, 13-17; 24:1-4, 5-12, 13-17, 18-20, 21-25.

absent deity and by affirming his innocence. This also rejects the call to repentance; the advice is irrelevant for a blameless and innocent sufferer like Job and protest prayer is proper when God is absent and silent. The third stanza, 23:13-17, is marked by וְהוּא, shifting the focus to God, and closed by Job's conviction, articulated by כִּי־לֹא.[8] This stanza revisits some of Job's complaints from his third speech (cf. 9:11-24), but closes with his conviction that he is dismayed but not destroyed. This analysis of Job 23 indicates it is a response to Eliphaz's call to repentance. In the face of such advice, Job maintains his integrity, asserting he has no need for their counsel because of his righteousness and steadfastness.

Job 24 subdivides into two sections. In 24:1-17 Job issues a thesis through a rhetorical question, followed by an elaborate defense of the thesis with evidence for the affliction and marginalization of the poor. The argument is that God does not judge justly, clearly a response to Eliphaz's strict retributive framework. In the second section, 24:18-25, Job continues to take aim at the comforters' arguments of strict retribution and justice by summarizing their views in 24:18-20, 24, and refuting them in 24:21-23, 25. This is a notoriously difficult section because what is articulated does not align with Job's statements from 24:1-17 or his other speeches (e.g., Job 21).[9] Accordingly, some scholars remove these verses, attribute all of this chapter or this section to a friend (usually Zophar) (e.g., Clines 2006: 547–8, 661, 667–73), interpret this section as a quotation of the friends (e.g., Gordis 1978: 269, 531–4), or make an argument for these being Job's words (Lo 2003: 108–18). There is no textual evidence for moving these verses to another location in the book, as Clines does, where he places these verses after 27:17 (2006: 661–3). Lo argues that 24:18-24 can be interpreted as Job's words in accordance with the author's rhetorical strategy in the third cycle, employing contradictory juxtaposition (2003: 119–26).

In my view, vv. 21-23 and Job's closing rhetorical question in v. 25 can be read as his words without any issue. Furthering his argument of injustice from vv. 1-17, he again highlights the injustice of the wicked as they harm the barren woman and the widow (v. 21), he states that God preserves the wicked so they do not despair in life (v. 22), and that he aids them by providing security even as he has "his eyes on them" (v. 23). He closes the argument with a provocative and effective question that affirms he cannot be proven a liar (v. 25). Interspersed through these arguments is Job's quotation of the friends, characterizing them as affirming the

---

8. Regarding כִּי־לֹא, see Hartley 1988: 341 n. 3.
9. For a comparison of the ideas, see Lo 2003: 104–8.

short-lived life of the wicked and their accursed condition (v. 18), the sure descent of the wicked into Sheol as they are overcome by drought (v. 19), and the wicked's lot as forgotten by the community (v. 20). "Injustice is broken like a tree," as the friends would articulate, at least thematically (24:20). Immediately preceding his closing question, Job reiterates their position again, namely, that they think the exalted life of the wicked is short-lived; the wicked will be humbled and will wither (v. 24). In this reading, the final section can be read coherently within Job's argument in the book, while not applying all of 24:18-24 to Job's friends or excising the entire passage.[10] The major objection to this understanding of the use of quotation arises from the lack of any marking of quotation. None of Fox's criteria fit these verses (1980a: 416–31).[11] It seems the obvious contradiction in viewpoint, not only within this speech but in others (e.g., Job 21), is thus the virtual marker for a quotation.[12]

Job's refutation of their views builds on images of divine injustice, thus also linking Job's speech in Job 24 with Eliphaz's argument in 22:12-20. This analysis shows Job's second major movement also corresponds to Eliphaz's previous speech.

By means of a two-fold argument, corresponding to major movements in Eliphaz's speech in Job 22, Job justifies his protest prayer by rejecting the call to repentance in Job 23 and criticizes the friends' strict retributive framework in Job 24. This latter emphasis is also an argument in favor of his use of protest prayer in that it reveals that their arguments used to encourage repentance are built on a faulty foundation.

Strategies

Characterization and Lexical Repetition. Despite the claim that Job does not address anyone in this speech (e.g., Clines 2006: 589), Job's use of characterization and lexical repetition are two rhetorical strategies that would indicate otherwise. By characterizing the friends'

10. A similar, though slightly different, interpretation is offered by Davidson 1895: 177–9 and Janzen 1985: 169, though neither develop their interpretation much (cf. ESV, NRSV, NET). Wilson (2015: 124–5) offers a similar interpretation to that outlined here. Wilson does not consider 24:24 a quotation, but does see vv. 18-20 as a virtual quotation with vv. 21-25 as Job's argument.

11. See also Ho's recent analysis, where he adds additional insight from Greenstein (2009: 703–15).

12. This is admittedly tenuous, but no other interpretation is adequate. Other proposals include reading 24:18-24 as a curse (cf. Hartley 1988: 343, 352–4 and Newsom 1996: 512), but the grammatical features of the passage make this hard to sustain, as Newsom admits: the verbal forms are not jussives.

arguments through quotation and by using words from Eliphaz's previous speech, Job employs two strategies intended to change the friends' views regarding the ethics of Job's protest prayer.

Though disputed, the best interpretation of Job 24:18-20, 24 seems to be that Job is quoting the friends in his argument to reject their rigid understanding of divine justice, an argument going back to 24:1. By citing the friends' views, using images and themes that correlate to the friends' description of the fate of the wicked, Job highlights their arguments regarding divine justice. Job's point is that their arguments lack cogency, refuting their characterized arguments with his own arguments in 24:21-23 and the closing rhetorical question in 24:25. The friends contend that the wicked's life is transient and cursed (24:18; cf. 8:11-15; 15:20-22, 28-30, 32-34; 18:5-7, 12-15, 18-21; 20:5-28).[13] The wicked are overcome by drought and heat in the same way that Sheol overcomes sinners: swiftly and completely (24:19; cf. 8:12-13, 15; 15:30-35; 18:5-7, 13-15, 18; 20:5-28).[14] The wicked are also forgotten and overcome by death because wickedness is "broken like a tree" (24:20; cf. 8:15; 15:34; 18:17, 19; 20:7-9). Job counters that the wicked harm the widow (24:21). The verb, though disputed, can be read as רעה I, "to pasture," a verb Job had used to describe the actions of the wicked oppressors in 24:2.[15] Despite the wicked's oppression, God preserves (משך) the "mighty" (אַבִּירִים) so that the wicked are secure, protected by God's care (24:22-23).[16] Returning to his main argumentation from the first movement of chapter 24, Job again marshals evidence to refute the doctrine of retribution. God does not hold the wicked accountable, Job says; he preserves them. Job returns to characterize the friends' arguments in 24:24, again reflecting their

---

13. Job's use of חֶלְקָה, echoing Zophar's use of חֵלֶק in 20:29, amplifies the association of this quotation with the friends' views. See also Lo 2003: 105.

14. On this imagery, see Clines (2006: 670), who highlights how the combination of images perhaps emphasizes "the rapidity of disappearance" or the complete disappearance. These are not mutually exclusive, and perhaps both should be seen.

15. For the different views on this verb, see ibid.: 656–7. Clines does not mention this as a repetition of the verb from 24:2. Substantiating this link is the use of אַלְמָנָה in 24:21b (cf. 24:3). This reading fits within the parallelism of the verse as well, with the second colon articulating that the wicked person causes harm for the widow. Cf. NIV11: "[The wicked] prey upon the barren and childless woman, and to the widow they show no kindness."

16. משך is also disputed. See Clines' discussion (ibid.: 657). He seems to dismiss the view that this means to "prolong" or "preserve" because it usually takes a thing, rather than a person, as its object. But as he points out, a person as an object is not impossible (see Neh. 9:30). The adversative conjunction on the verb accentuates this statement, indicating its contrast to the previous verse.

position, that the prosperity of the wicked does not last; they "wither" (מלל; cf. 8:12; 15:33; 18:16). The images from the friends' speeches are used to characterize their argument. Job's argument uses their imagery, juxtaposed with his own, to drive home his argument that God does not rigidly apply a doctrine of retribution. As a response to Eliphaz's previous speech (cf. 22:12-20), Job disputes that God judges justly. For Eliphaz, this point was a major part of convicting Job of sin and thus part of his argument that Job needed to repent. Job is not innocent; he has no right to protest in prayer, Eliphaz insists. Job counters, arguing that the very premises upon which the friends' ethical critique of Job's discourse are based are faulty.[17]

The second rhetorical strategy that indicates Job 23–24 is a disputation in response to Eliphaz's argument is Job's re-use of lexemes from Job 22 (see Course 1994: 143). There are forty-six lexemes shared between the two speeches, many of which are rhetorically significant as refutations of Eliphaz's arguments. In his introduction, Job immediately rejects Eliphaz's advice in 22:22. Using פֶּה, Job rejects any notion of retributive suffering rooted in divine chastisement as relevant for him in 23:4: Job will fill his "mouth" with arguments, not instruction. Using פֶּה again, Job states why: "the commandment of his lips—I have not departed; more than my portion I have treasured the words of his mouth" (23:12).[18] Job asserts that he will fill his mouth with arguments because he has not sinned; his behavior, whether in action or verbal, is innocent of wrongdoing and thus he has no need to accept instruction to repent. Another shared lexeme is יכח. Eliphaz sarcastically references Job's piety, again referring to his suffering as a divine rebuke (22:4). Job responds by affirming his right to protest prayer: "the upright can argue with God" (23:7).[19] Job further refutes Eliphaz's rebuke regarding Job's piety using דֶּרֶךְ (cf. 22:3). Job insists God knows his innocent "ways" (23:10-11). Job's "way" is not the

---

17. The conclusion of this analysis does not differ much from Lo's, but it does attribute some of these words to Job as a quotation, the rhetorical effect of which is to silence the friends by exposing the bankruptcy of their position. By this snarky sarcasm, the friends are left without much of a response, as evidenced by Bildad's next speech.

18. This reading retains מֶחְקִי in v. 12 in light of its use in v. 14. Job affirms in the latter verse that God will fulfill Job's "lot." Job cares more about his piety than whatever God has in store for him—a powerful affirmation of his integrity.

19. While Eliphaz does not use יָשָׁר, he uses the other three descriptions of Job from 1:1 in 22:3-5: תמם (cf. תָּם), יִרְאָה (cf. ירא), and רעע (cf. רָע) (Course 1994: 142). While the use of יָשָׁר is not strictly a lexical repetition, it is another indication of the author's use of Job's argument as a response to Eliphaz.

way of the wicked, as Eliphaz asserted in 22:15; his "way" is the way of the pious. Thus, Job again asserts that he has no need to repent, thereby defending his protest prayer.[20]

Job uses other lexemes from Eliphaz's speech. He uses בהל and the verbal form פחד in 23:15 to admit that he is terrified, but following Job's preceding statements regarding his innocence, he recasts why he is terrified (note the use of עַל־כֵּן). It is not because of his mistreatment of the poor, the conclusion Eliphaz had drawn in 22:10 (using בהל and the nominal form פַּחַד), but because God has attacked him (23:16). Likewise, Job uses חֹשֶׁךְ and כסה in 23:17, closing his argument with an emphatic statement that he is not wholly dismayed. Though not as strong a link given the plethora of occurrences in the book, Job seems to be using שַׁדַּי and אֱלוֹהַּ to recast Eliphaz's portrayal of God. Eliphaz uses the former epithet for God in 22:3, 17, 23, 25, and 26. The latter two occurrences inform his advice: it is שַׁדַּי who will be Job's delight. Job counters by saying it is שַׁדַּי who has harmed him (23:16) and who demonstrates injustice (24:1). Regarding the latter epithet, אֱלוֹהַּ, Job provocatively accuses God of "charging no one with wrong" (24:12)—a refutation of Eliphaz's portrayal of אֱלוֹהַּ's justice (22:12, 26). Reiterating the lack of justice, Job uses עֵת in 24:1 in response to Eliphaz's contention that the wicked are eradicated justly in 22:16. Job expands on this argument, while also asserting his innocence, by repeating רעב, אַלְמָנָה, חבל, עָרוֹם, and יָתוֹם. Eliphaz uses these words to condemn Job for social injustice (22:6, 7, and 9); Job uses these words to portray the wicked and thereby argue against Eliphaz's views of divine justice (24:3, 7, 9, 10, and 21).

These two strategies, characterization and lexical repetition, counter the friends' arguments about Job's sin and God's retributive justice. Their arguments are invalid on both accounts. Job uses these strategies to defend his prayer of protest and to undermine their theology. Because of this flawed foundation, their advice against Job's protest prayer has no basis.

Tropes. Job also uses tropes in his eighth speech to accomplish his rhetorical goals.[21] He reminds his friends of his suffering in 23:2 and 17, describing his rebellious complaint in 23:2a, the burden that weighs him down in 23:2b, and his emotional and spiritual darkness in 23:17. The use

---

20. Hartley (1988: 341) and Newsom (1996: 507) also read Job's avowal of innocence as a rebuttal of Eliphaz's call for repentance.
21. This analysis focuses on the tropes in 23:2–24:17, 25. The tropes of 24:18-24 are analyzed in the section on characterization above since they are so intimately related to Job's rhetoric of characterizing and refuting the friends' arguments.

of אֲנָחָה recalls Job's opening complaint (3:24). Together, these two cola reiterate his argument that he should complain by placing his suffering at the forefront of the discussion again. Recalling his complaint that initiated the dispute, Job reminds them what his complaint is seeking: relief. He admits he is in a dark place (23:17), using the trope of darkness to describe his suffering. Coming after his use of divine attack imagery in 23:15, where divine attack is implied, and 23:16, Job stresses that his terror is caused by God's attacks. The vivid imagery of Job's suffering, rooted in God's attack, is once again put into service to justify his complaint.

The justification of protest prayer is also the effect of the litigation trope in 23:4-7. Job will argue—he must argue—given his condition and its cause. He rejects any notion of admitting sin he has not committed in order to achieve restoration.[22] Restoration will come through protest prayer. This illuminates his integrity and his faith in God. Also justifying his protest prayer is his use of divine absence imagery in 23:3, 8-9; 24:1, 12. Because God has yet to respond to Job's complaint, because God remains silent and absent, Job reminds his friends that his exigency has yet to be resolved. Job also uses purification imagery (i.e., the simile of gold) and the metaphor of life as a journey, in which he has held fast to God's ways, in 23:10-12 to justify his protest prayer (Hartley 1988: 340), refuting the false accusations Eliphaz made in Job 22. Mutually reinforcing, the imagery of Job 23—Job's suffering, the divine attack, the darkness trope, God's absence, the litigation trope, the purification trope, and Job's righteousness—is used to reject Eliphaz's call for repentance and reflects Job's justification for protest prayer.

The dominant trope in this speech, however, is the trope of divine injustice. This trope is a complex amalgamation of imagery that takes up most of chapter 24. The trope of divine injustice emerges in 24:1, 12c, and 21-23. Job asserts that God does not hold wrongdoers accountable; in fact, he preserves them in his delayed execution of justice. Job illustrates (and thereby develops) his argument with a provocative and vivid back-and-forth description of wicked oppression (24:2-4a, 9)[23] and the afflicted

---

22. In 23:6 Job implies a belief in divine justice by affirming his confidence in achieving restoration and relief. This seems at odds with the use of divine injustice imagery in Job 24:1-17, 21-23. Once again, this tension emerges in Job, revealing his ultimate belief in divine justice, using the trope of divine injustice in his argumentation with the friends (i.e., as a rhetorical device).

23. The objects in 24:2a, b, 3a are fronted for emphasis. The object in 24:9a is in the final position in the clause, with the prepositional phrase עַל־עָנִי fronted in 24:9b, forming a chiasm with the verbs of oppression. This highlights the oppression by placing the afflicted inside the verbs.

poor (24:4b-8, 10-12), supplementing it with an extended discussion of three typical sinners, namely, the murderer, the adulterer, and the thief (24:13-17). These tropes employ further imagery. Imagery of the loss of property and possessions (24:2-3), food imagery (24:5),[24] animal imagery (24:5),[25] unjust work environments (24:6, 10-11),[26] clothing imagery (24:7, 10),[27] rain and rock imagery (24:8),[28] city imagery (24:12),[29] and light and dark motifs (24:13-17) combine to present a vivid picture of wicked oppression and sin that are left unchecked. Clines is attuned to Job's internal rhetoric when he writes (1998: 248), "The sufferings of the poor are not depicted for the sake of the poor but for the sake of Job's theological program." This imagery reinforces Job's argument against the retributive justice that Eliphaz expounds in 22:12-20. Eliphaz condemned Job by arguing for God's rigid application of justice; Job responds with an elaborate picture of God's justice neglected (or deferred?). But this imagery of wickedness also justifies Job's innocence. As noted above, Eliphaz had claimed that Job harmed the widow and the orphan through unjust pledges (22:6-9), and linked Job with the wicked in 22:13-19. Job takes these same images and applies them to the wicked, rejecting any association with these actions (23:10-12; 24:2-12; cf. 21:16). Job's use of tropes has an important effect rhetorically: it reinforces Job's rejection of Eliphaz's two main arguments.

More than that, though, the elaboration of divine injustice implies a petition that God should act.[30] A rhetorical effect similar to Job's use of allusion, the imagery provides an implicit appeal. By portraying divine injustice, he appeals to God implicitly to do something—to act in accordance with what Job believes to be true. If Job did not have this kind of faith, he would not maintain his integrity. He would accept the friends' advice and move on; or worse, he would "curse God and die" (see 2:9).

24. See Newsom 1996: 510.
25. See Hawley 2018: 152–7.
26. See Clines 2006: 608.
27. See Hartley 1988: 347.
28. See Clines 2006: 606.
29. See Hartley 1988: 349.
30. Clines suggests this as the primary rhetorical aim of these images (2006: 609). This does not account for Job's rhetorical situation, in which the primary exigency he faces relates to the friends' comforting practices.

Allusion. Job uses four allusions in this speech for rhetorical effect. In 23:8-10 Job alludes to Ps. 139:5, 7-10, 23-24. Verses 8-9 recall Ps. 139:5, 7-10, using קֶדֶם and אָחוֹר.[31] The double merism links Job's statements with Zophar and the psalm (Kynes 2012: 116). Zophar had last alluded to Psalm 139 in response to Job's use of the psalm (cf. Job 10:8-10; 11:7-9) (102–15). In 23:8-10 Job reverses the imagery of the psalm: God is not omnipresent but absent (ibid.; see also Hartley 1988: 340). With this allusion Job refutes the friends' certainty of knowing God's ways (cf. 11:7-9, though also a fitting retort to 22:12-20); he rejects their epistemological hubris (115). Crucial, though, is that this (116–17)

> does not necessarily imply that Job has rejected the psalmist's view of God. In fact, he is more likely presenting it as the norm from which his current experience of God has departed… Once again, Job's antithetical allusion to the psalm involves a desire to see its depiction of intimate relationship with God actualized. And thus, he searches for a God who is no longer there (23:3), reversing roles with the God of the psalm, whose pursuit was inescapable.

Job's parody seems to lead him to confidence in the psalm's ending (117).

Job 23:10 alludes to Ps. 139:23-24, using the words דֶּרֶךְ, ידע, and בחן (Kynes 2012: 117).[32] Job asserts that he can withstand divine scrutiny like the psalmist; the parody incisively undercuts Eliphaz's accusations of sin. Kynes suggests that the purpose of this allusion is to move God to act and be the God Job believes him to be, to remind God of who he is supposed to be in an attempt to procure relief (118). Given Job's rhetorical situation, however, it seems that this is a secondary effect. Since Zophar utilized the psalm to silence Job's protest prayer, Job reprises the psalm to defend it (ibid.). Job does not feel as if God is omnipresent, as Zophar argued using this psalm and as Eliphaz implies (cf. 11:8-9; 22:12); according to Job, those who cannot find God lament or complain. Nevertheless, Job is certain his piety matches the psalmist, a piety that demands God be who he is supposed to be (119).

The second allusion occurs in 23:11a, where Job alludes to Ps. 73:2. Three lexical links establish this connection: רֶגֶל, אָשֻׁר, and נטה (Kynes 2012: 173). Eliphaz just alluded to the psalm in Job 22 to associate Job with the wicked; Job replies by associating himself with the righteous psalmist. Kynes writes (174, italics original):

---

31. These words only occur elsewhere together in Isa. 9:11 and Ezek. 8:16 (Kynes 2012: 116).

32. Kynes points out that these words occur in two adjacent verses in only three other places: Jer. 6:27; 17:9-10; Ps. 95:9-10.

> In contrast to Eliphaz's implied accusation that Job is among the wicked of Psalm 73, Job uses this allusion to claim for himself a righteousness even greater than the psalmist's. Whereas the psalmist admits that he almost "stumbled" (נטה) and his feet had "nearly slipped," Job claims his foot has held fast to God's steps, and he has not "turned aside" or "stumbled" (נטה)... [A]lthough [the psalmist's] steps almost slipped, Job has held fast to *God's* steps.

By linking himself with the psalmist, Job refutes the friends' application of this psalm to him and their insinuations that he is wicked.

The third allusion also occurs in this context, with Job alluding to Ps. 1:1, 6 in 23:10-11 (Kynes 2012: 155–6). Continuing the use of Psalm 1 and the argument over its interpretation from Job 21 and into Job 22, Job reprises this allusion in his rhetoric. Together, the allusions to Psalm 139 and Psalm 1 provide the reason for God's absence: God knows Job is righteous (156). Job is certain of vindication because he understands and believes the theology of Psalm 1, and, according to Kynes (157), "he turns the promise of God in the psalm into an accusation against God for not living up to it." This implied petition is once again secondary in Job's rhetorical situation, though. In response to Eliphaz's accusations, this is a refutation of the need to repent, and thus a defense of protest prayer as a pious way to interact with God in his case. The friends' rigid application of the psalm is corrected, again, by Job's rhetoric.

The fourth allusion is another reprise, with Job's rhetorical question וּמִי יְשִׁיבֶנּוּ in 23:13 alluding to Isa. 43:13. Job and Zophar used this passage against each other in the first cycle (cf. 9:12; 11:10).[33] Job uses the allusion in this case to recast the rigidity of the friends' retributive framework. God is free, Job declares, and recalls the discussion from the first cycle as well as the Isaianic traditions (cf. 9:2-12 and 12:9, 17). With his statements in vv. 12 and 14, Job affirms God's freedom while also maintaining his innocence and integrity: his piety is more important to him than whatever God has decreed.

Emphatic Statements. A major rhetorical strategy in this speech is Job's use of particles to mark key statements in his argument. The first emphatic statement occurs in 23:2 with the use of גַּם, marking Job's opening statement, a thesis regarding his protest prayer, which emerges clearly in Job's statements of resolve in vv. 4-5.[34] Job draws attention to

---

33. See Chapter 3 above for a discussion of the allusion in those speeches.
34. Clines (2006: 574) thinks the גַּם in 23:2 makes the entire section emphatic. Fohrer (1963: 364–5) highlights how Job's rejection of Eliphaz's advice is related to his conviction to protest.

his suffering, his opening complaint (see 3:24), and his resolve to protest in prayer. Continuing this trajectory is Job's second emphatic statement in 23:6, marked by אַךְ. After answering his own question, Job states his conviction that God will pay attention to him, will hear his protest prayer. The wish builds into a resolve which culminates in a conviction. This conviction is marked for emphasis in his dispute, and corresponds to his defense of protest prayer. He has no reason to seek to manipulate God and violate his integrity in accordance with Eliphaz's advice when he is certain God will grant him the ability to argue in prayer.

Also justifying his protest prayer is the third emphatic statement, with Job's emphasis on divine absence marked with הֵן in 23:8. Job persists in his arguments because God is absent. This particle highlights Job's allusion to Psalm 139. The כִּי in 23:10 marks an emphatic statement as well.[35] In fact, it marks Job's avowal of innocence that comprises 23:10-12. A number of the clauses in vv. 10-12 utilize marked syntax with fronted objects to reinforce the emphatic nature of these verses.[36] This avowal of innocence plays a major role in Job's rhetoric in this speech. This avowal includes allusions to Psalms 1 and 73, while also incorporating other psalmic language. Clines writes (2006: 598), "Job is the embodiment of psalmic piety." This refutes Eliphaz's accusations of Job's sin, and rejects any insinuation (remaining from the second cycle) that he is wicked.

Job draws a conclusion for Eliphaz and the friends in 23:15 using עַל־כֵּן. Admitting his dread, this marked statement draws attention to God's freedom (23:13-14), God's attack (23:15-16), and Job's resolve (23:17). Thus, it marks Job's use of tropes and prepares for another emphatic statement.[37] The כִּי־לֹא in 23:17 marks the final emphatic statement of Job 23.[38] Job is shrouded in darkness, and this causes him suffering; but the terse poetry in the flow of the argument implies that Job is not going to give up his complaint. As Balentine writes (1999a: 291, italics original), "Even if 'thick darkness' should cover his face so that he can neither see nor be seen, he will be a *presence* that God cannot ignore." Fohrer is clearer regarding protest (1963: 364; cf. 367): "In dieser Lage bleibt dem Leidende nichts als Klage und Anklage."

---

35. It seems best to take it as asseverative, *pace* Clines (2006: 578), who interprets it as causal.

36. See vv. 11a, 11b, 12a, 12b. On the syntax of v. 12a, see Hartley 1988: 339 nn. 4–5, citing GKC §143d.

37. This may also draw attention to Job's apprehension in respect of the argument he is about to make, a move that recalls Job 21:5-6. For this interpretation, see Westermann 1981b: 57.

38. On the function of כִּי־לֹא, see Hartley 1988: 341 n. 3.

Job also uses emphatic statements in the second movement. He draws attention to his evidence of oppression in 24:5 with הֵן, and he highlights the disputatious nature of his final rhetorical question in 24:25 with כִּי לֹא אֵפוֹ. Another emphatic statement corresponds to Job's thesis in this movement. In 24:12c, Job emerges from his trope to state that "God does not charge wrongdoing."[39] As the first tricolon of the movement and being outside the elaboration of the trope, this clause is marked.[40] This statement has two effects in Job's rhetorical situation: (1) it refutes the theological dogma of the friends which includes a reductionistic view of divine justice, and (2) it implies a petition for God to act—to charge wrongdoing.

Wish. Job uses a wish in 23:3 for rhetorical effect. The wish, indicated by מִי־יִתֵּן, expresses Job's desire for God to respond to his protest prayer and suffering (Magary 2005: 286). After recalling his suffering in 23:2, the wish is meant to remind Eliphaz and the friends what Job is seeking: restoration and relief. He will find relief by protest prayer (23:4-5), not penitential prayer, as Eliphaz suggested. He will present (עָרַךְ) his arguments (תּוֹכָחוֹת) to God in prayer (cf. 13:3, 15-18).

Rhetorical Questions. There are three rhetorical questions that Job employs to accomplish his rhetoric in his disputation.[41] The first occurs in 23:6. As a part of Job's opening movement, this question builds on Job's resolve to continue to argue in prayer (23:4-5). To bring the argument to a conclusion, Job asks and answers a rhetorical question: "Would he contend with me with much strength?" "No!"[42] By answering his question he does not allow the friends to answer the question as they would like, as they have affirmed (cf. 22:12-20). This leads Job to his emphatic statement in v. 6c.

---

39. Some emend תְּפִלָּה to תְּפִלָּה, "prayer." This is unnecessary (Clines 2006: 610). This word also occurs in 1:22, an ironic intratextual link.

40. The God-talk of Job 24 forms a kind of frame around Job's other strategies. He questions divine justice (24:1), affirms divine injustice (24:12), and documents it (24:22-23).

41. The interrogative מִי in 23:3 is used as a wish, and so is treated in the analysis of Job's rhetoric of his wish. The interrogative מָה in 23:5 indicates the object of the verb. The interrogative מִי in 23:13 is a part of an allusion, so its rhetoric is explored above. De Regt lists 23:17 as an unmarked interrogative (1994: 362), but it seems better to see it as an emphatic statement given כִּי־לֹא.

42. Magary (2005: 290) notes that this is the second (of two) rhetorical questions which Job answers himself (cf. 14:4).

The second question Job asks occurs in 24:1. This question initiates a new movement in Job's argument and implies that God does not hold the wicked accountable (24:1a). The result is that those who know God do not see his judgment (24:1b). The interrogative מַדּוּעַ may create a lament-like effect; Job implies an appeal that God might act justly so that he himself might see God's justice done. But in the context of Job's rhetorical situation, this question articulates a thesis which Job develops through the imagery of the afflicted, a thesis which argues against the friends' rigid theological system (Westermann 1981b: 58). This rhetorical question with its resulting development lays a foundation for Job's final rhetorical question in 24:25.

The final rhetorical question brings Job's argument to a close: "And if this is not so, then who will confute me, and make my words nothing?" (24:25). A challenge, the question asserts that Job's argument, as developed in chapter 24, is unimpeachable. The emphatic introduction to the rhetorical question (וְאִם־לֹא אֵפוֹ) confirms that the previous question in 24:1 had disputatious aims (cf. 9:24).

Summary of Job 23–24

In Job's eighth speech he has two main goals: to reject Eliphaz's advice to repent and to undermine the foundation upon which that advice is built, namely, his dogmatic commitment to the retribution principle. Job accomplishes his rhetorical goals through a number of strategies: characterization, lexical repetition, tropes, allusion, emphatic statements, wish, and rhetorical questions. Job reaffirms his commitment to protest prayer and argues that divine justice is not as well-established as Eliphaz and the friends make it out to be.

"How You Have Helped Him Without Power!":
The Rhetoric of Job's Ninth Speech (Job 26:2-4)

Introduction

Following Job's excoriation in his eighth speech, Bildad is so shaken he has a hard time uttering more than a "platitudinous reiteration" of Eliphaz's arguments (Walton 2012: 249; cf. Yu 2011: 342–4). Bildad juxtaposes divine transcendence with a low anthropology to silence Job; very quickly, however, Job interrupts Bildad to mock him.

Identifying the Rhetorical Unit[43]

Given the brevity of Bildad's speech in Job 25 and incongruence of the style and content of 26:5-14 with Job's discourse elsewhere in the dispute, a number of proposals for how to understand these verses have been suggested.[44] Newsom (1996: 516), drawing upon the textual clues in the variation of narratorial introduction in 27:1 and 29:1, suggests that there has been an interruption, namely, Job interrupting Bildad in 26:1-4. Bildad, however, is determined to finish his speech, and so continues in 26:5-14. Newsom writes (ibid.), "Such a situation may be the author's attempt to represent the interruptive and even overlapping speech of the parties to a conversation that has broken down."[45]

Five considerations strengthen this analysis, suggesting that 25:2-5 and 26:5-14 are spoken by Bildad, with 26:2-4 reflecting Job's frustrated interjection. First, 25:2-6 and 26:5-14 are unified by the theme of the great creator (Habel 1985: 366; Clines 2006: 626). Second, the use of this hymn contrasts with the obviously parodic nature of Job's other hymns (cf. 9:5-10; 12:13-25) (Habel 1985: 366; Newsom 1996: 516). Third, the continued use of the participles in the hymnic style in 26:7-9 recalls 25:2, while the repetition of the 3ms pronominal suffix in 26:6, 8, 9, 11, 12, 13, 14 recalls its use in 25:2-3, 5—God is mentioned explicitly only in 25:4. Fourth, the mention of Sheol imagery (i.e., maggots and worms) in 25:6 leads seamlessly to the use of Sheol imagery in 26:5. Fifth, the repetition of הֶן and מַה also links 25:2-6 with 26:5-14 (cf. 25:4-5; 26:14). This analysis indicates that Job's ninth speech is limited to 26:2-4. Accordingly, the following analysis identifies Job's literary rhetorical situation by examining 25:2-6 and analyzes the form(s) and rhetorical strategies of 26:2-4.

The Literary Rhetorical Situation of Job 26:2-4

Bildad is left dazed by Job's rhetorical tour de force of Job 23–24. Following his defense of his protest prayer in Job 23 and his refutation of their premises regarding God's justice in 24:1-17, Job characterized the friends' arguments and closed with a rhetorically powerful taunt (24:25). This leaves Bildad with few options for his rebuttal. He chooses

---

43. See p. 13 n. 28.
44. For a helpful summary of proposals, see Lo (2003: 127), though her assessment of Clines is mistaken.
45. See also Cheney (1994: 45–7, 102–3, 116, 123–4), who argues along the same lines. Cheney calls the lack of narratorial intrusion a "0-marker" transition.

to emphasize divine transcendence (25:2-3, 5) and to reprise Eliphaz's low anthropology (25:4, 6; cf. 4:17-19; 15:14-16) to refute Job. Framing his introduction with a chiasm, which places 25:2 and 6 in an antithetical relationship and links vv. 3 and 5 with their focus on the heavens, Bildad highlights 25:4 as his key statement: "Then how can a human be right with God, and how can one born of woman be pure?"[46] The rhetorical force of this question is to assert his low anthropology, a refutation of Job's asseveration of innocence from Job 23 (Clines 2006: 631). In other words, following Job's rejection of one of the premises of the friends' arguments (24:1-17), Bildad attempts to refute one of Job's premises. For Job, his innocence is part of the basis for defending his right to protest prayer. If Bildad can document that no human can be innocent, the key premise in Job's argument has no warrant. The hymn, thus, is a rhetorical strategy to silence Job's protest prayer.[47] By stressing so clearly the ontological sinfulness and corrupt nature of humanity, Bildad is suggesting that Job can never achieve restoration without repentance; protest is not only unbecoming but also ineffective.[48] Thus, Job still faces the exigency of defending his protest prayer, which has been called into question yet again.

The Forms of Job 26:2-4

The form of this short speech is a disputation (Murphy 1981: 36; Clines 2006: 627). This is confirmed by the use of the interrogatives and the tonality of scathing sarcasm.[49] There are six clauses of disputation in this short speech. This confirms the rhetorical situation just identified; Job is arguing with the friends.

---

46. On the chiasm, see Hartley 1988: 355.

47. Newsom (1996: 519–20) notes that Bildad finds Job's protest prayer abhorrent and uses his hymn to silence this kind of religious expression.

48. There is a self-defeating element to Bildad's argument regarding the otherness of God that implies God cannot be affected by humans. Berger (1990: 55–7, 74) calls this "religious masochism" and "transcendentalization"; as Berger points out, this allows individuals to deal with the existential pain of suffering (56). The friends utilize this to silence protest prayer: "the implicit accusation against God is turned around to become an explicit accusation against man" (74). Job rejects this at all costs (contra Berger).

49. These are also the reasons given by Murphy (1981: 36), who cites the sarcasm, and Clines (2006: 627), who cites the interrogatives. Clines thinks these words are uttered by Bildad, but his form-critical label is not affected by his identification of the speaker.

The Rhetorical Strategies of Job 26:2-4

Structure

This speech, given its brevity, does not divide into major movements. Job uses interrogatives to make exclamations (26:2-3), followed by a climactic rhetorical question (26:4). The different syntax of 26:3b marks it for emphasis in the middle of the short speech, highlighting Job's point that mocks the wisdom of Bildad and his companions.[50]

Strategies

Direct Address to the Friends, Lexical Repetition, Interrogatives, Tropes, and Tonality. In this brief speech Job accomplishes his rhetorical goal mainly through sarcasm (Good 1990: 284). The sarcasm emerges from Job's other rhetorical strategies: his use of second person forms in direct address, the use of interrogatives (which recall Bildad's use of מַה in 25:4; cf. 26:7, 14), and the use of tropes. Job's rhetorical strategies in this speech are interrelated and mutually reinforcing.

Job uses six second person forms in 26:2-4, two in each verse.[51] Five of these occurrences are verbal forms, which are obviously sarcastic in the present context. Job has repeatedly noted that the friends have offered no help or wisdom (cf. 6:14-30; 13:5-19; 16:2-6; 19:2-6). Job's use of the interrogative מַה confirms this. Bildad had used מַה twice to emphasize his main argument, namely, that humans cannot be righteous or pure with God since they are ontologically sinful (25:4). Job's exclamations with מַה mock Bildad's argument (26:2-3). Job's use of מִי in 26:4 also confirms the sarcasm in his speech. Job asks Bildad rhetorically from whom he has developed his arguments. Scholars have highlighted Job's rejection of Bildad's words as divinely inspired (Hartley 1988: 363; Newsom 1996: 517). But given the close affinity of Bildad's main argument in 25:4 with Eliphaz's statements in 4:17-19 and 15:14-16 it is likely that Job is also mocking Bildad's lack of creativity. Job taunts Bildad's rhetorical move to rehash arguments from another interlocutor, arguments which Job has already dismissed. Accordingly, with this question in 26:4, Job also

---

50. The fronted object in 26:3b does not follow the pattern of *qatal* verb followed by לֹא.

51. Each of these is a 2ms form, giving the impression that Job is specifically addressing Bildad. This may be another indication of Job interrupting Bildad's speech, angered by Bildad's religious masochism and by the theological foundation for his advice.

condemns the friends as a whole.[52] Job is mocking the rhetorical force of Bildad's arguments as Bildad is speaking.

The two tropes that emerge in this brief speech also indicate the sarcasm with which Job is speaking. He uses a motif of strength in 26:2 and a motif of wisdom in 26:3. These tropes echo Job's presentation of himself in 6:11-13, which recalls Job's first criticism and instruction regarding comforter ethics in 6:14.[53] The wisdom motif also recalls Job's denunciation of the friends' wisdom in 13:5-19. The ambiguity of the syntactical function of the clauses which contain these tropes also points to Job's sarcasm. Newsom notes that the phrases זְרוֹעַ לֹא־עֹז, לְלֹא־כֹחַ, and לְלֹא חָכְמָה could be read as verbal modifiers (1996: 517): "how you helped without strength," "how you saved with an arm without strength," and "how you counseled without wisdom."

The effect of these strategies, then, is to create pointed sarcasm to deride the theology (and advice upon which that theology is constructed) of Bildad through the second person forms, interrogatives, lexical repetition, and the tropes.[54] By this sarcasm Job rejects Bildad's arguments that he anticipates will be used to silence his protest prayer.[55]

---

52. Hartley draws a similar conclusion but from a different direction (1988: 363).

53. The use of כֹּחַ and תּוּשִׁיָּה recall 6:11 and 6:13, respectively.

54. If one were to interpret 26:5-14 as Job's words, another strategy would be Job's use of the hymn. The rhetorical effect of the hymn would be to reject the friends' wisdom. Given God's transcendence, Job avers that the friends would have no access to his wisdom and thus have no basis upon which to criticize and instruct him. Lo suggests that the sarcasm evident in 26:2-4 provides the framework for reading the hymn ironically. Ingenious though it may be, Lo's argument fails to convince. For this interpretation of the hymn, see Lo 2003: 160–5; Yu 2011: 345; Walton 2012: 264; Wilson 2015: 128–9.

55. Bildad's intention to silence Job's protest prayer emerges most clearly in his final statement in 26:14 (see Habel 1985: 374; Clines 2006: 640). Newsom writes (1996: 519), "One can deduce what Bildad finds unacceptable in Job's speech. From his perspective, Job has let the 'personal' quality of God become an intimacy that destroys the necessary and proper sense of awe that should be present in religious experience. Job has made God accountable to Job himself and talks as though they were two neighbors in a quarrel." This captures how Bildad's theology is driving toward silencing Job's lament, a form of discourse that undermines the otherness that Bildad wants so desperately to maintain. Newsom reflects how this kind of a response can be helpful for sufferers, which in some sense is true (519–20). For example, the movement of the Psalter, which answers the dominance of lament by pointing to the kingship of Yahweh in Book IV (see Wilson 1985; 1986: 85–94; 1993: 72–82; McKelvey 2010), reflects this tendency as an invitation to trust the

Summary of 26:2-4

With this short speech, Job interrupts Bildad in the midst of his hymn in order to ridicule his wisdom and comforting practices. Job rejects the religious masochism that undergirds Bildad's implied advice, a turn to repentance. Job uses the strategies of direct address, interrogatives, lexical repetition, and tropes to heighten his sarcasm and rejection of Bildad's argument.

"Until I Die I Will Not Turn My Integrity Away from Me":
The Rhetoric of Job's Tenth Speech (Job 27)

Introduction

After Bildad's hymn, Job brings the dialogue to an end with his tenth speech in Job 27. He reaffirms his commitment to true speech and rejects his comforters, bringing them to silence.

The Literary Rhetorical Situation of Job 27

The literary rhetorical situation for Job's tenth speech remains the same as Job's previous short speech in 26:2-4. With Bildad's hymn continuing his argument from 25:2-6, Job faces the same exigency, namely, to refute Bildad's argument of divine transcendence and human corruption that encourages repentance—in other words, the necessity of defending his protest prayer. Bildad maintains his position that in order for Job to achieve the restoration he wants, he must confess his sin (i.e., penitential prayer), though the illocution of Bildad's speech is somewhat subtle. The power of God and the physical (and therefore moral) corruption of all humans demands a change in the mode of prayer (Clines 2006: 626; cf. Habel 1985: 368–70; Newsom 1996: 517). Tracing the movement of the last few speeches, then, it becomes clear that with Eliphaz's manufactured list of sins and call to repentance (Job 22), Job offers an avowal of innocence to reject the call to repentance (Job 23), to which Bildad replies with his religious masochism in order to silence Job's protest prayer and encourage penitence. Job's primary audience, therefore, in Job 27 remains the friends.

---

creator king. But when this kind of theology makes humanity worthless—as Bildad's notion of humanity as worms and maggots does—in order to silence protest prayer, it is not an appropriate response.

The Forms of Job 27

In typical fashion, Job combines forms in his tenth speech. There is no consensus regarding these forms among interpreters.[56] Nevertheless, it seems that this speech is a disputation, noting the arguments made regarding true speech, the main topic of dialogue. In other words, Job is presenting an argument. He states his position clearly in 27:5c-6. Furthermore, the rhetorical questions play a major role in this speech, as does his stated intention to instruct them (27:11). Disputation is thus found in 27:5c-6, 8-23, a total of forty-five clauses. The jussive form in 27:7 indicates a wish (two clauses), while the oath form (marked by חַי with a divine name and חָלִילָה לִי) in 27:2-5b comprises ten clauses. The oath and the wish function within the argument to emphasize Job's resolve and to invoke divine affirmation for his position. This confirms the rhetorical situation just identified as Job uses forms appropriate to his exigency.

The Rhetorical Strategies of Job 27

Structure

This speech divides into three sections: (1) 27:2-6, Job's oath and opening argument; (2) 27:7-10, Job's curse and rhetorical questions; and (3) 27:11-23, Job's instruction regarding the friends "instruction."[57] The jussive form in v. 7 coupled with the rhetorical questions and a shift to the wicked demarcate vv. 7-10 from the oath in vv. 2-6. The resolve to

---

56. One major challenge for identifying the forms of this speech lies in the difficulty in identifying the speaker. There are several proposals for the speaker which tends to influence how scholars view the forms of these verses. Hartley (1988: 40–1) suggests that 27:2-6 are an avowal of innocence and 27:7-10 are a petition for deliverance from enemies. He does not list 27:11-12 and thinks 27:13-23 belong to Bildad. Clines (2006: 644) suggests that 27:2-6, 11-12 are disputation speech, made up of an oath, an accusation, a negative wish, and an assertion. He suggests 27:7-10 and 13-23 comprise Zophar's final speech. Murphy (1981: 36) is also attentive to multiple forms, suggesting that two, oath and complaint, come together to comprise a disputation. Westermann (1981b: 98–9) is reticent to comment on the third cycle in detail but does suggest that 27:2-6 are an avowal of innocence, related to Job's oath in Job 31.

57. This division corresponds with the view of most interpreters. Most see vv. 2-6 and 7-10 as major units. Even those who see Zophar or Bildad speaking in 27:13-23 group this section based on thematic coherence. The question emerges as to how vv. 11-12 relate, whether as a short unit creating four sections in this speech or as connected to either the second or third movement. See, e.g., Habel 1985: 377; Newsom 1996: 522; Lo 2003: 168; Clines 2006: 643, 661. Wilson (2015: 129) divides the chapter into three movements as well, though slightly differently: 27:2-6, 7-12, 13-23.

teach and the direct address in vv. 11-12 mark another shift. It seems best to see vv. 11-12 as the preface to vv. 13-23; the instruction Job intends to give sarcastically to correct their false teaching (vv. 11-12) is developed in vv. 13-23.

This structure reveals Job's major emphases in this speech. He begins with the oath to establish his resolve for true and pious speech (27:2-6). He then moves to reject the comforters by cursing them (27:7-10), and closes by mocking their teaching and advice (27:11-23). Clines notes, this speech "strongly [resists the friends'] positions. Formally speaking, it is a denial that they are in the right"; in this speech, Job affirms his "intention of not surrendering his position of innocence" (2006: 644). This captures the function of the speech, but not quite the whole picture. Given the calls—whether implicit or explicit—for Job's repentance, this speech is Job's rejection of the friends' position, particularly as it relates to repentance.[58]

Strategies

Oath and Emphatic Statements. Job begins his tenth speech with an oath, marked by חַי אֵל in 27:2 and חֲלִילָה לִי in 27:5a.[59] Notably, Job's oath relates directly to his verbal expression and its ethics. Job will not speak unjustly, nor will he speak deceit (27:4).[60] This statement recalls two other places where Job rejected the friends' counsel as a part of his justification of protest prayer: Job uses עַוְלָה in 6:30, while in 13:7 he uses עַוְלָה and רְמִיָּה as a word pair. Functionally, Job is affirming his true speech and the friends' deceit, as in 6:30 and 13:7 (note the use of שָׂפָה and לָשׁוֹן). Job draws a conclusion from his oath to stress his point, an emphatic statement marked by the fronted object: "To my righteousness I will hold fast, and I will not let it go; my heart will not reproach me all my days" (27:6).[61] The illocution of the oath in this rhetorical context is to reject completely the friends' arguments and advice, in that Job will not heed their advice as long as he is living (27:3, 5) (Yu 2011: 353); the reference

---

58. Clines highlights that Job's purpose is "to affirm his innocence as strongly as he can" (2006: 645).

59. See Joüon §165 e, f, and k; Arnold and Choi 2003: 188; WO §40.2.2b-c. There is a two-part structure to the oath, with corresponding components: oath formula (v. 2 // v. 5), reference to life/death (v. 3 // v. 5b-c), speech ethics concerns (v. 4 // v. 6).

60. The presence of אִם in this oath indicates the negative actions. See Arnold and Choi 2003: 188.

61. The focus on Job and his integrity in speech is emphasized by the twenty-two 1cs forms in this speech. The effect of this is a stark juxtaposition of Job's speech with that of the friends.

to death in 27:5b, עַד־אֶגְוָע, is also fronted, marking it for emphasis.[62] This is a defense of his protest prayer in that it rejects their call for repentance. This provocative move silences the friends, while also implying a petition for God to act (Hartley 1994: 88). But in so doing, Job also effectively elevates himself over God by forcing God into action and impugning God's justice. When Job takes the oath in the name of God, "who has turned aside my justice" and "who has made my soul bitter" (27:2), he explicitly links his suffering with the general suffering he described in Job 24.[63] The implications of the oath are significant in regards to Job's God-talk. Nevertheless, Job's faith in God, who violates his justice and attacks, emerges as he continues to hold out hope that God will act on his behalf (Newsom 1996: 523).

Job also marks an emphatic statement in v. 12 with the use of the particle הֵן. The emphasis is reinforced by the superfluous use of the pronouns: הֵן־אַתֶּם כֻּלְּכֶם חֲזִיתֶם ("Behold, you yourselves—all of you—have surely seen"). This marks the rhetorical question in which Job accuses the friends of vain, that is, false, teaching.

Tropes. Relatively speaking, this speech employs fewer tropes than Job's other speeches. Nevertheless, Job still uses them to reinforce his other rhetorical strategies. Immediately, and provocatively, Job reuses the images of divine injustice and divine attack in 27:2. As a part of the oath, these images reinforce Job's perceived disconnect between who he believes God should be (one who vindicates him) and what he experiences. The epithet הֵמַר נַפְשִׁי recalls Job's description of bitterness earlier in the dispute (3:20; 7:11; 10:1). In the context of Job's oath regarding his blamelessness in deed and discourse, these epithets also recall Job's description of divine attack in 16:7-17 and 19:7-20. Job is innocent; God is the source of his bitterness. Thus, Job believes protest prayer is the best option; repentance is irrelevant.[64]

---

62. This interpretation reads the verse differently than indicated by the Masoretic accentuation (see Clines 2006: 642).

63. The use of מִשְׁפָּט anticipates 40:8 (Hartley 1994: 83–4).

64. As is the case elsewhere when Job uses these images, there may be an element of implied petition (Hartley 1988: 369). But the rhetorical situation makes this a secondary aspect of Job's rhetoric. Job's rhetoric is designed for disputation, not protest prayer.

Job also uses images of life and death in the oath to reinforce his rejection of the friends' advice. His breath (נְשָׁמָה) and God's Spirit (רוּחַ אֱלוֹהַּ) form a metonymy for his life (Clarke 2011: 111–21).[65] Conversely, the trope of death emerges in v. 5, the second part of the oath. Job affirms with these tropes that as long as he is living he will never accept the theology and advice of the friends. Another metonymy is Job's use of his "heart" (לֵבָב) to refer to himself in v. 6. These tropes thus function within Job's emphatic statements.

Job also uses the verb/noun combination of הבל and הֶבֶל metaphorically (Johnston 1997: 1003; Fredericks 1997: 1005; Fox 1999: 27–9). Different from Job's other uses, where they are used to describe the nature of his life as a sufferer (7:16; 9:29), Job uses these words to stress the false and empty nature of the friends' theology and advice (21:34). This trope reinforces Job's characterization and rhetorical question in 27:12.[66]

Curse. Job also issues a wish, marked by the use of the jussive in 27:7. Since this wish invokes a negative outcome, it is, more specifically, a curse. Job curses his enemy (אֹיְבִי), wishing for his experience to be like the wicked. The identification of this enemy is disputed to some degree, but the context would seem to indicate that Job is referring to his friends.[67] Three points support this: (1) the parallel description of the one who rises against Job (מִתְקוֹמְמִי) fits the description of the friends' actions against Job; (2) the use of the friends' terms and teaching, specifically the fate of the wicked, which would be odd to wish upon God; and (3) the use of the second person plural in vv. 11-12, as Job builds on his curse to apply it to the friends. In Job's rhetorical context this curse silences the friends as he condemns them as wicked. This curse, thus, functions in the same way as Job's condemnations of the friends in 13:4-5, 16:3, and 19:3, and his characterization of the friends in this speech and elsewhere. As a curse, God is invoked by the rhetoric as well—an implied petition for deliverance from the enemies, Job's friends. Like the oath, Job's curse leaves the friends in silence.

---

65. Hartley notes that this depicts Job's recognition that his very life depends on Yahweh, an image of trust (1994: 85).

66. Job's use of the fate of the wicked in vv. 13-23 is another trope, but is intimately related to Job's tonality and characterization, and so will be developed below.

67. See, e.g., Andersen 1976: 238; Habel 1985: 381–2; Newsom 1996: 523; Lo 2003: 190. Andersen, Newsom, and Lo consider the enemy Job's friends, while Habel suggests it is God.

Rhetorical Questions. Job builds on this curse with a series of rhetorical questions in 27:8-10. Having wished his comforters would experience the fate of the wicked, Job, through these rhetorical questions, avers they will be cut off as the wicked (27:8). Moreover, God would not hear their cries because of their wickedness (27:9-10). Eliphaz used עָנָג עַל in 22:26 in his exhortation to Job regarding repentance. Job, mocking his advice, shows how futile this advice has been (27:10): will the friends desire God when they face hardship? Furthermore, with his avowal of innocence in the background, Job reminds them that he does have hope when he calls on God; God will vindicate and restore Job as one who is blameless, not wicked. These questions, then, are intimately related to Job's curse, with the curse setting up Job's argument for their demise. Through these strategies he rejects the friends, condemning them as wicked. This rejection of the friends leaves them in silence, while also justifying his approach to God by rejecting their advice.[68]

Direct Address to the Friends, Characterization, and Tonality. Job brings together a number of rhetorical strategies following his oath and his curse to accomplish his rhetorical goals of defending his protest prayer and silencing his comforters. His direct address to the friends, characterization of the friends (as false teachers, mocking their instruction), and tonality (sarcasm) work together as Job brings his speech to a close. Job takes up a "didactic manner of speaking," but one riddled with sarcasm (Newsom 1996: 524).[69]

Beginning with Job 27:11, Job articulates his intention to instruct the friends. The direct address in v. 11 recalls Job's address in 27:5: "I will not declare you (אֶתְכֶם) right,"[70] indicating these strategies (oath, direct address, and tone) are related. With this in mind, Job's intention in instruction becomes clear: their theology and related advice are flawed: Job "will teach [them] about the hand of God" (27:11). Job reinforces his teaching with the emphatic particle (הֵן) and superfluous use of 2mp forms (אַתֶּם כֻּלְּכֶם) to mark his rhetorical question in 27:12: "why then have you become so vain?" With this question, Job focuses on "the inanity of what the friends have said" (Newsom 1996: 524). The use of לָמָּה here

---

68. There is one additional rhetorical question, in 27:12, which will be addressed below because of its connection to Job's direct address and characterization of the friends.

69. The sarcasm, as noted below, is indicated by the repurposing of the friends' language. Noteworthy as well is the obvious sarcasm from Job's previous speech as preparation for reading the same sardonic style in Job 27.

70. On the declarative sense of the Hiphil of צדק, see GKC §53c.

indicates an accusation with an implied petition: stop teaching falsely. Job's sarcasm continues in v. 13 as Job quotes Zophar's final words in 20:29 almost verbatim, while also employing a number of themes and images from the friends' speeches throughout the book.[71] Job is calling the friends out as liars (Lo 2003: 191).

Job builds on this direct address by also characterizing the friends and their teaching. The characterization of the friends in 27:12-13 builds on the foundational characterization in 27:7. Job depicts the friends as the "overt enemies of God" by bringing together the word pair of אָדָם רָשָׁע and עָרִיצִים in 27:13 (cf. 15:20) (Habel 1985: 385). Job also characterizes their teaching in a semi-quotation of the fate of the wicked, imitating their theology and instruction.[72] This reveals how empty (הֶבֶל) their teaching is. Parodying their teaching, his instruction in vv. 13-23 recalls a number of passages from the friends' speeches in the book.[73] Even more, the rhetoric of Job's mocking instruction recalls his characterization of them as wicked; wishing for them this same fate, he uses their words against them (Lo 2003: 193).[74]

---

71. Presenting the texts alongside each other helps to highlight the parallels:

Job 20:29 זֶה חֵלֶק־אָדָם רָשָׁע מֵאֱלֹהִים וְנַחֲלַת אִמְרוֹ מֵאֵל
Job 27:13 זֶה חֵלֶק־אָדָם רָשָׁע עִם־אֵל וְנַחֲלַת עָרִיצִים מִשַּׁדַּי יִקָּחוּ

72. Janzen (1985: 171–4, 185–6) suggests that Job makes Zophar's speech for him in 27:13-23. Newsom argues similarly, though with an important nuance. Rather than Job giving Zophar's speech for him, Newsom is attentive to the imitative quality of 27:13-23, by which Job rejects "such drivel as the friends have been speaking" (1996: 522–4, quote from 522). Lo appreciates these two interpretations as they read 27:13-23 as Job's words but does not agree that there is quotation or imitation in view. Rather, Lo suggests the contradiction is an intentional juxtaposition to highlight the bankruptcy of the friends' views (2003: 183–93). On the different approaches to Job 27:13-23, see ibid.: 167, though she errs in her categorization of Clines and Newsom.

73. 27:13 recalls 4:8 and quotes almost verbatim 20:29. 27:14 recalls 15:22-23 (cf. 4:11; 5:4). 27:15 recalls 18:12, 13, 19. 27:16-17 recall 20:10, 15, 18-19. 27:18 recalls 8:14-15 (on the text-critical questions, see Clines 2006: 659). 27:19 recalls 15:29; 20:21, 26, 28; 22:20. 27:20 recalls 15:21, 24; 18:11, 14; 20:25. 27:21 recalls 8:2; 15:2. 27:23 recalls 22:19-20. 27:13-23 recall 8:22; 11:20; 20:7-9; 22:10-11. I am indebted to Lo's study for some of these parallels. See Lo 2003: 172–5. The ending of the speech seems rather abrupt, perhaps to indicate Job's recognition that he has said enough, or that he is perhaps even uncomfortable with what he has already said.

74. Lo's suggestion regarding the rhetorical strategy of contradictory juxtaposition is unconvincing, even if her conclusions are insightful. In my view, the rhetoric of Job's speech in Job 27 involves the sarcastic tone and the parodic characterization of the friends' teaching in direct address, rather than contradictory juxtaposition.

Following Job's oath (27:2-6) and curse (27:7-10), this characterization and sardonic instruction directed at the friends further emphasizes their false speech when juxtaposed with his true speech. With these strategies, Job thus rejects the friends as sages and comforters, thereby defending his verbal expression in protest prayer. In this rejection Job silences the friends with a rhetorical flourish.

Summary of Job 27

Following Bildad's tone-deaf hymn, Job takes an oath to assert his true words and accuse the friends of being liars. He drives home his argument regarding the appropriateness of his speech with a curse, rhetorical questions, direct address in sardonic instruction, and characterization of the friends as wicked and false teachers. Job rejects the friends as comforters, and thus defends the ethics of his own discourse. His rhetoric in this speech is so effective, it brings an end to the dispute. Alter (1981: 79) notes that silence can be significant in a narrative's plot as a rhetorical device with respect to the reader. In this case, it stresses the friends' inability to win the dispute over the ethics of Job's God-talk, and in particular the ethics of protest prayer.

This is a significant point in terms of the overall movement of the book. As some scholars note, key terms in this speech recall the events of the prologue; moreover, Yahweh's second speech will reference this speech in 40:8 (see Habel 1985: 378; Hartley 1994: 83–4).[75] At this critical juncture, Job's rhetoric that rejects the friends as a way of defending his protest prayer emerges as a significant datum in the book's contribution to speech ethics.

"Does Not One on a Heap of Ruins Stretch Out His Hand?":
The Rhetoric of Job's Eleventh Speech (Job 29–31)

Introduction

Following Job's speech in Job 27, the friends are left in silence. The narrator then returns to assess for the reader the preceding dispute in Job 28.[76] Job 29–31 provides Job's final speech, a prayer of protest to move God to act on his behalf.

---

75. As Hartley points out, it is significant that this oath recalls the prologue with the repetition of סוּר, חָזַק, תֻּמָּה, and שָׂפָה (see 1:1, 8; 2:3, 9, 10).

76. See Chapter 2 for the rhetoric of Job 28.

The Literary Rhetorical Situation of Job 29–31

With the friends' silence, Job no longer faces their criticism and advice. In this case, the friends' silence is indicative of their failure to convince Job to adopt a penitential mode rather than a protesting one. With that exigency no longer a factor, Job returns to his remaining exigency: his suffering. It was the motivating factor in Job's opening complaint in Job 3; it also was a motivating factor throughout the first cycle. In the second and third cycles, Job's primary exigency has been the one caused by the friends' advice, and so his suffering played a less prominent role in motivating his speeches. Job depicts his suffering throughout Job 30, recalling images and language used throughout his speeches. Of particular note is 30:26, which recalls 3:26.[77]

This analysis indicates Job's audience and goal. As an innocent sufferer, Job turns to address God to protest in prayer with the goal of achieving relief from his suffering and the restoration of his relationship with God. The constraints are the same as those that were in effect in Job's opening speech.

The Forms of Job 29–31

Interpreters identify the forms of Job 29–31 variously.[78] An examination of the forms indicates that, even though six different forms comprise this speech, this speech is protest prayer (lament and complaint). There are 227 clauses in this speech, with 34% of the clauses being either lament or complaint (seventy-seven of 227)—more than any other form. Notably the wish form creates an inclusio around the entire speech (29:2; 31:35), with Job's complaint at the center of the entire speech.[79] The following analysis will proceed along the chapter divisions, which correspond to the major movements of the speech.

---

77. Recall the use of בוא in Job 3 as a way of revealing Job's rhetorical situation following the prologue (see p. 46 n. 5).

78. E.g., Murphy (1981: 39) describes Job 29–31 as a soliloquy, made up of complaint (Job 30) and an avowal of innocence or purificatory oath (Job 31); Hartley (1989: 41–2) interprets Job's final speech as an avowal of innocence; Habel (1985: 404–5) suggests the speech is a formal public testimony with a complaint; Westermann (1981b: 38–42, 67–70) argues the speech is a lament, with 31:35-37 being a wish to encounter God; Clines (2006: 978–9) outlines Job 29 as a description of experience, Job 30 as a lament, and Job 31 as an oath of purification; Seow (2013: 59–61), building on the work of Dobbs-Allsopp on the Meṣad Ḥashavyahu ostracon, understands Job 29–31 as a judicial complaint.

79. The complaint is most pronounced in 30:20-23. The final clause of 30:23 brings the reader to the exact middle point of the speech in terms of number of clauses.

Job 29 includes fifty-eight clauses, comprised exclusively of the wish form. This is usually described in terms of a statement of remembrance (e.g., Hartley 1988: 385; Clines 2006: 978). Westermann connects Job 29 with statements of remembrance in communal laments (1981b: 39–40). But the מִי־יִתֵּן of 29:2 governs the entire chapter, indicating that the whole chapter is a wish.[80] This wish works with the prayer of protest that emerges with the וְעַתָּה of 30:1. This wish does two things: (1) it indicates Job's former life as a contrast to the prayer of protest, and (2) expresses Job's desired goal, namely, to return to the life he had with God and within society before his suffering.

Job 30 is protest prayer. This is almost unanimously agreed upon.[81] There are seventy-seven clauses in Job 30, with sixty-one clauses being lament (30:1-10, 11c-18, 24-31) and sixteen clauses being complaint (30:11a-b, 19-23). The complaint emerges to the foreground explicitly in 30:19-23 with the direct accusations against God.

Job 31 has ninety-two clauses, in which four types of forms are found. Avowal of innocence occurs in twenty-three clauses (31:1-4, 14-15, 28, 30-32), oath occurs in forty-nine clauses (31:4-10, 13, 16-17, 19-22, 24-27, 29, 33, 38-40b); twelve clauses are motive clauses (31:11-12, 18, 23, 34), and wish occurs in eight clauses (31:35-37). The motive clauses give the reasons for the ethical conduct to which Job attests, whether by oath or avowal of innocence. These motive clauses reveal his fear of God and his accountability to God. The illocutions of the oath and of the avowal of innocence are the same: to testify to his innocence and thus to move God to act. The wish of 31:35-37 reveals his goal (cf. 29:2). The forms of Job 31 also function to supplement the protest prayer, just as the wish of Job 29 did.

The most frequently employed form in this complex speech is protest prayer (seventy-seven clauses). It sits in the middle of the speech, indicating its prominent role. The second most common form is the wish (sixty-six clauses), also holding a prominent structural place at the beginning and at the end. The third most common form is the oath (forty-nine clauses). These latter two forms work together under the dominant forms of lament/complaint.

---

80. The repetition of temporal constructions indicates that 29:3-25 elaborate Job's wish from 29:2. Job's remembrance is thus subordinated to Job's wish, with מִי־יִתֵּן governing the whole chapter.

81. See the literature in n. 78 above.

This is confirmed by Seow's genre analysis (2013: 59–61). Seow connects Job 29–31 to the Meṣad Ḥashavyahu ostracon, which F. W. Dobbs-Allsopp argues is a judicial complaint.[82] This coheres with the analysis above, namely, that this is a complaint with judicial elements; there is a petition in this speech.[83] Job is appealing to God, the highest authority, against God—in the vein of the God-laments—in order to achieve the restoration he desires.

This confirms the literary rhetorical situation identified above. As an innocent sufferer—and one who believes himself to be suffering at God's hands—Job engages in protest prayer in order to move God to act on his behalf, to bring relief. The wish, oath, and avowal of innocence function rhetorically within the prayer of protest. Job employs the appropriate form in his situation. Job's goal is to move God into action (Dick 1979: 49; Hartley 1988: 386; Clines 2006: 979). This also implies that Job's audience must be God.

The Rhetorical Strategies of Job 29–31

Structure

The structure of Job's final speech at the macro-level divides along the chapter divisions: Job 29 looks to the past, Job 30 is a prayer of protest over his current experience, and Job 31 is an oath.

Job 29 begins with the wish in v. 2.[84] The wish is then developed and illustrated throughout the rest of the chapter. Job wishes for "the months of old" or "the days God watched over me." Job describes his relationship

---

82. This is also known as the Yavneh Yam ostracon. See *COS* 3.41:77–78; cf. Dobbs-Allsopp 1994: 49–55; Seow 2013: 60.

83. The jussive form of 31:35 ("let the Almighty answer me" [יַעֲנֵנִי]) is a petition. See Dobbs-Allsopp (1994: 49–51) on the petition element in the Meṣad Ḥashavyahu ostracon, indicated by various volitional forms in conjunction with a rehearsal of the acts and accusation. Seow acknowledges that there is an "implicit accusation" in Job's avowal of innocence, but does not recognize—at least explicitly—that the accusation contains petition (2013: 69).

84. There is broad agreement among interpreters on the structure of Job 29. See, e.g., Clines (2006: 976), Habel (1985: 402–3), Hartley (1988: 387), Newsom (1996: 537), and Wilson (2015: 140–1). There are minor divergences. For example, Habel separates v. 2 and v. 25 from the rest of the poem as an introduction and conclusion, while Clines makes two strophes out of 29:11-17, vv. 11-14 and vv. 15-17. Each of these interpreters is agreed on 29:7-10 as a unit. My analysis includes v. 11 with this unit, noting the presence of the temporal indicators (בְּ in 29:7 and כִּי in 29:11),

with God and his family in 29:3-6, his role within the community in 29:7-11, his role as a guarantor of justice in 29:12-17, his past confidence and hope in 29:18-20, and concludes with a return to his role in the community in 29:21-25. This return to focus on the community sets Job up for his emphasis on his alienation from this community in Job 30.

Job 30 is divided by the repetition of וְעַתָּה in 30:1, 9, and 16, with אַךְ marking the final unit.[85] Thus, Job opens with a lament over his experience as one who is mocked and launches into a description of these mockers (30:1-8), then returns to his experience as one who is mocked in 30:9-15. He laments and complains about the attack from God in 30:16-23, and closes with a final lament with justification in 30:24-31.

Job 31 divides into nine sections: 31:1-4 (an avowal of innocence), 5-8 (an oath of innocence regarding deceit), 9-12 (an oath of innocence regarding adultery), 13-15 (an oath of innocence regarding his household), 16-23 (an oath of innocence regarding the marginalized of society), 24-28 (an oath of innocence regarding idolatry), 29-34 (an oath of innocence of any other sins, a "catch-all"), 35-37 (his wish), and 38-40b (an oath of innocence regarding the land).[86]

This analysis reveals Job's major emphases within each chapter. As noted above, Job's wish forms an inclusio around the speech, indicating his goal of a restored relationship (Wilson 2015: 140). Job's complaint is found in a prominent place in the middle of the speech, as Job seeks to move God to act. This structural analysis also reveals how the wish and the oath/avowal of innocence serve the prayer of protest to reveal his goals and his innocence, reinforcing the prayer of protest over his suffering.

---

forming an inclusio. Moreover, 29:11 is better connected thematically to the preceding material than the subsequent material. The temporal כִּי in 27:12 begins a new section. Clines considers 29:2 the node for the entire chapter (2006: 980).

85. This division is suggested by Clines (2006: 976) and Newsom (1996: 544). Hartley groups 30:1-15 together (1988: 544). Habel (idiosyncratically) divides the chapter into three sections: 30:1-11, 12-19, and 20-31 (1985: 413–14). This ignores the repetition of וְעַתָּה, while disconnecting verses that are linked thematically. Wilson (2015: 144–8) takes 30:1 as a topic sentence, and structures the chapter thus: 30:1, 2-8, 9-15, 16-19, 20-23, 24-31.

86. There is agreement on these divisions. Newsom (1996: 552) groups some of these small divisions together, forming the following structure: 30:1-12, 13-23, 24-28, 29-34, 35-37, and 38-40. Wilson aligns with the analysis presented here (2015: 149), as do Hartley (1988: 409–25) and Clines (2006: 976), though they rearrange vv. 38-40 before vv. 35-37. Habel's division is once again unique: 30:1-6, 7-12, 13-23, 24-28, 29-34, and 35-40 (1985: 423–5).

Strategies

Tropes. The most pervasive rhetorical strategy in Job's final speech is the use of tropes. In fact, both Job 29 and 30 are primarily extended, complex tropes.

Job 29 depicts Job's life prior to his extensive suffering. He opens with two similes in parallel: "as the months of old" and "as the days God watched over me." These similes bring to mind days of order, rest, protection, and joy. This image of Job's previous life is thus developed and illustrated further in a number of ways throughout the rest of the chapter. In fact, every verse is related to Job's wish for "months of old."

Job builds on this simile by incorporating a number of other tropes. He uses light imagery, juxtaposed with imagery of darkness, in 29:3 to describe his past; he uses light imagery again in 29:24 to illustrate his civic prominence. Job uses clothing imagery in 29:14 to describe his role regarding justice. This imagery is royal as well, which also comes to the foreground in 29:15-16: Job procures justice for the marginalized, acting as a father-figure, a protector, a guarantor in the administration of justice.[87] Royal imagery is found explicitly in 29:25.[88] Water imagery occurs in 29:19, 23, with 29:19 depicting Job's days as thriving and vibrant, and with 29:23 depicting how his vitality provided refreshment to others. Job provided comfort where it was needed (29:25).[89] Job also employs body imagery to depict the respect he held in the community (29:9, 10, 11, and 15). Job's days of old were days of prominence and ease.

It is the trope of ease that most characterizes Job 29. This trope is also variously depicted: in 29:4 Job describes his ease in terms of his intimate relationship with God; in 29:5 he recounts his life in terms of his relationship with God and his children; in 29:6 he portrays his life in terms of luxury; in 29:7-11 he outlines his life in terms of his civic prominence; in 29:12-17 he depicts his life in terms of his active lifestyle in establishing

---

87. On the royal nature of the image of the robe and the turban, see Clines 2006: 989.

88. Hartley even suggests, though does not develop, a possible allusion to Ps. 72:12 in 29:12 (1988: 12). Newsom writes (1996: 540), "It is striking how many of Job's images for himself in chap. 29 are elsewhere applied to kings and even to God." That Job is a royal figure in his depiction of his pre-suffering days testifies further to the description of his intimacy with God, as he reflected God to his community.

89. Job's imagery of mourners and comfort is not superfluous (*pace* Clines 2006: 995). It fits within the movement of the book quite well since a major theme throughout the dialogue has been on the comforting practices of the friends. Even in Job's prayer of protest, he takes a rhetorical dig at the friends, noting his superiority to them (6:14; 16:4-6). So also Newsom 1996: 539–40.

justice; in 29:18-20 he describes his strength and security;[90] in 29:21-25 Job returns to portray his civic prominence. Job commanded respect as a prominent figure in society who actively—aggressively (29:17)—fought for justice.[91] The emphasis is not on Job's obligation but his acts of supererogation. Life for Job was socially, religiously, and emotionally stable.

Job thus describes his previous life of ease, one in which life was ordered, restful, and whole. The effect of these images is to emphasize Job's great life before his current suffering befell him. Job 29 is one long, complex amalgamation of images of ease, prominence, service, and recognition—the good life. This complex use of images sets up the imagery of suffering depicted in Job 30, marked by וְעַתָּה in 30:1. The description of Job's life of ease in Job 29 provides a jarring backdrop for the description of his suffering in Job 30 (Newsom 1996: 537). Job 30 develops imagery of suffering as Job describes his physical, emotional, spiritual, and social unrest.

Job describes his emotional and spiritual suffering in 30:15, 16, 19, 24-25, 26, and 31. Job's possibility of deliverance is ephemeral (30:15). His soul is overturned within him (30:16). Job cries out as a heap of ruins (30:24), and laments the hardship of others and himself (30:25). He experiences complete unrest (30:26; cf. 3:25-26).[92] He uses dust and ashes as a metonymy for his whole life as an act of lamentation (30:19; cf. 42:6), using the instruments of mourning to describe his lamentation as well (30:31). Night, with its connection to darkness imagery, is personified in 30:17 to describe the physical harm it does to Job, creating restless nights (cf. 7:3-5, 14). Job combines this darkness imagery with body imagery ("bones") to describe his emotional state, his unrest; this fusion of images recurs in 30:27 (using "innards") and in 30:28, 30 (using darkened "skin" and "bones").[93] Job's "garment," using clothing imagery as a metonym for his body, is disfigured (30:18). This disfigurement is the result of

---

90. On the imagery of the קֶן, see Wilson 2015: 143.

91. The depictions of Job's civic role, as one who establishes justice, describe the ease he enjoyed as a respected member of the society. He uses further imagery of warfare and animals to describe his aggressive and intentional lifestyle to root out injustice as he "shattered the fangs of injustice" and "from its teeth cast out prey" (29:17). As Wilson writes, recalling 29:14, "It is in this active lifestyle sense that he was clothed with justice and righteousness" (ibid.).

92. This unrest is reinforced with the light and darkness imagery, recalling Job 29, where light was used to describe his pre-suffering days. This imagery also recalls Job 3, with the וַיָּבֹא recalling 3:26. Darkness (אֹפֶל) came, like turmoil (רֹגֶז).

93. Newsom notes that Job is experiencing gloom, not skin disease (1996: 547).

divine attack, which Job also depicts in 30:11, 15, 19, 21, 22, and 23.[94] God undoes Job's cord (Job 30:11),[95] is the presumed source behind the personified attacking terrors (30:15; cf. 7:14; 9:34; 13:11, 21; 21:6; 23:15-16), casts Job into the mire to result in Job's lamentable state (30:19; cf. 9:30-31), is cruel toward Job (30:21), hates Job (30:21; cf. 16:9), harmfully lifts Job to the wind (30:22), melts Job before the storm (30:22; cf. 9:17; 30:15),[96] and leads Job to death (30:23). This last example combines divine attack imagery with death imagery.[97] Paradoxically, Job depicts God not only as an attacker, but also as absent (30:20).[98]

The divine attack is portrayed as the foundation for the community attack and the alienation which Job experiences. God's attack in 30:11 is given as the reason for the community's attack as indicated by the causal כִּי in v. 11a and the parallelism that links God's attack with the community's actions in v. 11b. The community mocks him (30:9; cf. 12:4; Jer. 20:7; Lam. 3:14, 63), shows no restraint toward Job (30:11; cf. 17:6), rises against him (30:12; cf. 16:10-11), sets traps for him (30:12; cf. 18:7-10; 19:6), builds siege ramps against him (30:12), breaks up his path (30:13), promotes his calamity (30:14), breaks in upon him (30:14; cf. 16:14), and rolls over him (30:14). This has left Job socially marginalized (30:1, 9-14, 29; cf. 19:13-19). Job reinforces this alienation with animal imagery in 30:29. Job uses an extended and complex series of images in 30:2-8 to describe the lowest of society: they are weak, scavengers, and outcasts. He uses strength imagery (30:2), plant imagery (30:3-7), and

---

94. The subject of the verbs in 30:18 is ambiguous. It could be either night (cf. 30:17) or God (cf. 30:19). This recalls the ambiguity of the subject that closes wombs in Job 3:10.

95. This reading follows the *qere* (see Hartley 1988: 399 n. 4). Job depicts God's life-threatening action with this imagery (cf. Job 4:21). If one were to read the *kethib*, Job depicts how God has armed himself against him. The rhetorical effect is roughly the same as reading the *qere*.

96. This reading follows the *kethib* (see Clines 2006: 956); cf. Job 36:29.

97. Westermann (1981b: 41) connects 30:23 with 3:11, 20. See also 7:15.

98. This divine attack imagery is rhetorical, as elsewhere in Job's speeches. Thus, Walton (2012: 332–4) misunderstands the nature of protest prayer when he interprets Job's statements here as Job making God out to be a chaos creature. If Job really thought God was a chaos creature, he would no longer talk to God, and he certainly would not express his wish for a restored relationship. This wish, with its accompanying oath, testifies to Job's belief in the righteousness and justice of God. The imagery gives Job's rhetoric bite. Hartley writes (1988: 400), "By vividly recounting the misery that God's harsh treatment causes him, Job is desperately seeking to arouse God's sympathy for him."

animal imagery (30:1, 7) to reinforce this description. This nameless, foolish group merits nothing but disdain (30:8), and Job has become more alienated than these.[99]

Job truly is a "heap of ruins," as he characterizes himself in 30:24, calling out to God for help. The imagery of Job 30 reverses in almost every respect the imagery from Job 29. The tropes of ease become tropes of unrest; the tropes of divine friendship are now tropes of divine attack; the tropes of social prominence and inclusion become tropes of alienation and community attack. Job's life is now characterized by suffering and complete unrest. He is the object of scorn, treachery, and violence; he is socially marginalized. As Hartley notes (1988: 406), "Job suffers totally. His body is bent over by pain. His emotions are distraught. He is disgraced, being taunted by the dregs of society. The contrast between his former glory and his present disgrace is stark. Abandoned by all, Job laments the full scope of his misery."[100] Notably, Job's description of his suffering brackets his complaint and accusations in 30:20-23, which provides a clue as to how this depiction of total suffering functions rhetorically. It serves as the evidence upon which God should respond to Job's complaint; he experiences emotional and spiritual suffering as a result of his perceived treatment by God.

The rhetorical effect of the tropes in Job 29–30 is to present Job's suffering in stark and vivid ways. As a part of a complaint in which Job is seeking to move God to action, the juxtaposition of the imagery from Job's former days and the imagery of Job's current reality both document his suffering as a justification for his protest prayer, and create an emotional appeal for God to act on Job's behalf (Lo 2003: 219). This vivid imagery is intended to establish a renewed relationship. Because God has not responded to Job's previous cries, Job continues his lament (30:20, 24).

Tropes are employed less frequently in Job 31, but are nonetheless still a part of Job's rhetoric. He uses imagery of scales (31:6) and body imagery to reinforce his blamelessness (31:7, 27). His upright actions are depicted through tropes by portraying his actions with the poor and marginalized (31:16-21, 31-32) and plant imagery (31:38-40b). Job notes his equal status with those of a lower status using creation imagery in 31:15. Job

---

99. Wilson (2015: 145) notes that there is a sense of hyperbole in this description: Job is even marginalized by those on the margins. In other words, this description is a rhetorical move to heighten his own suffering. The repetition of וְעַתָּה in 30:9 and 16 reinforces this by directing renewed attention to his suffering.

100. See also Wilson 2015: 148.

also makes vivid the curse through various images. Accordingly, he uses sexual imagery (double entendre) in 31:10 and images of fire and death (Abaddon) in 31:12 to make vivid the consequences of his oath regarding adultery. He also uses body imagery in 31:22 to portray provocatively the consequences of injustice. The litigation imagery undergirds this whole chapter as an oath and avowal of innocence but comes to the foreground in the wish of 31:35. Job also uses body and clothing imagery in his final wish: Job would parade his innocence for all (31:36). This imagery thus is used to portray his upright actions (31:6, 7, 16-21, 27, 31-32, 38-40b), to reinforce the consequences of his oath (31:10, 12, 22), and to fortify his wish for God to hear him (31:35-36). In other words, while the tropes of Job 29–30 work with the rhetorical strategies of Job's protest prayer, the tropes of Job 31 reinforce Job's avowal of innocence and oath.

Wish and Inclusio. As noted above, Job uses the wish form in this speech in a significant way: it forms a frame around the entire speech. Job opens his speech with his wish that he could return to his former days, the time before his suffering in which he experienced the joy and ease of life in fellowship with God and with his family (29:2; cf. 29:4-5). Job closes his speech with the wish that God would hear him.[101]

Job's wish indicates Job's rhetorical goal: he desires a restored relationship with God, a life in which he no longer experiences his current suffering (cf. 14:13-17) (see Hartley 1988: 388; Clines 2006: 979; Wilson 2015: 237).[102] Job's focus on restoration includes his relationship with God (29:4-5). Job desires restoration to when the Almighty was "with [him]" (29:5)—a clear statement of relationship.[103] Job's renewed relationship with God entails his restoration to the community (29:7-25). With this restoration and the alleviation of his suffering, Job can resume his prominent place in the community. Job closes with an expression

---

101. As a number of interpreters point out, the identity of the שֹׁמֵעַ is connected to the identity of Job's witness and redeemer from Job 16:19 and 19:25, respectively. E.g., Wilson 2015: 154.

102. Furthermore, Magary (2005: 286–7) notes the frequency with which the מִי יִתֵּן formula is used to describe Job's yearning for God to respond to him.

103. Clines suggests that סוֹד in 29:4 is not a reference to relationship but protection, following the LXX and the BHS proposed emendation (2006: 935). His justification lies in the difficulty with the preposition עַל in 29:4. But the context, with the use of the preposition עִם in 29:5, indicates the MT should be read as סוֹד. As Wilson writes of this word, "It speaks to those in the intimate inner circle ('circle of trust') who hear the private or secret conversations" (2015: 141).

of his desire for God to respond to his prayer of protest (30:20). So he demands in this wish that God would answer him (31:35), something Job has desired throughout the book (cf. 9:14-16; 13:22; 23:5).

Job's wish thus articulates Job's petition: to have his relationship with God restored and his suffering removed. It is not an accident that Job begins and ends his speech with this petition, seeking to move God to act on his behalf, using the inclusio as a rhetorical device to reinforce the wish and petition.

Direct Address to God. At the very middle of Job's speech, Job turns to address God directly. This address confirms Job's protest prayer: he addresses God directly to move God to act. Job uses eleven 2ms forms in four verses (30:20-23).

Job reminds God that he cries to him (30:20a). The verb, שוע, is a verb of protest prayer, and indicates Job's ongoing attempt to move God to act (cf. Ps. 88:14 [13]).[104] Despite Job's cries, God has remained silent (30:20b). The effect of Job's juxtaposition of these two clauses in 30:20 is to emphasize that Job will continue to complain because God has not responded to him (30:24; 31:35). Job accuses God of divine absence (30:20) and divine attack (30:21-23). These accusations in the context of complaint are rhetorical, implying a petition for God to cease such actions. Job desires to return to a time when God watched over him with care (29:2), and the accusations are intended to move God to act. Westermann writes, "[E]ven this accusation against God which stands on the very brink of blasphemy, of which one assumes that it can be spoken *only* here, has its obvious parallels in the Psalter" (1981b: 42, italics original).[105]

Rhetorical Questions. Job also asks rhetorical questions in his protest prayer to persuade God to act. His first question occurs in 30:2, where he denigrates the strength of those who are marginalized from society, those to whom he compares himself (30:2-8). The effect of this question is to reinforce Job's alienation. Job's second question, though not marked by an interrogative particle, is marked by אך in 30:24.[106] In this question Job speaks metaphorically to compare himself to one on a heap of ruins who

---

104. On the persuasive nature of the statement "I cry out to you," see Howard 2008: 142.
105. Westermann (1981b: 63 n. 35) cites Pss. 88:7 [6] and 102:11 [10].
106. On 30:24 as an unmarked rhetorical question, see de Regt 1994: 362.

stretches out his hand for help. This is an admittedly difficult verse.[107] The 3ms pronominal suffix on פִּיד in v. 24b indicates the subject of שלח in v. 24a and clarifies that the gesture of stretching out the hand is a gesture of pleading for help in complaint.[108] Job, as one on a heap of ruins, is crying out. Job uses this question to justify the complaint and accusations which he has just levied in 30:20-23. Job continues this justification with his third question in 30:25: "Have I not wept for the one experiencing hardship; did not my soul grieve for the poor?" With this question Job argues two things: (1) that he has empathized with those who have suffered, showing a pattern of lament, and thus (2) justifies his current prayer of protest as he himself now experiences hardship.

There are a number of rhetorical questions in Job 31. Questions cluster in 31:1-4 as Job turns to his avowal of innocence. Job drives home his avowal of purity with his rhetorical question in 31:1b. Recalling 20:29 and 27:13, with his questions in 31:2-3 Job reminds God that he would expect to suffer if he had been guilty of wrongdoing. He asserts he would expect his portion from God above to be calamitous as a sinner. Job then avers through his question is 31:4 that he knows that God knows his blameless ways (cf. 23:10-12), thus invalidating calamity as an appropriate judgment.[109] Each of these questions thus reinforces his blamelessness, rhetorically serving the avowal of innocence. Job does not think he deserves the suffering he has experienced and is using the questions with the avowal of innocence of 30:1-4 to move God to act in accordance with his justice, something to which Job still holds or he would not be seeking to move God to act at all.

Job likewise uses rhetorical questions in 31:14-15 to reinforce the rhetoric of his oath regarding his treatment of his household servants. He demonstrates his accountability to God, asserting through the questions that he could not mistreat his own servants based on God's own judgment of those who mistreat the less fortunate (v. 14) and his equal status as one of God's creation (v. 15). The inclusio in v. 14, with the two questions

---

107. Nevertheless, the BHS proposed emendation is unnecessary and without any textual warrant. Clines' discussion of this textual problem is unfortunately rather unclear (2006: 957), but his use of 30:25 to understand 30:24 does not seem like the most natural reading.

108. ESV and NASB capture the sense: "Yet does not one in a heap of ruins stretch out his hand, and in his disaster cry for help?" (ESV); "Yet does not one in a heap of ruins stretch out *his* hand, or in his disaster therefore cry out for help?" (NASB).

109. On the flow of logic in 30:1-4, see de Regt 1994: 370.

framing Job's statement of God rising in judgment, draws attention to Job's rhetoric. Job recognizes he is accountable to God for all his actions, and thus emphasizes his blamelessness. The assumption that lies beneath this rhetorical question is that God is just and Job is seeking to encourage God to act in accordance with this justice through this question and its corresponding oath.

Emphatic Statements. Job uses particles to emphasize his arguments in this speech as he has in many other speeches. Job uses וְעַתָּה three times, all in the prayer of protest in chapter 30 (30:1, 9, 16). This repetition not only provides structure to his speech, but also draws attention to his current suffering. He is alienated even more than those whom society already shuns (30:1-15) as well as suffering emotionally, physically, and spiritually (30:16-23). Job uses גַם in 30:2, 8, in a similar way as וְעַתָּה. Occurring in 30:2 and 8, גַם marks the unit of Job's digression which develops the motif of the dregs of society.[110] Thus, this particle highlights this shunned group by separating out this unit and drawing attention to it as a comparison for Job—Job is more shunned than this foolish and nameless brood. Both of these particles thus highlight Job's suffering as he contrasts his current experience with his previous life depicted in Job 29. Job also draws attention to his justification of protest prayer in 30:24, using אַךְ in 30:24.[111] Job highlights his status as one "on a heap of ruins" (בְּעִי) with אַךְ to justify why he is calling out—if even one on a heap of ruins calls for help, so also should Job. These particles in Job 30 thus work with the tropes and the prayer of protest, reinforcing Job's rhetorical goal to move God to act.

Job uses emphatic statements in Job 31 as well. He highlights his blamelessness with emphatic statements in 31:20, 28, 31, and 36. In 31:20 Job describes the certainty that he has not violated the justice of his household (using אִם לֹא); in 31:28 Job uses גַם at the end of his oath regarding his idolatry; in 31:31 Job returns to his upright practice of justice within his household (also using אִם לֹא); in 31:36, in the context of Job's wish, he highlights his actions to parade his innocence before all (also using אִם לֹא). Each of these uses of particles relates to Job's blamelessness, thus reinforcing his oath and his avowal of innocence. The final particle in Job 31 also occurs in the context of Job's wish (31:35), using הֵן to draw attention to his "mark" (תָו). Thus, Job draws attention to his rhetorical goal with this particle, his petition: "let the Almighty answer me."

---

110. The גַם in 30:2 highlights Job's rhetorical question.
111. See the rhetorical effect of this question above.

Avowal of Innocence and Oath. One of Job's major rhetorical strategies in his final speech is his use of the avowal of innocence and oath in Job 31.[112] These two forms have the illocution of highlighting Job's blamelessness, which he uses to persuade God to respond to his prayer of protest.[113]

Job's use of the avowal of innocence occurs in 31:1-4, 14-15, 28, and 30-32. In these statements, he does not use the oath formula (אִם), but makes statements in the indicative about his innocent behavior. He asserts his purity in 31:1, and then reiterates this through a series of rhetorical questions. In 31:14-15 Job also uses rhetorical questions to articulate his accountability to God for his treatment of his household. Job affirms God's justice in these verses, using it as a basis upon which to claim innocence and move God to alleviate his suffering and restore their relationship. Job's use of the emphatic statement in 31:28 likewise affirms his blamelessness: Job will not engage in idolatrous worship (31:24-27) because it is punishable by judges; Job has not denied God. Job turns to a quick succession of statements in 31:29-34, in which he avers that he has not sinned in speech by asking for an oath on his enemy (31:30), his household servants are well fed (31:31), and he has taken appropriate action to shelter the sojourner (31:32). In each of these statements Job affirms his innocence of wrongdoing and as a lamenting, innocent sufferer wants God to act in accordance with his innocence.

Job's oath has the same rhetorical effect (Newsom 1996: 551). Job employs the oath formula in 31:5-10 to reveal his honesty and his purity.[114]

---

112. Witte (2013: 54–65) has recently suggested an allusion to Deuteronomy in Job 31. He outlines a number of links between these texts, mainly focused around the Decalogue in Deut. 5 (57–9). Unfortunately, most of these links are thematic rather than having strong lexical connections; because of this, I am not inclined to see an allusion. He writes, "The Decalogue in Deut. 5 is framed by a reflection on an encounter with God… The moral conduct (הלך דרך) of the pious demanded in 5:32-33 is exactly the subject of Job 31" (59). If one were to accept an allusion, the rhetorical effect would be relatively clear: Job frames his life as one of Torah observance, and hence should live a life of blessing. His reality, however, is quite different—his life is better described as under the curses of covenant violation. Thus, there would be an implicit petition in this collective allusion: God must restore Job and act as Job knows God is. In any case, this kind of rhetorical effect emerges clearly through the use of the avowal of innocence and the oath.

113. Westermann (1981b: 61 n. 17) notes that similar avowals of innocence and oaths can be found in lament psalms (cf. Ps. 7:4-6 [3-5]).

114. A number of interpreters point out that Job's focus is on internal motivations, not external actions. See, e.g., Hartley 1988: 407–8; Clines 2006: 1013; Wilson 2015: 358–9.

He grounds his oath in the reason that behavior described in these verses results in judgment (31:11-12). Since Job has not committed these acts, he does not deserve to be judged accordingly, and so he seeks to persuade God to respond to his prayer of protest. Job takes an oath regarding his justice toward the less fortunate in 31:13, 16-17, 19-22. Job's oath in this case attests to his innocence regarding his servants and the poor. Once again he weaves in reasons for his oath: as a fellow human being he is equal to them (31:18) and he has a holy fear of God's judgment for mistreating the marginalized (31:23) (Wilson 2015: 151–3). Job takes an oath regarding the purity of his worship (31:24-27), as well as his inner motives regarding any enemies (31:29). Job is blameless on these fronts. Moreover, Job has not committed deceit by hiding any sin (31:33-34).[115] Finally, Job avers he has treated his land appropriately (31:38-40). Each of these oaths is taken to prove Job's innocence.

These two forms, the avowal of innocence and the oath, are used by Job in conjunction with his prayer of protest. The effect of Job recounting his innocence with such thoroughness is to move God to act on his behalf, to bring an end to his suffering and to restore their relationship. It is noteworthy that Job's wish comes at the end of his declaration of innocence because it reminds God (and the reader) of Job's ultimate goal. Job wants God to answer him (31:35) and is seeking any strategy by which he can accomplish this goal—especially given God's prolonged silence (30:20). Daniel O'Connor (1985: 94) notes that Job's oath derives from his trust in God's justice; Job entrusts himself to the God who he believes to be one who rights wrongs, even if he does not experience that justice at the moment. In the context of a protest prayer, the oath and the avowal of innocence imply a plea for God to respond to Job, and is thus an "act of trust in the righteousness of God" (ibid.).[116] Job is turning to God

---

115. This oath also includes a motive clause, but is cut off. The quick transitions and the abbreviated oath in 31:33-34 seem to indicate Job's excitement as he recalls anything he can to demonstrate his blamelessness and then turns to his wish. The wish is often seen as out of place (e.g., Hartley 1988: 406–25; Clines 2006: 976, 1030–3), but there is no textual evidence to justify moving it. It seems better to read the quick succession of statements, the sudden shift to the wish, and the return to the final oath as a literary device to reveal Job's excited and emotional state. Longman argues similarly (2012: 363).

116. See also Dick 1979: 48–9. The wish replaces a standard petition, but it is still a petition and thus functions as a prayer of protest overall. Westermann (1981b: 39; cf. 61 n. 21, 67–70) connects petitions and wishes, writing of this speech, "[D]irect petition yields primacy of place to indirect wish."

for justice, knowing his own blamelessness and seeking to move God to act in accordance with what he believes about God's justice.

Summary of Job 29–31

With this final speech, Job returns to address God and thus modify the exigency of his ongoing suffering. This speech is a prayer of protest (direct address to God), and it includes wishes (as petitions) and an avowal of innocence and oath to supplement Job's protest prayer. These forms function as major rhetorical strategies—reinforced by tropes, rhetorical questions, inclusio, and emphatic statements—to move God to act on Job's behalf. Specifically, Job is seeking the alleviation of his suffering (29:2) and a restored relationship with God (29:4-5; 31:35). Job's faith undergirds this final prayer of protest—a daring act of trust to persuade God to show up (Hartley 1988: 386, 426). God will do just that in Job 38–41, the external rhetorical effect of which will be addressed in the next chapter.

Summary of the Third Speech Cycle and Job's Final Speech

Following Job's effective rebuttal of the use of the *topos* of the wicked to close the second cycle (Job 21), the third cycle begins with Eliphaz moving from insinuation to blatant accusation of sin (Job 22). The purpose of this accusation is to turn Job away from protest prayer. Job is not innocent; God is just; thus Job is judged appropriately and must repent in order to find restoration (Job 22:21-30). Job defends his protest prayer by rejecting repentance in light of his innocence (Job 23) and highlights perceived divine injustice (Job 24), refuting Eliphaz's argument. Bildad repeats Eliphaz's arguments (Job 25), and argues through the use of a hymn for a low anthropology to encourage Job toward repentance (26:5-14). Job interrupts Bildad to mock his help (26:2-4), and completes his speech with an argument that testifies to his ethical speech (27:2-6) and a condemnation of the friends and their instruction (27:7-23). With the friends' silence, Job turns his attention to God in Job 29–31. This concluding prayer of protest seeks to move God to act on Job's behalf to remove his suffering and restore his relationship with God. Job addresses the friends exclusively in the third cycle (Job 22–27) and addresses God exclusively in Job 29–31.[117]

---

117. In the third cycle combined with his final speech, Job addresses the friends in argumentation 44% of the time (176 of 403 clauses) and God 56% of the time (227 of

Job's use of verbal forms provides insight into Job's goals as well. Job uses a cohortative form six times (23:4 [2×], 5 [2×], 7; 31:8). Five of these six (23:4-5, 7) indicate Job's resolve toward protest prayer, each occurring in the introduction to his first speech of this cycle. In contrast to the first two cycles, Job does not use any imperatives or negated jussives to persuade God or the friends. On two occasions Job uses a jussive form as a petition: he asks for God to make his friends like the wicked (27:7) and he asks for the Almighty to answer him (31:35). The rest of Job's rhetoric relies on implication in order to accomplish his desired goals.

An examination of Job's rhetorical strategies in the third cycle reveals certain rhetorical emphases. His use of tropes is once again a dominant part of his rhetoric. Job uses the trope of divine injustice, all in the context of dispute (24:1-17, 21-23; 27:2). Job also uses the fate of the wicked trope exclusively in his dispute as he mocks his friends' instruction (27:13-23). Job's use of images of suffering and ease, on the other hand, are used almost exclusively in the context of his protest prayer.[118] Job's use of body imagery is also almost exclusively used in his address to God (29:9-11, 15; 30:17-18, 24, 27-28, 30; 31:7, 22, 27, 36), though its effect varies from describing the respect he receives (e.g., 29:9-11) to describing his suffering (30:17-18, 24, 27-28, 30) to reinforcing his oath (e.g., 31:7, 22, 27, 36). Divine attack is another trope almost exclusively used in his protest prayer; only in 23:15-16 and 27:2 does Job use this image in the dispute—both times to stress his innocent suffering. The remaining instances all occur in Job 30 to complain of God's actions as Job seeks to move God to act on his behalf (30:11, 15, 18-19, 21-23). The vivid imagery in the accusation heightens Job's rhetoric as he pleads with God to cease such actions.[119] This pattern of using images of divine injustice and the fate of the wicked in dispute and rest/ease, suffering, and divine attack in protest prayer is consistent with the first and second cycles, and is not surprising given Job's rhetorical goals.

---

403 clauses). Of the 176 clauses that comprise Job's speeches in the third cycle, 153 (87%) are disputation, highlighting his argumentative rhetoric, with all other forms (wish, oath, and avowal of innocence) supplementing rhetorically the disputation. Of the 227 clauses in which Job is protesting in prayer, sixty-one are lament and sixteen are complaint (34%). As noted above in the analysis of Job 29–31, Job uses wish, oath, avowal of innocence, and motive clauses to supplement his protest prayer.

118. Only five of fifty-two clauses in which Job uses images of suffering occur in the context of his dispute (23:2, 17; 27:2).

119. Eight of these sixteen occurrences include direct address to God (30:21-23).

Looking more specifically at Job's God-talk, Job describes God's attack in 23:15-16 and pejoratively adumbrates God's power, wisdom, and freedom in 23:13-14. Other more negative talk about God includes statements about divine absence (23:3, 5, 8-9) and divine injustice (24:1, 12, 22-23). Yet, as in the previous two cycles, Job's negative statements are balanced by his view of divine justice over against the views of the friends (27:8-11) and an expression of hope and faith that God will grant Job a hearing with his protest prayer (23:6-7). Job also talks about God in the context of his avowals of innocence and oaths (23:10-12; 27:2-3). As in the first two cycles, Job's talk about God to the friends is intimately related to his rhetorical goals in defending his protest prayer.

Job only speaks to God explicitly in thirteen clauses (30:20-23; 31:35b). Yet, the infrequency of explicit talk to God in this section is not indicative of its significance. To the contrary, it is these clauses of address that provide a clue as to Job's addressee in his final speech. When Job speaks to God in this speech he accuses him of divine attack and absence (30:20-23) and calls for him to act (31:35). Job speaks about God in twenty-five clauses in the context of his protest prayer (29:2, 4-5; 30:11, 18-19; 31:2, 6, 14-15, 23, 35, 37). These include his desire for his former relationship (29:2, 4-5), accusations (30:11, 18-19), and statements of divine justice that prove Job's innocence (31:2, 6, 14-15, 23) and play a role in his petition (31:35, 37). Job also describes his suffering (30:1-19, 24-31) in the context of his protest prayer. Job's God-talk in his protest prayer thus combines talk to God and talk about God, indicating Job's goals, accusations, and faith in God as one who upholds justice and should respond to Job's petition.

Job's rhetoric in this cycle and in his final speech continues the emphases from the previous cycles. When Job is addressing his friends, he is disputing their arguments that encourage penitence, and, thereby, defends his protest prayer. When Job is addressing God, he is seeking to move God to bring relief in accordance with the goals of protest prayer. Given the conclusion of Chapter 2—that the (implied) author uses Job's internal rhetoric to accomplish external rhetorical goals—it is clear that the fact that Job is either protesting in prayer or defending protest prayer indicates a major emphasis of the book. Job's God-talk is used for both of these aspects of Job's discourse. Determining the ethics—that is the rights and wrongs—of what Job has said, however, cannot be evaluated without turning to the external rhetorical effect of the Elihu and Yahweh sections.

Chapter 6

"WORDS WITHOUT KNOWLEDGE"?
THE EXTERNAL EFFECT OF THE ELIHU
AND YAHWEH SPEECHES

It was established in Chapter 2 that the primary way in which the book of Job makes its contribution to ethical God-talk is through Job's verbal expression. Then, in Chapters 3 through 5, it was demonstrated that Job's verbal expression seeks to move God to act through protest prayer or to refute the friends' attempts to eschew protest for penitence. In light of these conclusions, an analysis of how the Elihu speeches (Job 32–37) and Yahweh speeches with Job's responses (Job 38–42:6) shape the reader is required to finalize an answer to the question of the book's contribution to the theme of ethical God-talk. As noted in Chapter 2, both Elihu and Yahweh focus on Job's verbal expression. The placement of these so-called monologues in the narrative sequence plays a role in the reader's understanding of Job's internal rhetoric. This chapter analyzes the external rhetorical effect of the Elihu and Yahweh speeches by investigating the internal rhetoric of each character as a foundation for their external rhetorical contribution regarding the ethics of God-talk.

The Elihu Speeches (Job 32–37)

Following Job's final speech in Job 29–31, the narrator introduces a new character and a new movement in the plot of the book: Elihu and his speeches (32:1-6a). Elihu's contribution to the book has received much, and varied, treatment. His focus on Job's verbal expression is made clear by both the narrator in his introduction (32:2) and Elihu's speeches themselves (33:9-11; 34:5-9, 35, 37; 35:2-3, 16). Elihu's focus on Job's words forces the reader to (re)consider Job's verbal expression. Providing a summary and reflection on Job's discourse to and about God, Elihu's speeches reiterate ethical God-talk as a primary interpretive question in the book. Moreover, Elihu prepares the reader for Yahweh's assessment. Elihu's external rhetorical role, then, is to reiterate the ethics of God-talk as a theme and prepare the reader for part of the answer that is given by the book as a whole. The analysis of Elihu begins by discussing the originality and placement of Elihu in the book, followed by a brief internal rhetorical summary, and closes with an assessment of his external rhetorical effect.

The Originality and Placement of the Elihu Speeches

There has been much discussion regarding the originality and placement of the Elihu speeches. For example, G. B. Gray has suggested that the Elihu speeches are secondary, based on two main arguments: (1) the speeches are superfluous: there is no mention of Elihu elsewhere in the book, Elihu repeats the ideas of the friends, and there would be a seamless move from Job 31 to 38 if Elihu's speeches were removed; and (2) there are a number of stylistic and linguistic idiosyncrasies in Elihu's speeches, including his preference for the divine name אֵל, his use of אֲנִי, the less frequent use of archaic forms of prepositions, unique vocabulary, and Aramaisms (Driver and Gray 1921: xl–xlvii).[1] Newsom also suggests the Elihu speeches are secondary, proposing that they were added by a "dissatisfied reader" who "literally wrote himself into the text" (2003: 201–2, quote from 202).[2] Though Clines does not find arguments for Elihu as secondary convincing, he does argue that the Elihu speeches have been misplaced. He attributes Job 28 to Elihu, forming his conclusion. Thus, he suggests Elihu speaks after the conclusion of the debate (Job 27) before Job's final speech (Job 29–31) (2006: 908–9; cf. Clines 2005: 243–53).

Despite these suggestions, the Elihu speeches should be seen as original and in the location as presented in the canonical form of the book. Regarding the argument that Elihu is superfluous, Seow (2013: 34–7), McCabe (1997: 47–80), Habel (1984: 81–98; 1985: 36–7), and Wilson (1996b: 91–4) have shown how Elihu's speeches play an important literary and theological role in the book.[3] Seow suggests Elihu's view of wisdom and revelation confirms his location in the book; both Habel and Seow highlight how Elihu's use of the forensic metaphor transitions

1. Gray's discussion is used here because it is considered the strongest case made for the secondary nature of the Elihu chapters of the book (Seow 2013: 31).

2. Newsom argues that to take Elihu as original is to be required to read him as a self-destructing parody, undermined by himself and the narrator (2003: 201; cf. 1996: 558–9). She rejects this as a possibility, though this seems to be the best reading of the book, as argued below.

3. Furthermore, Ticciati's analysis of the מוֹכִיחַ testifies to Elihu's fit (2005: 119–37).

seamlessly from Job's final speech in Job 29–31; McCabe outlines Elihu's transitional role as one who summarizes previous narrative action, while also anticipating Yahweh's speeches. Moreover, as Clines notes (2006: 709), an author with the literary ability of the one who wrote the book of Job could create characters with different styles, thereby mitigating Gray's list of stylistic and linguistic idiosyncrasies.[4] Seow (2013: 31–3), in fact, argues cogently against Gray's stylistic and linguistic considerations, showing that in each case, they are inconclusive at best. On top of all of this, regarding the presence and placement of the Elihu speeches, there is no extant textual evidence that suggests any other form of the book than the canonical form (Seow 2011a: 257). Accordingly, the Elihu speeches will be interpreted as they sit in the narrative sequence in the canonical form.

A Summary of Elihu's Internal Rhetoric

Elihu makes four speeches (Job 32:6b–33:33; 34:2-37; 35:2-16; 36:2–37:24), and each needs a brief examination.

Elihu's first speech begins as an address to the friends (32:6b-22), as he issues an apology for his intrusion (32:6b-22); he is constrained by divine revelation (32:8) and internal compulsion (32:18-20). The primary addressee, however, is Job, to whom he turns in 33:1, addressing him by name. A disputation (Clines 2006: 706), Elihu's first speech seeks to instruct Job regarding his verbal expression (33:1, 31-33). Through imperatives (33:1, 5, 31-33) and a pointed rhetorical question (33:12), Elihu seeks to instruct Job about the (im)piety of his verbal expression. Elihu disapproves of Job's protest prayer, and encourages Job toward repentance.[5] This emerges not just from the pointed question in 33:13, but from his primary rhetorical strategy of citation and refutation (McCabe 1997: 51). Elihu cites Job's words in 33:8-11, highlighting Job's claims of blamelessness (33:9), divine attack (33:10-11a), and divine vigilance (33:11b). In 33:9 Elihu refutes Job's claims of blamelessness from 9:20-21, 13:23, 23:10-12, 27:5-6, and 31:1-40 (ibid.: 52). In 33:10-11a Elihu refutes Job's statements from 13:24, 27 specifically regarding divine enmity, though

---

4. Even Dhorme (1984: ciii), who considers the Elihu speeches secondary, admits this.

5. On Elihu's view that Job's speech is impious, see Newsom 2003: 211. Newsom casts Elihu's goals in the terms of lament rather than litigation, but a more accurate view is that Elihu is seeking to move Job toward penitence rather than protest. In fact, Newsom acknowledges Elihu's dependence on penitential psalms in this speech (213).

Job also uses the theme of divine attack in a number of other speeches.⁶ In 33:11b Elihu refutes Job's statements of divine vigilance, which Job developed most incisively in his complaint in Job 7:12, 18-21 (cf. 10:6, 14; 13:27; 14:5-6). These are foundational elements to Job's protest prayer: as a blameless sufferer whom God attacked (through relentless vigilance) Job protests in prayer, and defends his protest prayer. Elihu concludes that Job's verbal expression is wrong (33:12). Job's arguing with God in protest prayer is inappropriate (33:13). But Elihu's work is not entirely deconstructive; he offers a solution: repent (33:26-28). The corrective function of the suffering leads to entreaty (v. 26), which leads to confession (v. 27),⁷ which leads to restoration (v. 28). Confession of sin is the means by which Job can achieve the restoration he seeks, Elihu contends (McCabe 1997: 53–4).⁸ The citation of Job's words sets up Elihu to refute Job's position and correct Job's impious speech.

Elihu's second speech follows the same rhetorical strategy: citation and refutation. Also a disputation (Clines 2006: 765), Elihu turns to challenge and dispute the ethics of Job's God-talk, specifically the rhetoric of divine injustice. The ethical critique emerges clearly in 34:4, where he calls for the wise men, presumably a group of men listening to the dispute, to "choose what is right" (מִשְׁפָּט נִבְחֲרָה־לָּנוּ) and "know what is good" (נֵדְעָה בֵינֵינוּ מַה־טּוֹב), with both objects in syntactically emphatic positions. The address to these wise men can almost be read as Elihu's address to the reader.

Elihu summarizes Job's position regarding blamelessness and divine injustice in 34:5, highlighting in 34:6 Job's accusations regarding the injustice of God's attack. He continues the summary of Job's verbal expression in 34:9, characterizing Job as a defeatist in light of divine injustice.⁹ Elihu's summary in 34:5b is a virtual quotation of 27:2a (cf. 19:7) (McCabe 1997: 55). This quotation brings to mind Job's oath of 27:2-6, by which he has emphasized his blamelessness (ibid.; cf. Wilson 2015: 166). According to McCabe (1997: 56), Elihu's source for condemning Job is the statements he makes about his suffering being a witness against him (cf. 10:17; 16:8).¹⁰ Elihu's summary from 34:9 recalls

---

6. As McCabe points out (1997: 53), 33:10b is a virtual quotation of 13:24b while 33:11a is a virtual quotation of 13:27a.

7. It seems best to follow the proposed emendation, reading יָסֹר for יָסֻר. The repentant sinner "sings" his confession publicly. See Clines 2006: 703.

8. See also Habel 1985: 460; Clines 2006: 708, 742; Wilson 2015: 164.

9. The aside of rhetorical questions in 34:7-8 is a nice rhetorical move, as Elihu prejudices the jury.

10. The repetition of כזב also recalls 6:28 and 24:24.

Job's statements in 9:22-24 and 21:5-13 (ibid.; cf. Wilson 2015: 166). As McCabe writes of Elihu's summary (1997: 57), "Job's blasphemous words, according to Elihu, are an extension and a reflection of his sinfulness." Elihu then refutes Job's claims: God is just (34:10-12, 17-19, 23; cf. 8:3) (Habel 1985: 477–8; Newsom 1996: 575; 2003: 217–19). Elihu's refutation in 34:10-12 recalls Job's strongest affirmations of divine injustice, indicating that he has in mind other passages than those discussed in his citation. These may include Job's statements in Job 12:13-25 and 24:1-17. Elihu's rhetorical question in 34:17 focuses specifically on Job: "will you condemn (תַּרְשִׁיעַ) the mighty and righteous one?"[11] Job's inflamed rhetoric condemns Yahweh, and this is problematic. Elihu concludes that Job speaks unethically, with the five-fold characterization of Job's words in 34:35-37 as "without knowledge" (לֹא־בְדַעַת), "without insight" (לֹא בְהַשְׂכֵּיל), "responses of wicked men" (תְּשֻׁבֹת בְּאַנְשֵׁי־אָוֶן), "rebellion" (פֶּשַׁע), and "against God" (לָאֵל). So Elihu offers Job advice to conclude his second speech, namely, repentance (34:32-33).[12] For Elihu, any speech that insinuates that God acts poorly is sin (Clines 2006: 775); in Elihu's perspective, Job has erred in his complaint, which Elihu equates with unbelief and thinks will never achieve the restoration Job desires (Hartley 1988: 461–2).[13]

In his third speech, Elihu again rebukes Job for his God-talk related to divine justice.[14] Following the pattern from the first two speeches, Elihu cites Job's words in 35:2-3. His summary of Job's position portrays Job as accusing God of injustice: "Do you think this is justice? You have said, 'I am more right than God.' Indeed, you say, 'What use is it to you? What do I profit if I refrain from sin?'" The summary from 35:2 embellishes Job's position; Job has never said he is more right than God, but Elihu has understood Job's claims of blamelessness and his argument defending his right to protest in this way (cf. 4:17; 15:14; 25:4) (McCabe 1997: 58). Elihu draws upon Job's statements in 7:19-20, 9:22-31, and 21:7-13 for his summary in 35:3 (ibid.; cf. 13:18). Elihu's criticism is that Job has impugned God's majesty and justice with his complaints. Elihu presents two arguments to refute Job: God is just and wholly other (35:4-8; cf.

---

11. Elihu's rhetorical question follows two imperatives from 34:16 that intend to draw Job's attention to Elihu's conclusion. The question in 34:17 anticipates Yahweh's question in 40:8. Clines (2006: 765) suggests this is the node of the second speech.

12. On the notion of confession and repentance, see ibid., 782. Cf. Wilson 2015: 169.

13. In this Elihu has completely misunderstood complaint by not recognizing that protest prayer seeks restoration; cf. Wilson 2015: 167.

14. This speech is also a disputation (Clines 2006: 794).

25:2-6), and does not hear the cry of the wicked (35:9-13).[15] From these arguments, Elihu draws a conclusion: how much less will he hear Job's cry when Job has articulated such impious words (35:14)![16] He summarizes his position in 35:16 with his description of Job's verbal expression as vacuous (הֶבֶל; cf. 21:34; 27:12) and "without knowledge" (בִּבְלִי־דָעַת; cf. 34:35). Elihu's third speech thus also cites Job's position and refutes it, drawing conclusions for Job about his God-talk. The implication is that Job should cease his protest prayer because it impugns God's justice.

Elihu's fourth speech does not follow the citation and refutation pattern of the first three speeches. Nevertheless, Elihu's goal is to rebuke Job's impious speech and offer instruction. Elihu develops a hymn that celebrates God's creative majesty by which he invites "Job to 'stop' his complaint against God and marvel…at divine justice and revelation" (Clines 2006: 853). Elihu returns to God's justice, strength, and kingship (36:2-15). He then asserts that Job's experience is commensurate with his wickedness (36:17), arguing that Job's protest prayer will be to no avail (36:19). McCabe (1997: 60) suggests 36:16-21 are Elihu's application to Job, his "last appeal for Job to repent." Elihu calls Job to sin with his lips no more (36:21) (Wilson 2015: 175; cf. McCabe 1997: 61). Elihu then turns to his hymn (36:22–37:13).

Newsom is attentive to the rhetoric of the hymn, comparing it to a similar hymn in Sir. 42:15–43:33. Elihu uses the hymn to invoke awe and instruct piety (2003: 228–32).[17] From this hymn, Elihu draws a conclusion for Job: "stand and consider the wonderful works of God" (37:14). The proper response to God is not complaint, but silent awe (Diewert 1991: 606).

This internal analysis reveals Elihu's rhetorical goals are to turn Job from protest prayer to repentance, to modify his verbal expression (Diewert 1991: 576–9, 590–5). Elihu finds Job's God-talk unethical and inappropriate because it degrades God. He uses a number of strategies to accomplish his rhetorical goals, including rhetorical questions, direct address, citation of Job's words, and a hymn that is designed to invoke

---

15. This latter argument in 35:9-13 might have in mind Job's argument in 24:1-12 (McCabe 1997: 59).

16. Elihu builds his argument from v. 9, suggesting that people cry out in distress, to vv. 12-13, where he suggests that God does not respond to the cry of the wicked. He then draws an *a fortiori* argument: how much less (אַף כִּי) will he hear Job's cries in light of Job's blasphemous God-talk. McCabe also notes the *a fortiori* argumentation (ibid.). Job 35:14 is marked by the return of direct address to Job.

17. The use of rhetorical questions in the hymn anticipates the same rhetorical strategy Yahweh will use in Job 38 (McCabe 1997: 63–4).

awe. Seow summarizes Elihu's argument thus (2011a: 267): "Faced with suffering that finds no easy explanation, the faithful ought not to mouth empty words and speak ignorantly, as Job did (35:16), but to come before God in acknowledgement of God's transcendent goodness (ch. 36) and sovereign freedom (ch. 37)."[18] Elihu's primary goal in his speeches is to turn Job's impious discourse toward piety. More specifically, Elihu desires Job to eschew protest in favor of penitence (see 33:9-11, 26-33; 34:31-37; 35:9-12; 36:19, 21; 37:14).

The External Effect of the Elihu Speeches

The focus on Job's speech throughout Elihu's speeches creates a noticeable pattern, forcing the reader to (re)consider Job's verbal expression. Elihu's speeches reiterate the theme of ethical God-talk, forcing renewed (or continued) engagement from the reader. Nevertheless, Elihu's arguments are undermined by the narrator and by Elihu himself, indicating he is not providing the (implied) author's assessment of Job's God-talk.[19]

The narratorial introduction of 32:1-6a provides the hermeneutical lens for interpreting the speeches while also linking Elihu to the preceding material. The narrator repeats four times that Elihu is angry (32:2 [2×], 3, 5), a description which would place him in the camp of the fool, specifically the אֱוִיל (the brash fool) (Habel 1984: 88–90). The narrator provides a window into Elihu's internal motivation, indicating the reasons why Elihu is angry with the friends and with Job; in both cases Elihu's anger stems from speech-ethical concerns. He is angry with the friends because their discourse was ineffective and unethical: they failed to answer Job, condemning him without cause (32:3; cf. 32:11-22). Elihu is angry with Job "because he was righteous in his own eyes" (כִּי הוּא צַדִּיק בְּעֵינָיו) and "because he justified himself before God" (עַל־צַדְּקוֹ נַפְשׁוֹ מֵאֱלֹהִים) (see 32:1-2). The narrator's omniscience describing Elihu's anger shapes the reader,[20] the effect of which is to read Elihu cautiously and critically. The (implied) author depicts "Elihu as an impatient individual, he is more emotional than rational... The discrepancy between the author's presentation of Elihu's motives and Elihu's words [in 32:6b-22] is an example of dramatic irony... The Joban author's use of irony causes

---

18. See also Diewert 1991: 605–6.

19. For alternative interpretations, see Newsom 1996: 559; 2003: 201; Clines 2006: 716–17. Their interpretations seem to undervalue the authoritative voice of the narrator in 32:1-6a.

20. See Sternberg 1987: 121–2, 477–8. For the narrator giving Elihu's perspective and not his own, see, e.g., Clines 2006: 712–14.

us to question Elihu's claims of speaking on behalf of God" (McCabe 1997: 66–7).[21]

Elihu's self-portrayal also raises questions about his wisdom and truth value, confirming the narrator's views. Elihu's comical self-description and the analogical patterning that links him to the friends' argumentation lead the reader to question Elihu's arguments.[22] Moreover, Elihu's hubris undermines his arguments; he sees himself as "perfect of knowledge," a phrase he also uses of God (36:4; 37:16). Yu notes (2011: 378), regarding 36:4, "It seems impossible that anyone could make such a statement and still be taken seriously." Thus, Elihu is not providing the book's assessment of Job's speech. Yet, there is a literary effect of the speeches: to force the reader to (re)focus on the issue of the ethics of protest prayer. Not only are specific passages recalled (7:12-21; 9:20-21, 22-24; 13:23-27; 21:5-13; 23:10-12; 24:1-17; 27:2-6), but also these passages recall others that are related thematically and lexically.

Another literary effect of Elihu's speeches is to anticipate the Yahweh speeches.[23] There are a number of connections between Elihu and Yahweh: (1) both focus on Job's verbal expression and the propriety thereof (34:35, 37; 35:16; 38:2), (2) both focus on justice issues (34:17; 40:8), and (3) Elihu's final speech with its theophanic language and rhetorical questions prepare for Yahweh's arrival and mode of discourse. Elihu's theophany in particular prepares the reader to hear from God, a seamless transition as the storm rolls in (37:1-13; 38:1) (Gordis 1965: 108–9).[24]

This literary effect has theological implications. Elihu and his speeches are overwhelmed by Yahweh's speeches, another indication that Elihu does not provide the book's decisive contribution to ethical God-talk. Wilson suggests "[Elihu's] evaluation is thus a rival explanation to the later words of Yahweh, causing the reader to question Elihu's seemingly orthodox answer in the light of God's wider viewpoint. Elihu is…a theological foil for Yahweh" (2015: 157, 169). Wilson is perceptive on this point: despite the similarities between Elihu and God, they do not have the same

---

21. See also Habel 1984: 88, 92.

22. On analogical patterning, see Sternberg 1987: 268–70, 479–80. Regarding Elihu's self-description, see Cheney 1994: 164. On the analogical linking, see McCabe 1997: 57 n. 48; Habel 1984: 91.

23. Similar arguments have been made by Gordis 1965: 108–9; cf. McCabe 1997: 47–80; Habel 1984: 81–98; and Wilson 1996b: 81–94. The argument here teases out the implications of these scholars' work in more detail by highlighting Elihu's role in relation to the theme of ethical God-talk.

24. There is also a connection between the rhetorical questions and issues regarding knowledge (ידע); cf. 37:14-24; 38:2–39:30.

perspective on the issue of ethical God-talk. Elihu seeks to silence protest prayer. For Elihu, "Job's cries of outrage are a dark and anguished form of prayer, but one that Elihu cannot recognize… [B]ecause Job's radical departure from the language of tradition frightens Elihu, he hurries to declare it illegitimate and to suggest that God only hears cries when they are addressed in the traditionally approved form ([35:]12-13)" (Newsom 1996: 582).[25] Yahweh's argument is vastly different. Elihu seeks to defend God's justice against Job's complaints to silence Job's complaints; Yahweh defends his wisdom, sovereignty and freedom to invite Job out of his protest prayer and back into a restored relationship.

Thus, Elihu's focus on Job's verbal expression seems to be the primary effect of his speeches,[26] as he provides a transition from the dispute regarding the ethics of protest prayer to Yahweh's theophany. By summarizing Job's key complaints and arguments, Elihu encourages the reader to (re)consider Job's words in light of Elihu's arguments. By evaluating Elihu's arguments in light of the narrator's perspective, by Elihu's self-portrayal, and by revisiting Job's verbal expression, the reader is led to the (implied) author's perspective. This kind of meditative process—constant and consistent engagement with the text—is something the psalmist affirms as formative (Ps. 1:2); the reader's engagement with Job's words is formative in light of the narrative sequencing and engagement of multiple perspectives. This engagement is enhanced as Yahweh, whom Elihu anticipates, speaks. Not only does Elihu prepare Job to hear from Yahweh (unwittingly), but so also the reader.

The Yahweh Speeches and Job's Responses (Job 38–42:6)

Emerging out of Elihu's burgeoning storm, Yahweh appears in a whirlwind to answer Job—overwhelming the human verdict represented by Elihu. God answers (ענה) Job. Job has sought God's attention from as early as

---

25. Newsom captures excellently the relationship between Elihu's arguments and ethical God-talk (1996: 582–3). She notes how Elihu is critical of Job's form of prayer, and writes, "Although a challenge like Job's may be disturbing and disruptive, a vibrant and healthy religious community is invigorated by the presence of a Joban voice, faithful in its protest, even if irritating in its manner of speaking. Elihu is potentially the more dangerous to the faith, because he secures his own voice by silencing others. Although sincerely believing himself to serve God, Elihu arrogantly attempts to usurp God's role, declaring what language God finds acceptable."

26. See also Diewert 1991: 604; McCabe 1997: 64; Clines 2006: 767; Wilson 2015: 156, 165.

Job 3 and requested an answer as recently as Job 31:35. Job has been "clamoring" for Yahweh to respond (Job 3; 9:14-20, 32-35; 13:3, 15-24; 23:3-8, 15-17; 31:35-37) (Seow 2013: 38). Yahweh's reply to Job is a response to Job's most recent speech (Job 29–31) as well as his protest prayer throughout the book.[27] As with the Elihu speeches, the internal rhetoric of Yahweh's speeches provides the foundation for understanding the external effect regarding ethical God-talk. Yahweh's two speeches both highlight Job's verbal expression for the reader and provide an important evaluation of Job's verbal expression. Taken together with Job 42:7-8, Yahweh approves of Job's protest prayer, indicating its appropriateness, while nonetheless criticizing Job for impugning his justice and impinging upon his freedom.

A Summary of Yahweh's Internal Rhetoric and Job's Responses

Yahweh gives two speeches in his answer to Job, to which Job issues two responses. Together, Yahweh's speeches have three purposes: (1) to refute Job's obscuring of Yahweh's divine עֵצָה with verbal expression that accuses (and implies) widespread divine injustice; (2) to refute Job's attempt at coercion through his oath; and (3) to reveal a wise and compassionate creator who sovereignly reigns over the cosmos and so to invite Job back into relationship.

Yahweh's First Speech (38:1–40:2)

The purpose of Yahweh's first speech is to correct aspects of Job's verbal expression, as indicated by the thesis (38:2) and the conclusion (40:2).[28] Job has uttered "words" (מִלִּין) that are "without knowledge" (בְּלִי־דָעַת), and thereby "darkened counsel" (מַחְשִׁיךְ עֵצָה). Some aspect of Job's verbal expression has obscured Yahweh's design in the cosmos[29]—his wisdom, sovereignty, and freedom. As Wilson writes (2015: 182), "God is not claiming that this was Job's intention [i.e., to darken counsel], but it was the effect of his words." Job has found fault (יִסּוֹר) with Yahweh in his arguments (רָב and מוֹכִיחַ); Yahweh requests that Job respond to Yahweh's

---

27. On parallels between Job 29–31 and the Yahweh speeches, see Newsom 2003: 238–9.

28. While the narratorial introduction to another Yahweh speech act occurs in 40:1, I take this as an indication of the closing of the first speech. The words of 40:2, then, reiterate the point that Yahweh was intending Job to hear. 38:1 and 40:6 are distinct from 40:1 in light of the prepositional phrase מִן סְעָרָה as well as the shared opening imperatives in 38:3 and 40:7.

29. On עֵצָה as divine design, see, e.g., Clines 2011: 1089.

correction.³⁰ Yahweh's first speech employs two main rhetorical strategies to correct Job's verbal expression: rhetorical questions and imagery.

Yahweh states in 38:3 that he will question (שאל) Job, and this is exactly what Yahweh does, with rhetorical questions dominating the first speech.³¹ These questions play an important role in determining the tone and effect of this speech. Fox (1981: 58–60; 2013: 1) argues that the rhetorical questions indicate Yahweh's pedagogical mode: he is a wisdom teacher. These questions have obvious answers, revealing that, as Fox puts it (1981: 60), "God is saying to Job, You know very well that I and I alone created order and maintain it in the world, and I know that you know, and you know that I know that you know." The tone is not one of a bully or of intimidation, but of invitation to a restored relationship.³² Yahweh is criticizing (through instruction) Job's words, showing Job how he uttered unethical speech, while also responding to Job's criticisms and complaint by inviting Job to reconsider what Job already knows. A restored relationship is exactly what Job has desired since his suffering befell him (Job 14:13-17).

Yahweh's tone is also seen in his use of imagery. Yahweh uses cosmogonic, meteorological, astronomical, and zoological imagery. This exploration of the created order has a "kindly playfulness" to it, which has a goal "not to crush Job" but to reveal "God in his constant care for his world" (Andersen 1976: 292).³³ The panoramic tour of creation explodes Job's myopia to show that there is nothing which God does not control (Alter 1985: 96–7; Hartley 1988: 515–16).³⁴ The implied argument moves

30. I read יְסוֹר as an adjective, functioning substantively as the subject of the infinitive רֹב (from ריב), having the force of a finite verb. On רֹב, see GKC §113ee; on יְסוֹר, see *HALOT*, 417–18. I read יַעֲנֶנָּה as a jussive, with the suffix referring to God's argument as a whole.

31. See Clines 2011: 1087. The non-questions in the first speech include 38:3, 4b, 5aβ, 14-15, 18b, 21, 30; 39:4, 7-8, 13a, 14-18, 21-25, 28-30. As the frequency of rhetorical questions diminishes in the second half of the speech, each new animal is introduced with rhetorical questions (see 38:39, 41; 39:1, 5, 9, 13, 19, 26, and 27), indicating that the interrogative mode remains in effect.

32. Fox juxtaposes the tonality of the questions against the tonality of the same statements made in the indicative (1981: 59). The latter reveals a much more severe tone than the former. See also Ham (2013: 527–41), though his argument is less convincing; Balentine 1998: 267–8; Hartley 1988: 518; Andersen 1976: 290; Wilson 2015: 181; *pace* Clines 2011: 1088–9; cf. the literature cited in Fox 2013: 2 nn. 5–8.

33. See also Wilson (2015: 180–201), who consistently notes Yahweh's use of humor to soften the tone.

34. Fox (2005: 353) suggests that Job and the reader "are to infer God's goodness" from these speeches.

from the lesser to the greater: Job is able to see through this vivid imagery Yahweh's care, wisdom, and sovereign control over the uninhabitable places and to reason from this that Yahweh also cares for Job as a sufferer—his suffering falling under his wise and sovereign control. The imagery provides Job the foundation upon which to revise his theological thinking (Newsom 1996: 625).

The thinking Job needs to revise emerges in the details of this speech. Given Yahweh's focus in this speech, any suggestion that runs counter to Yahweh's wisdom, care, and goodness "darkens" his עֵצָה. The use of this word recalls Job's usage in 12:13. Job affirms that Yahweh possesses עֵצָה, and proceeds to detail what this means in a reverse doxology in 12:13-25. This "hymn," as noted in the analysis in Chapter 3 above, is used rhetorically to respond to Zophar, to highlight divine destruction and divine injustice in order to defend his protest prayer. Yahweh criticizes Job for obscuring Yahweh's design in speaking like this. This is unethical speech because the propositional content—God is unjust at a cosmic level—is false (i.e., not true of reality), and Job should know better. Other places in which Job has impugned Yahweh's wise and sovereign rule in the cosmos include Job 9:2-24, 21:7-33, and 24:1-17, 21-23.[35] Significantly, these passages are dominated by the tropes of divine destruction and divine injustice and are directed at the friends, employed to defend his right to protest in prayer. Job's verbal expression at this point is blameworthy because it is culpably ignorant. Job should know better than to denounce God as cosmically unjust; he reasoned out from his personal situation to a global conclusion. Nevertheless, it seems the pedagogical mode (i.e., the rhetorical questions) might be evidence of Yahweh's recognition that Job was pushed into this rhetoric by the friends, who were the first to introduce the issue of divine justice (8:3; 11:6-8). Other connections emerge. The links between Yahweh's speech and Job's oath indicate that Job's oath is problematic because it limits Yahweh's freedom.[36] The lexical

---

35. Brinks Rea (2010: 224–6, 228–31) has noted parallels between Yahweh's first speech and Job 9 and 12. Cf. 38:6 // 9:6; 38:12-13 // 9:7; 38:9-11 // 9:8; 38:2 //12:13, 22, 25; 38:4-11 // 12:14; 38:25-27 // 12:15. See also Hartley 1988: 491. Yahweh's non-interrogative statements in 38:14-15 challenge Job's statements about divine injustice (cf. 9:22-24; 21:17-20, 30-31; 24:1, 12). See also Timmer 2009: 286–305, esp. 294–6.

36. Wilson highlights how the Elihu speeches preserve Yahweh's freedom in the book by creating space between Job's oath and Yahweh's response (Wilson 1996b: 93). Both Yahweh's critique of Job's oath and the literary effect of narrative sequence of Elihu's speeches testify to Yahweh's freedom as a key theological point the book is making.

connections between 40:2 and 31:35 in particular criticize Job's use of the oath to constrain divine action. In this specific instance, the illocution of Job's oath impinges upon Yahweh's freedom. Job's verbal expression, then, is blameworthy in two respects: his inappropriate tropes to defend his protest prayer and his oath where he limits Yahweh's freedom.

This is not to say that Job's protest prayer is inappropriate as a whole; Yahweh's appearance and answer to Job's protest prayer testify otherwise. But where Job used language that obscured Yahweh's wisdom, sovereignty, freedom, and goodness in creation as a whole, Job erred. Job found fault with Yahweh's governance of the world in these passages by reasoning out from his personal situation to the entire cosmos; Yahweh requests Job address these concerns (40:2; cf. 38:3). But the request, with the questions and the imagery, invites Job into a restored relationship. Yahweh's first speech strikes a balance of criticism and invitation (Wilson 2015: 181). Job is not asked to repent of any sin, but to respond to Yahweh's arguments, which points to the fact that Yahweh does not reject Job's protest prayer outright. The correction merely regards aspects of Job's verbal expression.

Job's First Response (Job 40:3-5)

Job declines to oblige Yahweh's request for an answer (40:4-5). He acknowledges his insignificance before Yahweh (קלל), and shows deference to the one who asked him questions (40:4). Using a numerical saying, he then highlights his desire to remain silent (40:5). Job's response indicates his intention not to retract his words, though neither does he desire to push the matter further. Yahweh's first speech has made an impact on Job (Hartley 1988: 518; Clines 2011: 1138–9). This enigmatic response does not satisfy Yahweh, however, precipitating his second speech (Wilson 2015: 191–2).

Yahweh's Second Speech (40:6–41:24 [40:6–41:34])

Yahweh's second speech builds on the first. Yahweh issues the thesis of the speech in 40:8, arguing that aspects of Job's verbal expression have condemned (רשע) Yahweh. Some of the things Job has said have annulled (פרר) Yahweh's rule (מִשְׁפָּט).[37] This recalls Job's oath in 27:2, indicating that, like the first speech, Yahweh is pointing to Job's statements of divine injustice. Yahweh's challenge to Job in 40:9-14 (note the rhetorical question and imperatives) reminds Job that he does not have the power to "tread the wicked" (40:12). This indicates that Yahweh's criticisms relate,

---

37. On the sense of מִשְׁפָּט as royal prerogative in 40:8, see Scholnick 1982: 521–9.

once again, to Job's articulations of widespread divine injustice (9:2-24; 21:5-34; 24:1-17).³⁸ Job has utilized these rhetorical strategies in order to argue for the appropriateness of his protest prayer; Yahweh criticizes Job's use of these strategies.

Yahweh instructs Job through mythological imagery, the primary rhetorical strategy of his second speech. Interpretations of the references to Behemoth and Leviathan are legion, but the hyperbolic language points to their mythological nature. The images used to describe these creatures seem to combine parts of numerous animals, thus leading to a number of proposals as to the identity of these beasts. Furthermore, if taken as mythological, there is a progression of the rhetoric from wild, untamable animals in the first speech to heightened mythological creatures in the second. Fox suggests that the effect of these creatures is to bring about awe not intimidation (2012: 261–7; 2013: 1–23). Yahweh's rhetorical questions in 40:24–40:31 [40:24–41:7] and 41:5-6 [41:13-14] point to Job's (or any human's) inability to control these chaos creatures. On the other hand, Yahweh as the preeminent king of creation can and does: "everything under the heavens belongs to me" (תַּחַת כָּל־הַשָּׁמַיִם לִי־הוּא). Recalling Psalm 104, Yahweh reminds Job that Yahweh can "play with Leviathan like a bird" and "bind him" (40:29 [41:5]).³⁹ Yahweh interrupts his description of the might and uniqueness of Leviathan to make clear his point: "none is fierce enough that he should arouse him. Who then can stand before me? Who comes before me that I should repay him?" (41:2-3 [41:9-10]). Yahweh's imagery in his second speech thus reinforces his thesis, pointing to his kingship, freedom, and sovereign control over every aspect of creation. As Hartley writes (1988: 518), "By continuing to question Job Yahweh is expressing his care for his servant. He is seeking to overcome Job's resistance by gently and persuasively leading him into submission."⁴⁰ The purpose is to humble Job and invite Job into a restored relationship.⁴¹

---

38. Hartley also suggests 40:11-12 responds to 21:30-33 and 24:1-17 (1988: 520).
39. Cf. Ps. 104:26: לִוְיָתָן זֶה יָצַרְתָּ לְשַׂחֶק־בּוֹ.
40. See also Fox 2012: 261–7; 2013: 1–23; 2018: 11–15.
41. Another notable interpretation of these figures originates with Gammie and has been subsequently developed by Balentine. Gammie (1978: 217–31), pointing to textual clues like Behemoth being "made with you" (עָשִׂיתִי עִמָּךְ) and Leviathan's majestic nature, argues that Behemoth and Leviathan are didactic models for Job to consider. In particular, the images of fire or sneezing coming from Leviathan's mouth indicate that Yahweh is commending Job's verbal expression in protest prayer. Balentine argues similarly (1998: 259–78), highlighting Yahweh's reframing of Ps. 8 from the dialogue to commend Job's courage to protest in prayer.

Yahweh's arguments, then, in both speeches point to his cosmic kingship, his wisdom, his freedom, and his goodness as he controls every aspect of the cosmos. As a response to Job, Yahweh's speeches refute Job's statements where he has obscured these truths—most clearly in his statements of widespread divine injustice and in his oath that constricts Yahweh's freedom—while also responding to Job's protest prayer by inviting Job back into relationship. This restoration is what Job desired from the outset. This assessment indicates that these statements are unethical, sinful, a violation of what God desires and what Job knows to be true. Nevertheless, Yahweh's response to Job's protest prayer dignifies it, and the lack of a call for repentance is significant, pointing to the fact that the reader is not to regard all of Job's verbal expression as unethical.

Job's Second Response (Job 42:1-6)

Job's second response is more substantive than his first. It is comprised of two parallel movements. In the first movement, Job recognizes Yahweh's incomparable power and divine prerogative (42:2).[42] Job then cites Yahweh's words back to him, an acknowledgment that he has heard Yahweh's theses (42:3a; cf. 38:2). Job then draws a conclusion: "I declared—and cannot understand—things too wonderful for me—and I cannot know!" Job admits that he has spoken of things with a limited perspective. In the second movement, Job again cites Yahweh's words to acknowledge he has understood Yahweh's theses (42:4; cf. 38:3; 40:7). Job declares that Yahweh's speeches have made an impact on him (42:5) and he retracts his protest prayer (42:6). This last verse is an interpretive crux,[43] with the two verbal forms and the meaning of עַל־עָפָר וָאֵפֶר being ambiguous.[44] It seems best to read the first verb (אֶמְאַס) from מאס I ("to reject") and the second verb (וְנִחַמְתִּי) as a Niphal from נחם as a part of the idiom נחם על (Patrick 1976: 369–71). This idiom means to "change one's mind concerning" some action (ibid.). The Masoretic accentuation

---

42. This reading follows the *qere*. See Clines 2011: 1205.

43. See, e.g., Patrick 1976: 369–71; Kaplan 1978: 356–8; Curtis 1979: 497–511; O'Connor 1983: 181–97; Newell 1984: 298–316; Morrow 1986: 211–25; Muenchow 1989: 597–611; Dailey 1993: 205–9; van Wolde 1994: 242–50; Fox 2005: 364–6; 2013: 18–22; 2018: 15–16; Timmer 2009: 298–301; van der Lugt 2014: 623–39; Lambert 2015: 559–68; Martin 2018: 299–318. See also Fohrer 1963: 535–6; Gordis 1978: 492; Habel 1985: 576; Hartley 1988: 537; Newsom 1996: 628–9; Clines 2011: 1207–11, 1218–23; Wilson 2015: 204–7. Clines (2011) provides a robust outline of the possibilities for interpretation.

44. On the ambiguities, see Morrow 1986: 211–25.

indicates that עַל marks the object for both verbs (van Wolde 1994: 244, 249), namely, עָפָר וָאֵפֶר, "dust and ashes."[45] This is a rare pairing, only occurring elsewhere in Gen. 18:27 and Job 30:19.[46] The occurrence in Job 30:19 is most illuminating given its presence within the book of Job and that it comes from the same speaker—Job himself. In 30:19 Job had lamented God's actions in turning his life into an act of lamentation, with "dust and ashes" as a metonymy for lamentation.[47] Job, after Yahweh's speech, recalls that reference, and indicates his desire to retract his protest prayer (42:6)—to change his mind concerning his act of protest prayer.[48] Job recognizes his misstep and he retracts his protest prayer, recognizing Yahweh's wisdom, sovereignty, and freedom. Accordingly, he withdraws his act of lamentation, having reached a (re)new(ed) understanding of Yahweh through Yahweh's tour of creation (Wilson 2015: 204).[49] Yahweh's speeches invite Job back into relationship; Job accepts the invitation.

The External Rhetorical Effect of the Yahweh Speeches and Job's Responses

Yahweh's speeches also focus on Job's verbal expression in the book. Yahweh criticizes Job regarding aspects of his words.[50] Specifically, Yahweh corrects Job for impugning Yahweh's justice and freedom, as well as Yahweh's sovereign role in the cosmos (38:2; 40:8). This has a profound impact on the reader regarding ethical God-talk: it is blameworthy to condemn God's justice. The criticism, however, is tempered to some degree by Yahweh's questions, imagery, and tone, indicating that Yahweh recognizes that the friends instigated Job into inappropriate speech. Where Job has gone wrong has been in his verbal expression about God's injustice (9:2-24; 12:13-25; 21:5-33; 24:1-17; 27:2) and in his verbal expression to God that seeks to coerce Yahweh into action (31:1-40; cf. 27:2-6). In some

---

45. Recognizing this mitigates the fact that מָאַס I is almost always transitive.

46. It also occurs in Sir. 10:9; 40:3; 1QH 18:5; 4QD^a 1a-b:22-23; 4QD^b 1:5. It also may occur in 4QMyst^c 4:3; 4QShir^b 126:2.

47. A similar point is made by Lambert 2015: 567.

48. See also Patrick 1976: 370-1; van Wolde 1994: 249; Wilson 2015: 206-7; Lambert 2015: 564-8.

49. In light of Job's acknowledgment that he has spoken unethically in some ways (42:3), repentance is a viable interpretive option in some sense. The syntax and accentuation, however, seem to point in another direction.

50. Nevertheless, there is no explicit condemnation of Job's words, accusation of sin, or call to repentance (Hartley 1988: 488; Wilson 2003: 124).

of these cases Job seems to indicate that what he is saying is risky and potentially problematic (9:21; 9:35–10:1; 16:6; 21:4-5; 23:15-16). This may also explain Yahweh's tone: Yahweh knows that Job knows better. The propositional content of Job's God-talk regarding injustice as well as the illocution of Job's coercive oath are unethical. Simply put, it is unethical to impugn Yahweh's justice and to impinge upon Yahweh's freedom.

Nevertheless, that Yahweh responds to Job's protest prayer reveals that Yahweh has no issues with Job's protest prayer as such. Job's specific accusations of divine attack and divine injustice are not inappropriate because they are uttered in the context of prayer—in lament—as Job seeks to move God to action. This kind of language has parallels in the Psalter (e.g., Ps. 88) and also corresponds to the truth: Yahweh himself has admitted to attacking Job without cause (2:3). The response as such is an act of approval regarding Job's verbal expression in protest prayer. Yet, approval is tempered by criticism. Job, then, is not made a model for the reader, but is used as a rhetorical strategy for the (implied) author: Job's verbal expression commends protest prayer, even if not everything Job says is offered as a paradigm. Wilson writes (2003: 135–6), "Despite [Job's] need to move in a new direction, God clearly endorses the struggling words and persevering faith of Job... [That Yahweh does not] rebuke Job for his protesting complaints is understandable in the light of a significant Old Testament theme that regards protest to God as legitimate."

There is some tension between Yahweh's speeches and his assessment in the epilogue (42:7-8). The dissonance and ambiguity creates a subtlety to the book that requires the reader to engage the text. As the reader works to fill in these "gaps"—to alleviate the tension and interpret the subtleties—formation happens. The narrator ([implied] author) uses Yahweh's authoritative voice to engage and shape the reader, forcing the reader back to Job's verbal expression to (re)engage it in light of the narrative plot. The narrative sequencing forces the reader into further "meditation" on Job's verbal expression. Despite the dissonance, however, the narrative frame—especially Yahweh's assessment in Job 42:7-8— guides the reader's interpretation of Yahweh's speech from the whirlwind. The ambiguity, dissonance, and subtlety, with only the frame's guidance, and multiple perspectives establishes interest for the reader, leading to an active role in the discernment of the meaning, an engagement which has formative repercussions. Significantly, these poetics relate to Job's verbal expression in the book, indicating the (implied) author's goal to shape the reader in relation to the issue of the ethics of God-talk. Together, Yahweh's speeches with the frame indicate that Job's protest prayer and his defense of his protest prayer are approved, that is, ethical, though Job is not wholly paradigmatic given Yahweh's criticism from the whirlwind.[51] Aspects of Job's defense of his protest prayer—namely, propositional content regarding cosmic divine injustice—and aspects of his protest prayer—namely, the rhetorical goal of Job's oath that impinges upon Yahweh's freedom—are unethical.

The narrative sequencing not only relates to providing a corrective to Job's verbal expression, but also undermines Elihu's and the friends' attempts to silence protest prayer. Elihu's speeches are entirely overwhelmed by Yahweh from the moment he answers Job in 38:1. The authoritative divine voice indicates that, in fact, Yahweh will respond to Job's prayer of protest as Yahweh answers Job. The differences between Elihu's argument and Yahweh's argument require the reader to evaluate and engage these multiple perspectives as well. The reader is shaped away from Elihu's argument. Nevertheless, Elihu's role to focus on issues of justice and ethical God-talk prepares the reader to hear from Yahweh; Elihu's overall argument, however, is to be rejected since he ultimately seeks to silence Job's protest prayer.

Yahweh's speeches lead Job to retract his protest prayer, which also should have a profound impact on the reader. The God-centered focus of the speeches influences Job by reminding him of Yahweh's wisdom and sovereignty; the reader is also encouraged to remember these truths.[52] Both Job and the reader are invited to renewed trust in God, even in the midst of (innocent) suffering. Yahweh's presentation of his wisdom, freedom, and care for creation invite Job back into relationship with the cosmic king. In view of Yahweh's sovereignty, Job enters back into relationship with Yahweh, no longer needing to protest in prayer. In other words, the answer to Job's prayer of protest is Yahweh's kingship. In a move that is akin to the movement of the Psalter, where the laments of Books I–III are answered by Book IV's celebration of the cosmic kingship of Yahweh,[53] the book of Job shapes readers to see that, while protest prayer is an ethical mode of utterance in the midst of innocent suffering,

---

51. Job's defense of his protest prayer is not entirely blameworthy, since he is speaking truly in the sense of being consistent with reality and in the sense that it should be said. The friends' arguments *should* be addressed and refuted. See Härle 2011: 435–40.

52. See Wilson 2003: 125–6 on the God-centered nature of these speeches.

53. See Wilson 1985; 1993: 72–82; McKelvey 2010. Yahweh's speeches also have strong affinities with Isa. 40, in which Yahweh invites his suffering people (in this case due to their sin) back into relationship with him. They are comforted (40:1) by his sovereignty, wisdom, and freedom.

the act of lamentation is not a permanent posture. The reader is able to learn from Yahweh's speeches much as Job has. In sum, these speeches invite relationship and awe that reestablish what was lost in the midst of suffering. The suffering/lamenting reader is encouraged to trust God like Job.

Summary

The Elihu and Yahweh speeches shape the reader through a focus on Job's verbal expression. The narrator's ([implied] author's) use of these speeches forces the reader to engage and discern the ethics of Job's God-talk. The narrator's presentation of Elihu, Elihu's self-portrayal, and Yahweh's authoritative voice emerging from Elihu's burgeoning presentation of a storm overwhelm and undermine his attempt to silence Job's protest prayer. Yahweh's response, on the other hand, affirms Job's protest prayer as an answer and an invitation to a restored relationship. Job's protest prayer is affirmed, therefore, as ethical, even though the instruction qualifies Job's God-talk in significant ways, providing the book's contribution to ethical God-talk when read in light of the narrative frame.

Chapter 7

ETHICAL GOD-TALK:
CONCLUSIONS AND IMPLICATIONS

The foregoing analysis has engaged the book of Job with a literary-rhetorical approach, demonstrating the book's focus on the internal rhetoric of the character Job and Job's two emphases of protesting in prayer and defending his protest prayer. The analysis of Chapter 2 revealed that the theme of ethical God-talk is a prominent theme of the book of Job, intimately related to Job's discourse in the book. The saliency of the theme and the theme's correlation with established devices in biblical poetics indicate that the primary way in which the author of the book makes his contribution regarding ethical God-talk is through Job's verbal expression in the book. The internal rhetoric of Job is the foundation of the external rhetoric of the author.

The results of the first phase of investigation demonstrated the need for an internal rhetorical analysis of Job's speeches in the book, the concern of Chapters 3 through 5. The results of this analysis revealed that Job has two main exigencies: (1) his suffering and (2) the necessity of defending the ethics of his God-talk. The first exigency leads Job to protest prayer, beginning with Job 3 and continuing through each speech in the first cycle, concluding with Job's final speech in Job 29–31. As an innocent sufferer, Job turns to protest prayer as the means by which he can alleviate his suffering and achieve restoration with God; he appeals to God to respond. Job's protest prayer, especially in Job 3, matches the intensity and severity of his suffering. This "primordial lament" is not appropriate according to the friends, thus giving rise to the second exigency (Westermann 1981b: 61 nn. 14–15). Eliphaz, Bildad, and Zophar, in turn, criticize Job's God-talk and encourage penitence rather than protest (5:8; 8:5-6; 11:13-20; 15:2-6, 12-13, 25, 30; 18:2-4; 20:2-4, 29; 22:21-30; 25:4-6). Modifying this exigency becomes Job's primary focus in the second and third cycles; when the friends remain silent, Job returns to focus on the first exigency in his final speech. In other words, Job's suffering precipitates his protest prayer, while his ongoing suffering and his friends' comforting practices sustain Job's discourse throughout the book. This indicates Job's rhetorical goals: to alleviate his suffering and to defend his protest prayer against the arguments of the friends.

Job's protest prayer—his talk to God—is multifaceted. To God, he laments the difficulties and ephemerality of life (7:1-6, 8-10, 13-16, 21; 9:25-26, 29; 10:18-19, 21-22; 13:28; 14:1-2, 5-12, 18, 20-22; 17:1-2; 30:1-19, 24-31). To God, he complains of divine vigilance (7:17-19), divine injustice (9:28-29; 10:2-7, 14; 13:23; 14:3-4), divine absence (13:24; 31:20), and divine antagonism (7:12, 20; 9:30-31; 10:8, 10-13, 16-17; 13:24-27; 14:19; 16:7-8; 31:21-23). To God, Job expresses his desire for relief and restoration (3:13-15, 17-19, 24-26; 14:13-17; 29:2-25) and a commitment to protest prayer until God responds (7:11; 9:27). To God, Job uses rhetorical questions as accusations to move God to act on his behalf (3:11-12, 16, 20, 23; 7:1, 12, 17-21; 9:29; 10:3-6, 10, 18, 20; 13:23-25; 14:4; 17:3; 30:2, 24-25). Job explicitly petitions God to respond (7:7, 16; 10:2, 9, 15, 20; 13:20-23; 14:6; 17:3-4; 31:35). Job's wishes function similarly (6:8-10; 9:33; 14:13-17; 29:2-25; 31:35). These petitions reveal Job's continued faith in God as he struggles to move God to act; if Job rejected God, he would not continue to petition God to act or to respond to his prayer. Job also engages God with an oath/avowal of innocence to supplement his petition (31:1-34, 38-40); Job is innocent of wrongdoing and desires God to act according to this reality. Job's protest prayer is effective: God answers Job from the whirlwind (Job 38–41) and restores Job (42:10-17).

Job's talk about God is also multifaceted. Job uses his talk about God to defend his protest prayer and/or to reject the friends. Job defends his protest prayer by pointing out divine antagonism (6:4, 13; 9:17-18; 12:9; 16:7, 9, 11-14; 17:6; 19:6, 8-13, 21; 23:15-16), divine power and wisdom (9:8-10, 19; 12:10, 13, 16), divine destruction (9:5-7; 12:14-15, 17-25), divine anger (9:13), and divine absence (9:11; 23:3, 5, 8-9). He also defends his protest prayer through avowal of innocence and oath (23:10-12; 27:2-3); Job holds fast to God's ways and has no need of repentance. Job rejects the friends' arguments by outlining perceived divine injustice (9:12, 20, 22-24; 12:6, 9; 16:11; 19:6; 21:9, 17-20; 24:1, 12, 22-23). Nevertheless, Job also highlights divine justice as he corrects the friends through instruction (13:7-11; 21:22; 27:8-11); he asserts they will be judged for their comforter malpractice. He rejects the friends by comparing them to God's attack (19:22). Moreover, Job states his resolve to protest in prayer (13:3). Most significantly, Job also talks about God in ways that reveal his faith and hope in him (13:15-16; 16:19-21; 19:25-27; 23:6-7). Job's God-talk is a consequential aspect of Job's rhetorical goals to both audiences.

The (implied) author uses two additional collections of speeches to aid the reader in evaluating the ethics of Job's God-talk, both of which are analyzed in Chapter 6. The Elihu speeches cite Job's words, criticizing Job for speaking "words without knowledge" (35:16). Nevertheless, the narrator's presentation of Elihu undermines Elihu's arguments (i.e., these speeches do not give the authoritative view regarding the ethics of Job's speech); yet, these speeches prepare the reader for Yahweh's speeches (which also criticize Job's verbal expression as "words without knowledge" [38:2]), which evaluate aspects of Job's discourse for the reader. While both Elihu and Yahweh are critical of Job's words, their intentions are entirely dissimilar. The former is critical in order to silence protest prayer; the latter is critical to instruct and invite back into relationship. Yahweh's assessment provides a divine perspective that indicates that Job's verbal expression of cosmic divine injustice and an oath that impinges upon Yahweh's freedom are seen as unethical. Nevertheless, Job's protest prayer is dignified by Yahweh's response, after which Job retracts it (42:6). The criticism of Job's language focuses mostly on what Job says in his address to the friends—what he says about God, namely, alleging cosmic divine injustice. Nevertheless, Yahweh's commendation of Job's verbal expression in 42:7-8 leads the reader to see that Job's protest prayer is ethical, even encouraged.

The Book's Contribution to Ethical God-Talk

The (implied) author uses Job's verbal expression in protest prayer and in defense of protest prayer to shape the reader to see that this kind of God-talk is approved and encouraged for the innocent sufferer; though protest prayer may not be obligatory, it is at a minimum permissible. The narrator's affirmation of Job's verbal expression, Job's protest prayer, Job's defense of protest prayer, the condemnation of the friends' arguments (by Job, the narrator, and Yahweh), and Yahweh's statement that Job has spoken נְכוֹנָה, truth, commends protest prayer to the innocent sufferer. In other words, the narrative frame highlights the ethics of Job's protest prayer through the presentation of Job's character and the assessments of the narrator and Yahweh (1:22; 2:10; 42:7-8).

The extended focus on the issue of the ethics of Job's verbal expression also corresponds to protest prayer. The friends are critical of it and suggest penitence. Their arguments are rejected by Job (e.g., 13:3-4), the narrator (e.g., Job 28), and Yahweh (e.g., 42:7-8), which indicates that Job's protest prayer is ethical. Since Job's verbal expression is the primary way in which the book makes its contribution, his (divinely confirmed) criticism and rejection of the friends highlights the ethics of protest prayer in general. While aspects of Job's defense of his protest prayer may well be unethical, Job is not wrong to defend his protest prayer. In other words, Job's context, as one whose protest prayer is criticized by the friends, and form (disputation) are right. Moreover, the inclusio of Job's protest prayer around the dispute of the ethics concerning Job's God-talk highlights the significance of this mode of prayer. Finally, Yahweh's response to Job as an answer to Job's protest prayer dignifies his protest prayer as a whole, especially in conjunction with the lack of any explicit call to repentance. Job's verbal expression is not entirely ethical. The book reveals that certain things—such as asserting that God is cosmically unjust—are unethical in talk about God and to God. Even though the book highlights these, the overall emphasis is on commending protest prayer since it is only certain aspects of Job's language that are problematic. Yahweh never calls Job to repentance or sacrifice like the friends, and the friends are entirely rejected. It is they who require intercession and sacrifice (42:8).

Job's faith and relationship with Yahweh undergird his use of protest prayer; to lament or complain to God in the midst of chaos is an inherently faith-filled act. Significantly, Job's trust in God emerges explicitly at various points in the book. The divine assessment in Job 42:7-8 confirms Job's ethical God-talk.[1]

Nevertheless, many of the things Job says are difficult for the reader. Fox (1980b: 9) notes in his discussion of the rhetoric of Ezekiel 37 that "[s]trange, shocking, and bizarre images...are needed when one seeks to break down old frameworks of perception and to create new ones... Such images may attack our normal system of expectations in order to replace it with a new one."[2] Job's internal rhetoric, as the (implied) author's primary rhetorical vehicle in relation to ethical God-talk, has this exact effect.

---

1. Related to this point is the crucial distinction that lament is not a curse. The prospect of cursing God arises in the *satan*'s two statements in the prologue. Job is said to curse (קלל), but the object is his fate. To curse God would be to speak unethically. But Job's discourse, as protest prayer, is categorically distinct from cursing.

2. Fox acknowledges indebtedness to Tannehill's (1975: 53–4; cf. 25–6) discussion of "imaginative shock" in Jesus' teaching rhetoric.

Tannehill writes (1975: 54), "If speech is to induce 'imaginative shock,' effectively challenging the old structures and suggesting new visions, it must resist...digestion... Forceful and imaginative language can do its work only if it does not fit into our ordinary interpretive structures."[3] The shocking and difficult-to-embrace verbal expression of Job keeps the reader engaged, wrestling with how to understand it; when the narrative frame's affirmation of Job's verbal expression is given its due force, Job's verbal expression, by its hyperbolic character, shapes the reader, breaking down any notion that protest prayer is unethical. While Job is shown to speak unethically in some way by Yahweh's speeches, the book's focus with the narrative frame and the use of Job's verbal expression in protest prayer and in defense of his protest prayer highlights the book's emphasis on the ethical nature of protest prayer as its contribution. Thus, the Yahweh speeches at the end serve (ingeniously) to reframe the hyperbolic use of Job's internal rhetoric. In light of the correction of Job, it is difficult to conclude that Job himself is a paradigm for readers to emulate in every way, even if this kind of prayer language is approved.

The (Reconstructed) Rhetorical Situation of the Book of Job

The book's contribution to the ethics of God-talk should be understood in light of the book's rhetorical situation. Unfortunately, determining the date of the book is difficult, if not impossible. Nevertheless, a rhetorical situation can be derived from the ideas in the book itself, as previous scholars have suggested. After outlining and adding to these proposals, I propose a tentative, since somewhat hypothetical, reconstruction of the intellectual milieu to which the book might be addressed.

---

3. This explains why Job seems to be more vivid than the protest prayer of the psalter. See, e.g., Newsom 2003: 130–68; Seow 2013: 337, on subversion or parody; Dell (1991) on the misuse of forms. The (implied) author's use of Job's hyperbolic internal rhetoric is a vivid and provocative rhetorical device; the author is not subverting the protest prayer of the Hebrew Bible or offering a new tradition or understanding. As Kynes has shown, the parodies of various psalms are "antithetical allusions" that depend upon the traditional understanding of these psalms for their rhetorical provocativeness and effectiveness (2012; 2011: 276–310). Any "subversion" or parody is rhetorical on the internal level (i.e., intended for persuasion of characters within the narrative world). Another reason for missing psalmic elements is because a vow or statement of confidence would violate Job's integrity (Hartley 1994: 90–1).

Previous Proposals of the Rhetorical Situation for the Book

Lo lays a helpful foundation for a discussion of the rhetorical situation of the book of Job. In her inquiry as to the rhetorical role of Job 28, she suggests that the best evidence for the rhetorical situation of the book is found in the perspectives of the characters (2003: 62). This is necessary because of the lack of firm knowledge of its historical and geographic provenance. She concludes that there are three exigencies which the book intends to modify: (1) blind application of theodicies, manifested in three forms, (a) the concept of retribution, (b) human depravity, (c) chastisement of God; (2) proud claims to knowledge and reliance upon tradition; (3) misconceptions about God (62–9). The first two exigencies relate to the friends: the book criticizes and, therefore, seeks to shape readers away from hubristic comforting practices. Comforters need to recognize their own epistemic limits and cruel comforting practices, evident in their attempts to equate suffering and sin simplistically. The third exigency relates to Job, indicating the tendency of sufferers to impugn God's justice. Lo locates the audience of the book through the characters as well: Job and his friends reflect the kind of people to whom the book is addressed, suggesting that the exigencies specify the audience (69). Furthermore, she identifies the religious background of the characters as the primary constraint. She develops this by noting how the religious background of the characters includes views of justice vis-à-vis God, monotheism, the fear of Yahweh, and the act–consequence nexus (70–1).

Yu's work builds on this foundation, bringing clarity to the exigencies that relate to the hubristic and abusive comforting practices of sages and comforters. Like Lo, Yu acknowledges the difficulty in establishing with certainty the historical milieu out of which the book arose, yet suggests that "the intellectual milieu" from which the book springs can be identified by close attention to the ideas it contains (2011: 24). The ideas of the book reveal how "the author is in conversation with existing ideas of his day and is responding to known philosophical positions on the causes of suffering" (26). The depiction of the comforters as "callous and deceitful" reveals an exigency of comforter malpractice the book is seeking to modify; the book is written to sages, mourners, and comforters (26–7, 415–18). This dovetails well with Lo's conclusions noted above (especially her first two exigencies).

Methodologically speaking, using the internal data to establish the rhetorical situation of a book whose provenance is unknown has recently been defended by Joel Barker. Barker shows that the concept of the rhetorical situation as conceived by George Kennedy, itself rooted in Lloyd Bitzer's rhetorical theory, proves challenging for the biblical material; it is difficult to get at the "world behind the text" because of the temporal and geographic distance between text and interpreter (2014: 42–3). He illustrates the problem with two recent studies of prophetic books, and suggests that a better way forward is to establish the rhetorical situation from "the world of the text," "examining the situation or exigencies that the text appears to create and to which it responds" (43–51, quote from p. 47). Building on the work of Dennis Stamps (1993: 193–210), he notes that the rhetorical situation is "entextualized" (49). Barker further notes that this allows the text a "timelessness" that befits biblical narrative, "and potentially permits its persuasive power to have influence beyond the time and place of its original utterance" (47). In this way, the text itself provides the clues to the rhetorical situation, where the (implied) author as rhetor "shapes the rhetorical situation through the discourse and constructs the exigence that requires rhetorical response" (49). Barker cogently argues that determining the rhetorical situation at the synchronic level—"the world of the text"—is helpful, appropriate, and necessary, when establishing the rhetorical situation at the diachronic level—"the world behind the text"—proves challenging, or even impossible.[4] This is exactly what Lo and Yu have provided Joban scholars.

Thus, a close reading of the book can provide the necessary information for establishing the rhetorical situation of the book of Job. The proposals of the exigencies of the book by Lo and Yu are both valid and insightful in my view. They represent key issues to which the book of Job speaks and in relation to which the book of Job seeks to shape its readers. However, in light of the analysis of the issue of the ethics of God-talk in this study, it seems that both scholars have overlooked an important exigency, namely, the loss of protest prayer as an acceptable, ethical manner of speaking. The audience remains the same as both Lo and Yu have identified, namely, mourners and comforters. But an important constraint needs to be added: the interplay between the broader canonical view of protest prayer and the apparently current intellectual milieu in which protest prayer is eschewed. The friends and Elihu seek to persuade Job away from protest and toward

---

4. To be fair, Barker's methodological proposal is for prophetic literature, but the reasons why the model is necessary for prophetic literature are the same for a book like Job, namely, the lack of data for a concrete dating of the book. Because of this, his methodological proposal is appropriate and valid for Job as well. He further notes that this undercuts Bitzer's theory because Bitzer was adamant that rhetorical situations be historical and not fictive (2014: 48). He counters that Bitzer allowed for "persistent or recurring rhetorical situations," and the biblical text certainly fits that description (48). On this point, see also Yu 2011: 11.

penitence. It seems likely that the characters in the book represent ideas current in the intellectual milieu out of which the book arises. The book's contribution—that protest prayer is ethical, even encouraged, for the innocent sufferer—speaks to this intellectual milieu, seeking to shape its readers away from the ideas of the day and to return its readers to a view that accepts protest prayer in accordance with other biblical traditions and texts.

A Proposed Historical Reconstruction of the Rhetorical Situation of the Book of Job

Despite the methodological appropriateness of establishing the rhetorical situation of the book of Job from within the text, it is illuminating to consider the rhetorical situation of the book in light of its possible historical provenance. This is admittedly somewhat speculative, since there are no firm data from which to date the book (and thus no consensus on a date). Nevertheless, a case can be made to locate the book in a broad historical period, and this historical period exhibits trends that pertain specifically to the analysis of the book of Job in this study.

Most commentators suggest that the book likely reached its final form sometime between the seventh and second centuries BCE.[5] Seow offers a most comprehensive discussion of the date, noting that the mention of Tema and Sheba in Job 6:19 provides a clue for establishing a date for the book. He understands Sheba to refer to the Sabean trading colony that was founded near Tema sometime around the turn of the ninth to the eighth century BCE (2013: 40).[6] Noting the connection of the Sabeans in the prologue with Chaldean raiders (1:15, 17), and that the Chaldeans were known to have been raiders only about 550–540 BCE at the time of Nabonidus, he writes, "One might conjecture…that the Chaldeans who raided properties in the region were part of the retinue brought by Nabonidus" (ibid.). This, in turn, meant that the Sabeans were forced into "occasional banditry" as they lost control of the merchant activities in the region (ibid.). Seow suggests that the prologue thus resembles this historical period, namely, the mid-sixth century, making this the "earliest possible date of the book" (ibid.).[7]

---

5. See, e.g., Dhorme 1984: clxix; Habel 1985: 40; Hartley 1988: 18; Clines 1989: lvii; Newsom 1996: 325; Longman 2012: 26.

6. See Tadmor 1994: 142–3.

7. The evidence from Qumran, specifically 4QPalaeoJob[c], indicates that the *terminus ante quem* of the final form of the book is mid-second century (Seow 2013: 43–4).

Seow does not allow conclusions drawn from intertextuality or allusion between Job and other texts like the Psalms, Proverbs, or Ecclesiastes to play a part in his dating of the book. He is willing, though, to allow "parallels" in Jeremiah, Lamentations, and Isaiah 40–55 to play a role in the discussion (Seow 2013: 41–2). In light of Kynes' method and study of the intertextuality of Job and the Psalms, however, it seems best not to exclude allusions to the Psalter. Kynes' method accounts for the difficulty in dating OT poetic texts by his criterion of coherence, which inquires as to which text is more likely the original based on internal and external contexts (2012: 59). This question treats the diachronic nature of intertextuality in a way not dissimilar from textual criticism: which text more likely gave rise to the other? Kynes identifies Psalms 1, 8, 73, 107, and 139 as psalms that both Job and his friends allude to, with only Job alluding to Psalm 39. Each psalm except Psalm 39 is shown to be earlier than the book of Job based on his method, and in the case of Psalm 39 one could argue both possibilities.[8] Kynes notes something similar with the intertextual relationship between Job and Isaiah (2013b: 98; *pace* Hartley 1988: 13–15, 19).

Based on the geographical references from Job 6:19 and the allusions from Job to books like Psalms, Jeremiah, Lamentations, and Isaiah, it is likely that Job is postexilic, a view that accords with the (hedged) view of most interpreters.

In light of this proposed date, it is noteworthy that a number of scholars have shown that protest prayer was increasingly "eclipsed" in favor of penitential models. The word eclipse is used intentionally in light of Morrow's subtitle and significance in this discussion (2006b: 3). This view seems to have been first advanced by Westermann (1981a: 165–213, esp. 171–2, 206–7). Balentine summarizes Westermann's contribution thus: "The *third* or late stage in the history of lament coincides with the defeat of the state and the destruction of the temple, a calamitous political and religious loss for Israel that dramatically changed the way it prays… Westermann understood the shift to penitential prayer to signal the dissolution of the lament psalm as a fixed prayer form in ancient Israel" (2006b: 5).[9] Boda writes: "The legacy of the destruction of Jerusalem and the exile of the people is seen in the size of its impact on the prayer forms of Israel from this point forward. There is a fundamental shift in outlook

---

8. See Kynes 2012: 69, 84–5, 106–7, 149, 164–5; on Ps. 39, see 126–30.

9. This understanding has been developed and qualified by others; cf. Werline 1998: 11–64, 191–5; Boda 1999, 2001: 186–97; 2003: 51–75; Morrow 2006a. See also the collection of essays in Boda et al. 2006.

from this point on in the history of Israel" (2006b: 190). The exile shifted the focus of prayer in suffering to focus on the sin of the nation, thereby justifying God and his discipline. Repentance and confession thus play a major role in the prayer forms (Boda 2006a: 27–34; cf. Werline 2006: xv). Protest prayer, on the other hand, which focuses on God's antagonism or indifference, placing the blame on God for rhetorical purposes, would not be welcomed in the prayer life of Israel. As these scholars show, this shift had a significant impact on the use of complaint in this era. If this is the case, the book of Job is written in response to the shift of the dominance of penitential prayer—to encourage the persistence and ethical (i.e., right) nature of protest prayer for the innocent sufferer. The context of the book highlights Job's innocent suffering, and, in light of the narrative frame of the book, defends his right to protest over against the friends who insist on penitence. Job and his friends represent these vastly different approaches to God-talk in suffering.[10] If Westermann, Boda, and others are right to suggest that the exile transformed the perspective of prayer so that "complaint against God was absolutely disallowed" (Westermann 1981a: 171), the book of Job speaks into that historical situation to modify this exigency, using Job and his discourse as the means to that end. Thus, the book of Job serves as a reminder that protest prayer is an ethical mode of prayer depending on one's circumstances.[11]

While this may not be a firm conclusion, it seems probable given the foregoing discussion on the rhetorical situation that emerges from "the world of the text." Biblical books are especially amenable to persisting rhetorical situations because of their religious nature. This means the book of Job's message regarding ethical God-talk is applicable in many different eras. The book of Job speaks to us as much as it does to the postexilic word: it is ethically good and right to protest in prayer.

---

10. The friends and Elihu may even be portrayed as having a misunderstanding of protest prayer (Wilson 2015: 256; cf. Westermann 1981b: 21).

11. Boda's balance is helpful in reminding us that both types of prayer are appropriate, but the perspective of life (*Ausblick aufs Lebens*) determines when each prayer type is to be used (2006b: 189–90; cf. Boda 2003: 51–75).

BIBLIOGRAPHY

Aitken, James A. 2013. "The Inevitability of Reading Job Through Lamentations." Pages 204–15 in *Reading Job Intertextually*. Edited by Katharine Dell and Will Kynes. LHBOTS 574. New York: Bloomsbury.
Alter, Robert. 1981. *The Art of Biblical Narrative*. New York: Basic Books.
———. 1985. *The Art of Biblical Poetry*. New York: Basic Books.
Andersen, Francis I. 1976. *Job*. Downers Grove: InterVarsity.
Arnold, Bill T., and John H. Choi. 2003. *A Guide to Biblical Hebrew Syntax*. Cambridge: Cambridge University Press.
Averbeck, Richard E. 2004. "Ancient Near Eastern Mythography as it Relates to Historiography in the Hebrew Bible: Genesis 3 and the Cosmic Battle." Pages 328–56 in *The Future of Biblical Archaeology: Reassessing Methodologies and Assumptions: The Proceedings of a Symposium, August 12–14, 2001 at Trinity International University*. Edited by James K. Hoffmeier and Alan Millard. Grand Rapids: Eerdmans.
Baker, William R. 1995. *Personal Speech Ethics in the Epistle of James*. WUNT 68. Tübingen: Mohr.
Balentine, Samuel E. 1993. *Prayer in the Hebrew Bible: The Drama of Divine–Human Dialogue*. OBT. Minneapolis: Fortress, 1993.
———. 1998. "'What Are Human Beings That You Make So Much of Them?' Divine Disclosure from the Whirlwind: 'Look at Behemoth.'" Pages 259–78 in *God in the Fray: A Tribute to Walter Brueggemann*. Edited by Tod Linafelt and Timothy K. Beal. Minneapolis: Fortress.
———. 1999a. "Job 23:1–9, 16–17." *Int* 53: 290–3.
———. 1999b. "Who Will Be Job's Redeemer?" *PRSt* 26: 269–89.
———. 2006a. "Afterword." Pages 193–204 in *Seeking the Favor of God: Volume 1: The Origins of Penitential Prayer in Second Temple Judaism*. Edited by Mark J. Boda, Daniel K. Falk, and Rodney A. Werline. Atlanta: SBL.
———. 2006b. "I Was Ready to Be Sought Out by Those Who Did Not Ask." Pages 1–20 in *Seeking the Favor of God*. Vol. 1, *The Origins of Penitential Prayer in Second Temple Judaism*. Edited by Mark J. Boda, Daniel K. Falk, and Rodney A. Werline. Atlanta: SBL.
Barker, Joel. 2014. *From the Depths of Despair to the Promise of Presence: A Rhetorical Reading of the Book of Joel*. Siphrut 11. Winona Lake, IN: Eisenbrauns.
Bartholomew, Craig G. 1998. *Reading Ecclesiastes: Old Testament Exegesis and Hermeneutical Theory*. Rome: Editrice Pontificio Istituto Biblico.
———. 2009. *Ecclesiastes*. BCOT. Grand Rapids: Baker Academic.

Bastiaens, J. C. 1997. "The Language of Suffering in Job 16–19 and in the Suffering Servant Passages in Deutero-Isaiah." Pages 421–32 in *Studies in the Book of Isaiah: Festschrift Willem A. M. Beuken*. Edited by J. Van Ruiten and M. Vervenne. Leuven: Leuven University Press.

Bautch, Richard J. 2006. "Lament Regained in Trito-Isaiah's Penitential Prayer." Pages 83–99 in *Seeking the Favor of God*. Vol. 1, *The Origins of Penitential Prayer in Second Temple Judaism*. Edited by Mark J. Boda, Daniel K. Falk, and Rodney A. Werline. Atlanta: SBL.

Ben-Porat, Ziva. 1976. "The Poetics of Literary Allusion." *PTL: A Journal for Descriptive Poetics and Theory of Literature* 1: 105–28.

Berger, Peter L. 1990. *The Sacred Canopy: Elements of a Sociological Theory of Religion*. New York: Anchor Books.

Beuken, W. A. M. 1994. "Job's Imprecation as the Cradle of a New Religious Discourse: The Perplexing Impact of the Semantic Correspondences Between Job 3, Job 4–5, and Job 6–7." Pages 41–78 in *The Book of Job*. Edited by W. A. M. Beuken. Leuven: Leuven University Press.

Billings, J. Todd. 2015. *Rejoicing in Lament: Wrestling with Incurable Cancer and Life in Christ*. Grand Rapids: Brazos.

Billman, Kathleen D., and Daniel L. Migliore. 1999. *Rachel's Cry: Prayer of Lament and Rebirth of Hope*. Cleveland, OH: United Church Press.

Bitzer, Lloyd F. 1992. "The Rhetorical Situation." *Philosophy & Rhetoric* 25: 1–14.

Blumenthal, David R. 1993. *Facing the Abusing God: A Theology of Protest*. Louisville: Westminster John Knox.

Boda, Mark J. 1999. *Praying the Tradition: The Origin and Use of Tradition in Nehemiah 9*. Berlin: de Gruyter.

———. 2001. "From Complaint to Contrition: Peering Through the Liturgical Window of Jer 14,1–15,4." *ZAW* 113: 186–97.

———. 2003. "The Priceless Gain of Penitence: From Communal Lament to Penitential Prayer in the 'Exilic' Liturgy of Israel." *HBT* 25: 51–75.

———. 2006a. "Confession as Theological Expression: Ideological Origins of Penitential Prayer." Pages 21–50 in *Seeking the Favor of God*. Vol. 1, *The Origins of Penitential Prayer in Second Temple Judaism*. Edited by Mark J. Boda, Daniel K. Falk, and Rodney A. Werline. Atlanta: SBL.

———. 2006b. "Form Criticism in Transition: Penitential Prayer and Lament, Sitz Im Leben and Form." Pages 181–92 in *Seeking the Favor of God*. Vol. 1, *The Origins of Penitential Prayer in Second Temple Judaism*. Edited by Mark J. Boda, Daniel K. Falk, and Rodney A. Werline. Atlanta: SBL.

Boda, Mark J., Daniel K. Falk, and Rodney A. Werline, eds. 2006. *Seeking the Favor of God*. Vol. 1, *The Origins of Penitential Prayer in Second Temple Judaism*. Atlanta: SBL.

Booth, Wayne C. 1983. *The Rhetoric of Fiction*. Chicago: The University of Chicago Press.

Brenner, Athalya. 1989. "Job the Pious: The Characterization of Job in the Narrative Framework of the Book." *JSOT* 43: 37–52.

Brinks Rea, Christina L. 2010. "The Thematic, Stylistic, and Verbal Similarities Between Isaiah 40–55 and the Book of Job." PhD diss., University of Notre Dame.

Brown, Sally A., and Patrick D. Miller. 2005a. "Introduction." Pages xiii–xix in *Lament: Reclaiming Practices in Pulpit, Pew, and Public Square*. Edited by Sally A. Brown and Patrick D. Miller. Louisville: Westminster John Knox.

Brown, Sally A., and Patrick D. Miller, eds. 2005b. *Lament: Reclaiming Practices in Pulpit, Pew, and Public Square*. Louisville: Westminster John Knox.

Brown, William P. 2000. "*Creatio Corporis* and the Rhetoric of Defense in Job 10 and Psalm 139." Pages 107–24 in *The God Who Creates: Essays in Honor of S. Tibley Towner*. Edited by William P. Brown and S. Dean McBride Jr. Grand Rapids: Eerdmans.

Broyles, Craig C. 1989. *The Conflict of Faith and Experience in the Psalms: A Form-Critical and Theological Study*. JSOTSup 52. Sheffield: Sheffield Academic.

Brueggemann, Walter. 1985. "A Shape for Old Testament Theology, II: Embrace of Pain." *CBQ* 47: 395–415.

———. 1995a. "From Hurt to Joy, from Death to Life." Pages 67–83 in *Psalms and the Life of Faith*. Edited by Patrick D. Miller. Minneapolis: Fortress.

———. 1995b. "Psalms and the Life of Faith: A Suggested Typology of Function." Pages 3–32 in *Psalms and the Life of Faith*. Edited by Patrick D. Miller. Minneapolis: Fortress.

———. 1995c. "The Costly Loss of Lament." Pages 98–111 in *Psalms and the Life of Faith*. Edited by Patrick D. Miller. Minneapolis: Fortress.

———. 1995d. "The Formfulness of Grief." Pages 84–97 in *Psalms and the Life of Faith*. Edited by Patrick D. Miller. Minneapolis: Fortress.

Bryant, Donald C. 1953. "Rhetoric: Its Function and Scope." *Quarterly Journal of Speech* 39: 401–24.

Burnight, John. 2013. "The 'Reversal' of *Heilsgeschichte* in Job 3." Pages 30–41 in *Reading Job Intertextually*. Edited by Katharine Dell and Will Kynes. LHBOTS 574. New York: Bloomsbury.

———. 2014. "Does Eliphaz Really Begin 'Gently'? An Intertextual Reading of Job 4,2–11." *Bib* 85: 347–70.

Caws, Mary Ann. 1985. *Reading Frames in Modern Fiction*. Princeton: Princeton University Press.

Cheney, Michael. 1994. *Dust, Wind and Agony: Character, Speech and Genre in Job*. Stockholm: Almqvist & Wiksell International.

Chin, Catherine. 1994. "Job and the Injustice of God: Implicit Arguments in Job 13.17–14.12." *JSOT* 64: 91–101.

Clarke, Rosalind. 2011. "Job 27:3: The Spirit of God in my Nostrils." Pages 111–21 in *Presence, Power, and Promise: The Role of the Holy Spirit in the Old Testament*. Edited by David G. Firth and Paul D. Wegner. Downers Grove, IL: IVP Academic.

Clines, David. J. A. 1985. "False Naivety in the Prologue to Job." *HAR* 9: 127–36.

———. 1989. *Job 1–20*. WBC 17. Waco: Word.

———. 1998. "Quarter Days Gone: Job 24 and the Absence of God." Pages 242–58 in *God in the Fray: A Tribute to Walter Brueggemann*. Edited by Tod Linafelt and Timothy K. Beal. Minneapolis: Fortress.

———. 2005. "Putting Elihu in His Place: A Proposal for the Relocation of Job 32–37." *JSOT* 29: 243–53.

———. 2006. *Job 21–37*. WBC 18a. Nashville: Thomas Nelson.

———. 2011. *Job 38–42*. WBC 18b. Nashville: Thomas Nelson.

Cooper, Alan. 1990. "Reading and Misreading the Prologue to Job." *JSOT* 46: 67–79.

Corbett, Edward P. J. 1969. *Rhetorical Analysis of Literary Works*. Oxford: Oxford University Press.

Course, John E. 1994. *Speech and Response: A Rhetorical Analysis of the Introductions to the Speeches of the Book of Job (Chaps. 4–24)*. Catholic Biblical Quarterly Monograph Series 25. Washington, D.C.: Catholic Biblical Association of America.

Curtis, John B. 1979. "On Job's Response to Yahweh." *JBL* 98: 497–511.
———. 1983. "On Job's Witness in Heaven." *JBL* 102: 549–62.
Dailey, Thomas F. 1993. "And Yet He Repents—On Job 42:6." *ZAW* 105: 205–9.
Davidson, A. B. 1895. *The Book of Job: With Notes, Introduction, and Appendix*. Cambridge: Cambridge University Press.
de Regt, Lenart J. 1994. "Functions and Implications of Rhetorical Questions in the Book of Job." Pages 361–73 in *Biblical Hebrew and Discourse Linguistics*. Edited by Robert D. Bergen. Winona Lake, IN: Eisenbrauns.
Dell, Katharine J. 1991. *The Book of Job as Sceptical Literature*. Berlin: de Gruyter.
———. 2013. "'Cursed Be the Day I Was Born': Job and Jeremiah Revisited." Pages 106–17 in *Reading Job Intertextually*. Edited by Katharine Dell and Will Kynes. LHBOTS 574. New York: Bloomsbury.
Dhorme, Édouard. 1984. *A Commentary on the Book of Job*. Translated by Harold Knight. Nashville: Thomas Nelson.
Dick, Michael Brennan. 1979. "The Legal Metaphor in Job 31." *CBQ* 41: 37–50.
Diewert, David A. 1987. "Job 7:12: Yam, Tannin and the Surveillance of Job." *JBL* 106: 203–15.
———. 1991. "The Composition of the Elihu Speeches: A Poetic and Structural Analysis." PhD diss., University of Toronto.
Dobbs-Allsopp, F. W. 1994. "The Genre of the Meṣad Ḥashavyahu Ostracon." *BASOR* 195: 49–55.
Driver, S. R., and G. B. Gray. 1921. *A Critical and Exegetical Commentary on the Book of Job*. ICC. Edinburgh: T&T Clark.
Dubbink, Joep. 1999. "Jeremiah: Hero of Faith or Defeatist? Concerning the Place and Function of Jeremiah 20.14–18." *JSOT* 86: 67–84.
Erickson, Amy. 2013. "'Without My Flesh I Will See God': Job's Rhetoric of the Body." *JBL* 132: 295–313.
Fishbane, Michael A. 1971. "Jeremiah 4:23–26 and Job 3:3–13: A Recovered Use of the Creation Pattern." *VT* 21: 151–67.
———. 1992. "The Book of Job and Inner-Biblical Discourse." Pages 86–98 in *The Voice from the Whirlwind: Interpreting the Book of Job*. Edited by Leo Perdue and W. Clark Gilpin. Nashville: Abingdon.
Fohrer, Georg. 1963. *Das Buch Hiob*. KAT 16. Gütersloh: Gütersloher Verlagshaus Gerd Mohn.
Fokkelman, Jan P. 2012. *The Book of Job in Form: A Literary Translation with Commentary*. Leiden: Brill.
Forrest, Robert W. E. 1988. "The Two Faces of Job: Imagery and Integrity in the Prologue." Pages 385–98 in *Ascribe to the Lord: Biblical and Other Studies in Memory of Peter C. Craigie*. Edited by Lyle Eslinger and Glen Taylor. JSOTSup 67. Sheffield: JSOT.
Fox, Michael V. 1977. "Frame-Narrative and Composition in the Book of Qohelet." *HUCA* 48: 83–106.
———. 1980a. "The Identification of Quotations in Biblical Literature." *ZAW* 92: 416–31.
———. 1980b. "The Rhetoric of Ezekiel's Vision of the Valley of the Bones." *HUCA* 51: 1–15.
———. 1981. "Job 38 and God's Rhetoric." *Semeia* 19: 53–61.
———. 1999. *A Time to Tear Down and a Time to Build Up: A Rereading of Ecclesiastes*. Grand Rapids: Eerdmans.
———. 2005. "Job the Pious." *ZAW* 117: 351–66.

———. 2011. "Reading the Tale of Job." Pages 145–62 in *A Critical Engagement: Essays on the Hebrew Bible in Honour of J. Cheryl Exum*. Edited by David J. A. Clines and Ellen van Wolde. Sheffield: Sheffield Phoenix.

———. 2012. "Behemoth and Leviathan." *Bib* 93: 261–7.

———. 2013. "God's Answer and Job's Response." *Bib* 94: 1–23.

———. 2018. "The Meanings of the Book of Job." *JBL* 137: 7–18.

Fredericks, D. C. 1997. "הֶבֶל." Pages 1005–6 in vol. 1 of *NIDOTTE*. Edited by W. A. VanGemeren. 5 vols. Grand Rapids: Zondervan.

Frevel, Christian. 2009. "Dann wär' ich nicht mehr da. Der Todeswunsch Ijobs als Element der Klagerhetorik." Pages 25–41 in *Tod und Jenseits im alten Israel und in seiner Umwelt*. Edited by Jan Dietrich and Bernd Janowski. Tübingen: Mohr Siebeck.

Futato, Mark D. 2008. "Hymns." Pages 300–305 in *Dictionary of the Old Testament: Wisdom, Poetry, and Writings*. Edited by Tremper Longman III and Peter Enns. Downers Grove, IL: InterVarsity.

Gammie, John G. 1978. "Behemoth and Leviathan: On the Didactic and Theological Significance of Job 40:15–41:26." Pages 217–31 in *Israelite Wisdom*. Missoula, MT: Scholars.

Gerstenberger, Erhard S. 1988. *Psalms: Part 1 with an Introduction to Cultic Poetry*. FOTL 14. Grand Rapids: Eerdmans.

Good, Edwin M. 1990. *In Turns of Tempest: A Reading of Job with Translation*. Stanford, CA: Stanford University Press.

Gordis, Robert. 1965. *The Book of God and Man: A Study of Job*. Chicago: University of Chicago Press.

———. 1978. *The Book of Job: Commentary, New Translation, and Special Studies*. New York: Jewish Theological Seminary of America.

Greenstein, Edward L. 2004a. "Jeremiah as an Inspiration to the Poet of Job." Pages 98–110 in *Inspired Speech: Prophecy in the Ancient Near East, Essays in Honor of Herbert B. Huffmon*. Edited by John Kaltner and Louis Stulman. London: T&T Clark.

———. 2004b. "Review of Talking about God: Job 42:7–9 and the Nature of God in the Book of Job." *RBL* 7: n.p.

———. 2006. "Truth or Theodicy? Speaking Truth to Power in the Book of Job." *PSB* 28: 238–58.

Gutiérrez, Gustavo. 1987. *On Job: God-Talk and the Suffering of the Innocent*. Translated by Matthew J. O'Connell. Maryknoll, NY: Orbis Books.

Habel, Norman C. 1983. "The Narrative Art of Job: Applying the Principles of Robert Alter." *JSOT* 27: 101–11.

———. 1984. "The Role of Elihu in the Design of the Book of Job." Pages 81–98 in *In the Shelter of Elyon: Essays on Ancient Palestinian Life and Literature in Honor of G.W. Ahlstrom*. JSOTSup 31. Sheffield: JSOT.

———. 1985. *The Book of Job: A Commentary*. OTL. Philadelphia: Westminster.

Ham, T. C. 2013. "The Gentle Voice of God in Job 38." *JBL* 132: 527–41.

Harding, James E. 2010. "The Book of Job as Metaprophecy." *Studies in Religion/ Sciences Religieuses* 34: 523–47.

Härle, Wilfried. 2011. *Ethik*. Berlin: de Gruyter.

Hart, Roderick P., and Suzanne M. Daughton. 2005. *Modern Rhetorical Criticism*. Boston: Pearson.

Hartley, John E. 1988. *The Book of Job*. NICOT. Grand Rapids: Eerdmans.

———. 1994. "From Lament to Oath: A Study of Progression in the Speeches of Job." Pages 79–100 in *The Book of Job*. Edited by W. A. M. Beuken. Leuven: Leuven University Press.
Hawley, Lance R. 2018. *Metaphor Competition in the Book of Job*. JAJSup 26. Göttingen: Vandenhoek & Ruprecht.
van Hecke, Pierre. 2003. "From Conversation About God to Conversation with God." Pages 115–24 in *Theology and Conversation: Towards a Relational Theology*. Edited by J. Haers and P. de Mey. Leuven: Leuven University Press.
———. 2011. "'I Melt Away and Will No Longer Live': The Use of Metaphor in Job's Self-Descriptions." *ET Studies* 2: 91–107.
Ho, Edward. 2009. "In the Eyes of the Beholder: Unmarked Attributed Quotations in Job." *JBL* 128: 703–15.
Hoffman, Yair. 1981. "The Relation Between the Prologue and the Speech-Cycles in Job: A Reconsideration." *VT* 31: 160–70.
Holbert, John C. 1981. "'The Skies Will Uncover His Iniquity': Satire in the Second Speech of Zophar (Job XX)." *VT* 31: 171–9.
Howard, David M. 1994. "Rhetorical Criticism in Old Testament Studies." *BBR* 4: 87–104.
———. 2008. "Psalm 88 and the Rhetoric of Lament." Pages 132–46 in *"My Words Are Lovely": Studies in the Rhetoric of the Psalms*. Edited by Robert L. Foster and David M. Howard. LHBOTS 467. New York: T&T Clark.
Janowski, Bernd. 2009. *Arguing with God: A Theological Anthropology of the Psalms*. Translated by Armin Siedlecki. Louisville: Westminster John Knox.
Janzen, J. Gerald. 1985. *Job*. Interpretation. Atlanta: John Knox.
———. 1989. "Another Look at God's Watch Over Job (7:12)." *JBL* 108: 109–14.
Jimenez, Carlos Patrick. 2013. "The Enemy Lament: A Socio-Cognitive Approach to the Metaphors of Job 16:7–14." Pages 49–70 in *Spiritual Complaint: The Theology and Practice of Lament*. Edited by Miriam J. Bier and Tim Bulkeley. Eugene, OR: Wipf & Stock.
Johnston, Gordon H. 1997. "הבל." Pages 1003–5 in vol. 1 of *NIDOTTE*. Edited by W. A. VanGemeren. 5 vols. Grand Rapids: Zondervan.
Kaiser Jr., Walter C. 1983. *Toward Old Testament Ethics*. Grand Rapids: Zondervan Academic.
Kaplan, L. J. 1978. "Maimonides, Dale Patrick, and Job XLII 6." *VT* 28: 356–8.
Kennedy, George A. 1984. *New Testament Interpretation Through Rhetorical Criticism*. Chapel Hill, NC: The University of North Carolina Press.
Kitz, Anne Marie. 2007. "Curses and Cursing in the Ancient Near East." *Religion Compass* 1: 615–27.
Kline, Jonathan G. 2016. *Allusive Soundplay in the Hebrew Bible*. AIL 28. Atlanta: SBL.
Koops, Robert. 1988. "Rhetorical Questions and Implied Meaning in the Book of Job." *The Bible Translator* 39: 415–23.
Kynes, Will. 2011. "Beat Your Parodies into Swords, and Your Parodied Books into Spears: A New Paradigm for Parody in the Hebrew Bible." *BibInt* 19: 276–310.
———. 2012. *My Psalm Has Turned to Weeping: Job's Dialogue with the Psalms*. BZAW 437. Berlin: de Gruyter.
———. 2013a. "Intertextuality: Method and Theory in Job and Psalm 119." Pages 201–13 in *Biblical Interpretation and Method: Essays in Honour of John Barton*. Edited by Katharine Dell and Paul M. Joyce. Oxford: Oxford University Press.

———. 2013b. "Job and Isaiah 40–55: Intertextualities in Dialogue." Pages 94–105 in *Reading Job Intertextually*. Edited by Katharine Dell and Will Kynes. LHBOTS 574. New York: Bloomsbury.

———. 2013c. "Lament Personified: Job in the *Bedeutungsnetz* of Psalm 22." Pages 34–48 in *Spiritual Complaint: The Theology and Practice of Lament*. Edited by Miriam J. Bier and Tim Bulkeley. Eugene, OR: Wipf & Stock.

———. 2013d. "The Trials of Job: Re-litigating Job's 'Good Case' in Christian Interpretation." *SJT* 66: 174–91.

———. 2015. "The Modern Scholarly Wisdom Tradition and the Threat of Pan-Sapientialism: A Case Report." Pages 11–38 in *Was There a Wisdom Tradition? New Prospects in Israelite Wisdom Studies*. Edited by Mark R. Sneed. AIL 23. Atlanta: SBL.

———. 2018. "The 'Wisdom Literature' Category: An Obituary." *JTS* 69: 1–24.

———. 2019 *An Obituary for "Wisdom Literature": The Birth, Death, and Intertextual Reintegration of a Biblical Corpus*. Oxford: Oxford University Press.

Lambert, David A. 2015. "The Book of Job in Ritual Perspective." *JBL* 134: 557–75.

Laytner, Anson. 1990. *Arguing with God: A Jewish Tradition*. Lanham, MD: Rowman & Littlefield.

van Leeuwen, Raymond C. 2001. "Psalm 8.5 and Job 7.17–18: A Mistaken Scholarly Commonplace?" Pages 205–15 in *The World of the Aramaeans: Volume 1*. Sheffield Academic.

Lo, Alison. 2003. *Job 28 as Rhetoric: An Analysis of Job 28 in the Context of Job 22–31*. Leiden: Brill.

Long, V. Philips. 2012. "On the Coherence of the Third Dialogic Cycle in the Book of Job." Pages 113–25 in *Studies on the Text and Versions of the Hebrew Bible in Honour of Robert Gordon*. Edited by Geoffrey Khan and Diana Lipton. Leiden: Brill.

Longman III, Tremper. 1985. "Form Criticism, Recent Developments in Genre Theory, and the Evangelical." *WTJ* 47: 46–67.

———. 2008. "Disputation." Pages 108–12 in *Dictionary of the Old Testament: Wisdom, Poetry, and Writings*. Edited by Tremper Longman III and Peter Enns. Downers Grove, IL: InterVarsity.

———. 2012. *Job*. BCOT. Grand Rapids: Baker.

Lugt, Pieter van der. 1995. *Rhetorical Criticism and the Poetry of Job*. Leiden: Brill.

———. 2014. "Who Changes His Mind about Dust and Ashes? The Rhetorical Structure of Job 42:2–6." *VT* 64: 623–39.

Lundbom, Jack R. 1997. *Jeremiah: A Study of Ancient Hebrew Rhetoric*. Winona Lake, IN: Eisenbrauns.

Luyten, Jos. 1990. "Psalm 73 and Wisdom." Pages 59–81 in *La Sagesse de L'Ancien Testament*. Edited by Maurice Gilbert. Leuven: Leuven University Press.

Magary, Dennis R. 2005. "Answering Questions, Questioning Answers: The Rhetoric of Interrogatives in the Speeches of Job and His Friends." Pages 283–98 in *Seeking Out Wisdom: Essays Offered to Honor Michael V. Fox on the Occasion of His Sixty-Fifth Birthday*. Edited by Ronald L. Troxel, Kelvin G. Friebel, and Dennis R. Magary. Winona Lake, IN: Eisenbrauns.

Martin, Troy W. 2018. "Concluding the Book of Job and Yahweh: Reading Job from End to Beginning." *JBL* 137: 299–318.

McCabe, Robert V. 1997. "Elihu's Contribution to the Thought of the Book of Job." *DBSJ* 2: 47–80.

McKelvey, Michael G. 2010. *Moses, David and the High Kingship of Yahweh: A Canonical Study of Book IV of the Psalter*. Gorgias Dissertations in Biblical Studies 55. Piscataway, NJ: Gorgias.

Mettinger, Tryggve N. D. 1993. "Intertextuality: Allusion and Vertical Context Systems in Some Job Passages." Pages 257–80 in *Of Prophets' Visions and the Wisdom of the Sages: Essays in Honour of R. Norman Whybray on his Seventieth Birthday*. Edited by Heather A. McKay and David J. A. Clines. JSOTSup 162. Sheffield: Sheffield Academic.

Miller, Patrick D. 1993. "Prayer as Persuasion: The Rhetoric and Intention of Prayer." *WW* 13: 356–62.

———. 1994. *They Cried to the Lord: The Form and Theology of Biblical Prayer*. Minneapolis: Fortress.

———. 1998. "Prayer and Divine Action." Pages 211–32 in *God in the Fray: A Tribute to Walter Brueggemann*. Edited by Tod Linafelt and Timothy K. Beal. Minneapolis: Fortress.

Moberly, R. W. L. 1997. "Lament." Pages 866–84 in vol. 4 of *NIDOTTE*. Edited by Willem VanGemeren. 5 vols. Grand Rapids: Zondervan.

Moore, Rick D. 1983. "The Integrity of Job." *CBQ* 45: 17–31.

Morrow, William S. 1986. "Consolation, Rejection, and Repentance in Job 42:6." *JBL* 105: 211–25.

———. 2006a. *Protest Against God: The Eclipse of a Biblical Tradition*. Hebrew Bible Monographs 4. Sheffield: Sheffield Phoenix.

———. 2006b. "The Affirmation of Divine Righteousness in Early Penitential Prayers: A Sign of Judaism's Entry into the Axial Age." Pages 101–17 in *Seeking the Favor of God*. Vol. 1, *The Origins of Penitential Prayer in Second Temple Judaism*. Edited by Mark J. Boda, Daniel K. Falk, and Rodney A. Werline. Atlanta: SBL.

Muenchow, Charles. 1989. "Dust and Dirt in Job 42:6." *JBL* 108: 597–611.

Muffs, Yochanan. 1992. "Who Will Stand in the Breach? A Study of Prophetic Intercession." Pages 9–43 in *Love and Joy: Law, Language and Religion in Ancient Israel*. New York: Jewish Theological Seminary of America.

Muilenburg, James. 1961. "The Linguistic and Rhetorical Usages of the Particle כי in the Old Testament." *HUCA* 32: 135–60.

———. 1969. "Form Criticism and Beyond." *JBL* 88: 1–18.

Murphy, Roland E. 1981. *Wisdom Literature: Job, Proverbs, Ruth, Canticles, Ecclesiastes, and Esther*. FOTL 13. Grand Rapids: Eerdmans.

Nam, Duck-Woo. 2003. *Talking About God: Job 42:7–9 and the Nature of God in the Book of Job*. Studies in Biblical Literature 49. New York: Peter Lang.

Newell, B. Lynne. 1984. "Job: Repentant or Rebellious?" *WTJ* 46: 298–316.

Newsom, Carol A. 1996. "The Book of Job: Introduction, Commentary, and Reflections." Pages 317–637 in vol. 4 of *New Interpreter's Bible*. 12 vols. Nashville: Abingdon.

———. 2003. *The Book of Job: A Contest of Moral Imaginations*. Oxford: Oxford University Press.

O'Connor, D. J. 1983. "Job's Final Word—'I am Consoled…' (42:6b)." *ITQ* 50: 181–97.

———. 1985. "Reverence and Irreverence." *ITQ* 51: 85–104.

O'Connor, M. 1987a. "The Pseudo-Sorites in Hebrew Verse." Pages 239–53 in *Perspectives on Language and Text: Essays and Poems in Honor of Francis I. Andersen's Sixtieth Birthday*. Edited by Edgar W. Conrad and Edward G. Newing. Winona Lake, IN: Eisenbrauns.

———. 1987b. "The Pseudosorites: A Type of Paradox in Hebrew Verse." Pages 161–72 in *Directions in Biblical Hebrew Poetry*. Edited by Elaine R. Follis. JSOTSup 40. Sheffield: JSOT.

O'Dowd, Ryan P. 2008. "Frame Narrative." Pages 241–5 in *Dictionary of Old Testament: Wisdom, Poetry, and Writings*. Edited by Tremper Longman III and Peter Enns. Downers Grove, IL: InterVarsity.

Oeming, Manfred. 2000. "Ihr habt nicht recht von mir geredet wie mein Knecht Hiob: Gottes Schlusswort als Schlüssel zur Interpretation des Hiobbuchs und als kritische Anfrage an die moderne Theologie." *Evangelische Theologie* 60: 103–16.

Oosthuizen, M. J. 1991. "Divine Insecurity and Joban Heroism: A Reading of the Narrative Framework of Job." *OTE* 4: 295–315.

Osborne, Grant R. 1983. "Genre Criticism—*Sensus Literalis*." *TrinJ* 4: 1–27.

Oswalt, John N. 1988. *The Book of Isaiah: Chapters 40–66*. NICOT. Grand Rapids: Eerdmans.

Patrick, Dale. 1976. "Translation of Job 42:6." *VT* 26: 369–71.

———. 1979. "Job's Address of God." *ZAW* 91: 268–82.

Patrick, Dale, and Allen Scult. 1990. *Rhetoric and Biblical Interpretation*. JSOTSup 82. Sheffield: Sheffield Academic.

Patrick, Dale, and Kenneth Diable. 2008. "Persuading the One and Only God to Intervene." Pages 19–32 in *"My Words are Lovely": Studies in the Rhetoric of the Psalms*. Edited by Robert L. Foster and David M. Howard. LHBOTS 467. New York: T&T Clark.

Patterson, Richard D. 2010. "An Overlooked Scriptural Paradox: The Pseudosorites." *JETS* 53: 19–36.

Pinker, Aron. 2015. "A New Interpretation of Job 19:26." *JHS* 15: 1–23.

Pohl IV, William C. 2018. "Arresting God's Attention: The Rhetorical Intent and Strategies of Job 3." *BBR* 28: 1–19.

Powell, Mark Allan. 1990. *What is Narrative Criticism?* Guides to Biblical Scholarship. Minneapolis: Fortress.

———. 2010. "Narrative Criticism." Pages 239–55 in *Hearing the New Testament*. Edited by Joel B. Green. 2nd ed. Grand Rapids: Eerdmans.

Pyeon, Yohan. 2003. *You Have Not Spoken of Me What is Right: Intertextuality and the Book of Job*. Studies in Biblical Literature 45. New York: Peter Lang.

Roberts, J. J. M. 1973. "Job's Summons to Yahweh: The Exploitation of a Legal Metaphor." *Restoration Quarterly* 16: 159–65.

Rom-Shiloni, Dalit. 2006. "Socio-Ideological Setting or Settings for Penitential Prayers?" Pages 51–68 in *Seeking the Favor of God: Volume 1: The Origins of Penitential Prayer in Second Temple Judaism*. Edited by Mark J. Boda, Daniel K. Falk, and Rodney A. Werline. Atlanta: SBL.

Ross, Allen P. 2013. "The 'Thou' Sections of Laments: The Bold and Earnest Prayers of the Psalmists." Pages 135–50 in *The Psalms: Language for All Seasons of the Soul*. Edited by Andrew J. Schmutzer and David M. Howard. Chicago: Moody.

Scheindlin, Raymond. 1998. *The Book of Job: Translation, Introduction, and Notes*. New York: Norton.

Scholnick, Sylvia Huberman. 1982. "The Meaning of *Mišpāṭ* in the Book of Job." *JBL* 101: 521–9.

Schultz, Richard L. 1999. *The Search for Quotation: Verbal Parallels in the Prophets*. JSOTSup 31. Sheffield: Sheffield Academic.

Seow, C. L. 2004. "Job's *gōʾēl*, Again." Pages 689–709 in vol. 2 of *Gott und Mensch im Dialog*. Edited by Markus Witte. Berlin: de Gruyter.

———. 2010. "Poetic Closure in Job: The First Cycle." *JSOT* 34: 433–46.

———. 2011a. "Elihu's Revelation." *Theology Today* 68: 253–71.

———. 2011b. "Speaking Rightly: The God-Talks of Job and His Friends." *TTJ* 19: 70–92.

———. 2013. *Job 1–21: Interpretation and Commentary*. Illuminations. Grand Rapids: Eerdmans.

Simons, Herbert W. 1986. *Persuasion: Understanding, Practice, and Analysis*. New York: Random House.

Sneed, Mark R., ed. 2015. *Was There a Wisdom Tradition? New Prospects in Israelite Wisdom Traditions*. AIL 23. Atlanta: SBL.

Sommer, Benjamin D. 1998. *A Prophet Reads Scripture: Allusion in Isaiah 40–66*. Stanford, CA: Stanford University Press.

Stamps, Dennis L. 1993. "Rethinking the Rhetorical Situation: The Entextualization of the Situation in New Testament Epistles." Pages 193–210 in *Rhetoric and the New Testament: Essays from the 1992 Heidelberg Conference*. Edited by Stanley E. Porter and Thomas H. Olbricht. JSNTSup 90. Sheffield: Sheffield Academic.

Sternberg, Meir. 1987. *The Poetics of Biblical Narrative: Ideological Literature and the Drama of Reading*. Bloomington, IN: Indiana University Press.

Strawn, Brent A. 2008. "Imprecation." Pages 314–20 in *Dictionary of the Old Testament: Wisdom, Poetry, and Writings*. Edited by Tremper Longman III and Peter Enns. Downers Grove, IL: InterVarsity.

Sweeney, Marvin A. 2008. "Form Criticism." Pages 227–41 in *Dictionary of the Old Testament: Wisdom, Poetry, and Writings*. Edited by Tremper Longman III and Peter Enns. Downers Grove, IL: InterVarsity.

Tadmor, Hayim. 1994. *The Inscriptions of Tiglath-Pileser III, King of Assyria: Critical Edition, with Introductions, Translations, and Commentary*. Jerusalem: Israel Academy of Sciences and Humanities.

Tannehill, Robert C. 1975. *The Sword of His Mouth*. Philadelphia: Fortress.

Ticciati, Susannah. 2005. *Job and the Disruption of Identity: Reading Beyond Barth*. London: T&T Clark.

Timmer, Daniel. 2009. "God's Speeches, Job's Responses, and the Problem of Coherence in the Book of Job: Sapiential Pedagogy Revisited." *CBQ* 71: 286–305.

Trible, Phyllis. 1994. *Rhetorical Criticism: Context, Method, and the Book of Jonah*. Guides to Biblical Scholarship. Minneapolis: Fortress.

Vanhoozer, Kevin J. 1998. *Is There A Meaning in this Text? The Bible, The Reader, and The Morality of Literary Knowledge*. Grand Rapids: Zondervan.

Vogels, Walter. 1994. "Job's Empty Pious Slogans." Pages 369–76 in *The Book of Job*. Edited by W. A. M. Beuken. Leuven: Leuven University Press.

Walton, John. 2012. *Job*. NIVAC. Grand Rapids: Zondervan.

Watson, Duane F., and Alan J. Hauser. 1994. *Rhetorical Criticism of the Bible: A Comprehensive Bibliography with Notes on History and Method*. Biblical Interpretation Series 4. Leiden: Brill.

Watts, James W. 2001. "The Unreliable Narrator of Job." Pages 168–80 in *The Whirlwind: Essays on Job, Hermeneutics, and Theology in Memory of Jane Morse*. Edited by Stephen L. Cook, Corrine L. Patton, and James W. Watts. JSOTSup 336. New York: Sheffield Academic.

Weeks, Stuart. 2013. "The Limits of Form Criticism in the Study of Literature, with Reflections on Psalm 34." Pages 15–25 in *Biblical Interpretation: Essays in Honour of John Barton*. Edited by Katharine J. Dell and Paul M. Joyce. Oxford: Oxford University Press.

———. 2015. "Wisdom, Form and Genre." Pages 160–77 in *Was There a Wisdom Tradition? New Prospects in Israelite Wisdom Studies*. Edited by Mark R. Sneed. AIL 23. Atlanta: SBL.

Wenham, Gordon J. 2000. *Story as Torah: Reading Old Testament Narrative Ethically*. Grand Rapids: Baker Academic.

Werline, Rodney A. 1998. *Penitential Prayer in Second Temple Judaism: The Development of a Religious Institution*. Atlanta: SBL.

———. 2006. "Defining Penitential Prayer." Pages xiii–vii in *Seeking the Favor of God*. Vol. 1, *The Origins of Penitential Prayer in Second Temple Judaism*. Edited by Mark J. Boda, Daniel K. Falk, and Rodney A. Werline. Atlanta: SBL.

Westermann, Claus. 1974. "The Role of the Lament in the Theology of the Old Testament." *Int* 28: 20–38.

———. 1981a. *Praise and Lament in the Psalms*. Translated by Keith R. Crim And Richard N. Soulen. Atlanta: John Knox.

———. 1981b. *The Structure of the Book of Job: A Form-Critical Analysis*. Translated by Charles A. Muenchow. Philadelphia: Fortress.

———. 1998. "The Complaint Against God." Pages 233–41 in *God in the Fray: A Tribute to Walter Brueggemann*. Translated by Armin Siedlecki. Edited by Tod Linafelt and Timothy K. Beal. Minneapolis: Fortress.

Whitekettle, Richard. 2010. "When More Leads to Less: Overstatement, *Incrementum*, and the Question in Job 4:17a." *JBL* 129: 445–8.

Williams, James G. 1971. "'You Have Not Spoken Truth of Me': Mystery and Irony in Job." *ZAW* 83: 231–55.

Wilson, Gerald H. 1985. *The Editing of the Hebrew Psalter*. Chico: Scholars.

———. 1986. "The Use of Royal Psalms at the 'Seams' of the Hebrew Psalter." *JSOT* 35: 85–94.

———. 1993. "Shaping the Psalter: A Consideration of Editorial Linkage in the Book of Psalms." Pages 72–82 in *The Shape and Shaping of the Psalter*. Edited by J. Clinton McCann. JSOTSup 159. Sheffield: JSOT.

———. 2007. *Job*. New International Bible Commentary. Peabody, MA: Hendrickson.

Wilson, Lindsay. 1996a. "Realistic Hope or Imaginative Exploration? The Identity of Job's Arbiter." *Pacifica* 9: 243–52.

———. 1996b. "The Role of the Elihu Speeches in the Book of Job." *RTR* 55: 81–94.

———. 2003. "Job 38–39 and Biblical Theology." *RTR* 62: 121–38.

———. 2005. "Book of Job." Pages 384–9 in *Dictionary for Theological Interpretation of the Bible*. Edited by Kevin J. Vanhoozer. Grand Rapids: Baker.

———. 2015. *Job*. Two Horizons Old Testament Commentary. Grand Rapids: Eerdmans.

Witte, Markus. 2013. "Does the Torah Keep Its Promise? Job's Critical Intertextual Dialogue with Deuteronomy." Pages 54–65 in *Reading Job Intertextually*. Edited by Katharine Dell and Will Kynes. LHBOTS 574. New York: Bloomsbury.

Wolde, Ellen J. van. 1994. "Job 42,1–6: The Reversal of Job." Pages 223–50 in *The Book of Job*. Edited by W. A. M. Beuken. Leuven: Leuven University Press.

Wolterstorff, Nicholas. 2001. "If God Is Good and Sovereign, Why Lament?" *Calvin Theological Journal* 36: 42–52.

Wright, Christopher J. H. 2004. *Old Testament Ethics for the People of God*. Downers Grove, IL: IVP Academic.
Yeung, Maureen Wing-sheung. 1990. "Speech Ethics in the Book of Proverbs: A Test-Case for Utilizing the Literary Context in Formulating Christian Ethical Principles." MA thesis, Trinity Evangelical Divinity School.
Yu, Charles. 2011. "To Comfort Job: The Speeches in the Book of Job as Rhetorical Discourse." PhD diss., University of Wisconsin-Madison.
Zuckerman, Bruce. 1991. *Job the Silent: A Study in Historical Counterpoint*. Oxford: Oxford University Press.

Index of References

Hebrew Bible/
Old Testament
Genesis
4:10   146
12:18   48
16:2   51
18:10-15   22
18:27   243
20:18   51
25:22   46
27:46   46
29:31   51
30:22   51
43:23   145
46:30   57

Exodus
6:6   163
15:13   163
16:3   57

Numbers
11:11   48
14:2   57
22:37   48

Deuteronomy
5   223
5:26   163
13:14 Heb. 29
13:15   29
17:4   29
32:21   67

Joshua
3:10   16

Judges
9:54   57
16:30   57

Ruth
1:13   46
1:20-21   46
2:4   65
2:9   65

1 Samuel
1:5   51
1:6   51
7:3   101
15   24
15:19   48
17:26   163
17:36   163
23:23   29
26:4   29
26:10   45
26:15   48
31:4   57

2 Samuel
7:7   48
16:17   48

1 Kings
15:30   67
19:4   57
21:22   67

2 Kings
19:4   163
19:16   163
23:26   67

1 Chronicles
17:6   48

2 Chronicles
32:31   145

Job
1–2   26, 31, 35
1   139
1:1   27, 36–8,
            40, 47,
            190, 210
1:5   25, 28
1:8   27, 28, 38,
            40, 47,
            113, 210
1:9-11   28, 40
1:9   25
1:10   25, 52
1:11   25, 28
1:14-19   46
1:15   254
1:17   254
1:20   45
1:21   1, 25, 28,
            44, 46
1:22   28, 29,
            197, 249
2   28
2:3   27, 28, 40,
            47, 90,
            113, 210,
            244
2:5   25
2:8   45
2:9   25, 28,
            193, 210

Job (cont.)		3:11-26	49	3:26	46, 52, 120, 129, 211, 216
2:10	1, 28, 29, 44, 210, 249	3:11-24	49		
		3:11-19	47, 49		
		3:11-12	47, 52, 85, 248	4–31	36
2:11-13	45			4–27	15
2:11	173	3:11	48, 53, 55, 58, 123, 217	4–14	127
2:15	28			4–5	33, 44, 59, 126, 127
3–27	31				
3–14	44	3:12	48, 58	4	44
3	13, 19, 20, 31–3, 35, 39, 40, 44, 45, 48, 49, 52, 53, 56–61, 63, 67, 72, 73, 75, 76, 78, 79, 95, 121, 127, 185, 211, 216, 237, 247	3:13-15	47, 50, 51, 130, 131, 248	4:2-33	35
				4:2-6	60, 166
				4:2	33, 68
		3:13-14	49	4:4	68
		3:13	47, 49	4:5	67, 68
		3:14-26	49	4:6-11	59
		3:14	49	4:6-7	116
		3:16	47, 52, 53, 58, 123, 248	4:6	35, 60, 67, 68
				4:7	67
		3:17-19	47, 50, 51, 130, 131, 248	4:8	209
				4:9	67
				4:10	59, 60
3:1-3	40	3:17	52, 120	4:11	67, 209
3:1	31, 45, 155	3:19	37	4:12-21	60
3:2	40	3:20-26	49	4:12	68
3:3-26	144	3:20-23	47	4:17-21	133
3:3-13	49	3:20	52, 58, 76, 77, 88, 123, 129, 206, 217, 248	4:17-19	200, 201
3:3-10	49			4:17	60, 232
3:3-9	47–50, 55, 56, 131			4:19	67
				4:20	67
3:3	40, 51, 53, 55, 128			4:21	217
		3:21-22	52, 130	5	176
		3:23	1, 45, 49, 51, 52, 57, 58, 119, 123, 129, 130, 248	5:1-8	60
3:4	49, 50, 58, 128, 129			5:2-8	110
				5:2-7	71
3:4-6	52			5:2-5	112
3:4-5	50, 184			5:2	61, 67
3:5	40, 46, 51, 128	3:24-26	47, 50, 131, 248	5:4	67, 209
				5:5	112, 171
3:6	50, 51, 128	3:24	46, 47, 52, 59, 60, 192, 196	5:6-8	60
3:7	50, 128			5:6	74
3:8	51, 55, 75, 128			5:7	67
		3:25-26	49	5:8-16	60
3:9	50–2, 128	3:25	46, 47, 52, 129, 184	5:8	33, 37, 44, 60, 108, 247
3:10-19	49				
3:10	47, 49–52, 55, 58, 77, 129, 217			5:9	91

5:12-13	112	6:8-10	60, 61, 64,	6:26	68-70, 80,
5:12	67		71, 75, 98,		166
5:13-14	94, 177		131, 248	6:27-29	127
5:15	158	6:8	67, 125,	6:27	62, 66, 68
5:16	112		129	6:28-30	62
5:17-26	67	6:9	63, 64, 67,	6:28-29	61, 66, 72
5:17	60, 64, 68		129, 130	6:28	168, 231
5:18	63, 89	6:10	60, 67–70,	6:29	33, 60, 61,
5:19-22	63, 89		72, 128,		66
5:20	68, 158		166	6:30	205
5:21-22	60	6:11-23	61	6:30	33, 59,
5:24	171	6:11-13	62–4, 70,		61–3,
5:25	171		202		69–73
5:26	68	6:11	69, 202	7	61, 62, 73,
5:27	38, 110	6:12	69		74, 76–9,
5:32-33	223	6:13	63, 64, 67,		98, 159
6–7	19, 44,		69, 70,	7:1-21	33
	59–62,		129, 202,	7:1-11	62
	127, 138		248	7:1-6	52, 62, 77,
6	8, 14–17,	6:14-30	33, 62, 67,		129, 248
	20, 61–5,		103, 105,	7:1-4	130
	71, 72, 79,		108, 127,	7:1-2	61, 74, 130
	99		201	7:1	62, 74, 77,
6:2-30	169	6:14	62, 64, 65,		126, 136,
6:2-13	62		137, 138,		248
6:2-7	64, 72		202, 215	7:2	75
6:2-4	33, 44, 59,	6:15-30	137	7:3-6	61
	61, 69, 71,	6:15-29	66	7:3-5	216
	76	6:15-17	66	7:3	74, 129
6:2-3	62	6:17-18	68	7:4	74–6, 120,
6:2	60–2, 67,	6:18-20	66		129, 130
	72	6:18	68	7:5	74
6:3-4	71	6:19	254, 255	7:6-10	130
6:3	33, 60, 63,	6:21-29	72	7:6-8	79, 93
	68	6:21-22	61	7:6	74
6:4	60, 63, 64,	6:21	64, 66, 68,	7:7-21	33
	67, 68, 73,		72	7:7-16	62
	76, 79,	6:22-30	61	7:7-8	61
	129, 136,	6:22-23	70	7:7	61, 62,
	248	6:22	69, 70		73–6, 78,
6:5-7	61, 63, 72	6:23	68		79, 128,
6:5-6	62, 69	6:24	61, 62, 69,		131, 144,
6:5	69, 70		70		248
6:6	69, 70	6:25-29	72	7:8-10	129, 248
6:7	70	6:25-27	61	7:8-9	73
6:8-13	72	6:25-26	33, 66, 70	7:8	74, 75, 79
6:8-11	93	6:25	68-70, 166	7:9-10	61

Job (cont.)		7:20	76–8, 123,	9–10	19, 44,
7:9	73–5, 184, 248		129, 139, 248		79–84, 86, 89, 100, 127
7:10	62, 74, 248	7:21	60, 61, 73, 75, 76, 78,	9	5, 57, 82,
7:11-21	61		129, 144,		83, 87, 88,
7:11	33, 59, 62, 75, 76, 88, 128, 129, 133, 174, 206, 248	8	248 83, 88, 96, 127	9:2-24	91, 92, 239 82–4, 239, 241, 243
7:12-21	62, 77, 119, 235	8:2-6 8:2-3	166 33, 80	9:2-12 9:2-10	91, 195 83
7:12-19	136	8:2	66, 80, 97, 133, 136,	9:2-4	83, 84, 88, 129
7:12-15	1		154, 166,	9:2-3	82
7:12	62, 73, 75–7, 79, 129, 130, 231, 248	8:3	209 85, 89, 94–6, 100, 154, 157, 232, 239	9:2 9:3-4 9:3	87, 94, 96 86 82–4, 86, 94
7:13-14	75, 129			9:4-24	82, 95
7:13	73, 133, 174	8:4 8:5-10	172 80	9:4-13 9:4	82 86, 88, 91, 94, 97
7:14	76, 79, 130, 184, 216, 217	8:5-6 8:5	80, 96, 108, 247 33, 44, 80, 81, 85	9:5-13 9:5-10	82–4 82, 86, 94, 199
7:15-16	75, 129, 130	8:6	86, 96, 97	9:5-9	88
7:15	73, 217, 248	8:8-10 8:8	38 108	9:5-7 9:6	129, 248 239
7:16	60–2, 73–5, 78, 79, 105, 128, 130, 131, 144, 207, 248	8:10 8:11-19 8:11-13 8:11-15 8:12-13 8:12	81 80 177 189 189 190	9:7 9:8-10 9:8 9:10 9:11-12 9:11	239 129, 248 91, 239 88, 91 92, 96 86, 89, 129, 248
7:17-21	52, 62, 77, 79, 130, 144, 248	8:13 8:14-15 8:14	80, 137 209 97	9:11-24 9:12	83, 187 86, 89, 91, 92, 94,
7:17-20	1	8:15	189		101, 129,
7:17-19	129, 248	8:18	95		195, 248
7:17-18	76–8	8:19-20	96		
7:17	73, 74, 78	8:19	155	9:13-17	88
7:18-21	231	8:20-22	80, 108	9:13	86, 88,
7:18-19	73	8:20	81, 89, 96		129, 248
7:18	78, 79	8:21	33, 81, 89,	9:14-24	83
7:19-20	76, 232		97	9:14-20	84, 237
7:19	77, 79	8:22	209	9:14-16	88, 92, 129, 220

9:14-15	86	9:27-28	80, 85		100, 128, 133, 174, 206
9:14	82, 84, 86, 96, 128	9:27	46, 84, 128, 133, 174, 248	10:2-22	33, 82, 84, 85, 88, 95, 98, 99
9:15	86, 87, 96				
9:16	84, 86, 89	9:28-35	85		
9:17-31	83	9:28-31	82, 98		
9:17-20	89	9:28-29	87–9, 129, 248	10:2-17	83, 85, 136, 144
9:17-18	1, 82, 89, 100, 129, 248	9:28	85, 98, 130	10:2-7	129, 248
		9:29-31	94	10:2-3	88
9:17-19	86	9:29	83, 123, 129, 130, 207, 248	10:2	82, 84, 98, 128, 131
9:17	90, 217			10:3-8	82
9:18	89, 120			10:3-6	248
9:19-21	88	9:30-31	89, 129, 217, 248	10:3	89, 90, 94–6, 98, 100, 125, 130, 176
9:19-20	86				
9:19	88, 94–6, 129, 248	9:30	84, 87		
		9:31	85, 87, 89, 98, 130		
9:20-21	87, 96, 230, 235	9:32-35	237	10:4-6	95
9:20	96, 97, 129, 133, 248	9:32-34	88	10:4-5	86, 91
		9:32-33	85	10:6	90, 231
		9:32	82, 86, 96	10:7	88, 90, 96, 98
9:21-24	82, 84	9:33-34	87, 131		
9:21	40, 83, 84, 89, 90, 97, 99, 100, 244	9:33	6, 82, 87, 98, 128, 144, 248	10:8-17	83
				10:8-12	82, 83, 92
				10:8-10	194
		9:34	82, 85, 89, 99, 128–30, 146, 217	10:8-9	90
9:22-31	232			10:8	1, 90, 98, 129, 130, 248
9:22-24	1, 82, 86, 89, 91, 100, 117, 129, 232, 235, 239, 248				
		9:34-35	83	10:9-15	82
		9:35–10:22	84	10:9	82, 90, 128, 130, 131, 144
		9:35–10:1	33, 84, 85, 87, 89, 92, 97, 116, 136, 244		
				10:10-13	1, 129, 248
9:22	96			10:10	90, 95, 98, 248
9:23	89				
9:24	83, 84, 89, 95, 96, 198	9:35	80, 84, 87, 97, 99, 100, 128	10:11-13	90, 99
				10:11-12	99
9:25–10:22	83			10:11	90
9:25-35	33, 83–5	10	87, 88, 90, 93, 98	10:13-17	82
9:25-34	84, 85			10:13	90, 98, 99, 130
9:25-33	82	10:1-22	33, 82, 83		
9:25-28	82	10:1-17	84		
9:25-26	89, 129, 130, 248	10:1-7	82, 83	10:14-15	88
		10:1-2	82	10:14	90, 98, 129, 231, 248
9:25	82, 83	10:1	80, 83–5, 87, 97, 99,		
9:27-31	33				

Job (cont.)

Reference	Pages
10:15	82, 88, 90, 96, 98, 120, 128–31
10:16-20	82
10:16-17	98, 129, 248
10:16	90, 128, 130
10:17	90, 126, 128, 130, 231
10:18-22	82–5
10:18-20	83
10:18-19	90, 129, 130, 248
10:18	84, 85, 95, 123, 248
10:19	184
10:20-22	130
10:20-21	90, 93, 130
10:20	82, 90, 93, 95, 98, 105, 128, 130, 131, 248
10:21-22	82, 90, 117, 129, 144, 184, 248
10:21	90
11	44, 59, 100, 114, 126, 127
11:2-12	110
11:2-6	106, 166
11:2-4	33
11:2-3	101, 107
11:2	101, 102, 107
11:3	102, 107
11:4	101, 165
11:5-6	101, 107
11:5	101, 107
11:6-8	239
11:7-12	101
11:7-11	103, 104, 106, 107
11:7-9	92, 194
11:7	106
11:8-9	194
11:9	106
11:10	101, 195
11:11	101
11:12-13	106
11:13-20	33, 108, 247
11:13-19	101
11:13-14	44
11:18	106, 117
11:20	101, 122, 209
12–14	19, 44, 100–102, 104, 126, 127
12–13	102
12	57, 239
12:2–13:19	102, 103, 107
12:2–13:5	104
12:2-6	102–4, 107, 109
12:2-3	102, 109, 114
12:2	103, 106, 109, 110, 114
12:3	103, 109, 110, 114
12:4-6	102
12:4	113, 116, 117, 217
12:6	106, 107, 110, 117, 129, 248
12:7-25	91
12:7-12	103, 104, 106, 109, 110, 114
12:7-8	107, 117, 136
12:7	102-104, 107–9, 114
12:8-12	102
12:8	103, 107, 174
12:9	107, 110, 111, 113, 114, 117, 129, 195, 248
12:10	129, 248
12:11	104, 110, 117
12:12-13	114
12:12	104, 106, 109
12:13–13:2	176
12:13-25	102, 104, 109, 111, 117, 129, 199, 232, 239, 243
12:13	106, 109, 129, 239, 248
12:14-15	103, 114, 129, 248
12:14	111, 117, 239
12:15	106, 111, 117, 239
12:16	109, 129, 248
12:17-25	117, 129, 248
12:17-20	111
12:17	112, 195
12:20	107
12:21	111, 176
12:22	106, 111, 117, 239
12:23	111
12:24	106, 111, 176
12:25	111, 239
13:1-19	33
13:1-4	102, 104

13:1-3	103	13:20-21	105, 118, 130, 131, 144		116, 179, 250
13:1	103, 104, 114, 117			13:3	33, 105, 107, 117, 118, 129, 132, 136, 197, 237, 249
13:2	103, 104, 106, 108, 109, 114	13:20	104, 118, 121, 124, 128, 144		
13:10	105, 117	13:21-22	103		
13:11	110, 217	13:21	120, 128, 217		
13:12	105, 109, 117	13:22-23	121, 131	13:4-12	33
13:13-15	136	13:22	107, 122, 128, 220	13:4-5	207
13:13-14	116			13:4	105, 107–10, 113, 117, 132
13:13	33, 103, 105, 107, 108, 111, 116, 118, 128	13:23-27	105, 122, 144, 235		
		13:23-25	248	13:5-19	71, 104, 105, 108, 153, 201, 202
		13:23-24	123		
		13:23	103, 106, 120, 122, 123, 126, 128, 129, 230, 248		
13:14-16	102			13:5-6	107, 116
13:14	111, 118			13:5	103, 104, 106–8, 132, 137
13:15-24	237				
13:15-18	197				
13:15-16	126, 129, 144, 145, 249	13:24-27	103, 118, 121, 129, 130, 248	13:6-28	104
				13:6	33, 103, 105, 107, 108, 117
13:15	1, 33, 103, 115, 116, 118, 147	13:24	118, 122, 129, 230, 231, 248		
				13:7-12	102, 103
				13:7-11	129, 248
13:16	103, 116	13:25-26	119	13:7-9	6, 110
13:17-19	104, 117	13:25	118, 120, 122, 123, 125	13:7	33, 105, 107, 108, 205
13:17-18	108				
13:17	103–5, 108, 168	13:26-27	124	13:8	105
13:18-19	102, 116	13:26	118, 120, 122	13:9	106
13:18	103, 104, 106, 116			14	98, 102, 106, 124
		13:27	118, 119, 122, 230, 231		
13:19	104, 107, 111			14:1-22	33, 104
				14:1-6	105
13:20–14:22	33, 102, 103, 105, 118, 121, 123, 124, 126	13:28	105, 120, 125, 129, 248	14:1-2	120, 129, 130, 248
				14:1	120, 129
		13:28–14:6	93	14:3-5	103
		13:28–14:2	103	14:3-4	129, 248
13:20-28	1, 33, 105, 136	13:28–14:1	130	14:3	121, 123, 124, 144
		13:3-19	39		
13:20-23	122, 248	13:3-4	103, 105, 107, 115,	14:4	123, 197, 248
13:20-22	103			14:5-12	129, 248

Reference	Pages	Reference	Pages	Reference	Pages	Reference	Pages
Job (cont.)		14:21-22	103	15:25	34, 133, 247		
14:5-6	119, 231	14:21	106, 119				
14:6	103, 105, 106, 121, 122, 125, 128, 130, 131, 248	14:22	104, 120, 124, 130	15:27	160		
		14:27	119	15:28	170, 171		
		15–21	132	15:28-30	189		
		15	34, 127, 133, 134, 136, 143, 159	15:29	209		
14:7-12	103, 105, 120, 126, 130			15:30-35	189		
				15:30	34, 137, 143, 150, 170, 174, 247		
14:7	105, 124	15:2-16	133				
14:8	106, 120, 130	15:2-6	34, 35, 143, 166, 179, 247	15:32-34	189		
				15:32	45		
14:9	120			15:33	136, 190		
14:10	123	15:2	136, 137, 209	15:34	137, 170, 171, 189		
14:11	120						
14:12	105, 130	15:3	133, 137	15:35	136		
14:13-17	106, 121–3, 125, 130, 131, 219, 238, 248	15:4-6	150	16–17	19, 34, 132, 133, 135, 149, 178, 179		
		15:4	35, 133				
		15:5	133, 137				
		15:6	133, 137				
		15:7-11	133	16	5, 135, 140, 149, 156, 157, 159, 160		
14:13	103, 120, 122, 126	15:10	38				
		15:11	136, 137, 169, 170				
14:14-17	103						
14:14	103, 118, 120, 123, 125, 126, 130, 144, 145	15:12-13	133, 150, 170, 174, 247	16:2-7	134, 135		
				16:2-6	134, 135, 137, 143, 201		
		15:13	34, 137, 143				
14:15	120–2, 125	15:14-16	78, 133, 159, 200, 201	16:2-5	135, 181		
14:16-17	120, 122, 126			16:2	45, 136, 138, 142, 149, 169, 180, 181		
14:16	119, 124, 126	15:14	143, 232				
		15:17-35	133	16:3-6	33		
14:18-22	106, 136	15:17	136	16:3	136, 138, 146, 207		
14:18-20	103	15:18	137				
14:18-19	119	15:20-35	133	16:4-6	180, 215		
14:18	124, 129, 248	15:20-27	171	16:4-5	136, 138, 142, 180		
		15:20-24	171				
14:19-20	130	15:20-22	189	16:4	142, 145, 146		
14:19	106, 119, 120, 122, 129, 157, 184, 248	15:20	136, 137, 209				
				16:5	146		
		15:21	171, 209	16:6-17	135		
		15:22-23	209	16:6-8	181		
14:20-22	129, 248	15:22	157, 158				
14:20	119, 122	15:24	176, 209				

16:6	136, 138, 146, 147, 244	16:15 16:16 16:17-21	139, 140 139–41 141	17:4	179, 181, 248 135, 136, 141, 142,
16:7–17:16	135	16:17-18	181		145, 180,
16:7-22	135	16:17	33, 34,		181
16:7-17	1, 135, 140, 142, 143, 146, 206		134–6, 140, 141, 146–9, 181 135	17:5-16 17:5-9 17:5	135 134, 135 137, 138, 181
16:7-16	34, 143, 144, 156, 161	16:18–17:1 16:18-22 16:18	135 139, 141, 143, 146,	17:6	1, 138–40, 147, 148, 181, 182,
16:7-14	138–40		181		217, 248
16:7	134, 135, 137–9, 143, 144, 150, 182, 248	16:19-21 16:19	16, 134, 141, 143, 145, 146, 182, 249 1, 147, 148, 219	17:6-10 17:6-9 17:6-8 17:6-7 17:7	135 137 181 137, 140 67, 139, 141, 144
16:7-9	138, 182			17:8-10	137
16:7-8	134, 135, 141, 181, 182, 248	16:20	139, 141, 145, 147, 181, 182	17:8 17:9 17:10-16	137–9, 148 137 134, 135
16:8-22	135	16:21	137, 143,	17:10	134–7,
16:8-17	134		144, 146,		143, 147,
16:8	134, 138, 139, 141, 181, 231	16:22	148 134, 136, 140, 181		180, 181
16:9	139, 144, 147, 154, 156, 182, 217, 248	17 17 17:1-5	135, 140 26 135	17:11-16 17:11 17:12	135 140, 147, 150, 181 137, 138,
16:10-11	137, 141, 144, 147, 181, 217	17:1-4 17:1-2	135, 137, 142, 145, 147 134, 181,	17:13-16 17:13	141 140, 147 134, 147,
16:10	138, 148, 181, 182	17:1	248 140, 141,	17:14	184 141, 181
16:11-14	138, 181, 182, 248	17:2-10	181 135	17:15-16 17:15	147 134, 147
16:11	137, 139, 147, 154, 182, 248	17:2	137, 138, 142, 147, 181	17:16 17:17 18	147 134 149, 154
16:12-13	181, 182	17:3-4	39, 134,	18:2-4	150, 166,
16:12	139, 140		141, 142,		179, 247
16:13	139		146, 248	18:2	34, 154,
16:14	139, 217	17:3	134, 141,		155
16:15-16	139, 140, 181, 182		142, 147,	18:3	160

278   *Index of References*

Job (cont.)
18:4   34, 150, 154, 170, 174
18:5-21   150
18:5-7   189
18:5-6   170, 174
18:5   170
18:6   155, 171
18:7   150
18:8-10   154, 155
18:8   150
18:11   154, 160, 209
18:12-15   189
18:12   209
18:13-15   189
18:13   155, 209
18:14-15   171
18:14   150, 155, 160, 209
18:15-21   170
18:15   155
18:16   177, 190
18:17   189
18:18-21   189
18:18   136, 189
18:19   171, 189, 209
18:20   45, 155
19   5, 19, 34, 149–52, 155, 158–62, 164, 178, 179
19:2-20   151
19:2-6   151, 152, 154, 158, 201
19:2-5   152
19:2-3   152, 153, 180, 181
19:2   153–5, 158, 160, 180
19:3   153, 155, 207
19:4-22   152
19:4   155, 161
19:5-6   153, 161
19:5   152, 153, 161, 180, 181
19:6-22   1
19:6-21   181
19:6-13   156, 181, 182
19:6-12   152
19:6-7   157, 181
19:6   34, 151–6, 159, 161, 180, 182, 184, 248
19:7-20   34, 151–3, 161, 206
19:7-13   156
19:7-12   151, 152, 156
19:7   156, 158, 159, 231
19:8-13   156, 182, 248
19:8   157, 159, 184
19:9   78, 159
19:10   154, 157, 159
19:11   156, 159
19:12   154–6, 159
19:13-22   152
19:13-20   151, 152, 181, 182
19:13-19   73, 157, 217
19:13   152, 154, 157, 160, 161
19:14   154
19:18   161
19:20   152, 155, 157
19:21-29   152
19:21-27   152
19:21-22   151, 152, 161, 164
19:21   34, 151–6, 158, 160–2, 180, 182, 248
19:22   153, 154, 156–8, 161, 180, 181, 249
19:23-29   152
19:23-27   152, 154
19:23-24   151, 161, 164
19:23   151, 125
19:25-27   16, 151, 160, 162, 164, 182, 249
19:25-26   152, 155
19:25   1, 154, 162, 163, 219
19:26   155, 157, 181
19:27   151, 157, 162
19:28-29   151–4, 164
19:28   153, 154, 156, 158, 180, 181
19:29   153, 154, 162, 180, 182
20   165, 169
20:2-4   247
20:2-3   165, 179
20:2   165
20:3   34, 165
20:4-29   165
20:4-28   166
20:5-28   189
20:5   169, 172
20:7-9   189, 209
20:8   160
20:10   209
20:11-12   170

20:11	170, 171	21:6	184, 217	21:21	167, 172, 174, 175
20:12-14	170	21:7-33	1, 168, 181, 182, 239	21:22-26	167, 168
20:15-18	171			21:22	172, 175, 182, 248
20:15	209				
20:18-19	209	21:7-26	171		
20:20	170	21:7-21	177	21:23-26	170
20:21	170, 209	21:7-13	167, 170, 171, 173, 174, 232	21:23-24	170, 172
20:23	170			21:23	170, 177
20:25	209			21:25	171, 172
20:26-28	170	21:7	167, 169, 171, 174, 175, 177	21:26	170, 172
20:26	170, 171, 209			21:27-34	167, 170
				21:27-33	168
20:28-29	170	21:8	171, 172, 177	21:27-28	169, 173, 180, 181
20:28	169–71, 209	21:9	169, 171, 172, 182, 184, 248	21:27	167, 168, 171, 178
20:29	34, 37, 165, 169, 179, 189, 209, 221, 247			21:28-33	171
		21:11-13	169	21:28	168–70, 173
		21:11	175–7		
		21:12	169, 171, 172	21:29-30	168, 170, 173–5
21:10-11	171	21:13	169, 171, 172	21:29	180
21	5, 19, 34, 165–7, 171, 175, 178, 180, 184, 187, 188, 195, 225			21:30-33	241
		21:14-21	167	21:30-31	239
		21:14-16	167	21:30	170, 173
		21:14-15	173, 177	21:31	173, 175
		21:14	167, 176, 177, 180	21:32-33	172
				21:34	33, 167–9, 171, 173, 175, 180, 181, 207, 233
21:2-6	167	21:15	169, 173		
21:2-3	167–9, 173, 180	21:16	94, 169–71, 174, 176–8, 193		
21:2	167, 169, 170				
		21:17-26	170	22–27	183, 225
21:3	107, 168, 169, 171	21:17-20	172, 182, 239, 248	22	183, 188, 190, 192, 194, 195, 203, 225
21:4	33, 133, 168, 169, 171, 173–5, 179, 181	21:17-19	172		
		21:17-18	168, 170, 174, 175	22:2-5	35
		21:17	169, 170, 174	22:3-5	190
21:4-5	167, 244			22:3	184, 190, 191
21:5-34	241	21:18-21	167, 168		
21:5-33	243	21:18	169, 176, 177	22:4	35, 184, 190
21:5-13	232, 235				
21:5-6	167, 196	21:19-21	174	22:5-11	35
21:5	167, 168, 180	21:19-20	175	22:5	184
		21:19	172	22:6-9	184, 193
21:6-17	167			22:6	184, 191

Job (cont.)		23:13-14	185, 196, 227	23:8-10	92, 186, 194
22:7	191				
22:9	191	23:13	195, 197	23:8-9	185, 192, 194, 227, 248
22:10-11	184, 209	23:14	190, 195		
22:10	191	23:15-17	185, 237		
22:12-20	184, 186, 188, 190, 193, 194, 197	23:15-16	1, 196, 217, 226, 227, 244, 248	23:8	185, 186, 196, 227
				23–24	19, 36, 184–6, 190, 198, 199
22:12	191, 194	23:15	185, 186, 191, 192, 196		
22:13-19	193				
22:13-14	184			24	5, 186–9, 192, 197, 198, 206, 225
22:15	191	23:16	191, 192		
22:16	191	23:17	185, 186, 191, 192, 196, 197, 226		
22:17	191				
22:18	94, 176, 177, 184			24:1-25	185
				24:1-17	1, 185–7, 192, 199, 200, 226, 232, 235, 239, 241, 243
22:19-20	209	23:2–24:17	191		
22:19	112, 176, 184	23:2-13	185		
		23:2-7	186		
22:20	209	23:2-6	35		
22:21-30	35, 185, 186, 225, 247	23:2	133, 185, 186, 191, 195, 197, 226		
				24:1-12	233
				24:1-4	186
22:21	185			24:1	186, 189, 191, 192, 197, 198, 227, 239, 248
22:22	166, 172, 190	23:3-8	237		
		23:3-7	185		
22:23	185, 191	23:3	125, 185, 186, 192, 194, 197, 227, 248		
22:25	191				
22:26	191, 208			24:2-17	186
23	187, 188, 192, 196, 199, 203			24:2-12	193
		23:4-9	185	24:2-4	192
		23:4-7	192	24:2-3	193
23:10-12	185, 192, 193, 196, 221, 227, 230, 235, 248	23:4-5	186, 195, 197	24:2	189, 192
				24:3	189, 191, 192
		23:4	33, 190, 226		
				24:4-8	193
		23:5	197, 220, 226, 248	24:5-12	186
23:10-11	190, 195			24:5	185, 186, 193, 197
23:10	194, 196	23:6-7	227, 249		
23:11-12	186	23:6	185, 186, 192, 196, 197	24:6	193
23:11	194, 196			24:7	191, 193
23:12	6, 166, 190, 195, 196			24:8	193
		23:7-17	35	24:9	191, 192
		23:7	186, 190, 226	24:10-12	193
23:13–24:25	185			24:10-11	193
23:13-17	185–7	23:8-12	186	24:10	191, 193

24:12	191–3, 197, 227, 239, 248	26:2-4	19, 35, 107, 198–203, 225	27:8-23	204
				27:8-11	227, 248
				27:8-10	208
24:13-17	186, 193	26:2-3	201	27:8	37, 208
24:18-25	186, 187	26:2	202	27:9-10	208
24:18-24	37, 186–8	26:3	201, 202	27:9	37
24:18-21	191	26:4	201	27:10	37, 208
24:18-20	186–9	26:5-14	35, 37, 199, 202, 225	27:11-23	204, 205
24:18	188, 189			27:11-12	204, 205, 207
24:19	188, 189				
24:20	188, 189	26:6	199	27:11	37, 204, 208
24:21-25	186, 188	26:7-9	199		
24:21-23	1, 186, 187, 189, 192, 226, 239	26:7	201	27:12-13	209
		26:8	199	27:12	33, 35, 206–8, 214, 233
		26:9	199		
		26:11	199		
24:21	187, 189, 191	26:12	199	27:13-23	37, 204, 205, 207, 209, 226
		26:13	199		
24:22-23	189, 197, 227, 248	26:14	199, 201, 202	27:13	37, 209, 221
24:22	187	27	19, 37, 186, 203, 204, 208–10, 229	27:14	209
24:23	187			27:15	209
24:24	186–9, 231			27:16-17	209
24:25	36, 185–7, 189, 191, 197–9	27:1	36, 199	27:17	187
		27:2-6	35, 204, 205, 210, 225, 231, 235, 243	27:18	209
25	26, 36, 199, 225			27:19	209
				27:20	209
25:2-6	35, 199, 203, 233			27:21	209
		27:2-5	204	27:23	209
25:2-5	199	27:2-4	35	27:23	36
25:2-3	199, 200	27:2-3	227, 248	28	26, 36–9, 210, 229, 250, 252
25:2	199, 200	27:2	1, 37, 144, 205, 206, 226, 231, 240, 243		
25:3-6	36				
25:3	200			28:1	36
25:4-6	247			28:12	36, 37
25:4-5	199	27:3	37, 205	28:20	36, 37
25:4	199–201, 232	27:4	33, 205	28:23	37
		27:5-6	204, 230	28:28	36–8
25:5-14	199	27:5	205–8	29–31	19, 37, 39, 183, 210, 211, 213, 225, 226, 228–30, 237, 247
25:5-6	78	27:6	205, 207		
25:5	199, 200	27:7-23	225		
25:6	199, 200	27:7-12	204		
26–33	41	27:7-10	204, 205, 210		
26	13				
26:1-4	199	27:7	204, 207, 209, 226	29–30	218, 219

Job (cont.)

Reference	Pages
29	26, 36, 37, 39, 212, 213, 215, 216, 218
29:1	36, 199
29:3-25	212
29:3-6	214
29:3	215
29:4-5	219, 225, 227
29:4	37, 215, 219
29:5	37, 215, 219
29:6	215
29:7-25	219
29:7-11	214, 215
29:7-10	213
29:7	213
29:9-11	226
29:9	215
29:10	215
29:11	213–15
29:11-14	213
29:11-17	213
29:12	215
29:12-17	214, 215
29:14	215, 216
29:15	215
29:15	226
29:15-16	215
29:15-17	213
29:17	216
29:18-20	214, 216
29:19	215
29:2-25	248
29:2	37, 125, 211–14, 219, 220, 225, 227
29:21-25	214, 216
29:23	215
29:24	215
29:25	213, 215
30	36, 39, 211–14, 216, 218, 222, 226
30:1-19	227, 248
30:1-15	214, 222
30:1-12	214
30:1-11	214
30:1-10	212
30:1-8	214
30:1-6	214
30:1-4	221
30:1	212, 214, 216–18, 222
30:2-8	214, 217, 220
30:2	217, 220, 222, 248
30:3-7	217
30:7-12	214
30:7	218
30:8	218, 222
30:9-15	214
30:9-14	217
30:9	214, 217, 218, 222
30:11-18	212
30:11	212, 217, 226, 227
30:12-19	214
30:12	217
30:13-23	214
30:13	217
30:14	217
30:15	216, 217, 226
30:16-31	39
30:16-23	214, 222
30:16-19	214
30:16	214, 216, 218, 222
30:17-18	39, 226
30:17	216, 217
30:18-23	1
30:18-19	226, 227
30:18	216, 217
30:19-23	212
30:19	216, 217, 243
30:20-31	214
30:20-23	39, 211, 214, 218, 220, 221, 227
30:20	39, 217, 218, 220, 224
30:21-23	220, 226
30:21	217
30:22	217
30:23	211, 217
30:24-31	212, 214, 227, 248
30:24-28	214
30:24-25	216, 248
30:24	39, 216, 218, 220, 221, 222, 226
30:25-26	216
30:25	216, 221
30:26	211, 216
30:27-28	226
30:27	39, 216
30:28-29	39
30:28	216
30:29-34	214
30:29	217, 222
30:30	39, 216, 226
30:31	39, 216
30:35-40	214
30:35-37	214
30:38-40	214
31	36, 39, 40, 204, 211–14, 218, 219, 221–3, 229, 230, 243
31:1-40	248
31:1-34	248
31:1-4	212, 214, 221, 223
31:1	221, 223

31:2-3	221	31:35-37	211, 212, 214, 237	33:26-28	231		
31:2	227			33:26	231		
31:4-10	212	31:35-36	219	33:27	231		
31:4-5	226	31:35	39, 125, 211, 213, 219, 220, 222, 224–7, 237, 240, 248	33:28	231		
31:4	221			33:31-33	230		
31:5-10	223			34:2-37	230		
31:5-8	214			34:4	231		
31:6	218, 219, 227			34:5-9	40, 228		
				34:5	231		
31:7	218, 219, 226	31:36	219, 222, 226	34:6	231		
				34:7-8	231		
31:8	226	31:37	227	34:9	37, 231		
31:10	219	31:38-40	212, 214, 218, 219, 224, 248	34:10-12	232		
31:11-12	212, 224			34:12	154		
31:12	219			34:16	232		
31:13-15	214	31:40	40	34:17-19	232		
31:13	212, 224	32–37	19, 228	34:17	41, 232, 235		
31:14-15	212, 221, 223, 227	32	26				
		32:1-6	228, 234	34:23	232		
31:14	221	32:1-5	40	34:31-37	41, 234		
31:15	218, 221	32:1-2	234	34:32-33	232		
31:16-23	214	32:2	37, 228, 234	34:34-37	41		
31:16-21	218, 219			34:35-37	232		
31:16-17	212, 224	32:3	234	34:35	42, 228, 233, 235		
31:18	212, 224	32:5	234				
31:19-22	212, 224	32:6–33:33	230	34:37	166, 228, 235		
31:20	222, 248	32:6-22	230, 234				
31:21-23	248	32:8	230	35:2-16	230		
31:22	219, 226	32:11-22	234	35:2-3	40, 228, 232		
31:23	212, 224, 227	32:12	166				
		32:14	166	35:2	232		
31:24-28	214	32:18-20	230	35:3	232		
31:24-27	212, 223, 224	33:1	230	35:4-8	232		
		33:3	166	35:9-15	41		
31:27	218, 219, 226	33:5	230	35:9-13	233		
		33:8-11	230	35:9-12	41, 234		
31:28	212, 222, 223	33:9	230	35:9	233		
		33:9-11	40, 41, 228, 234	35:12-13	233, 236		
31:29-34	214, 223			35:14	233		
31:29	212, 224	33:10-11	230	35:16	41, 42, 228, 233–5, 249		
31:30-32	212, 223	33:10	231				
31:31-32	218, 219	33:11	230, 231				
31:31	222, 223	33:12	230, 231	36	234		
31:32	223	33:13	41, 230, 231	36:1	37		
31:33-34	224			36:2–37:24	230		
31:33	212	33:23	145	36:2-15	233		
31:34	212	33:26-33	234	36:4	235		

Job (cont.)		39:1	238	42:5	242
36:13	41	39:4	238	42:6	45, 90,
36:16-21	233	39:5	238		216, 242,
36:17	233	39:7-8	238		243, 249
36:19	41, 233,	39:9	238	42:7-17	26
	234	39:13	238	42:7-9	164
36:21	233, 234	39:14-18	238	42:7-8	1, 4, 29,
36:22–37:13	233	39:19	238		31, 36, 42,
36:22-24	41	39:21-25	238		47, 105,
36:29	217	39:26	238		237, 244,
37	26, 234	39:27	238		249, 250
37:1-13	235	39:28-30	238	42:7	28, 29, 113
37:14-24	235	40:1	41, 237	42:8	28, 113,
37:14	233, 234	40:2	41, 237,		250
37:16	235		240	42:10-17	248
38–42	19	40:3-5	240	42:11	45
38–41	95, 225,	40:4-5	20, 240		
	248	40:4	240	Psalms	
38	229	40:5	240	1	57, 94,
38:1–42:6	228, 236	40:6–41:34 Heb.	240		174, 176–
38:1–40:2	237	40:6–41:24	240		8, 184,
38:1	41, 235,	40:6	41, 237		195, 196,
	237, 245	40:7	41, 237,		255
38:2–39:30	235		242	1:1	176, 184,
38:2	42, 235,	40:8	42, 210,		195
	237, 239,		232, 235,	1:2	236
	242, 243,		240, 243	1:3-4	125
	249	40:9-14	240	1:4	176
38:3	41, 237,	40:11-12	241	1:6	195
	238, 240,	40:12	240	5:9	29
	242	40:24–41:7 Heb.	241	5:10	29
38:4-11	239	40:24–40:31	241	6:7	67
38:4	238	40:29	241	6:8	67
38:5	238	41	26	7:1-2 Heb.	163
38:6	239	41:2-3	241	7:2-3	163
38:7	37	41:5-6	241	7:3-5 Heb.	223
38:9-11	239	41:5 Heb.	241	7:4-6	223
38:12-13	239	41:9-10 Heb.	241	8	57, 77–9,
38:14-15	238, 239	41:13-14 Heb.	241		159, 255
38:18	238	41:25	51	8:5	78
38:21	238	41:33	51	10:14	67
38:25-27	239	42:1-6	242	19:14	40
38:30	238	42:2-6	20	19:14 Heb.	163
38:39	238	42:2	242	19:15	163
38:41	238	42:3	242, 243	22:1	52, 60
39	26	42:4	242	22:2	52, 60

24:3	147	73:2	194	89:41	139
24:4	147	73:11	176, 184	95:9-10	194
24:5	147	73:14	79	95:10	97
31:10	67	73:17-28	160	102:1	46
32:2	52, 60	73:23-26	160, 164	102:10 Heb.	220
32:3	52, 60	77:3 Heb.	46	102:11	220
33:28	68	77:4	46	103	46
35:5	176	77:15 Heb.	163	103:4	163
35:16	147	77:16	163	104	241
35:17	77	78:35	163	104:24	241
35:22-24	163	78:37	29	104:34	46
37:12	147	80:12 Heb.	139	106:10	163
37:13	45	80:13	139	107	57, 111, 113, 176, 177, 184, 255
39	57, 69, 93, 94, 125, 255	83:13 Heb.	176		
		83:14	176		
		84:2 Heb.	163		
39:2	147	84:3	163	107:6	176
39:4	79	85:4 Heb.	67	107:10-14	111
39:5	69	85:5	67	107:10	111
39:5 Heb.	79	88	16, 73, 98, 244	107:13	176
39:7	79			107:14	111
39:8	69, 79	88:5	73	107:16	111
39:9	147	88:6 Heb.	73, 220	107:17	112
39:13 Heb.	79, 93	88:6	73	107:19	176
39:14	79, 93	88:7 Heb.	73	107:28	176
42:2 Heb.	163	88:7	73, 220	107:33-37	111
42:3	163	88:8 Heb.	73, 160	107:38-41	111
44:23-26	163	88:8	73	107:40	111
44:24-27	163	88:9	73, 160	107:41	175, 176
51:10 Heb.	29			107:42	112, 184
51:12	29	88:10-12	52, 73, 123	108:1	29
55:2 Heb.	46	88:10-12	73	108:2	29
55:3	46	88:11-13	52, 123	112:7	29
55:17 Heb.	46	88:13 Heb.	220	119	69
55:18	46	88:14	73, 220	119:28	147
57:7 Heb.	29	88:15	73	119:50	68, 69, 72
57:8	29	88:16	73	119:51	69
64:1 Heb.	46	88:16	73	119:69	113
64:2	46	88:16-17	119	119:73	92
69:18 Heb.	163	88:17	73	119:84	77
69:19	163	88:17 Heb.	73	119:103	68, 69
72:12	215	88:17-18	119	119:121-122	147
73	57, 94, 164, 176, 177, 184, 195, 196, 255	88:18	73	119:154	163
		88:18 Heb.	73, 160	119:158	97
		88:19	73, 160		
		89:40 Heb.	139		

Psalms (cont.)		44:22-23	163	29:27	48
139	57, 92, 93, 97, 100, 195, 196, 255	44:24	91, 163	45:3	46
		44:25	112	45:4-5	46
		45:9	86, 91, 92, 94	50:34	163
139:5	194	47:4	163	*Lamentations*	
139:7-10	194	48:20	163	2:2	159
139:13-16	92	49:4	148	2:4-5	159
139:21	97	49:7	163	3	159
139:23-24	194	49:26	163	3:2	159
142:2	46	50:4-9	148	3:4	159
142:3	46	50:6	148	3:5	159
144:3	78	50:7-9	148	3:6	159
146-150	46	52:9	163	3:7-9	159
		52:13–53:12	160	3:7	159
Proverbs		52:14–53:12	148	3:14	113, 159, 217
1:7	38	52:14	148		
8:14-16	112	53:3	148	3:43	159
9:10	38	53:4	148, 160	3:58	163
23:11	163	53:5	160	3:63	217
		53:9	148	5:16	159
Isaiah		53:10	160		
9:11	194	54:5	163	*Ezekiel*	
17:13	176	54:8	163	6:9	97
26:21	146	59:20	163	8:16	194
37:4	163	60:16	163	19:7	60
37:17	163	63:16	163	20:43	97
40–55	91, 92, 148, 163, 255			21:25	45
		Jeremiah		21:30	45
40	245	6:27	194	24:7-8	146
40:1	245	10:10	163	36:31	97
40:26	91	11–20	56	37	250
40:27	57	12:1	86, 177		
40:28	91	17:9-10	194	*Daniel*	
41:8	113	20	113	6:20	163
41:14	113, 163	20:7	113, 217	6:21	163
41:20	113, 114	20:8	158	6:26	163
43:1	163	20:11-13	56	6:27	163
43:13	91, 94, 101, 195	20:14-18	55–8, 86, 113		
				Hosea	
43:14	163	20:14	55	1:10	163
43:27	145	20:15	55	2:1	163
44	112	20:16	55	5:4-6	53
44:6	163	20:17-18	55	9:11-16	53
		23:36	163	13:14	163

Jonah		APOCRYPHA		*4QD^b*	
1:12	57	*Ecclesiasticus*		1:5	243
4:3	57	10:9	243		
4:9	57	40:3	243	*4QMyst^c*	
		42:15–43:33	233	4:3	243
Micah					
4:10	163	DEAD SEA SCROLLS		*4QShir^b*	
6:14-15	53	*1QH*		126:2	243
		18:5	243		
Zechariah					
11:3	60	*4QD^a*			
		1a-b:22-23	243		

Index of Authors

Aitken, J. A. 159
Alter, R. 12, 22–4, 53, 74, 139, 210, 238
Andersen, F. I. 36, 77, 207, 238
Arnold, B. T. 17, 205
Averbeck, R. E. 75

Baker, W. R. 2, 3, 6, 25
Balentine, S. E. 6, 9, 11, 152, 157, 161, 162, 196, 238, 241, 255
Barker, J. 253
Bartholomew, C. G. 26, 31
Bastiaens, J. C. 148, 160
Bautch, R. J. 11
Ben-Porat, Z. 54
Berger, P. L. 200
Beuken, W. A. M. 31, 44, 52, 59, 60
Billings, J. T. 9
Billman, K. D. 9
Bitzer, L. F. 6, 13, 47, 253
Blumenthal, D. R. 10
Boda, M. 11, 255, 256
Booth, W. C. 12, 26, 27
Brenner, A. 27
Brinks Rea, C. L. 91, 113, 148, 160, 239
Brown, S. A. 9, 10
Brown, W. P. 92, 93
Broyles, C. C. 9, 14–17, 53, 74, 78, 130, 144
Bryant, D. C. 13
Brueggemann, W. 9
Burnight, J. 57, 60, 70

Caws, M. A. 26
Cheney, M. 5, 25, 26, 30, 35, 36, 199, 235
Chin, C. 121
Choi, J. H. 17, 205
Clarke, R. 207
Clines, D. J. A. 6–8, 27, 31, 34, 36, 39–41, 44–50, 52, 53, 61, 63–7, 69, 70, 72–4, 78, 80–7, 89, 97, 99, 101–5, 107–9, 111–13, 115, 116, 118, 121, 123, 124, 133–7, 139, 143–5, 150–3, 156, 157, 159, 162, 164–7, 170–2, 174, 175, 178, 185–9, 193, 195–7, 199, 200, 202–6, 209, 211–15, 217, 219, 221, 223, 224, 229–32, 234, 236–8, 240, 242, 254
Cooper, A. 27
Corbett, E. P. J. 12
Course, J. E. 33, 59, 60, 67, 74, 75, 80, 97, 101, 154, 155, 190
Curtis, J. B. 144, 242

Dailey, T. F. 242
Daughton, S. M. 18
Davidson, A. B. 188
Dell, K. J. 55, 56, 86, 113, 158, 177, 251
Dhorme, E. 230, 254
Diable, K. 49, 53
Dick, M. B. 39, 213, 224
Diewert, D. A. 41, 75, 233, 234, 236
Dobbs-Allsopp, F. W. 213
Driver, S. R. 229
Dubbink, J. 56

Erickson, A. 157

Fishbane, M. A. 49, 78
Fohrer, G. 60, 66, 73, 76, 83, 89, 119, 145, 155, 195, 196, 242
Fokkelman, J. P. 49
Forrest, R. W. E. 27, 29
Fox, M. V. 6, 12, 13, 18, 22, 26, 27, 30, 32, 42, 107, 136, 172, 175, 184, 207, 238, 241, 242, 250
Fredericks, D. C. 173, 207
Frevel, C. 71, 72, 74
Futato, M. D. 16

Index of Authors

Gammie, J. G. 241
Gerstenberger, E. S. 15–17, 50, 58
Good, E. M. 59, 104, 133, 137, 157, 161, 201
Gordis, R. 144, 145, 163, 184, 187, 235, 242
Gray, G. B. 229
Greenstein, E. L. 5, 29, 33, 55, 56, 136, 158, 159, 177
Gutièrrez, G. 5, 21

Habel, N. C. 7, 12, 31, 34, 36, 39, 44, 45, 48–50, 52, 55, 59, 64, 70–2, 75, 81, 83, 84, 88, 101, 102, 104, 109, 112, 115, 119, 133, 135, 144, 145, 150, 152, 154, 156, 162, 165, 167, 169–72, 186, 199, 202–4, 207, 209–11, 213, 214, 229, 231, 232, 234, 235, 254
Ham, T. C. 238
Harding, J. E. 5
Härle, W. 2, 245
Hart, R. P. 18
Hartley, J. E. 8, 27–9, 36, 39, 41, 42, 45, 48, 49, 51, 55, 56, 58, 61, 66, 67, 69, 70, 72, 74, 76, 77, 81–4, 88–90, 99, 101–4, 106, 108–10, 115, 123, 124, 133–7, 139–47, 150–7, 159, 161–4, 166–8, 171, 172, 174, 175, 178, 185–8, 191–4, 196, 200–202, 204, 206, 207, 210–15, 217–19, 223–5, 232, 238–41, 243, 251, 254, 255
Hauser, A. J. 11, 12, 22
Hawley, L. R. 7, 33, 66, 80, 133, 138, 139, 193
van Hecke, P. 6, 52, 105, 141
Ho, E. 107, 136, 172, 188
Hoffman, Y. 27
Holbert, J. C. 34, 150, 165
Howard, D. M. 6, 13, 16, 21, 98, 220

Janowski, B. 9
Janzen, J. G. 75, 188, 209
Jimenez, C. P. 138, 139
Johnston, G. H. 207

Kaiser Jr., W. C. 2
Kaplan, L. J. 242
Kennedy, G. A. 13, 18
Kitz, A. M. 17
Kline, J. G. 69

Koops, R. 42
Kynes, W. 3, 6, 7, 18, 54–7, 69, 78, 79, 91–4, 97, 101, 111–13, 125, 147, 159, 160, 175–7, 184, 194, 195, 251, 255

Lambert, D. A. 6, 10, 45, 242, 243
Laytner, A. 10
van Leeuwen, R. C. 78
Lo, A. 29, 31, 36–8, 47, 187, 189, 199, 202, 207, 209, 218, 252
Long, V. P. 183
Longman III, T. 6, 14, 15, 25, 31, 32, 45, 46, 49, 59, 60, 69, 85, 89, 101, 144, 152, 162, 167, 186, 224, 254
van der Lugt, P. 7, 242
Lundbom, J. R. 13, 18
Luyten, J. 160

Magary, D. R. 7, 26, 42, 70, 77, 95, 111, 123, 125, 140, 197, 219
Martin, T. W. 242
McCabe, R. V. 40, 41, 229–33, 235, 236
McKelvey, M. G. 202, 245
Mettinger, T. N. D. 148, 149, 159
Migliore, D. L. 9
Miller, P. D. 9, 10, 15, 16, 25, 48, 49, 58
Moberley, R. W. L. 9
Moore, R. D. 27
Morrow, W. S. 9, 11, 15, 16, 46, 47, 118, 158, 242, 255
Muenchow, C. 242
Muffs, Y. 144
Muilenburg, J. 13, 68
Murphy, R. E. 8, 14–17, 31, 48, 61, 62, 82, 101, 102, 134, 151, 167, 185, 200, 204, 211

Nam, D.-W. 6, 29
Newell, B. L. 6, 242
Newsom, C. A. 7, 32, 35, 36, 38, 41, 42, 45, 49, 51, 61, 63, 76, 86, 101, 107–10, 112, 115, 120, 133, 135, 138, 139, 144, 150, 153, 157, 162, 167, 168, 183, 186, 188, 191, 193, 199–204, 206–9, 213–16, 223, 229, 230, 232–4, 236, 237, 239, 251, 254

O'Connor, D. J. 224, 242
O'Connor, M. 7, 53
O'Dowd, R. P. 26

Oeming, M. 6, 29
Oosthuizen, M. J. 27
Osborne, G. R. 14
Oswalt, J. N. 148

Patrick, D. 7, 33, 49, 53, 127, 142, 242, 243
Patterson, R. D. 7, 53, 54, 88
Pinker, A. 162
Pohl IV, W. C. 45
Powell, M. A. 12
Pyeon, Y. 33, 49, 55, 56, 101, 113

de Regt, L. J. 42, 70, 77, 101, 174, 197, 220, 221
Roberts, J. J. M. 86
Rom-Shiloni, D. 11
Ross, A. P. 9

Scheindlin, R. 84
Scholnick, S. H. 240
Schultz, R. L. 54
Scult, A. 7
Seow, C. L. 6, 8, 12, 27, 29, 33, 34, 41, 45–7, 51, 53, 60, 62, 64, 65, 67, 72, 74, 80, 82–4, 86–9, 91, 93–5, 101, 104, 105, 107–11, 115, 117–19, 123, 126, 133, 135, 136, 139–46, 148, 150, 152–8, 161–4, 166–71, 172–5, 178, 183, 211, 213, 229, 230, 234, 237, 251, 254, 255
Simons, H. W. 18
Sneed, M. R. 3
Sommer, B. D. 54
Stamps, D. L. 253
Sternberg, M. 12, 21–4, 31, 35, 40, 234, 235
Strawn, B. A. 17
Sweeney, M. A. 15

Tadmor, H. 254
Tannehill, R. C. 250, 251

Ticciati, S. 87, 144, 229
Timmer, D. 239, 242
Trible, P. 13, 18

Vanhoozer, K. J. 12, 14, 21
Vogels, W. 27

Walton, J. 6, 29, 36, 101, 144, 198, 202, 217
Watson, D. F. 11, 12, 22
Watts, J. W. 27
Weeks, S. 3, 14
Wenham, G. J. 12
Werline, R. A. 11, 255, 256
Westermann, C. 8, 9, 11, 15–17, 39, 40, 45, 48, 56, 71, 78, 80, 82, 102, 103, 105, 112, 122, 132, 134, 149, 151, 159, 167, 168, 185, 196, 198, 204, 211, 212, 217, 220, 223, 224, 247, 255, 256
Whitekettle, R. 60
Williams, J. G. 29
Wilson, G. H. 177, 202, 245
Wilson, L. 8–10, 40–2, 44, 49, 83, 98, 125, 144, 162, 185, 186, 188, 202, 204, 213, 214, 216, 218, 219, 223, 224, 229, 231–3, 235–40, 242–5, 256
Witte, M. 223
Wolde, E. J. van 242, 243
Wolterstorff, N. 9, 10
Wright, C. J. H. 2

Yeung, M. W.-s. 25
Yu, C. 6, 7, 13, 27, 33, 34, 38, 39, 45, 46, 50, 57, 60, 77, 80–4, 86, 88, 95, 99, 101, 102, 104, 107, 133, 135, 140, 150, 151, 165–8, 173, 174, 184, 185, 198, 202, 205, 235, 252, 253

Zuckerman, B. 56